Mac Multimedia & CD-ROMs For...

The Best Multimedia Macs

This list includes currently available models that you can buy new as well as discontinued models that you may be able to buy used.

Model Name	Advantages
Centris 660AV	Video input and output, CD-quality stereo sound recording
LC 630	Optional cable-ready TV input, optional video input, medium-quality stereo sound recording
Performa 630, 635, 636, or 638	Optional cable-ready TV input, optional video input, medium-quality stereo sound recording
Performa 6100, 6112, 6115, 6117, or 6118	Optional video input and output, CD-quality stereo sound recording
PowerBook 520c, 540c	Color screen, CD-quality stereo sound recording
Power Mac 5200LC	Optional cable-ready TV input, optional video input, medium-quality stereo sound recording
Power Mac 6100AV, 7100AV, 8100AV	Video input and output, CD-quality stereo sound recording
Power Mac 7500	Video input, CD-quality stereo sound recording
Power Mac 8500, 9500	Video input and output, CD-quality stereo sound recording
Quadra 630	Optional cable-ready TV input, optional video input, medium-quality stereo sound recording
Quadra 660AV, 840AV	Video input and output, CD-quality stereo sound recording

AppleCD Audio Player Shortcuts

Operation	Shortcut
Play or pause CD	Spacebar or Enter key
Stop CD	Delete or Escape key
Eject CD	⌘-E
Skip to next track	Right-arrow key
Skip to previous track	Left-arrow key
Rename CD and tracks	Return or Tab key
Raise and lower volume	Up- and down-arrow keys

... For Dummies: #1 Computer Book Series for Beginners

Mac Multimedia and CD-ROMs For Dummies

QuickTime Movie Shortcuts

Operation	Shortcut
Play or pause movie	Spacebar, Return key, or double-click inside movie
Play movie backwards	⌘-left arrow or Shift-double-click inside movie
Play at custom speed	Control-drag on frame buttons
Go one frame backward	Left-arrow key
Go one frame forward	Right-arrow key
Go to first frame in movie	Option-left arrow
Go to last frame in movie	Option-right arrow
Raise and lower volume	Up- and down-arrow keys
Mute volume	Option-click on speaker icon

Apple Video Player Shortcuts

Note: Video Player is included only with the junior AV Macs (Quadra, LC, and Performa 630 series and PowerMac 5200LC).

Operation	Shortcut
Start Apple Video Player	Option-Tab or TV/Mac button on remote
Change to next or previous channel	Right- or left-arrow key
Skip to specific channel	Enter channel number
Skip between current and last channel	Tab
Expand TV to full screen	⌘-3 or Display button on remote
View TV at quarter-screen size	⌘-2
Raise and lower volume	Up- and down-arrow keys
Mute volume	⌘-M or Mute button on remote
Shut down computer	Power button on remote

Copyright © 1995 IDG Books Worldwide, Inc. All rights reserved.
Cheat Sheet $2.95 value.
For more information about IDG Books, call 1-800-762-2974.

... For Dummies: #1 Computer Book Series for Beginners

References for the Rest of Us

COMPUTER BOOK SERIES FROM IDG

Are you intimidated and confused by computers? Do you find that traditional manuals are overloaded with technical details you'll never use? Do your friends and family always call you to fix simple problems on their PCs? Then the ... *For Dummies*™ computer book series from IDG is for you.

...*For Dummies* books are written for those frustrated computer users who know they aren't really dumb but find that PC hardware, software, and indeed the unique vocabulary of computing make them feel helpless. ...*For Dummies* books use a lighthearted approach, a down-to-earth style, and even cartoons and humorous icons to diffuse computer novices' fears and build their confidence. Lighthearted but not lightweight, these books are a perfect survival guide for anyone forced to use a computer.

> "I like my copy so much I told friends; now they bought copies."
> — Irene C., Orwell, Ohio

> "Quick, concise, nontechnical, and humorous."
> — Jay A., Elburn, Illinois

> "Thanks, I needed this book. Now I can sleep at night."
> — Robin F., British Columbia, Canada

Already, hundreds of thousands of satisfied readers agree. They have made ... *For Dummies* books the #1 introductory level computer book series and have written asking for more. So, if you're looking for the most fun and easy way to learn about computers, look to ... *For Dummies* books to give you a helping hand.

MAC® MULTIMEDIA & CD-ROMs FOR DUMMIES®

MAC MULTIMEDIA & CD-ROMs FOR DUMMIES

by Deke McClelland

IDG Books Worldwide, Inc.
An International Data Group Company

Foster City, CA ♦ Chicago, IL ♦ Indianapolis, IN ♦ Braintree, MA ♦ Dallas, TX

Mac® Multimedia & CD-ROMs For Dummies®

Published by
IDG Books Worldwide, Inc.
An International Data Group Company
919 E. Hillsdale Blvd.
Suite 400
Foster City, CA 94404

Text and art copyright © 1995 by IDG Books Worldwide, Inc. All rights reserved. No part of this book, including interior design, cover design, and icons, may be reproduced or transmitted in any form, by any means (electronic, photocopying, recording, or otherwise) without the prior written permission of the publisher.

Library of Congress Catalog Card No.: 95-77666

ISBN: 1-56884-910-9

Printed in the United States of America

10 9 8 7 6 5 4 3 2 1

1A/RX/QX/ZV

Distributed in the United States by IDG Books Worldwide, Inc.

Distributed by Macmillan Canada for Canada; by Computer and Technical Books for the Caribbean Basin; by Contemporanea de Ediciones for Venezuela; by Distribuidora Cuspide for Argentina; by CITEC for Brazil; by Ediciones ZETA S.C.R. Ltda. for Peru; by Editorial Limusa SA for Mexico; by Transworld Publishers Limited in the United Kingdom and Europe; by Al-Maiman Publishers & Distributors for Saudi Arabia; by Simron Pty. Ltd. for South Africa; by IDG Communications (HK) Ltd. for Hong Kong; by Toppan Company Ltd. for Japan; by Addison Wesley Publishing Company for Korea; by Longman Singapore Publishers Ltd. for Singapore, Malaysia, Thailand, and Indonesia; by Unalis Corporation for Taiwan; by WS Computer Publishing Company, Inc. for the Philippines; by WoodsLane Pty. Ltd. for Australia; by WoodsLane Enterprises Ltd. for New Zealand.

For general information on IDG Books Worldwide's books in the U.S., please call our Consumer Customer Service department at 800-762-2974. For reseller information, including discounts and premium sales, please call our Reseller Customer Service department at 800-434-3422.

For information on where to purchase IDG Books Worldwide's books outside the U.S., contact IDG Books Worldwide at 415-655-3021 or fax 415-655-3295.

For information on translations, contact Marc Jeffrey Mikulich, Director, Foreign & Subsidiary Rights, at IDG Books Worldwide, 415-655-3018 or fax 415-655-3295.

For sales inquiries and special prices for bulk quantities, write to the address above or call IDG Books Worldwide at 415-655-3200.

For information on using IDG Books Worldwide's books in the classroom, or ordering examination copies, contact Jim Kelly at 800-434-2086.

For authorization to photocopy items for corporate, personal, or educational use, please contact Copyright Clearance Center, 222 Rosewood Drive, Danvers, MA 01923, or fax 508-750-4470.

Limit of Liability/Disclaimer of Warranty: The author and publisher have used their best efforts in preparing this book. IDG Books Worldwide, Inc., and the author make no representation or warranties with respect to the accuracy or completeness of the contents of this book and specifically disclaim any implied warranties of merchantability or fitness for any particular purpose and shall in no event be liable for any loss of profit or any other commercial damage, including but not limited to special, incidental, consequential, or other damages.

Trademarks: All brand names and product names used in this book are trademarks, registered trademarks, or trade names of their respective holders. IDG Books Worldwide is not associated with any product or vendor mentioned in this book.

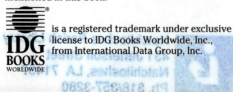 is a registered trademark under exclusive license to IDG Books Worldwide, Inc., from International Data Group, Inc.

About the Author

Deke McClelland is the author of more than 30 books about desktop publishing and graphics programs for the Mac and Windows, including IDG's best-selling *Macworld Photoshop 3 Bible, Photoshop 3 For Macs For Dummies, CorelDRAW! 5 For Dummies, Macworld FreeHand 4 Bible,* and *PageMaker 5 For Windows For Dummies.*

He is also a contributing editor to *Macworld* magazine and frequently pops up in *Publish* and *PC World.* He received the Ben Franklin Award for the Best Computer Book in 1989 and won prestigious Computer Press Awards in 1990, 1992, and 1994. When he isn't writing, he hosts the television series "Digital Gurus" for the Jones Computer Network. In his few minutes of spare time, he lives with his wife and aging cat in Boulder, Colorado.

Welcome to the world of IDG Books Worldwide.

IDG Books Worldwide, Inc., is a subsidiary of International Data Group, the world's largest publisher of computer-related information and the leading global provider of information services on information technology. IDG was founded more than 25 years ago and now employs more than 7,500 people worldwide. IDG publishes more than 235 computer publications in 67 countries (see listing below). More than 60 million people read one or more IDG publications each month.

Launched in 1990, IDG Books Worldwide is today the #1 publisher of best-selling computer books in the United States. We are proud to have received 8 awards from the Computer Press Association in recognition of editorial excellence, and our best-selling ...For Dummies™ series has more than 17 million copies in print with translations in 25 languages. IDG Books Worldwide, through a recent joint venture with IDG's Hi-Tech Beijing, became the first U.S. publisher to publish a computer book in the People's Republic of China. In record time, IDG Books Worldwide has become the first choice for millions of readers around the world who want to learn how to better manage their businesses.

Our mission is simple: Every one of our books is designed to bring extra value and skill-building instructions to the reader. Our books are written by experts who understand and care about our readers. The knowledge base of our editorial staff comes from years of experience in publishing, education, and journalism — experience which we use to produce books for the '90s. In short, we care about books, so we attract the best people. We devote special attention to details such as audience, interior design, use of icons, and illustrations. And because we use an efficient process of authoring, editing, and desktop publishing our books electronically, we can spend more time ensuring superior content and spend less time on the technicalities of making books.

You can count on our commitment to deliver high-quality books at competitive prices on topics consumers want to read about. At IDG Books Worldwide, we value quality, and we have been delivering quality for more than 25 years. You'll find no better book on a subject than an IDG book.

John J. Kilcullen

John Kilcullen
President and CEO
IDG Books Worldwide, Inc.

IDG Books Worldwide, Inc., is a subsidiary of International Data Group, the world's largest publisher of computer-related information and the leading global provider of information services on information technology. International Data Group publishes over 235 computer publications in 67 countries. More than sixty million people read one or more International Data Group publications each month. The officers are Patrick J. McGovern, Founder and Board Chairman; Kelly Conlin, President; Jim Casella, Chief Operating Officer. International Data Group's publications include: **ARGENTINA'S** Computerworld Argentina, Infoworld Argentina; **AUSTRALIA'S** Computerworld Australia, Computer Living, Australian PC World, Australian Macworld, Network World, Mobile Business Australia, Publish!, Reseller, IDG Sources; **AUSTRIA'S** Computerwelt Oesterreich, PC Test; **BELGIUM'S** Data News (CW); **BOLIVIA'S** Computerworld; **BRAZIL'S** Computerworld, Connections, Game Power, Mundo Unix, PC World, Publish, Super Game; **BULGARIA'S** Computerworld Bulgaria, PC & Mac World Bulgaria, Network World Bulgaria; **CANADA'S** CIO Canada, Computerworld Canada, InfoCanada, Network World Canada, Reseller; **CHILE'S** Computerworld Chile, Informatica; **COLOMBIA'S** Computerworld Colombia, PC World; **COSTA RICA'S** PC World; **CZECH REPUBLIC'S** Computerworld, Elektronika, PC World; **DENMARK'S** Communications World, Computerworld Danmark, Computerworld Focus, Macintosh Produktkatalog, Macworld Danmark, PC World Danmark, PC Produktguide, Tech World, Windows World; **ECUADOR'S** PC World Ecuador; **EGYPT'S** Computerworld (CW) Middle East, PC World Middle East; **FINLAND'S** MikroPC, Tietoviikko, Tietoverkko; **FRANCE'S** Distributique, GOLDEN MAC, InfoPC, Le Guide du Monde Informatique, Le Monde Informatique, Telecoms & Reseaux; **GERMANY'S** Computerwoche, Computerwoche Focus, Computerwoche Extra, Electronic Entertainment, Gamepro, Information Management, Macwelt, Netzwelt, PC Welt, Publish, Publish; **GREECE'S** Publish & Macworld; **HONG KONG'S** Computerworld Hong Kong, PC World Hong Kong; **HUNGARY'S** Computerworld SZT, PC World; **INDIA'S** Computers & Communications; **INDONESIA'S** Info Komputer; **IRELAND'S** ComputerScope; **ISRAEL'S** Beyond Windows, Computerworld Israel, Multimedia, PC World Israel; **ITALY'S** Computerworld Italia, Lotus Magazine, Macworld Italia, Networking Italia, PC Shopping Italy, PC World Italia; **JAPAN'S** Computerworld Today, Information Systems World, Macworld Japan, Nikkei Personal Computing, SunWorld Japan, Windows World; **KENYA'S** East African Computer News; **KOREA'S** Computerworld Korea, Macworld Korea, PC World Korea; **LATIN AMERICA'S** GamePro; **MALAYSIA'S** Computerworld Malaysia, PC World Malaysia; **MEXICO'S** Compu Edicion, Compu Manufactura, Computacion/Punto de Venta, Computerworld Mexico, MacWorld, Mundo Unix, PC World, Windows; **THE NETHERLANDS'** Computer! Totaal, Computable (CW), LAN Magazine, Lotus Magazine, MacWorld; **NEW ZEALAND'S** Computer Buyer, Computerworld New Zealand, Network World, New Zealand PC World; **NIGERIA'S** PC World Africa; **NORWAY'S** Computerworld Norge, Lotusworld Norge, Macworld Norge, Maxi Data, Networld, PC World Ekspress, PC World Nettverk, PC World Norge, PC World's Produktguide, Publish& Multimedia World, Student Data, Unix World, Windowsworld; **PAKISTAN'S** PC World Pakistan; **PANAMA'S** PC World Panama; **PERU'S** Computerworld Peru, PC World; **PEOPLE'S REPUBLIC OF CHINA'S** China Computerworld, China Infoworld, China PC Info Magazine, Computer Fan, PC World China, Electronics International, Electronics Today/Multimedia World, Electronic Product World, China Network World, Software World Magazine, Telecom Product World; **PHILIPPINES'** Computerworld Philippines, PC Digest (PCW); **POLAND'S** Computerworld Poland, Computerworld Special Report, Networld, PC World/Komputer, Sunworld; **PORTUGAL'S** Cerebro/PC World, Correio Informatico/Computerworld, MacIn; **ROMANIA'S** Computerworld, PC World, Telecom Romania; **RUSSIA'S** Computerworld-Moscow, Mir - PK (PCW), Sety (Networks); **SINGAPORE'S** Computerworld Southeast Asia, PC World Singapore; **SLOVENIA'S** Monitor Magazine; **SOUTH AFRICA'S** Computer Mail (CIO),Computing S.A.,Network World S.A., Software World; **SPAIN'S** Advanced Systems, Amiga World, Computerworld Espana, Communicaciones World, Macworld Espana, NeXTWORLD, Super Juegos Magazine (GamePro), PC World Espana, Publish; **SWEDEN'S** Attack, ComputerSweden, Corporate Computing, Macworld, Mikrodatorn, Natverk & Kommunikation, PC World, CAP & Design, Datalngenjoren, Maxi Data,Windows World; **SWITZERLAND'S** Computerworld Schweiz, Macworld Schweiz, PC Tip; **TAIWAN'S** Computerworld Taiwan, PC World Taiwan; **THAILAND'S** Thai Computerworld; **TURKEY'S** Computerworld Monitor, Macworld Turkiye, PC World Turkiye; **UKRAINE'S** Computerworld, Computers+Software Magazine; **UNITED KINGDOM'S** Computing /Computerworld, Connexion/Network World, Lotus Magazine, Macworld, Open Computing/Sunworld; **UNITED STATES'** Advanced Systems, AmigaWorld, Cable in the Classroom, CD Review, CIO, Computerworld, Computerworld Client/Server Journal, Digital Video, DOS World, Electronic Entertainment Magazine (E2), Federal Computer Week, Game Hits, GamePro, IDG Books Worldwide, Infoworld, Laser Event, Macworld, Maximize, Multimedia World, Network World, PC Letter, PC World, Publish, SWATPro, Video Event; **URUGUAY'S** PC World Uruguay; **VENEZUELA'S** Computerworld Venezuela, PC World; **VIETNAM'S** PC World Vietnam.

05/17/95

Dedication

To EP, the best interactive multimedia experience a guy could ever want.

Acknowledgments

Heartfelt thanks to the vendors who supplied me with the piles and piles of hardware and software required to put together this book, including Keri Walker, Doedy Hunter, Katie Boos, Debbie Riveness, and Jamie Curtis from Apple; Bruce Berkoff from Radius and Morgan Littlefield from A&R Partners; Karen Saper at APS Technologies; Teresa Mahler from Connectix; Chris Smith from VideoLabs; Patricia Pane and LaVon Peck at Adobe Systems; and Jane Chuey and Steve Cherneff at Macromedia. Thanks also to the countless folks in PR departments across the country who participated in Part V by sending us their company's CD-ROMs for review.

A special thanks to the people whose Herculean efforts made this book possible. I could not have done it without the hard work of editor and occasional collaborator Julie King. I feel extremely lucky to have had her able assistance throughout six books in a row. Thanks also to Diane Steele, Milissa Koloski, John Kilcullen, and the others who made this long-term idea bear fruit. And a big "way to go" to Suki Gear, who gave up a small part of her life to the thankless job of calling multimedia vendors during the E3 blackout, and to Megg Bonar, who gave Suki free rein and did all the other things Megg is so wonderful at doing. A final thanks to Beth Jenkins and the A-#1 IDG production crew, which is known to have once laid out a page and bluelined it in less time than it takes a hummingbird to make a single downstroke.

Thanks to Jim Martin for his wealth of CD-ROM vendor contacts. I still owe you. Thanks to *Macworld*'s Marjorie Baer, Carol Person, Galen Gruman, and Wendy Sharp for coming through in times of digital duress. I honestly can't imagine a better magazine to work for. And thanks to Marcus Woziwodzki at PC Brokers for homing in on the most baffling computer problem I've ever encountered.

If this book is accurate, it's in large part because of the over-the-top technical editing and general all-around wisdom of Tim Warner, lab guy supreme at *Macworld* magazine. And, of course, a special thanks to the Deiter family for giving over one room and a special nine-year-old named Jessica to review children's CD-ROMs.

(The Publisher would like to give special thanks to Patrick J. McGovern, without whom this book would not have been possible.)

Credits

Senior Vice President and Publisher
Milissa L. Koloski

Editorial Director
Diane Graves Steele

Acquisitions Editor
Megg Bonar

Brand Manager
Judith A. Taylor

Editorial Manager
Kristin A. Cocks

Editorial Executive Assistant
Richard Graves

Editorial Assistants
Stacey Holden Prince
Kevin Spencer

Acquisitions Assistant
Suki Gear

Production Director
Beth Jenkins

Supervisor of Project Coordination
Cindy L. Phipps

Pre-Press Coordinator
Steve Peake

Associate Pre-Press Coordinator
Tony Augsburger

Media/Archive Coordinator
Paul Belcastro

Project Editor
Julie King

Technical Reviewer
Tim Warner

Production Staff
Gina Scott
Carla C. Radzikinas
Patricia R. Reynolds
Melissa D. Buddendeck
Dwight Ramsey
Robert Springer
Theresa Sánchez-Baker
Kathy Schnorr
Megan Briscoe
Brandt Carter
Angie Hunckler
Laura Puranen
Anna Rohrer
Michael Sullivan

Proofreader
Kathleen Prata

Indexer
Sharon Hilgenberg

Book Design
University Graphics

Cover Design
Kavish + Kavish

Contents at a Glance

Introduction *1*

Part I: Meet Your Awesome Multimedia Mac *7*
Chapter 1: "Big Tub o' Media" Just Doesn't Have the Same Ring 9
Chapter 2: Adding the All-Important CD-ROM Drive 23
Chapter 3: Building a Computerized Stereo 41
Chapter 4: See All that You Can See 51
Chapter 5: What in the World is Going on with AV? 65
Chapter 6: You Can Never Have Enough Digital Closet Space 81

Part II: The Glorious World of Digital Images *91*
Chapter 7: Putting Your Photo Albums on CD 93
Chapter 8: Taking Computer Pictures 103
Chapter 9: Keeping Track of Your Images (and Other Media) 113
Chapter 10: Playing with Pictures 123

Part III: Teaching Your Mac to Sing, Record, and Speak *137*
Chapter 11: Listening to Your Audio CDs 139
Chapter 12: Recording Sounds for Fun and Profit 155
Chapter 13: Editing Sounds Like a Pro 173
Chapter 14: Conversing with Your Computer 193

Part IV: Hollywood in a Box *205*
Chapter 15: TV Meets Monitor 207
Chapter 16: A New Kind of Picture Show 223
Chapter 17: Recording Your Own QuickTime Movies to Disk 233
Chapter 18: Cutting Room Meets Special Effects Factory 249
Chapter 19: Sending Your Movies Back to Videotape 267

Part V: The Part of Tens 275

Chapter 20: Ten Ways to Make Your CD-ROMs Perform like Champs 277
Chapter 21: Top Ten CDs — Interactive Coffee-Table Books 283
Chapter 22: Top Ten CDs — Educational Resources 299
Chapter 23: Top Ten CDs — Games and Entertainment 319
Chapter 24: Top Ten CDs — Great Stuff for Kids 341

Index 359

Reader Response Card .... Back of Book

Cartoons at a Glance
By Rich Tennant

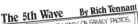

page 122

page 205

page 172

page 137

page 275

page 248

page 91

page 7

page 50

page 339

Table of Contents

Introduction 1

What Do I Have to Know to Use This Book? 2
What's in This Book? 3
    Part I: Meet Your Awesome Multimedia Mac 3
    Part II: The Glorious World of Digital Images 3
    Part III: Teaching Your Computer to Sing, Record, and Speak ... 4
    Part IV: Hollywood in a Box 4
    Part V: The Part of Tens 4
What's with All the Margin Icons? 4
Where Do I Go Next? 6

Part I: Meet Your Awesome Multimedia Mac 7

Chapter 1: "Big Tub o' Media" Just Doesn't Have the Same Ring 9

What Does Multimedia Mean to You? 10
The World's Number One Multimedia Computer 11
    Mac multimedia milestones 11
    Just how multimedia is your Mac? 14
    Multimedia on the go 18
    My computer got a "stinky"! What do I do? 21

Chapter 2: Adding the All-Important CD-ROM Drive 23

CDs are Much Simpler than You Think 24
    So what's so special about CDs? 24
    The care and feeding of your CDs 25
All about CD-ROM Drives 27
    Why speed doesn't matter 27
    Internal or external? 29
What to Look for in an External Drive 29
    The front of the drive, in all its splendor 30
    The drive's more important rear end 31
    Does it support all kinds of CDs? 33
How to Make the Right SCSI Connections 33
What to Expect from an Internal Drive 37
CD Software Stuff 38
How to Get the CD the Heck Out of the Machine 39

Chapter 3: Building a Computerized Stereo 41

Meet Your Mac's Sound-Out Port 42
What Can the Sound-Out Port Do? 42
The Serpentine World of Cables 43
    The secrets of the miniplug 44
    Channel-splitting 45
    What about my external CD-ROM drive? 46
Treat Yourself to a Set of Powered Speakers 47
    Mighty morphing power speakers 47
    How low can you go? 47
    More criteria for the savvy shopper 49
What Now? 50

Chapter 4: See All that You Can See 51

Mac Screen Facts 52
The Curious World of Computerized Color 53
    Some CDs like color more than others 54
    Explore your personal crayon box 56
How to Get More Colors 59
    Vroom! Vim! VRAM! 59
    When everything else fails, buy a board 60
    Some Macs need special care 63
My CD-ROM Won't Play 64

Chapter 5: What in the World is Going on with AV? 65

The Primo Multimedia Macs 66
    Big AVs on campus 66
    The spunky AV junior 68
What Makes AV Tick, Whir, and Flicker? 69
Get Out Your VCRs! 71
    Plug it again, Jack 72
    How do I play video into my computer? 73
    And how do I send computer signals to the VCR? 75
Make Your AV Even Better 77
    A technology named DAV 77
    How to get hitched to DAV 77
Can You Add AV to Your Old Mac? 79

Chapter 6: You Can Never Have Enough Digital Closet Space 81

Your Mac Can't Think Straight without Memory 82
    How much RAM is enough? 83
    If I only had some RAM 84
Space on the Platter 85
    Give me space, lots of space 86
    Tips for buying that new digital parcel 87
Storage on the Run 88

Part II: The Glorious World of Digital Images 91

Chapter 7: Putting Your Photo Albums on CD 93
Getting Those Pics on the Discs 95
Keeping Abreast of Your Thumbnails 96
Sticking the Photo CD in the Drive 97
    Take a stroll through your digital album 98
    How to get a closer look 100
    Print, edit, have a ball 102
    When was this photo scanned? 102

Chapter 8: Taking Computer Pictures 103
Shooting Computerized Polaroids 104
    The quickest shooter in the West 105
    Who needs a digital camera? 106
Comparing a Couple of Cameras 107
Snapping Philmless Fotos 108
Turning Your Camcorder into a Digital Camera......................110

Chapter 9: Keeping Track of Your Images (and Other Media) 113
Creating an On-Screen Image Album in PhotoFlash 114
Amassing Your Digital Imagery in Fetch 116
Playing with Your Catalog 118
Figuring Out Files and Files of Formats 120

Chapter 10: Playing with Pictures 123
Just What Can Photoshop Do? 124
Stilt the Tilt 126
    Putting the image on the up and up 127
    Making the tower go straight 128
Clip Away the Excess Gunkage 129
Sharpen the Focus 131
Breathe New Life into Dead Colors 133
    Taking colors to new levels 134
    Doing the color correction five-step 135

Part III: Teaching Your Mac to Sing, Record, and Speak 137

Chapter 11: Listening to Your Audio CDs 139
Hear the Music 139
Spin the Silver Platters 143
Take My CD Remote, Please 145

The Just Plain Better CD Audio Player 148
    Naming the tracks 149
    Customizing the album 149
    Fooling around with the options 151
How Long's that Song? 152
My Sound is Cutting Out! 153

Chapter 12: Recording Sounds for Fun and Profit 155

Bonding with Your Microphone 157
    Mike in the box 157
    Which mike is right for your Mac? 159
Recording from That Crazy External CD-ROM Drive 160
Setting Up a Recording Session 161
Creating That Perfect Error Beep 163
    Sound advice 165
    How to play an alert scale 167
Teaching Your Files to Speak 169

Chapter 13: Editing Sounds Like a Pro 173

Editing Sound for Pennies on the Dollar 174
Grasping the Semantics of Cybernetic Sound 175
    Inside every sound bite is a bunch of bits 175
    Blips per second 177
    Yes, well, very nice, but so what? 177
Recording in Style 178
    Recording monophonic stuff 178
    Reading the sound wave 181
    Recording two channels at a time 183
Wreaking Havoc on Your Sounds 186
Messing about with the System's Innards 188
    Lifting a sound right out of the System 188
    Pilfering sounds from other programs 191

Chapter 14: Conversing with Your Computer 193

How to Install Your Computer's Vocal Cords 194
Computer's First Words 196
    Some voices are smarter than others 198
    Meet the cast 199
    Speaking tips 200
Some Ways to Put Speech to Practical Use 201
    Getting your computer to tell you every little thing 201
    Getting a rise out of a few keys 202
I'm So Glad You've Had This Time Together 203

Part IV: Hollywood in a Box 205

Chapter 15: TV Meets Monitor 207

The Couch Potato's Dream Machine 208
    Getting to TV-watching headquarters 210
    Introducing the Video Player to the neighborhood 211
    Fine-tuning the setup 212
    Protecting impressionable minds 213
Other Stuff You Can Do with a Computerized TV 215
How to Watch TV on the Big AV 219

Chapter 16: A New Kind of Picture Show 223

The QuickTime Collection 225
Where to Find Movies and a Program to Play Them 226
Take a Crack at the QuickTime Projector 227
QuickTime Movies on a CD-ROM 229
QuickTime's Virtual World 230

Chapter 17: Recording Your Own QuickTime Movies to Disk 233

Checking Your P's and Q's 234
Bringing Big Movies to the Small Screen 235
    Flying your colors at half mast 235
    Making a recording 236
    Grabbing a still image 242
Picking Up the Pace 243
Buying a Live Video Camera 244

Chapter 18: Cutting Room Meets Special Effects Factory 249

Premiere Just Wants to Be Understood 250
First, Carve Up Your Scenes 254
What to Do with All Those Clips 257
Fade to Bob, Alone by the Marigolds 259
Prelude to a Movie 261
Show Time 263

Chapter 19: Sending Your Movies Back to Videotape 267

How to Send Video Out to Your VCR 268
Where's My Menu Bar? 271
How to Fill the Screen with Movie 272
I Was Told We'd See Color Bars 273

Part V: The Part of Tens 275

Chapter 20: Ten Ways to Make Your CD-ROMs Perform like Champs 277

Install QuickTime and Its Cronies Once and Never Again 278
Turn off File Sharing, Virtual Memory, and RAM Doubler 278
Give HyperCard Player More Memory 278
Copy the Main Program File to Your Hard Drive 279
Set the Video to Thousands 279
Click to Skip the Introductory Movie 280
Don't Go Clicking Like a Madman 280
Move the Cursor away from the Movie 281
Press ⌘-Q to Skip the Closing Credits 281
What to Do When All Else Fails 282

Chapter 21: Top Ten CDs — Interactive Coffee-Table Books 283

Material World: A Global Family Portrait 284
American Visions: 20th Century Art from the
  Roy R. Neuberger Collection 285
OceanLife: Volumes 2 through 4 287
For All Mankind 288
Passage to Vietnam 289
The Complete Maus: A Survivor's Tale 291
Four Paws of Crab 292
Seven Days in August: Unfold the Drama of the Cold War 293
Comic Book Confidential 295
Oceans Below 296
The Next-Best Ten 297

Chapter 22: Top Ten CDs — Educational Resources 299

The First Emperor of China 300
The Crucible 301
A.D.A.M. 303
The Cartoon History of the Universe 304
How Animals Move 306
Microsoft Exploration Series 307
The Rosetta Stone Language Library 309
Exploring Ancient Cities 310
Macbeth 312
Learn to Speak Spanish 313
The Next-Best Ten 314

Chapter 23: Top Ten CDs — Games and Entertainment 319

    The Lost Mind of Dr. Brain 320
    Star Trek: The Next Generation Interactive Technical Manual 321
    The Daedalus Encounter 323
    Myst 325
    Gadget 326
    The Residents Freak Show 327
    SimCity Enhanced 329
    Lode Runner: The Legend Returns 331
    This Is Spinal Tap 332
    Rebel Assault 334
    The Next-Best Ten 335

Chapter 24: Top Ten CDs — Great Stuff for Kids 341

    Gahan Wilson's The Ultimate Haunted House 342
    The Trail Series 344
    Mario is Missing! Deluxe 345
    Welcome to Bodyland 347
    Putt-Putt Joins the Parade 348
    Bailey's Book House (and Friends) 349
    Math Workshop 351
    SimTown 353
    3-D Dinosaur Adventure 354
    The Living Books Series 355

Index 359

Reader Response Card... Back of Book

Introduction

By 2010, television as we know it will be dead, and you'll be responsible.

Okay, the passive TV experience won't be *completely* out of the picture, but nor will it enjoy the singular popularity it enjoys today. Consider the example of TV's audio-only cousin, radio. AM radio was invented in 1915, and the first radio shows were broadcast in 1920. Throughout the mid-30s and 40s, radio reigned as the most popular and pervasive means of entertainment in the world. Movie houses, the other overnight entertainment success of the day, closed down from 7:15 to 7:30 every weekday evening to pipe in "Amos and Andy." "The War of the Worlds" broadcast of 1938 scared millions silly and propelled Orson Welles into the headlines. And for the first time, a real war, World War II, was brought home in startling detail. And yet, by the 1950s, the world's most important media was on the way out. The last network radio dramas played in 1962, leaving only music, news, call-in shows, and "A Prairie Home Companion."

The culprit was television, the box that added pictures to the sound. By the time the first transcontinental broadcast went out in 1951, TV had become the major force in world culture, and color TV was under way. But after 40 years of dominance, TV continues to grow out but not up. Despite promises of higher screen resolution and hundreds of channels, TV remains a passive experience. The only way to "talk back" is to call "Donahue" or buy a product on QVC.

Television's interactive replacement is the computer. Sure, computers have been around for a long time — since the 40s — but although they occasionally found their way into news stories about cracking top-secret Nazi codes and predicting presidential elections, it wasn't until the 1970s that they became widely available to regular Dick and Jane users like us. In addition to replacing typewriters, calculators, and Rolodexes, computers achieved instant success as game machines. Ever since Pong, computers have competed with TV and have even affected television programming. You can see the impact of computer graphics in everything from the arcade-style edits of MTV to the montage of kiddy anarchy broadcast every Saturday morning. There are even shows and movies based on computer games (a messed up idea if there ever was one).

But you haven't seen anything yet. Multimedia CD-ROM titles are springing up like rabbits and are projected to outsell videotapes in the next decade. In ten years, computers will be integrated into home entertainment systems as regularly as cable boxes are now, and fiber-optic entertainment services will pipe in a gamut of fully interactive games and information vehicles for basic subscription fees. Participatory dramatic fare will come a few years after that. (For a contemporary example of what you can expect to see in spades in the future, read "The Daedalus Encounter" section of Chapter 23.)

The idea of so much change may seem scary, especially when it affects such basics as entertainment and communication. But in truth, the only reason multimedia will triumph is because *you* will take to it as naturally as a fish takes to water. Multimedia promises to offer a more rewarding and more absorbing entertainment and education experience than any passive form we've seen in the past (this book included).

With that in mind, *Mac Multimedia & CD-ROMs For Dummies* gets you ready for this brave new world by offering an exciting tour of multimedia as it exists today on the Macintosh computer. Frankly, I think that you'll be surprised to learn how far things have already come. All Macs offer built-in sound, most come with microphones and speaker ports, and the recent models offer video-input jacks for integrating TV signals. You can actually record a movie to disk or play a computer movie out to videotape. Most non-Macs don't begin to offer these amazing options as standard equipment. And it goes without saying that you can play interactive CD-ROMs until the cows come home. Your Mac is ready to entertain, educate, and interact right this minute. What your friends will be doing five years from now, you can do today.

What Do I Have to Know to Use This Book?

Not much. I want this book to be fully understandable, whether by you, your mom, your dad, your boss, your secretary, or whoever is the primary computer dummy in your particular sphere of influence. I assume that you have no primary knowledge whatsoever about sound, video, or CD-ROM technology. (You don't even have to know what a CD-ROM is; I'll tell you in Chapter 2.) If multimedia is Greek to you, then you're ready to start right in.

I do assume a smidgen of Macintosh experience, however:

- I assume that you're familiar with the *Finder desktop*, that place where all the file and folder icons hang out. It's the first thing you see after you turn on your computer.

- Hopefully, you know the three basic ways to use your mouse. Press the mouse button once to *click*; press twice in a row to *double-click*; and hold the button down while moving the mouse to *drag*.

- I also assume that you know how to start up a program, such as Microsoft Word, ClarisWorks, or one of those.

> ✔ I assume that you know how to choose commands from menus. In this book, if I say, "Choose File➪New," that means to choose the New command from the File menu.

I don't think that you'll have any problem keeping up — you look like a pretty savvy customer to me — but if you have any reservations, read *Macs For Dummies* by David Pogue. This delightful book explains the basic Mac stuff as clearly as any I've seen.

What's in This Book?

Of all the books I've written so far, this one is my personal favorite. Granted, I always feel this way when I finish a book, but this time, I'm ready to burst with sheer verve. *Mac Multimedia and CD-ROMs For Dummies* was the most exciting, the most demanding, and the most fun book I've had the pleasure to create. I sincerely hope the enthusiasm on my end translates to understanding and enjoyment on yours.

I've manifested my zest for Mac multimedia into five parts. The first part lays out all the nasty, persnickety hardware stuff. After that, you can skip to any chapter in any other part of the book you like without missing a beat.

Part I: Meet Your Awesome Multimedia Mac

Every Mac ever shipped offers some kind of multimedia capabilities. But some Macs are more blessed than others. In addition to explaining just what multimedia is and mapping out what different Macintosh computers can do, I offer specific advice for buying and installing CD-ROM drives, audio speakers, monitors, RAM, and hard drives. I also introduce you to the AV Macs, which can handle video and TV.

Part II: The Glorious World of Digital Images

The three primary cornerstones of multimedia are still images, sound, and video. This part of the book explains still images, the common everyday pictures that you can transfer to your computer screen. I show you how to put photos on a CD-ROM, how to take pictures with digital cameras, how to keep track of your images so that you can instantly find that special picture of Aunt Zelda 20 years from now, and how to edit pictures to make them look better (or weirder).

Part III: Teaching Your Computer to Sing, Record, and Speak

It's so funny to hear PC users talk about their new sound cards and all the great sounds they can hear. Hey, Earth to PC user: The Mac has been playing sound without any additional hardware since the first one hit the shelves in 1984, and it just keeps getting better. Now you can play your music CDs with your CD-ROM drive, record sounds from a microphone or from a CD, and edit sounds to delete stuff or add special effects. You can even make your computer talk — and I mean talk *well* — in one of 22 voices.

Part IV: Hollywood in a Box

Video is the newest Mac multimedia wave. The Mac has been able to handle on-screen movies since 1991, but now the movies are bigger, better looking, and more believable than ever. Provided that you have the proper hardware, you can watch TV on your monitor, record movies from videotape to disk, and play a digital movie out to your VCR. And even without special video hardware, you can play movies other folks have recorded and even edit them. I show you how in these chapters.

Part V: The Part of Tens

The term *CD-ROM* figures pretty prominently into the name of this book. But by this point in the book, I've discussed CDs in Chapters 2 and 11 — hardly what I'd call extensive coverage. Well, here are five more chapters devoted entirely to CD-ROMs. Learn how to get the most enjoyment and performance out of your CDs and read reviews of the top ten CD-ROM titles in four categories. With the help of the kind folks at IDG Books, I was able to round up more than 300 CD-ROMs from which to cull my top recommendations, as you can see in the upcoming figure. Even if you don't plan on buying any of these CDs right now, you can see what's new, what's hot, and where it's all going.

What's with All the Margin Icons?

There are purists in the world who believe that you should stick to written words when communicating on the printed page, and that's it. Well, phooey. If a picture tells a story of its own, I say use it. The following pictures are signposts that point out text that you'll want to read first, read last, read in order, or not read at all. It's totally up to you; I just want you to know what's coming. And as an added bonus, each icon is thoughtfully labeled in case you can't remember what the picture means.

Introduction 5

Some pictures of the 300 Macintosh CD-ROM titles that took over my house during the making of this book.

Multimedia does have its technical sides. Folks in the know are constantly slinging about terms like *16-bit graphics* and *22 kHz sound*. If you want to know precisely what these folks are talking about, look for this icon.

After you make sense of what's going on, you may start wishing that you could work faster and avoid a few steps. When you start yearning for a better way, check out the Tip icons.

This icon calls out some important bit of information that will keep you in good stead for years to come. Or it may remind you of something you may have forgotten. Never skip a Remember icon.

Mac Multimedia & CD-ROMs For Dummies

 Not much can go wrong when you're working with multimedia. But if you're venturing into dangerous territory, I spell it out with this icon, and I tell you exactly how to avoid trouble.

 Every so often, I feel compelled to share some silly bit of information that doesn't add a thing to your understanding of multimedia or computers in general. I'm just talking to hear myself talk. If you want to tune me out, skip this icon.

 Every year, Apple makes a bundle of breakthroughs in multimedia computing, and then the next year, a bunch of PCs follow suit. To see where the Mac has blazed new territory, keep an eye out for this icon.

 Okay, I've never appeared on the Psychic Friends Network, but every once in a while, I share an insight into how multimedia will change the way we entertain and educate ourselves in the future. This icon points out my predictions of things to come.

Where Do I Go Next?

One of the wonderful things about multimedia is that it's fully interactive. You click on a button, and the button takes you where you want to go.

Well, I don't know if you've noticed, but books are interactive, too. You look up a topic of concern in the index, go to the suggested page, and the mysteries of the universe unfold before you.

Certainly, I encourage you to read the book in the order I've laid it out. This isn't a book of boring facts; I wrote it to be read in a comfy chair by a crackling fire, with a warm glass of milk within easy reach. But if you just want the answer to a burning question, feel free to flip around. I'll do my best to snag you and teach you a couple of extra things in the bargain.

Part I
Meet Your Awesome Multimedia Mac

The 5th Wave By Rich Tennant

"I did this report with the help of a satellite view atmospheric map from the National Weather Service, research text from the Jet Propulsion Laboratory, and a sound file from 'The Barfing Lungworms' new CD."

In this part . . .

There's nothing like a good analogy to bring home a topic. With that in mind, imagine that multimedia is a potentially beautiful flowering plant seeking nourishment. The world of personal computers comprises two kinds of soil for this plant to choose from. Most of this soil is dry, flaky clay, or what we know as DOS and Windows-compatible PCs. To make the clay sustain life, you have to add a confusing array of fertilizer and compost — or what computer dealers call sound cards, video cards, special driver software, and so on. It's enough to make you give up on the flower and let it die.

But a lucky few were smart enough to buy the right kind of soil in the first place. Rich soil that came preconfigured with the essential ingredients that will make the flower bloom. You guessed it, my friend — the name of that soil is Macintosh.

Every Mac sold in the last three years is a multimedia planter box just waiting for you to sow the seeds and add water. (Older machines provide slightly poorer soil but can be made to support multimedia life with a little effort.) The chapters in this part explain how to start your garden, how to care for your new seedlings, and how to make sure that your multimedia takes root.

In the months that follow, try to be kind to your suffering PC friends. When they tell their stories of multimedia dying on the vine, when they explain with stiff upper lips that the crude multimedia that they've managed to craft is "good enough," offer a sympathetic ear and a shoulder to cry on. Because, as every Mac user does, you'll want like heck to say, "Neener neener neener."

Chapter 1
"Big Tub o' Media" Just Doesn't Have the Same Ring

In This Chapter
- An introduction to multimedia
- How to use multimedia
- A tour of Mac multimedia from 1984 to the present
- The sound and video capabilities of every Mac released since the Mac Plus
- Advice for upgrading your present Mac

*M*ultimedia is what your fifth-grade teacher would have called a *compound word,* with *multi* on one side of the aisle and *media* on the other. The latter part — media — is the linchpin of multimedia. It refers to any material on which you can record sound, video, graphics, and even text. A CD is a variety of media. So are videotapes, cassettes, books, laserdiscs, records, snapshots, 8-tracks, Super-8 home movies, slabs of rock with hieroglyphics chiseled into them — in short, anything you can use to capture information and convey it across the vast seas of time can be considered media.

The prefix *multi,* which is derived from the Latin word *multus* — meaning *much* or *many* — translates literally to *big tub o'*. Witness *multimillion,* which means *big tub o' millions,* or *multiplicity,* short for *big tub o' plicities.* Other examples are too *multitudinous* to mention.

It should come as no surprise, therefore, that *multimedia* means *big tub o' media* — that is, the integration of many different kinds of media into a single production. It's the kind of thing that film editors have been doing for years. They mix moving images from one source, sound effects from another, music from a third, and titles from a fourth to create a single work of art. (At least, *they* consider their stuff art, so who am I to judge?)

Naturally, your Macintosh computer isn't quite as well equipped as a film editing studio. But it is better suited to handling the rigors of multimedia computing than any other brand of personal computer. It reads CDs, it plays digital sounds and movies from disk, and it might even allow you to display video images on your monitor. Suffice it to say, the Mac eats media for breakfast (along with its *multigrade vitamin plus iron*).

What Does Multimedia Mean to You?

This may be very well and good for your Mac, but what about you? Here are a few ways you can use your Mac's media-snarfing capabilities to improve your general quality of life:

- **Play an interactive CD-ROM:** Hundreds upon thousands of CD-ROM titles abound for the Macintosh computer. Most are *interactive*, meaning that they obey your instructions (rather than just playing along whether you like it or not, like TV). For example, you can search through an encyclopedia, play a game, or explore an imaginary environment by clicking on buttons and choosing options from menus. Chapter 2 tells you how to get started. Part V reviews some of my favorite CD-ROM titles.

- **Play an audio CD:** If you have a CD-ROM drive hooked up to your computer, you can turn your computer into a cranking, state-of-the-art stereo system for less than $200. Chapter 3 tells you how to set things up; Chapter 11 tells you how to make it work.

- **Record and edit digital sounds:** Many Macs come with microphones so that you can record your voice to disk. You can also record sounds from CDs and other sources. After you record sounds, you can edit them by splicing out words, applying special effects, or mixing voice with music. Chapters 12 and 13 explain everything you need to know.

- **Open and edit photographs stored on CD:** Kodak's Photo CD technology lets you store your family snapshots in rich, beautiful color on a CD. Not only is a CD better able to withstand the scourges of time, but it also enables you to print as many copies of your photographs as you like and edit them as you see fit. See Chapters 7 and 10 for the whole story.

- **Play digital movies:** Your Macintosh system software includes a little something called QuickTime that lets you play movies stored on disk and view them on your monitor. Chapter 16 explains how QuickTime works and shows you how to play digital movies.

✓ **Record your own digital movies:** If you have an AV Mac or some other brand of video recording hardware — such as SuperMac's old VideoSpigot — you can record movies from videotape. You can then edit the movies, add titles, or mix in new soundtracks. Chapter 5 tells how to hook up your VCR to an AV computer. Chapter 17 shows how to capture movies to disk; Chapter 18 tells how to edit them; and Chapter 19 explains how to record them back to videotape.

The World's Number One Multimedia Computer

All Macintosh computers offer multimedia capabilities. The very first Mac, introduced more than 10 years ago, could play digital sounds right out of the box — a feat that many DOS- and Windows-based PCs still can't pull off without the aid of additional hardware. Other Macs can record sounds, play CD-ROM discs, display amazingly colorful graphics, and record movies. When it comes to multimedia, the Mac is in a league all its own.

Mac multimedia milestones

Just for fun, I thought that I'd include a list of historic blasts from the Mac's illustrious past. It's a little something you can show to your Windows friends and taunt "Can your PC do this?" while humming "*neener neener.*" I mean, what good is owning a Mac if you can't feel superior on occasion?

✓ **January 1984:** The original Mac (later dubbed the 128K) became the first personal computer to provide an internal speaker that played digitized sounds. At its unveiling, the Mac even spoke, starting off with a bit of well-timed levity: "It sure is great to get out of that bag."

✓ **January 1986:** The Mac Plus introduced the SCSI (pronounced *scuzzy*) port, which let you plug in an external hard drive. Years later, this same port enabled adventurous users to plug in CD-ROM drives so that they could play their favorite interactive titles.

✓ **March 1987:** The Macintosh II was the first machine to play stereo sound through a minijack at the back of the machine. You could plug in a pair of Walkman-type headphones or hook up special speakers.

The Mac II was also the first Mac to include interior slots that allowed you to enhance the capabilities of the machine by adding special upgrade boards. You could buy boards to hook up a color monitor or improve the computer's sound capabilities.

- **September 1989:** The IIci was the first Mac to include a video port so that you could hook up a color monitor without buying more hardware. This incredibly stalwart machine reigned as the most capable Macintosh model for more than a year. Hey, that's pretty good. A human year is equal to about 70 computer years. And most computers don't even live to see 50.

- **October 1990:** The Mac LC and IIsi were the first Macs to offer microphones so that you could enjoy the melodious sounds of your own voice. Both machines also included sound-input jacks so that you could capture sounds from CDs and tapes.

- **October 1991:** The Quadra 900 offered both a stereo microphone minijack and left and right RCA jacks, just like those built into standard stereo systems. The bad news was that the two stereo signals were combined into a single signal by the logic board, so the Mac remained limited to monophonic sound. Strange but true.

   That same month marked the introduction of the PowerBooks 140 and 170, which were the first Macintosh laptop models to provide sound-input jacks like those in the LC and IIsi.

- **September 1992:** The Performa 600 was the first Mac to offer an optional internal CD-ROM drive, the AppleCD 300i. This drive supported Kodak's Photo CD format so that you could open family snapshots and other electronic photos. (One month later, Apple released this same machine as the IIvx in the U.S. and as the IIvi abroad. What will those wacky marketing folks think of next?)

   The PowerBooks 160 and 180 also debuted in September. These models were the first Mac laptops to provide more than two colors, black and white. They also offered video-out ports so that you could hook them up to color monitors. As if that weren't enough, they sported built-in mikes at the top of their keyboards.

- **June 1993:** The LC520 was one of those strange creatures that came and went without much notice but had a big influence on the course of Macintosh development. It looked like a standard Mac with a monitor fused to the top. Below the screen were two stereo speakers — a first for the Mac — as well as a headphone jack with volume controls — another first.

- **July 1993:** The Centris 660AV (later slightly upgraded and renamed the Quadra 660AV) and the Quadra 840AV revolutionized Macintosh multimedia, enabling you to capture movies from videotape or laserdisc complete with CD-quality, stereo sound. You could then edit the movies on disk and play them back to videotape. Finally, some multimedia technology you could really sink your teeth into!

- **October 1993:** The PowerBook Duo 270c became the first Mac notebook to support thousands of colors on the built-in LCD screen (up from the standard 256 colors). Unfortunately, the image size shrunk slightly to accommodate the additional colors, making the screen look like a letterboxed movie with black stripes at the top and bottom. And the LCD screen wasn't capable of displaying all the colors properly. But progress isn't always perfect.

  No discussion of imperfect progress would be complete without mentioning the Macintosh TV. This unusual computer integrated a cable-ready tuner and remote control so that you could hook up a coaxial cable and actually change channels, just like on a real TV. The machine also had two RCA sound-output jacks, so you could hook it up to a stereo receiver. Sadly, it was limited and overpriced. For $2,000, you could display computer graphics *or* video, but not both at once, and you couldn't record QuickTime movies.

- **March 1994:** Apple released its new Power Macintosh line of computers, which included Motorola's super-fast PowerPC chip. The Power Macs 6100, 7100, and 8100 came with optional AV hardware, which endowed them with the full suite of options provided by the Quadra 840AV. This meant video-input and -output jacks and the ability to record CD-quality stereo sound.

- **May 1994:** The PowerBook 500 series was born. These machines allowed you to record CD-quality stereo sound just like the AV Macs. They also included built-in stereo speakers, like the LC520. The built-in microphone was still monophonic, but you could record stereo sound from tapes and CDs.

- **July 1994:** Apple introduced the Quadra 630, which was also released as the LC 630 and Performa 630 through 636. These systems could accommodate an optional video capture card and a TV tuner, making them a cross between the AV Macs and the Mac TV. Better yet, you could resize the TV window so that you could watch TV and work on your Mac. (Gosh knows, you can get a lot of work done that way.) However, it lacked the ability to output movies to videotape or record stereo sound.

- **April 1995:** The first computer to feature the upgraded PowerPC 603 chip was the Power Macintosh 5200/75 LC. Though actually slower than older Macs with 601 chips, it was less expensive. The entire computer was built into the equivalent of a monitor case — on a swivel stand, no less. This consumer model supported all the optional Quadra 630 hardware, including both video-capture card and TV tuner.

Wow, what a history! And as I write this in early 1995, Apple is poised to release all kinds of new models that will steer multimedia in new directions. What an exciting time to be alive (unless you have to knock yourself out trying to keep up with the new technology like I do, in which case you can replace the word "exciting" with "totally overwhelming").

Just how multimedia is your Mac?

Chances are better than even that you don't own any of the computers mentioned in my exhilarating timeline. After all, Apple has released more than 80 models, and I've only mentioned a quarter of them.

In case you're not sure what capabilities your particular Mac offers, check out Table 1-1, which describes each and every desktop Mac released since the Mac Plus in alphabetical order. (If you own a laptop Mac, such as a PowerBook or Duo, don't fret. I include another table just for laptops a few pages from now.)

If you're shopping for a new or used model, feel free to use the table as a buying guide. I even rate each machine from "poor" to "excellent" ("excellent" being the best, in case you're new to rating systems). It's a little extra you won't find in any other multimedia book. Ah shucks, don't mention it.

Table 1-1 The Amazing Capabilities of Desktop Macs

Macintosh Model	Internal CD-ROM	Sound In	Sound Out	Maximum Colors	Television In and Out	Multimedia Rating
II	no	NA	stereo	NA	no	fair
IIci	no	NA	stereo	256	no	fair
IIcx	no	NA	stereo	NA	no	fair
IIfx	no	NA	stereo	NA	no	fair
IIsi	no	mono	stereo	256	no	fair
IIvi	optional	mono	stereo	thousands	no	good
IIvx	optional	mono	stereo	thousands	no	good
IIx	no	NA	stereo	NA	no	fair
Centris 610	optional	mono	stereo	thousands	no	good
Centris 650	optional	mono	stereo	thousands	no	good
Centris 660AV	yes	stereo	stereo	thousands	yes	very good
Classic	no	NA	mono	2	no	poor
Classic II	no	mono	mono	2	no	poor
Color Classic	no	mono	mono	thousands	no	fair
Color Classic II	no	mono	mono	thousands	no	fair

Chapter 1: "Big Tub o' Media" Just Doesn't Have the Same Ring

Macintosh Model	Internal CD-ROM	Sound In	Sound Out	Maximum Colors	Television In and Out	Multimedia Rating
LC	no	mono	mono	256	no	fair
LC 475	no	mono	stereo	thousands	no	fair
LC 520	yes	mono	stereo	thousands	no	good
LC 550	yes	stereo	stereo	thousands	no	good
LC 575	yes	stereo	stereo	thousands	no	good
LC 580	yes	stereo	stereo	thousands	optional	good
LC 630	optional	stereo	stereo	thousands	optional	very good
LC II	no	mono	mono	256	no	fair
LC III	no	mono	mono	thousands	no	fair
Performa 200	no	mono	mono	?	no	poor
Performa 400	no	mono	mono	256	no	fair
Performa 405	no	mono	mono	256	no	fair
Performa 410	no	mono	mono	256	no	fair
Performa 430	no	mono	mono	256	no	fair
Performa 450	no	mono	mono	thousands	no	fair
Performa 460	no	mono	mono	thousands	no	fair
Performa 466	no	mono	mono	thousands	no	fair
Performa 467	no	mono	mono	thousands	no	fair
Performa 475	no	mono	stereo	thousands	no	fair
Performa 476	no	mono	stereo	thousands	no	fair
Performa 550	yes	stereo	stereo	thousands	no	good
Performa 560	yes	stereo	stereo	thousands	no	good
Performa 570	yes	stereo	stereo	thousands	optional	good
Performa 575	yes	stereo	stereo	thousands	no	good
Performa 577	yes	stereo	stereo	thousands	no	good
Performa 578	yes	stereo	stereo	thousands	no	good
Performa 580	yes	stereo	stereo	thousands	optional	good
Performa 600	optional	mono	stereo	thousands	no	good
Performa 630	optional	stereo	stereo	thousands	optional	very good

(continued)

Table 1-1 *(continued)*

Macintosh Model	Internal CD-ROM	Sound In	Sound Out	Maximum Colors	Television In and Out	Multimedia Rating
Performa 635	optional	stereo	stereo	thousands	optional	very good
Performa 636	optional	stereo	stereo	thousands	optional	very good
Performa 638	optional	stereo	stereo	thousands	optional	very good
Performa 6110	yes	stereo	stereo	thousands	no	good
Performa 6112	yes	stereo	stereo	thousands	no	good
Performa 6115	yes	stereo	stereo	thousands	no	good
Performa 6117	yes	stereo	stereo	thousands	no	good
Performa 6118	yes	stereo	stereo	thousands	no	good
Plus	no	NA	mono	2	no	poor
Power Mac 5200 LC	yes	stereo	stereo	thousands	optional	very good
Power Mac 6100	optional	stereo	stereo	thousands	no	good
Power Mac 6100AV	yes	stereo	stereo	millions	yes	very good
Power Mac 7100	optional	stereo	stereo	millions	no	good
Power Mac 7100AV	yes	stereo	stereo	millions	yes	excellent
Power Mac 7500	yes	stereo	stereo	millions	in only	very good
Power Mac 8100	optional	stereo	stereo	millions	no	good
Power Mac 8100AV	yes	stereo	stereo	millions	yes	excellent
Power Mac 8500	yes	stereo	stereo	millions	yes	excellent

Chapter 1: "Big Tub o' Media" Just Doesn't Have the Same Ring

Macintosh Model	Internal CD-ROM	Sound In	Sound Out	Maximum Colors	Television In and Out	Multimedia Rating
Quadra 605	no	mono	stereo	thousands	no	fair
Quadra 610	optional	mono	stereo	thousands	no	good
Quadra 630	optional	stereo	stereo	thousands	optional	very good
Quadra 650	optional	mono	stereo	thousands	no	good
Quadra 660AV	yes	stereo	stereo	thousands	yes	very good
Quadra 700	optional	mono	stereo	millions	no	good
Quadra 800	optional	mono	stereo	thousands	no	good
Quadra 840AV	yes	stereo	stereo	millions	yes	excellent
Quadra 900	optional	mono	stereo	millions	no	good
Quadra 950	optional	mono	stereo	millions	no	good
SE	no	NA	mono	2	no	poor
SE/30	no	NA	stereo	2	no	poor
TV	yes	mono	stereo	thousands	in only	good

Having looked up your particular Mac (along with four or five others just to see how it compares), it's quite possible that you're not clear about how some of the categories work. I mean, how is it that the Mac II can get "NA" in the "Maximum Colors" category? Just to make everything crystal clear, the following list elaborates:

- **Internal CD-ROM:** An internal CD-ROM affords the most benefits because you can automatically play the audio through the computer's speakers or through the sound-output jack without any additional fussing about. However, if your Mac doesn't support an internal drive, you can hook an external drive up to its SCSI port. For a world of additional info, check out Chapter 2.

- **Sound In:** If available, the sound-in jack is located at the back of the machine or, on rare occasions, on the monitor. An "NA" in the table means that there is no jack; "mono" means that you can record monophonic sound only (even from an internal CD); and "stereo" means that you can record in stereo. Chapters 12 and 13 tell you everything you need to know.

- **Sound Out:** You can hook up speakers or headphones to your Mac's sound-output jack, which is typically located at the back of your Mac. All desktop Macs provide output jacks, and nearly all Macs play sounds in stereo, which is especially useful for you folks with internal CD-ROM drives. To turn your Mac into a high-tech boom box, read Chapter 3.

- **Maximum Colors:** Every desktop Mac released in the last four years includes either a built-in monitor or a video port so that you can hook up an external monitor. Only a few Mac II models lack video ports, which is why they are marked "NA" in the table. Otherwise, the table lists the maximum number of colors that can be displayed on 14-inch monitors (or smaller, if the monitor is built into the computer). A value of 2 means that the computer supports black and white only. For more information on Macintosh video, read the eye-popping Chapter 4.

- **Television In and Out:** Most Macs wouldn't recognize a television signal if it came with formal papers of introduction signed by Jerry Seinfeld. But a privileged few do include special jacks for inputting TV signals. Some, including the Mac TV and Quadra 630, even let you change channels. The best — the AV models — let you input TV, edit it, and output it back to videotape. Read Chapter 5 to learn what's what.

Multimedia on the go

Where multimedia is concerned, desktop Macs can't be beat. But laptop Macs — particularly PowerBooks — are not without their own special multimedia capabilities. Table 1-2 lists all laptop Macs released so far, explains their capabilities, and rates them.

You'll notice that "good" is the best rating any laptop gets, and ratings go as low as "stinky," which means that the machine is in some respects worse than the original Mac 128K. Ouch.

You'll also notice that I judge the laptops according to different criteria than the desktop models. For example, no laptop Mac currently has room for an internal CD-ROM drive (though that will undoubtedly change in the future), so the "Internal CD-ROM" category is missing. "Television In and Out" is also beyond the means of today's laptops.

I explain the remaining categories at the end of the table. In the meantime, here are the laptop Macs in alphabetical order:

Chapter 1: "Big Tub o' Media" Just Doesn't Have the Same Ring

Table 1-2   The Less Amazing Multimedia Capabilities of Laptop Macs

Laptop Model	Sound In	Sound Out	Maximum Colors	Screen Matrix	Multimedia Rating
Duo 210	mono (mike only)	NA	16	passive	stinky
Duo 230	mono (mike only)	NA	16	passive	stinky
Duo 250	mono (mike only)	NA	16	active	stinky
Duo 270c	mono (mike only)	NA	256 (thousands)	active	poor
Duo 280	mono (mike only)	NA	16	active	stinky
Duo 280c	mono (mike only)	NA	256 (thousands)	active	poor
Duo with Duo Dock	mono	stereo	thousands	NA	fair
Duo with Duo Dock II	mono	stereo	thousands	NA	fair
Duo with MiniDock	mono	stereo	256	NA	fair
Portable	NA	stereo	2	active	stinky
PowerBook 100	NA	mono	2	passive	stinky
PowerBook 140	mono	stereo	2	passive	poor
PowerBook 145	mono	stereo	2	passive	poor
PowerBook 145B	mono	stereo	2	passive	poor
PowerBook 160	mono	stereo	16 (256)	passive	poor
PowerBook 165	mono	stereo	256 (256)	passive	fair

(continued)

Table 1-2 *(continued)*

Laptop Model	Sound In	Sound Out	Maximum Colors	Screen Matrix	Multimedia Rating
PowerBook 165c	mono	stereo	256 (256)	passive	fair
PowerBook 170	mono	stereo	2	active	poor
PowerBook 180	mono	stereo	16 (256)	active	fair
PowerBook 180c	mono	stereo	256 (256)	active	fair
PowerBook 520	stereo	stereo	16 (256)	passive	fair
PowerBook 520c	stereo	stereo	256 (thousands)	passive	good
PowerBook 540	stereo	stereo	64 (256)	active	fair
PowerBook 540c	stereo	stereo	256 (thousands)	active	good

As promised, it's time to explain the categories:

- **Sound In:** Nearly all PowerBooks and Duos have tiny microphones nestled above their keyboards. (The mike may look like three little holes or a vertical slit.) Only a few — including the original three, the PowerBooks 100, 140, 170 — lacked built-in mikes. All PowerBooks except the 100 also include sound-input jacks on the back of the machine for recording from tapes and CDs.

- **Sound Out:** As on a desktop Mac, the sound-output jack on a laptop lets you hook up headphones or speakers. Only the Duos lack sound-out jacks.

- **Maximum Colors:** This category explains the maximum number of colors that you can display on the internal LCD screen — the one built into the laptop's lid — when it's set to full-screen size. (The Duos 270c and 280c and the PowerBooks 520c and 540c support thousands of colors at a reduced screen size, but the LCD screen isn't capable of displaying the colors properly, so what's the point?)

If you can hook up the laptop to an external monitor, a number in parentheses lists the number of colors you can display. (The number is frequently higher because external monitors are more capable than LCD screens.)

✔ **Screen Matrix:** Ooh, here's an exciting one. LCD screens come in two basic flavors: *passive matrix* and *active matrix*. I could delve into all kinds of technical detail, but suffice it to say that a passive matrix screen is muddy and doesn't always keep up with your cursor movements, while an active matrix is bright, cheerful, and hunky-dory.

Before closing out this section, I should mention one more thing. Three items in the table — Duo with Duo Dock, Duo with Duo Dock II, and Duo with MiniDock — are not separate models but rather equipment that you can add to other models in the table.

"Huh?" you ask in a bewildered fashion, not unlike Goldilocks upon waking up to the unconventional sight of three drooling bears hungrily smacking their lips. Well, it's like this: The Macintosh PowerBook Duos — or just plain Duos for short — are special laptop computers that you can magically transform into desktop computers by sliding them into docking stations, much like a space shuttle might dock in a larger ship. Apple sells three docking stations: the Duo Dock, the Duo Dock II, and the MiniDock. Each dock provides additional output ports for sound, video, and other stuff. So, by combining any Duo model with one of these docks, you get the enhanced multimedia performance listed in the table. Pretty nifty, huh?

My computer got a "stinky"! What do I do?

At this point, more impatient readers might be tempted to drop everything and sink all the ready cash they possess into a Power Mac 7100AV or some equally obscenely-powerful machine. That's what I did, anyway. But those of you with a modicum of common sense might care to study the situation a little more closely before you abandon your current Mac.

Just for the record, here are a few words of friendly advice:

✔ If you own a Duo, dock it, preferably in a Duo Dock II. A docked Duo has access to way more stuff than a lost and lonely Duo out on its own.

✔ If your only computer is a PowerBook, you might want to get a desktop computer as well. Though PowerBooks provide limited multimedia capabilities, desktop Macs provide more bang for the buck.

- If your desktop Mac ranked "poor" in the first table, scrap it and upgrade to a better machine. Sorry, but those one-piece happy Macs such as the Plus and Classic simply don't qualify as multimedia machines.

- If your Mac received a "fair" rating, you might want to upgrade it by adding inexpensive pieces of hardware, such as an external CD-ROM or an enhanced video board. Read Chapters 2 through 6 to discover your options.

- If it costs more than $1,000 to upgrade your present "fair" Mac, buy a new one. Those tired old '80s Macs are about as worthy of expensive upgrades as a rusted Gremlin.

- Even if you own a "good" or "very good" Mac, you may want to spend a few hundred bucks upgrading the memory or investing in a larger hard drive. See Chapter 6 for more information.

The sad fact is that multimedia is one of the most demanding and therefore expensive pursuits that you can attempt with a computer. The good news is that it's also one of the most fun. When's the last time your word processor made you shriek with delight? When's the last time you stayed up into the wee hours playing with your spreadsheet? Multimedia can be exciting, addictive, enlightening, and memorable. If that's not worth laying out a little extra cash, I don't know what is.

Chapter 2
Adding the All-Important CD-ROM Drive

In This Chapter
- ▶ What's so special about CDs?
- ▶ Taking care of your CDs
- ▶ Purchasing a CD-ROM drive
- ▶ Understanding and ignoring drive speed
- ▶ Selecting between an internal or external drive
- ▶ Evaluating an external drive
- ▶ Hooking the drive up to your computer
- ▶ Installing the necessary extensions
- ▶ Ejecting a CD

No doubt you're aware of the newest media rage, CD-ROM. Huge conglomerates such as Time Warner and Sony have gotten into the act, and about a zillion more — MGM, Paramount, and others — are smacking their lips in the wings. In-depth encyclopedias, interactive catalogs, comprehensive maps and atlases, and spine-tingling games are now available on wafer-thin CDs, the very same CDs that you've been sticking in your stereo for years.

And it's no wonder. More than half of all Macintosh computers sold these days include CD-ROM drives. As if that weren't amazing enough, the sales of CD-ROM drives are expected to better than double throughout the remainder of the decade. By the time Dick Clark ushers in the next millennium, more than 15 million of us will be spinning the silver platters right next to our computers. Some crazed pundits are predicting that CD-ROM sales will eventually outpace video sales. Even loonier pundits think that CD-ROMs will make books obsolete. But whatever the future holds, CD-ROMs are bound to be a big part of it.

If I were an irritating geek on a late-night infomercial, I'd hasten to warn you, "Don't *you* miss out on this information revolution! Join our 12-product, lifetime-obligation program today!" Lucky for you, I'm not an irritating infomercial geek. I'm a kind and gentle geek who has your best interests at heart. So I'll lay it out like it is: A CD-ROM drive is the first step in any multimedia system. You just have to have one. It means shelling out a few hundred bucks, but you won't regret it.

This chapter explains what CD-ROM means and offers some advice for buying CD-ROM drives. I'll also tell you how to get a CD-ROM up and running on your computer. Whether you've never used a CD-ROM in your life or you're having problems with the old CD machinery, this chapter is here to help. On the other hand, if you use CD-ROMs every day without incident and you were hoping to learn something a little more interesting, skip this chapter and see what the next one has to offer.

CDs are Much Simpler than You Think

CD-ROM — pronounced *see dee rom* — stands for *Compact Disc, Read Only Memory*. The *Compact Disc* part simply means that a CD is smaller than an old LP record. *Read Only Memory* means that you can't use a CD to record music as you can with a cassette tape, nor can you write to it as you can a standard computer disk. After you buy the thing, you can play it, but you can't modify it.

A better way to think about CD-ROMs is that they're CDs for your computer. In fact, there is *no* physical difference between a music CD (also called an *audio CD*) and a CD-ROM. They both contain little bits of numerical data. It's just that the data on a music CD can be translated into sounds by your CD player, while the data on a CD-ROM can be translated to sound, pictures, and text by your computer.

So from now on, I'm going to forgo the "ROM" nonsense and call all CDs the same thing. If it's circular, flat, has a hole in the center, and makes pretty rainbow reflections when you hold it up to the light, it's a CD. Music CDs play music; multimedia CDs contain computer data. 'Nuff said.

So what's so special about CDs?

What with everyone but the Pope releasing a CD title — oops, I forgot, the Pope *does* have a CD, doesn't he? — you might think that the CD is an altogether unique breed of media. Not quite. Like a regular, old, everyday floppy disk — one of those $3^1/_2$-inch square plastic jobbies that isn't the least bit floppy — a CD holds computer files that folks much like you make using machines much like yours. Strictly speaking, you can't put anything on a CD that you can't put on any other kind of computer disk.

However, a CD does have certain properties that make it appealing to folks who like to make money distributing sounds, pictures, and text:

- A CD has the storage capacity of a large hard disk, so it can contain gobs and gobs of big, complex files (as explained in the sidebar "Just how much does a CD hold?"). Coincidentally, sound and video files are typically huge, so a CD is the logical medium for storing them.

- A CD can withstand the ravages of time. You can wipe out the contents of a computer disk by putting it next to a magnet. And as anyone over 30 knows, you can damage a vinyl record by exposing it to heat. To similarly harm a CD, you'd have to place it inside a microwave along with a magnet and nuke it on High for several minutes. (Don't do this at home, kids.) Knives, direct flame, and acid also have their detrimental effects, but the point is, a CD is pretty darn durable.

- CDs are inexpensive to manufacture — they cost about a buck apiece to produce, which is a far better deal than floppy disks when you factor in how much information CDs hold.

- It's cheaper for customers to buy a CD than to pirate it. If you have money dripping from your pockets, you can purchase special CD recording devices that cost anywhere from $3,000 to $5,000. But the rest of us can't afford to copy one CD to another. So we're forced to be honest and above board. (Quelle bummer!)

The care and feeding of your CDs

A CD is indisputably a tenacious creature. Though it isn't altogether indestructible — stepping on it, whacking it with a hammer, or using it for target practice does affect it adversely — you can get away with a surprising amount of abuse.

For example, you can do anything you want to the top of the CD (short of puncturing or cracking it). You can write on top of the CD or put labels on it. This goes for music CDs and CD-ROMs alike. The bottom side of the CD is the only side that gets read by the CD-ROM drive.

By the same token, you should take care when handling the bottom of the CD. The fewer smudges and goop applied to the CD's underbelly, the better it will work. If you do happen to slather strawberry preserves or some similar muck on the bottom side, wipe it off with a damp, soft cloth. Do *not* use paper towels, burlap, sandpaper, porcupine quills, or anything else that might scratch the acrylic coating.

Just how much does a CD hold?

Ludwig van Beethoven never could have predicted the things that would happen to his precious Ninth Symphony. It was prominently featured in Stanley Kubrick's ultraviolent *A Clockwork Orange,* which assigned the divine choral work a sinister flavor that would have made its composer scowl. But perhaps more bizarre is its impact on Japanese society and — as a result — consumer technology.

As the story goes, the triumphant Allied troops played Beethoven's Ninth as they marched on Tokyo, marking the end of World War II. Despite this seemingly negative introduction, the piece eventually became associated with the country's rebirth and economic renewal. Beethoven's Ninth is now firmly entrenched as the traditional New Year's anthem, much as "Auld Lang Syne" is in the U.S.

The only differences are that no one knows the words to the Ninth Symphony — well, very few folks know what's going on with "Auld Lang Syne" either, so I suppose it's not *that* different — and the Ninth is waaaay longer. Hence the maximum length for a music CD — 74 minutes — is just long enough to hold Japan's favorite European masterpiece. (Whether a CD would last only 4 minutes if it were developed in the U.S. — long enough to hold "Auld Lang Syne" — is a subject of continued speculation.)

Meanwhile, that same CD can hold as much as 650 megabytes (MB) of Macintosh computer data, more than many hard disks. Compare this with 1.4MB, which is the maximum amount of data that a standard floppy disk can hold. You can stuff 450 times as much stuff on a CD as on a floppy disk. A floppy disk can hold about eight seconds of CD-quality music, which may be the reason floppies never caught on with the Top 40 crowd.

(I've even had success completely submerging a CD in water and lovingly washing it with dish soap. Unfortunately, it is possible to harm the disk if the water seeps through the acrylic, so only resort to this technique if all other attempts to clean the CD fail.)

If the CD contains sequential information — as do music CDs — you may be able to isolate the section of the CD that's causing problems. Remember that CDs are read from the center outward, just the opposite of records. So if an early track won't play correctly, the problem is somewhere toward the center of the CD; if a late track gives you fits, examine the outer area — you know, for smudges, cigarette burns, and the like.

All About CD-ROM Drives

When it comes time to buy a CD-ROM drive for your Mac, my advice can be summed up as follows:

- If you're purchasing a new computer, go ahead and spring for an internal CD drive as well. Even if you already own an external drive, an internal drive provides more flexibility and less hassle.

- Don't pay any more than $350 for a new drive. I don't care what whiz-bang stuff the drive offers, you can find all you need in the $250 to $350 price range.

- Be very careful when buying a used drive. Don't buy anything that's more than two years old — the technology has advanced dramatically since then — and make sure that it's equipped with the stuff I mention in the following sections. Even then, I wouldn't pay more than $100. (If you want to pay more, call me first. I have a swell drive for you.)

If that's enough to get you going, then by all means, get going. If you'd like to be a little better informed before you venture out to get your CD-ROM drive, keep reading.

Why speed doesn't matter

Earlier, I mentioned a handful of the benefits associated with CDs. Now I'll tell you the one major drawback: speed. Opening and copying files from a CD can take nearly half again as long as opening or copying the same files from a hard disk. For reasons that you rightly don't care about, hard drive technology will always outpace CD drive technology because of differences in design.

I bring up this painful topic for the simple reason that speed is both one of the first criteria that drive manufacturers tout and arguably the least important. See, most multimedia CDs are optimized for the least common denominator, the slowest of all possible CD drives. They have to be. Multimedia producers don't want their customers to complain that the disk runs slowly or that the audio and video break up. If a CD runs well on a slow drive, it will also run well on a fast drive. Problem solved.

Thanks to the ever-quickening pace of technology, all drives sold today are fast enough to handle a typical multimedia title. (Currently, the basic model is a double-speed drive, as described in the sidebar "The fastest spin in the West.") These new drives can open and copy files from a CD more quickly than their crusty old counterparts, and they're better at playing on-screen movies, but most of the animated transitions and other multimedia stuff will plod along at the very same rate.

In other words, you don't have to worry about speed when purchasing a new CD-ROM drive. Oh sure, if you find two drives that cost about the same amount and provide absolutely identical features, you might as well go with the faster of the two. Otherwise, I've got more important stuff for you to worry about.

The fastest spin in the West

Guys in lab coats measure the speed of CD drives in two ways. First, there's the *spin rate*, which measures how fast the CD spins. This value is kind of like the old revolutions-per-minute rating applied to record players: A standard LP played at 33 rpm; the little singles with the big holes played at 45 rpm.

CD drives have to spin much more quickly than record players in order to transfer digital data. And in order to maintain a consistent flow of digital bits, the CD drive has to decelerate as it progresses from the inside to the outside of the disk. The music CD player in your living room spins at 530 rpm during the first track and slows down to 230 rpm by the last track. However, instead of being discussed in terms of these spin rates (530 to 230 rpm), your standard music CD player is simply called a *single-speed drive*.

If you spin music CDs any faster, they emit chipmunk-sounding songs, just like 33 rpm records played at 45 rpm. But by spinning CD-ROMs faster, you can transfer more data and therefore open and copy files faster. These days, CD drives come in various speed varieties — double-speed, triple-speed, and quad-speed, also known as 2x, 3x, and 4x — which spin CDs twice, three times, and four times as fast as a stereo CD player, respectively.

The second speed factor is *access time*, which is how fast the drive is able to locate data on the CD. Unlike a music CD, a multimedia CD contains hundreds or even thousands of files. A multimedia presentation must be able to quickly lift a file from any point on the CD. The faster the drive can bop around and pinpoint a file, the less you have to wait. Drive manufacturers frequently neglect to mention access times because it doesn't make good ad copy. But as a rule, drives with faster spin rates also provide faster access times.

After all that, the verdict is still the same: Speed just isn't an important issue. If I were to set two drives in front of you — one a double-speed and the other a quad-speed — I doubt that you could tell the difference. Both would run your multimedia titles just fine. The quad-speed drive would copy files faster, but I doubt that you'd notice unless you whipped out a stopwatch.

Internal or external?

An *external drive* is a drive that sits in a separate box outside your computer. An *internal drive* fits inside the computer's housing. I own one of each, and I can tell you from personal experience that an internal drive is preferable.

- An internal drive plays the sound from both music and multimedia CDs through the sound-out jack on the back of your computer, which is the most convenient way to hear all sounds through a single set of speakers. With an external drive, you have to hook up the drive independently, whether to your stereo or to a sophisticated speaker system that includes a separate amplifier or subwoofer. Both options are explained in Chapter 3.

- You have to hook up cables and worry about these messy things called SCSI-ID conflicts when using an external drive. An internal drive works hassle-free. (Well, *mostly* hassle-free.)

- An internal drive doesn't take up additional room on your desk. An external drive does.

Still, an external drive is not entirely without its advantages. It's portable, so you can use it on the job during the week and then take it home and hook it up to the family Mac over the weekend. Also, an external drive works with any kind of Mac. Many desktop models — most of the II, LC, and Classic series as well as the Performa 200 and 400s — aren't set up to hold an internal drive, and no portable currently offers internal CD. For a complete rundown of machines, check out Table 1-1 in Chapter 1. If you see a "No" in the "Internal CD-ROM" column for a particular computer, an external drive is your only option.

What to Look for in an External Drive

Figures 2-1 and 2-2 demonstrate all the physical stuff you should look for when purchasing an external CD-ROM drive. Figure 2-1 shows the front of the drive; Figure 2-2, which follows a few pages later, shows the back. The front is much prettier — not to mention less intimidating — but both the front and back contain some very important elements.

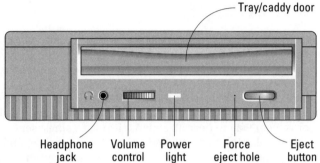

Figure 2-1: The minimum amount of stuff you should see on the front of your CD-ROM drive.

The front of the drive, in all its splendor

Here's one of those wonderfully exhaustive lists of the stuff you should find on the front of the drive:

- **Tray/caddy door:** The door itself isn't all that important — you couldn't stick a CD in the drive without some kind of opening — but what's behind the door is very telling. Many new drives now include trays that glide out when you press the eject button, just like music CD players. You stick the CD in the tray and give the tray a gentle push to send it back into the drive.

  A couple of recent drives offer flip-top access. As you do with portable CD players, you open the hood, set the CD in place, and close the hood. Who knows, it might catch on.

  Sadly, most older drives include independent CD cases called *caddies*. After ejecting the caddy, you have to take it out, open it up, stick the CD in, and push the caddy into the drive. Caddies can get lost, you can insert them incorrectly, and they're just plain stupid to boot. Look for a drive with a tray.

- **Headphone jack:** Just about every drive that supports audio CDs features a headphone jack up front so that you can listen to your tunes without connecting the drive to a stereo. Also, you don't have to reach around to the back of the drive to plug in your headphones.

  You can plug in a pair of Walkman-type headphones — the kind with the small plug. Incidentally, guys who work at Radio Shack call this kind of plug a *miniplug*. The jack into which the miniplug plugs is called — you guessed it — a *minijack*.

You can use the headphone jack to listen to music from audio CDs only; you *cannot* listen to sounds from multimedia CDs. I know, it's weird, but the two sounds are processed differently by the drive. I explain how this stuff works in Chapter 3.

- **Volume control:** The volume dial next to the headphone jack lets you control the volume of music from the CD. This dial affects the volume of the headphones only; if you have the drive hooked up to a stereo, the volume control doesn't do anything.

- **Power light:** When the light is on, the drive is on. Some drives include tiny little LCD readouts — like on a calculator — instead of a power light. As long as you can tell that the machine is on, you're in business.

- **Force eject hole:** The little hole next to the eject button lets you eject a CD when you can't get it out any other way. Straighten out a paper clip and gently but firmly stick the thing into the hole and push. The CD will obediently come out, even if the drive is turned off.

- **Eject button:** Press the eject button to spit out the tray or caddy so that you can insert a CD into the drive. If the drive contains a CD, it ignores you. The Mac system software requires you to eject the CD on-screen, as described in the section "How to get the CD the heck out of the machine." You can only evict an empty tray or caddy with the eject button.

The drive's more important rear end

As Figure 2-2 illustrates, the stuff on the back of the drive is a little more complicated. But it is also more important, because it contains all the essential connections. Here's what you should find and how it works:

- **SCSI connectors:** Every Macintosh-compatible CD-ROM drive includes two SCSI connectors — though they may not look exactly like the ones shown in Figure 2-2 — which let you hook up the drive to your computer without monkeying around with a lot of additional hardware, as you can with most Windows-based PCs. (SCSI stands for *Small Computer Systems Interface* — as if you care — but everyone just calls it *scuzzy*.)

    The drive should include at least one SCSI cable so that you can hook up the drive to your computer. If you're lucky, the drive will also include a second cable to hook up other pieces of hardware to the CD-ROM drive. (This second cable is a nice bonus but is not essential.)

    To learn how to hook up the external drive to your computer, read the upcoming section "How to Make the Right SCSI Connections."

- **Clasps:** Most SCSI connectors include clasps to keep the cable locked in place. (The only reason I labeled the clasps in Figure 2-2 is so that you'd know what they are.) Some drives include smaller connectors that have automatic clasps, saving you the anguish of manual clasping.

Part I: Meet Your Awesome Multimedia Mac

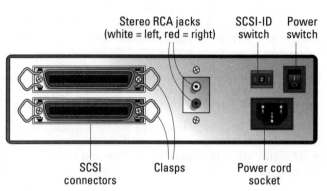

Figure 2-2:
If you don't see every one of these items on the back of your CD-ROM drive, throw a fit and demand to see the manager.

- **Stereo RCA jacks:** The two *RCA jacks* (also known as *phono jacks*) let you hook up your CD-ROM drive to a stereo, as explained in the next chapter. Like the headphone jack, the RCA jacks let you hear sounds from music CDs only.

  The jacks should be either colored — white for the left channel and red for the right — or labeled Left and Right. If there are no colors or labels, get a different drive.

- **Power cord socket:** Here's where you insert the power cord into the drive. If the drive doesn't include a power cord, something is dreadfully amiss.

- **SCSI-ID switch:** The SCSI system lets you hook up to eight different pieces of hardware to your computer. Each piece of hardware has to have a different *SCSI-ID number*, from 0 to 7. The ID 0 is always reserved for your internal hard drive; the ID 7 is for the computer's logic board. (Strange but true.) Therefore, you can really only choose 1 through 6.

  The best CD-ROM drives include little ID switches. The number in the center of the switch represents the ID number (2 in the figure). If this matches the ID number of some other external SCSI device, change it. Press one button on the switch to raise the ID number; press the opposite button to lower it.

  Some drives offer SCSI-ID dials, which require you to turn the dial with a tiny screwdriver. The worst drives make you change the ID number by messing around with a Byzantine collection of dip switches or these little plastic doohickeys called *jumpers*. My advice is to stay the heck away from any drive that lacks a SCSI-ID switch or at least a dial.

- **Power switch:** You turn on most CD-ROM devices by flipping a switch on the back of the drive. Be sure to turn on the drive before starting your computer. Otherwise, the computer may not notice that the drive is there, even if it is properly hooked up.

Incidentally, the little straight line on the switch means on; the little 0 means off. This is because in the boisterously entertaining world of binary logic, where the only digits left to mankind are 1 and 0, 1 means on and 0 means off. See how math influences our everyday lives?

Does it support all kinds of CDs?

If you're buying a used drive, you'll also want to make sure that the drive supports music CDs and Photo CDs. To test out a music CD, just insert a Sheryl Crow disc and see what happens. If you can't get the CD to appear on-screen, make sure that you installed the proper software (as explained in the "CD Software Stuff" section later in this chapter). If Sheryl still won't sing, it's time to leave Las Vegas. (That is, don't buy the drive.)

Testing Kodak's Photo CD format is a little more complicated, especially if you don't have a Photo CD handy. If the drive was made in 1994 or later, it's a safe bet that it supports Photo CD. If the drive was made in 1993 or earlier, be sure to ask. If the guy selling the drive says something like "Photo CD? Never heard of it," or "What do you need Photo CD for? Digital slide shows? Gimme a break," don't buy.

All new drives support both music CDs and Photo CDs. (In case you're wondering what all the fuss over Photo CD is about, check out Chapter 7.)

How to Make the Right SCSI Connections

The very initials SCSI are enough to chill the blood of any rational human being. But, in fact, hooking up a SCSI device such as an external CD-ROM drive to your Mac is surprisingly easy.

1. **Turn off both the CD drive and the computer.**

    If you change SCSI connections while the hardware is on, you run the risk of damaging the computer's power supply. You can get away with it, but you're better off playing it safe. (Granted, I personally do it all the time, but I'm a masochist.)

2. **Insert the smaller end of the cable into the SCSI port on the back of your computer.**

    The first example in Figure 2-3 shows me on the very brink of inserting cable into port. If you look carefully, you'll see that this end of the cable contains two rows of pins. There are 25 pins in all, which is why it's called a *25-pin connector*.

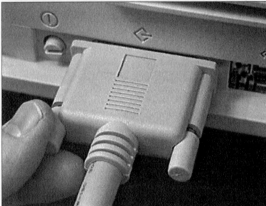

Figure 2-3: Insert the small end of the SCSI cable into the back of your computer (top) and then screw it in place (bottom).

   3. **Screw in the screws on either side of the cable connector to lock the cable into place.**

   The second example in Figure 2-3 shows me dutifully performing this very step.

   4. **Insert the larger end of the cable (called the *50-pin connector*) into either one of the SCSI connectors on the CD-ROM drive.**

   It doesn't matter which connector on the CD-ROM drive you use. But the bottom one is usually more convenient, as shown at the top of Figure 2-4.

Chapter 2: Adding the All-Important CD-ROM Drive

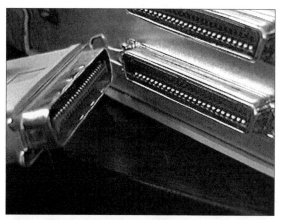

Figure 2-4: Insert the large end of the cable into the back of your CD-ROM drive (top) and then use the clasps to lock it in place (bottom).

   5. **Finally, press the clasps on either side of the drive connector into the notches on either side of the cable.**

   The bottom example of Figure 2-4 shows me pressing a clasp into place. This locks the cable to the drive. If there are no clasps, as on certain drives from NEC, just be sure that the connector is plugged in snugly.

The drive's second SCSI connector is provided so that you can hook up more SCSI devices. You'll need a second cable to pull this off — one that has a 50-pin connector at each end. In theory, you can hook up a total of six SCSI devices in tandem (a technique called *daisy chaining*, in case you're interested). But in reality, you're lucky to hook up three without running into some of the most baffling computer problems that exist.

The magic ingredient that puts the scuz in SCSI

SCSI is wonderful technology, and it's one of the prime factors that make the Mac a dream to use, but it isn't perfect. A little irritant known as *termination* can cause no end of frustrating problems.

A terminator (shown below) is a little device that tells the computer where a daisy chain of SCSI devices begins or ends. Theoretically, any time you hook up two or more SCSI devices in a chain, you should also hook up a terminator to the empty 50-pin SCSI connector on the last drive. If your computer lacks an internal hard drive — which is very unlikely — you'll also have to hook up a terminator to the 50-pin end of the cable coming out from the computer and into the first drive in the chain. (Many terminators have two sides to them, one that plugs into a cable, and the other that plugs into the SCSI device.)

Unfortunately, even if you attach a terminator to each end of the chain just like you're supposed to, you may still encounter problems. If a chain is improperly terminated, you won't be able to access one or more of the SCSI devices. Or worse, your computer might refuse to start.

If you absolutely can't decipher your termination woes, follow these steps:

1. **Whine and complain to your local computer wizard until he or she drops everything and agrees to see what's the matter.**

2. **Sit back and have a stifled chuckle or two as the wizard is likewise completely stumped and unable to resolve your problem.**

    Your computer still won't work, but at least you won't feel like such a bozo.

3. **Disconnect a SCSI device and try starting the computer.**

    If that doesn't work, disconnect another device and try again. When you get down to just one device, the termination error will haunt you no more.

I'm absolutely serious. As much as it hurts me to say it, you may have to accept the problem and work around it. For example, I have two SCSI devices that work fine together, and a third one that doesn't play well with others. At the beginning of each day, I decide if I want to use the two compatible devices or the lone difficult one. I then hook up the desired device(s), turn it (or them) on, and start my computer.

What to Expect from an Internal Drive

I can't begin to tell you how much easier internal drives are to deal with. If you bought the drive with your computer, you're ready to go. If you want to add the drive to your Mac, just take the computer into your local computer store and have a technician install the drive.

Inserting a drive by yourself is not impossible, but the process is complicated. It varies from one model to the next, and you can damage the logic board if you aren't careful. Also, if the Mac is less than a year old, installing your own drive may invalidate the warranty. All things considered, it's best to pay a qualified technician the extra $20 or $30 it costs to do the work for you.

If you buy an Apple drive — or if the drive came with your computer — it is automatically assigned a SCSI-ID number of 3. Keep this in mind if you decide to hook up an external SCSI device — such as a hard drive — in the future. It's also worth noting that all current Apple drives come with trays rather than caddies. We're talking quality craftsmanship.

Other manufacturers are not so predictable. Some provide trays; others require caddies. SCSI-ID numbers vary all over the place. More than one vendor has even been known to assign a SCSI-ID number of 0, which means that the CD-ROM drive is guaranteed to conflict with the internal hard drive. I guess the vendor wants to make sure that you call tech support and register the drive.

In any case, the technician who installs your drive should iron out all the wrinkles. Be sure to ask what ID number the drive has been assigned. You may even want to take some CDs with you — including a music CD or two — when you pick up the computer so that you can test out the drive and make sure that it works.

Internal drives can be set up to play all sounds — whether from music or multimedia CDs — through the internal speaker inside the computer. To listen to the sounds with headphones, plug the headphones into the sound-output jack at the back of the computer. (You'll need headphones with a long cord.) Music CDs can be a little tricky, so be sure to read Chapter 11 for the whole story.

CD Software Stuff

I neglected to mention one more item you will receive along with your new internal or external drive: a disk full of software. In order to get a CD to appear on-screen, you need to install six special files into the Extensions folder inside your System Folder. Like any other extensions, these six load with your system when you start your computer. If they don't load up properly, no CD.

If you somehow lose your CD-ROM software, all six extensions are included with System 7.5. Strange as it may seem, this is the first version of the system software to ship with the CD-ROM extensions.

Shown in Figure 2-5, the six precious extensions — listed in order of importance — work as follows:

- **Apple CD-ROM:** This extension is the primary *driver* — the piece of software that goes out and looks for a CD-ROM drive connected to your Mac. It also ensures that your Mac recognizes and mounts standard Macintosh multimedia CDs. To *mount* a disk, incidentally, is to display it on the desktop. (I know, I just missed a wonderful joke there, but this is a family book.)

The Apple CD-ROM extension isn't the only driver out there. In fact, this particular driver works only with Apple drives. Other CD-ROM drive vendors substitute a custom driver of their own. So be sure to use the driver that came with your drive.

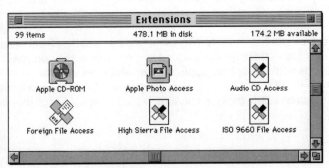

Figure 2-5: If these six files are present in your Extensions folder, your Mac will be able to load just about any variety of CD ever produced.

- **Foreign File Access:** If the CD is not a standard Macintosh CD — many, including music CDs, are not — your computer needs a translator. Foreign File Access is that translator. Without it, every one of the four files that follows is useless.

- **Audio CD Access:** This file represents the translator's first foreign language. It allows your Mac to mount any music CD, even if it contains something dreadful like Abba. Regardless of artist or title, every music CD appears on the desktop as *Audio CD* followed by a number. What can I say? Computers are cold creatures.

- **Apple Photo Access:** If you want to scan the family album onto a Kodak Photo CD, you need this file. Folks who have never tried Photo CD sometimes think that it's kind of corny, but it's actually one of the most exciting multimedia options around. So there.

- **ISO 9660 File Access:** International Standards Organization 9660 is a platform-independent CD-ROM publishing standard . . . oh, I forgot, you speak English. In that case, this extension ensures that you can run a multimedia CD designed for either the Mac or Windows platforms or mount a CD specifically designed for the PC. (If the CD is strictly for the PC, you won't be able to run any of the programs, but you'll be able to copy files and even open them if you have compatible software.)

- **High Sierra File Access:** Back in the early days of CD-ROM technology, there were no laws, and data was allowed to roam free. But then a whole mess of industry leaders — folks from both Apple and Microsoft, mind you — met in Stateline, Nevada, to rope in the data and establish a standard. They ultimately named the standard after their hotel, the rustic High Sierra. All computer CD standards, from the Macintosh format to our friend ISO 9660, have their beginnings in High Sierra.

  What does this trip down nostalgia lane have to do with you? Well, pardner, if you have a dusty old disk sitting around that conforms to the 10-year-old High Sierra standard, this little extension makes sure that your Mac can read it. Now isn't that a comforting thought?

How to Get the CD the Heck Out of the Machine

Earlier, I mentioned that you can't just press the eject button to remove a CD from the drive. You no doubt thought something along the lines of, "The eject button doesn't eject? What kind of eject button is that?" Well, it's not the eject button's fault, or even the CD-ROM drive's. It's your Mac's fault.

See, the Macintosh Finder — which is that part of the system software that greets you every time you start up the computer (you know, the part with all the files and folders and other icons) — likes to hold onto a disk once it mounts it. It complains vigorously if you try to eject the disk without its permission. The way to get permission to eject is to *unmount* the disk.

I know, you'd think it'd be *dis*mount. But we're not on the disk, which is how dismounting works. The disk is on us — in a manner of speaking, anyway. You see, it's kind of a transitive versus intransitive thing . . . oh, forget it.

Whatever you call it, you evict a CD just as you do a floppy disk — that is, in any of the following three ways:

- ✔ Drag the CD icon on the desktop onto the Trash icon. This doesn't harm the data on the CD — you can't change the data on the CD, remember? — but it does unmount the darned thing.

- ✔ Click on the CD icon to select it and choose File➪Put Away. When it comes to disks, "away" is out.

- ✔ Select the CD icon and press ⌘-Y, the keyboard shortcut for the Put Away command.

If a file on the CD is running, the system software won't let you unmount the CD until you close the file. Check all the programs that are running. If a program on the CD is running, quit the program. If a file from the CD is open inside any program, close that file. It's up to you to hunt around and figure out which file is to blame; your Mac doesn't give you any clues.

Chapter 3
Building a Computerized Stereo

In This Chapter
- Finding your Mac's sound-out port
- Distinguishing between mono and stereo miniplugs
- Hooking up your Mac to a stereo system
- Hooking up an external CD-ROM drive
- Purchasing powered speakers
- Hooking up speakers and subwoofers
- Evaluating speaker systems

You may not know it to look at it, but there's a home entertainment system lurking inside your Mac that's just itching to get out. As a little luck and a lot of forward-thinking engineering would have it, a pair of inexpensive speakers is all it takes to turn your Mac into a boom box with brains. In fact, though it may come as something of a surprise, most people who buy speakers these days are hooking them up to computers. It's just that kind of futuristic, Jetsons-type world.

Now at this point, you may be thinking, "Why would I want to hook up speakers to my Mac? So the darned thing can beep that much louder at me when I do something wrong?" Well, by golly, no, that's not it at all. I had the following multimedia-related benefits more in mind:

- First, if you intend to listen to music CDs, external speakers are a must. Even if you own some other piece of hardware with stereo speakers built in — such as an LC 550 or an AudioVision monitor — external speakers tend to sound much better than the built-in ones.
- Second, you wouldn't believe the sound on some interactive CD-ROMs. The music and movies really come to life when played through speakers.
- Third, you know that little chord that plays when you start up your Mac? Wait until you hear it at maximum volume on a full-blown, amplified pair of speakers with a subwoofer. It's enough to send you flying across the room.

Meet Your Mac's Sound-Out Port

Since the beginning of recorded time, Macintosh computers have been able to play sounds without any additional hardware. With the exception of the PowerBook Duo series, every Mac offers a *sound-out port*. (A *port* is a computer-geek term for a place that you plug stuff into.) As shown in Figure 3-1, this port is labeled with a little speaker icon so that you won't get it mixed up with the sound-in port, which is labeled with a little microphone. Go ahead, take a peek at your computer's backside. You may or may not see a sound-in port, but the sound-out port has been there all this time, patiently waiting for you to do something with it.

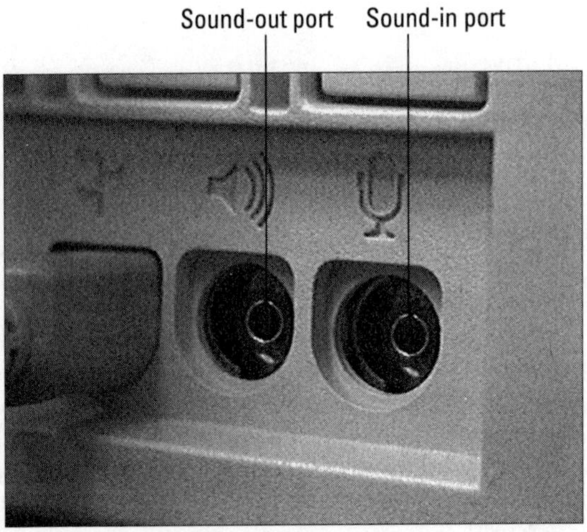

Figure 3-1: The sound-out and sound-in ports on the back side of a typical desktop Mac.

You can plug a pair of Walkman-style headphones into the sound-out port. Or you can cable the port to your stereo system. But you'll have the most fun hooking up a pair of speakers to it.

What Can the Sound-Out Port Do?

In all likelihood, your Mac comes with a single, monophonic speaker that sounds about as good as that AM transistor radio you dropped on the sidewalk and smashed to pieces when you were eight years old. So it may come as something of a shock that your sound-out port probably supports stereo sound. This isn't necessarily the case — many older models, including early LCs and Performas are limited to monophonic sound — but the stereo models are well in the majority.

Two ears are better than one

Audiophiles have spent the better part of this century listening to monophonic sound, which may be the reason why many folks don't even recognize the difference between mono and stereo sound. Just to make sure you understand what's going on, I offer the following insightful definitions:

- *Stereophonic* sound provides separate left and right signals for your left and right ears. Stereo has a richer, more realistic quality than its monophonic cousin, which is one of the reasons FM stations are more pleasurable to listen to than AM. No outrageous, supercilious, or flagrantly reprehensible talk-show hosts, either.

- *Monophonic* sound plays just one signal. This signal is generally the left signal, but it may also be both signals mixed together into one. Either way, it sounds flatter than stereo.

- *Monaural*, by the way, is just another word for monophonic. But I like plain old *mono* best because it reminds me of the infectious disease.

- The left and right signals are called *channels*. Stereo plays two channels; mono plays just one.

Now that I've set your ears on fire, you'll be better able to predict the exact kind of sound you ought to be getting out of your multimedia Mac.

To confirm the sound-out capabilities of your computer, consult the tables in Chapter 1. The "Sound Out" column lists "mono" or "stereo" for every model available when I wrote this book. If your model got a "mono," don't freak. You can still hook the computer up to speakers; it just won't sound as good.

None of the monophonic Macs permits an internal CD-ROM drive. And as I mention in the preceding chapter, sound from music CDs played on an external drive doesn't go through the computer. Therefore, you can still play music CDs in full stereo even if you own a mono Mac. By contrast, the sound from multimedia CDs always plays through the computer, so CD-ROMs play in mono on mono Macs and in stereo on stereo Macs.

The Serpentine World of Cables

Whether mono or stereo, the sound-out port on the back of your Mac is a *minijack*, the same kind of jack featured on a Walkman, a portable CD player or stereo, and the occasional television set. And what do you plug into a minijack? Why, a *miniplug*, of course.

The secrets of the miniplug

Miniplugs are tricky little devils. Like Macs, miniplugs come in two varieties, mono and stereo. It's very difficult to tell the difference between the two because they're never labeled. Oh, sure, the package that the cable comes in is labeled, but the cable itself is not. So if you have a bunch of cables lying around in a box in the basement, it can get a little frustrating.

In younger days, I applied for a job at an electronics store (one that I'm afraid must remain nameless). In the course of judiciously deciding not to hire me, the personnel guy assured me that electronic stores make a huge chunk of their cash on the sale of cables and other home entertainment paraphernalia. He went on to say that consumer confusion goes a long way toward increasing sales; it's easier to buy a new cable than to figure out what an old cable does.

That personnel guy and I never did see eye to eye, which is why I decided to whip up Figure 3-2. It shows you exactly how to tell a mono miniplug from its stereo twin. The mono plug has a single stripe near its tip; the stereo plug has a second stripe nearer to its base. Now that's what I call a subtle distinction worth remembering.

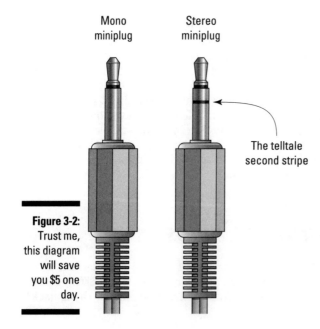

Figure 3-2: Trust me, this diagram will save you $5 one day.

If you hook up a mono plug to a stereo computer, you only get one channel. In fact, that lone top stripe represents the left channel. You still hear sound through both speakers, but they each play the left channel. The right channel gets lost in the shuffle.

If you hook up a stereo jack to a mono computer, the sound plays on the left speaker only. Because it's trying in vain to get sound from that second stripe, the right speaker remains silent.

Channel-splitting

Although a stereo Mac outputs both channels through a single jack, many speaker systems and all but a very few stereo systems are set up to receive each channel through a separate *RCA plug,* which is another type of audio-cable connector. As shown in Figure 3-3, each RCA plug is color-coded to show whether it carries the left or right channel. The right plug is always red; the left plug is usually white, but it might instead be black. (A yellow plug indicates a video connector, as I discuss in Chapter 5.)

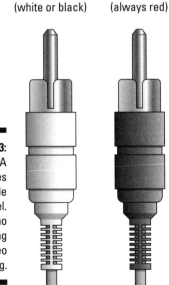

Figure 3-3: Each RCA plug carries a single channel. There is no such thing as a stereo RCA plug.

To hook up your computer to a conventional stereo system, you need a minijack-to-RCA conversion cable. The cable should have a miniplug at one end of it — either mono or stereo, depending on your computer — and should split off into two RCA plugs at the other end. It's called a *Y cable,* with the miniplug at the bottom of the Y and the two RCA plugs at the top.

- The Radio Shack part number for a three-foot Y cable with a stereo miniplug is 42-2475. The price is $4.39. For a six-foot version of that same cable, pay 60 cents more and get part number 42-2481.

- Radio Shack doesn't provide a long mono version, so you have to combine adapters. You can get a 6-foot cable with a mono miniplug on one end and a single RCA plug at the other (part number 42-2444). Then plug a short Y cable that splits off to two RCA plugs (part number 42-2435) onto the first RCA plug. The combined price is $5.08 before tax.

- A slightly more expensive option is to buy the six-foot stereo miniplug cable, 42-2481. Then add an adapter that converts the stereo miniplug to a mono miniplug, part number 274-368. The combined price is $6.18, but this way, you can use this same cable if you later upgrade to a stereo Mac.

- I hasten to mention that just because Radio Shack specializes in cables doesn't mean that it's the only place to find them, nor is it necessarily the best. You can most likely find every cable I've mentioned at K-Mart, CompUSA, and half a dozen other places, sometimes for less money. I provide the Radio Shack part numbers merely as a protective measure — if you do have to make a special trip to the Shack, you know exactly what to get.

Plug the left and right RCA plugs into the auxiliary input jacks on the back of your stereo amplifier or receiver. Many portable stereos also include auxiliary inputs.

What about my external CD-ROM drive?

If you want to hook an external CD-ROM drive to a stereo so that you can blare music CDs, you need a pair of cables with RCA plugs at both ends. Many drives include such cables. Even if your drive does not, you may have some extras lying around the house. After all, just about every piece of stereo equipment you've purchased over the years, from cassette decks to VCRs, includes RCA cables.

Though the industry standard is to color code the cables white and red, it doesn't matter what colors they are when you've got RCA plugs at both ends of the cable. The color coding, after all, is merely an aid to make sure you hook things up right. As long as the cables have RCA plugs at either end and you plug them in properly — one cable into both left jacks, the other into both right jacks — everything will work fine.

If you can't locate any extra RCA cables in the basement, attic, garage, or shed, you won't have any problems finding a pair for sale. Literally every stereo equipment store in the country carries these puppies in all lengths imaginable.

But in case you've become Radio Shack product number dependent, 15-1504 is a pair of medium-quality, three-foot RCA cables and 15-1505 is a pair of six-footers. The prices are $8.99 and $10.99, respectively.

Treat Yourself to a Set of Powered Speakers

If you can afford to spend the money, speakers are a great addition to any multimedia system. Unlike your stereo system, speakers are lightweight and portable. Computer speakers tend to be small enough to fit comfortably on a desk on either side of your monitor. If you're feeling particularly ambitious, you can even mount them on a wall. Best of all, you can buy a great set for under $200. If you aren't very picky, you can get by for $50 or less.

Mighty morphing power speakers

All computer speakers are *powered*, meaning that they plug into a wall power outlet. See, unlike a stereo system, which includes a built-in amplifier, your Mac offers no amplification. The low-level signal that flows out of the minijack port is barely loud enough to be audible when hooked up to standard stereo speakers. Powered speakers, on the other hand, provide their own amplification, allowing you to boost the signal many times over.

If you've ever hooked up speakers to a portable tape deck or CD player, you've used powered speakers. In fact, you can use those very same speakers with your Mac (assuming that you have the proper cable). The speakers may not provide a whole lot of amplification — certainly not enough to shatter your glasses during the start-up chord — but they'll be good enough to get you started.

By the way, you do not need to look specifically for Macintosh speakers. Though Apple puts out its own speakers — and I've read generally positive reviews — you can use the very same powered speakers for both Macs and PCs.

How low can you go?

Powered speakers come in basically two varieties. Shown in Figure 3-4, the first variety includes two speakers, each with its own stereo miniplug cable coming out the back. You plug one speaker — generally, the left one — into the sound-out port in the computer. Then you plug the second speaker into the first one. Power cables plug the speakers into an electric socket.

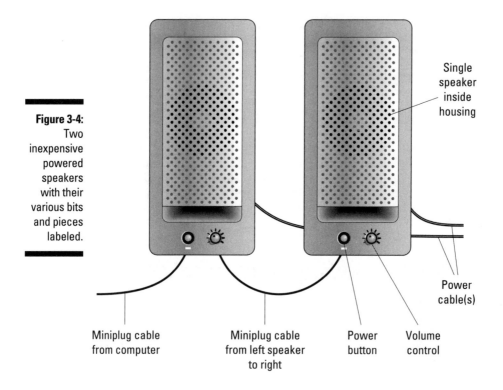

Figure 3-4: Two inexpensive powered speakers with their various bits and pieces labeled.

This variety of speakers tends to cost $100 or less, depending on its amplification. But the *bass response* — how well the speakers play low sounds — isn't very good. Unlike standard stereo loudspeakers, which actually house two speakers apiece — a tweeter for the high sounds and a woofer for the low ones — an inexpensive powered speaker contains a single speaker that handles the high and midrange sounds.

The second variety of speakers does a better job with low tones. It actually includes three items: a central *subwoofer,* which is a speaker devoted entirely to the very low notes, and two midrange speakers. The subwoofer very likely offers left and right RCA inputs along with a stereo minijack conversion cable so that you can hook up your computer. You then cable the subwoofer to the left and right speakers using either RCA cables or wires with bare ends, just like those provided with home speakers. You should find all cables you need inside the box your speakers come in.

Although computer speakers are typically petite, subwoofers can be massive, sometimes as big as the computer itself. Luckily, you don't have to put the subwoofer in any special place. Your ears have a hard time perceiving the origin of very low sounds. In fact, if a bass note is even slightly audible on the left or right midrange speaker, you will most likely associate the entire note with that speaker, even if the subwoofer is placed on the opposite side or in back of you. Therefore, feel free to position the subwoofer anywhere it fits. An out-of-the-way, partially enclosed place is ideal.

Regardless of what kind of speakers you decide to purchase, they will be set up to plug into a stereo computer. If you own a mono Mac, you also need to purchase an adapter to convert the stereo miniplug to a mono miniplug. That's Radio Shack part number 274-368, $1.19. In fact, you might as well buy the adapter before you get the speakers. That way, you won't have to endure a single moment of delayed gratification when your speakers arrive.

More criteria for the savvy shopper

Here are some other items to keep in mind when purchasing speakers for your Mac:

- For the best results, make sure that the speakers are *magnetically shielded*. This way, electromagnetic fields from the speakers won't interfere with the performance of your monitor, hard drive, or other elements. (By the way, just because your monitor reacts to occasional sounds doesn't mean that the speakers aren't shielded. More likely, you have the speakers turned up so loud that they're vibrating your desk.)

- The expense of the speakers is directly related to their amplification power. This power is measured in a little something called *watts per channel*. A typical pair of $50 speakers, for example, provides 2 to 3 watts per channel, enough to generate acceptable sound levels without disturbing the neighbors. For $150, you should be able to take home 10 to 12 watts per channel. That's what I have, and I've successfully disturbed the neighbors several times. I've seen systems as high as 40 watts per channel — enough to fill an entire house — but they cost $300 and more.

- If an amplification rating doesn't mention the per channel part, divide it in half and round down. For example, I own a 25-watt system, which translates to about 12 watts per channel. (Okay, so it's a little more, but it's always a good idea to round down.)

- Some speaker systems place all controls — volume, balance, pitch, and power — on a single unit. On my system, the controls are located on the subwoofer, making them hard to reach. In other systems, each speaker provides its own controls. You'll probably fuss with these controls a lot, so make sure that you're happy with their placement.

- If you own an external CD-ROM drive, look for a speaker system with a second pair of RCA inputs. The back of my subwoofer, for example, includes two sets of left and right RCA jacks. I can hook the computer into one set and the external CD-ROM into the other. An input switch on the front of the subwoofer lets me select between the two.

- ✔ Some speakers automatically power off when they haven't received a signal for a full minute and then snap back on when the signal returns. This means that you never have to turn off the speakers, but it also means that the sound cuts out on you at low volumes and comes back later than it ought to. Personally, I'd rather control the power switch myself.

- ✔ Many speakers include a stereo minijack up front so that you can plug in headphones. Of course, if you own one of the consumer multimedia computer models — like the Quadra 630 or Power Mac 5200 — you already have a headphone jack within easy reach. In any case, I consider a headphone jack a nice bonus, but hardly a requirement.

What Now?

If you're raring to play an audio CD through your new speakers, skip ahead to Chapter 11, which explains the many software issues that stand between you and your crankin' tunes. To get the most out of the QuickTime movies included on so many multimedia CDs, read Chapter 16. Either way, you're ready to hear your Mac produce sounds that I bet you never thought possible.

Chapter 4
See All that You Can See

In This Chapter
- How many colors can your Mac display?
- Do you need 32,000 colors, or are 256 okay?
- The strange connection between colors and bits
- How to add VRAM to get more colors
- Do you need to buy a new video board?
- The sordid details about NuBus and PCI
- What to do if your CD says you have too many colors

We've all heard the old saw about how massive computers used to fill warehouses and yet take days to figure out the simplest equations. (Story problems were especially challenging.) But the real weirdness with computers of yesteryear was the communication stuff — you know, how humans and computers would shoot the breeze with one another. The humans used punch cards and teletype machines to tell the computer what to do, and the computer printed out its response — usually, an itemized list of amenities and perks that it would require before participating.

The first personal computer that you could take home and enjoy in the privacy of your own warehouse was a hefty box called the Altair. It had no keyboard, no punch cards, and no printout. The intrepid user talked to the computer by flipping switches (that had intuitive names such as Deposit Next and Single Step) and then read a pattern of blinking lights (which had even more intuitive names, such as Prot and A14) to discover the computer's exciting responses. These people were known as "hobbyists"; they played with the Altair for "fun." By sheer coincidence, it was right about then that the term *nerd* came into popular usage.

Nowadays, thankfully, things are a little different. Rather than squinting at blinking lights, today's computer users — nerds and hipsters alike — view information on monitor screens. Early personal computers — such as the Apple II — relied on televisions as monitors, so it's no surprise that modern Mac monitors are little more than TVs that your mom lets you sit close to.

It goes without saying — but I'm going to say it anyway — that multimedia would never have come about if it weren't for the monitor. Can you imagine combing through a whiz-bang, sight-and-sound, interactive extravaganza on punch cards? Teletype machines, maybe. But punch cards, I don't think so.

This chapter, therefore, is a celebration of Macintosh screen options. You'll learn what color is, you'll learn how it's measured, and you'll learn why you care. As Ben Jonson said — right before Shakespeare went and ripped him off in *Hamlet* — "The screen's the thing!"

Mac Screen Facts

Back in the two Chapter 1 tables that I keep referring to — popularly known as Table 1-1 and Table 1-2 — I listed how many colors different Macs can display on a standard monitor screen. Check out the "Maximum Colors" column in both the first and second tables, and you'll see that I'm not fibbing. But if you're tired of flipping back and forth, here's a summary:

- Only a handful of old-model Macs — the II, IIx, and just about anything else with a *II* or an *x* in it — provide no video capabilities whatsoever. These systems are marked "NA" in the first table. You have to install special hardware in order to hook up a monitor (as explained later, in the section "When everything else fails, buy a board"). Of course, if you own one of these machines, you probably installed this hardware years ago, or you wouldn't be able to see a darn thing that your computer was doing.

- A few other old Macs include built-in screens but don't allow you to hook up external monitors. This is true for the Plus and Classic, for example, as well as many early PowerBooks. All of these machines offer two colors — black-and-white — and that's it. Most multimedia CD-ROMs won't run on black-and-white systems. The clever reader will therefore deduce that these computers are poor multimedia machines, as Table 1-1 happily verifies. The only way to upgrade these machines is to buy a new computer.

- The SE/30 — yet another one-piece computer with a black-and-white screen — is a special case. You can add a color monitor to this machine after installing special hardware, as discussed later in this chapter.

- Most PowerBooks issued in the last three years not only support lots of gray and colors on their internal screens but also let you hook up external monitors. This is true of the PowerBooks 165c, 180, and 500 series, for example, just to name a few.

✔ Several one-piece desktop Macs provide color screens but lack video-out ports. These systems include the Color Classic, LC 520, Performa 550, and others. As with the SE/30, you can attach an external monitor to one of these models only after installing special hardware.

Generally speaking, any Mac that can handle color can play just about any multimedia CD-ROM. If that's all you want to do, and you're not picky about how the CD's graphics look on-screen, you can skip this chapter and move on to the next. But if you want to display and edit images from Photo CD, play and record your own digital movies, or just make your multimedia CDs look better, you may want to add more colors to your screen. In which case, keep reading.

The Curious World of Computerized Color

Every Mac that supports a color monitor can display as many as 256 colors at any one time. This may sound like a lot of colors — after all, it's four of those jumbo boxes of crayons — but it's actually fairly limited. When you figure that your eyes are bombarded by billions upon trillions of distinct shades every day, 256 is rather trivial.

Many recent Macs can display 32,000 colors, more than one hundred times the standard 256. And a few models — most notably the Power Macs — can display as many as 16 million colors. That's 256 times 256 times 256! Better known as *gobs.*

The number of screen colors available affects your perception of the screen image. Say that you're looking at a picture of the freshly-born item in Figure 4-1. (This is a cheesy black-and-white book, so you'll have to use your imagination and pretend that the little duffer is displayed in beautiful Technicolor.) You'll see different things depending on the number of screen colors:

 ✔ If your screen can display 16 million colors at once, the baby looks smooth and lustrous, like the top tot in Figure 4-1. You can practically reach out and touch it, it's that realistic. The image looks even better than if it were shown on TV.

 ✔ If your monitor can display 32,000 colors, you see little, irregular dot patterns forming here and there. See, your Mac is trying to fake the colors it can't display by mixing other colors together. This mixing is called *dithering,* as in, "Those little jumbled screen dots are certainly in a dither."

 ✔ If your screen is limited to 256 colors, the dithering becomes more apparent. The bottom tike in Figure 4-1 is an example. Even though the image file itself contains millions of colors, the screen can only display a handful of them. So it has to dither colors like mad to keep up.

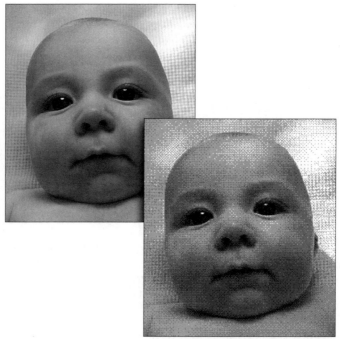

Figure 4-1: An innocent pawn of this book, displayed in millions of colors (top) and dithered for display in 256 colors (bottom).

The moral of the story is, if you want to edit photos or record movies, you want at least 32,000 colors. Some CD-ROM titles also look better when 32,000 or more colors are available. Suffice it to say, you just can't have enough colors.

Some CDs like color more than others

At this point, I thought I'd offer an example of a specific, well-known CD-ROM title that looks better when displayed on a more colorful screen. But I'm having a problem. The CD I'm thinking of comes from a popular musician who went and changed his name to a — what do you call it? — an ornament. You know, the fellow in Figure 4-2. His publicists didn't give me the special font I need to write his silly symbol — shown emblazoned on his face in the figure — so I don't know whether to call him "the artist formerly known to his mother as Prince Rogers Nelson," "the man with the large, purple ego," or what.

I'm told that at Warner Brothers, they just call him Mr. Doohickey. Sounds good to me.

Chapter 4: See All That You Can See

Did you know that colors come in bits?

If you've watched MTV or Saturday morning cartoons lately, you've undoubtedly seen one of those Sega or Nintendo commercials with some in-your-face kid hawking the benefits of 16-bit graphics. The televised youngster is referring to the number of colors you can display on-screen at once — the very stuff I've been droning on about in this very chapter. In this case, *16-bit* is just another way to say 32,000 colors.

Want to know how it works? Well, a *bit* is a single digit that can be 0 or 1, and that's it. One bit is enough to express two colors for every screen dot, or *pixel*. If the bit is 0, the color is white; if the bit is 1, the color is black.

So good so far. But what do you do if you want to express more colors? Add more bits, naturally. Two bits can express four colors, three bits can express eight colors, and so on. You figure it out by taking the number 2 and multiplying it by itself so many times. In the case of four bits, for example, you multiply 2 times itself 4 times to get 16. Math types express this as 2^4, or 2 to the 4th power.

Therefore, 8-bit video produces 2^8=256 colors; 16-bit video results in 2^{16}=32,000 colors; and 24-bit video makes 2^{24}=16 million colors.

Those of you who had your calculators out may have noticed my flagrant lie in that last paragraph. If the truth must be known, 2^{16}=65,536, not 32,000. Because monitors create colors by mixing red, green, and blue light — known by their initials, RGB — your Mac has to split the bits evenly between R, G, and B. (Otherwise they get all grumpy and whine that one got more than the others.) You can't evenly divide 16 bits by three, but you can evenly divide 15 bits. So the computer just ignores that last bit — better to throw it away than start a fight. So it's really 2^{15}=32,768, or 32,000 colors.

Figure 4-2: A still picture from the CD-ROM with the unpronounce-able name.

Anyway, whatever you call him, he has a multimedia CD with a name that's equally hard to pronounce, *[Doohickey] Interactive.* You wander around a fanciful mansion that has pictures of Mr. Doohickey tacked up to every wall (Figure 4-2 is just one of about 10,000 examples). You admire his hit songs, ogle his hit videos, and ingest more Doohickey trivia than any human being should have to tolerate in a single sitting. It's truly mind-numbing.

Although plodding around the mansion is tortuous enough to make you swear off "Paisley Park" for life, the graphics and videos are remarkably well done. They look okay in 256 colors, but you should really play the CD on a machine that can display 32,000 or 16 million colors to get the full effect. I mean, come on, you want to get just the right shade of violet, don't you?

Explore your personal crayon box

The tables in Chapter 1 tell you how many colors every Macintosh computer can display — "thousands" means 32,000 colors, and "millions" means 16 million. But these values have two problems.

- First, they indicate the *maximum* number of colors the computer can handle. Your particular computer might not be quite so well equipped. Specifically, you may need to install more VRAM into your computer, a topic I discuss at length in the section "Vroom! Vim! VRAM!" later in this chapter.

- Second, these numbers apply to 14-inch monitors only. If you own a larger monitor — such as a 17-incher — your computer will probably display fewer colors.

In other words, the values in the Chapter 1 tables are best-case scenarios. To find out exactly how many colors your Mac can handle, you have to display the Monitors control panel, like so:

1. **Choose the Control Panels command from the Apple menu.**

   This brings up the Control Panels window. In it, you'll find the Monitors icon, which appears spotlighted in Figure 4-3.

2. **Double-click on the Monitors icon.**

   The Monitors control panel appears, as shown in Figure 4-4.

Chapter 4: See All That You Can See   57

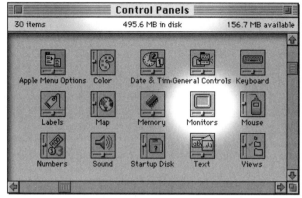

Figure 4-3: The Monitors icon hangs out in the Control Panels window.

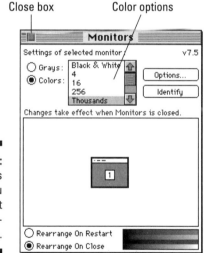

Figure 4-4: Here's where you control what you see on-screen.

Under System 7.5, you can make the Control Panels command display a submenu of additional commands. This way, you can access the control panel by choosing a single command instead of having to choose a command and then double-click on an icon. To do this, open up the Apple Menu Options control panel and select On from the Submenus options. From that point on, you can open up the Monitors control panel by choosing Apple➪Control Panels➪Monitors.

The Monitors control panel lets you change the number of colors displayed on-screen. The top-left corner of the control panel contains two options, Grays and Colors. Unless you're working on a PowerBook or Duo that can display only a few shades of gray, the Colors button should be selected.

Just to the right of Colors and Grays is a scrolling list of color options that starts with Black & White. The last number in the list is the maximum number of colors that you can display at once. In Figure 4-4, the number is Thousands, meaning that I can display up to 32,000 colors at a time.

- If the last number in the list is Millions, you have access to all 16 million colors. Congratulations, you can skip to Chapter 5.
- If the last number is Thousands, you can display 32,000 colors, which is probably good enough. You can skip to Chapter 5, too.
- If the last number is 256, you have to make a decision. Are 256 colors all you expect out of your computer? Or do you lust after more? If the latter is true, keep reading.

By the way, you can go ahead and close the Monitors control panel now. Just click on the close box in the upper-left corner of the control panel, and it disappears. (In case you can't find it, the close box is labeled in Figure 4-4.)

A monitor by any other name

Screen sizes — such as 14-inch and 17-inch — are misleading labels designed by marketing teams. The advertised size of any monitor is measured from the upper-left corner of the screen to the lower-right corner, just as with TV sets. That way, the screen sounds bigger than it actually is. A 14-inch screen, for example, is about 11 inches wide by 8 inches tall. Clever, huh?

Now, it used to be that screens went by smaller sizes. The first external Apple monitors sported 13-inch screens. That was because Apple measured the size of the screen image — the area that actually contains colored dots. Then some smart-alecky advertising type over at some other monitor company came up with a bright idea. "Let's measure the full size of the screen, all the way to the plastic. And let's round up. That way, we'll have a 14-inch monitor. It won't be any bigger, but it'll sound better."

Thanks to that little bit of technological ingenuity, everyone's screens have inflated. Your old 13-inch monitor is now a 14-inch monitor. What were once called 16-inch screens are now 17-inch screens; 19-inchers are now 20-inchers. The only ones that have stayed the same are the 12-inch and the 21-inch screens, but that's just because they were already exaggerating their sizes.

How to Get More Colors

If you can't display as many colors as you'd like, you can encourage a more thriving color population in two ways:

1. Install more VRAM in your computer.
2. Add a video board.

Both options involve turning off your computer, unplugging all the cables, and digging around inside the computer's guts. If you're not up to it, no problem. Just take your computer to an authorized dealer, where a qualified technician can do the work for you. In fact, when it comes to VRAM, that's usually the best advice.

Vroom! Vim! VRAM!

All right, you asked for it. We're in technical territory now.

Ever heard of RAM? (You pronounce it *ram*, just like it looks.) *RAM* is your computer's memory. RAM is where the computer sticks stuff that it wants to have within easy reach. Having lots of RAM allows you to run more than one program at a time and play complex interactive CDs. I discuss RAM in vivid detail in Chapter 6.

In the meantime, I bring up this topic because most Macs also have a second kind of RAM called *VRAM* (pronounced *vee ram*, short for *video RAM*). Adding more VRAM to your computer results in more on-screen colors.

Unfortunately, all computers have a VRAM limit. Let's say that you own an LC 550. It probably comes with 512 kilobytes (K) of VRAM, enough to display 256 colors on a 14-inch monitor screen. However, the LC 550 supports a total of 768K of VRAM, enough to display 32,000. If you want to go even higher, all the way up to 16 million colors, you have to add a video board.

The tables in Chapter 1 don't say anything about VRAM, but they do spell out the maximum video capabilities of your computer. If you aren't getting as many colors as the tables say that you should be getting, call your computer dealer and ask for some more VRAM.

Part I: Meet Your Awesome Multimedia Mac

Just how far does VRAM go?

VRAM is the heart and soul behind on-screen color. The best machines — such as the Power Mac 8100/100 — support as much as 4MB of VRAM, which is enough to display 16 million colors on a 21-inch monitor.

The problem is, even if you know how much VRAM your computer holds, there are so many monitor sizes and color options that it's hard to put everything together. I mean, what if you upgrade to 1MB of VRAM? How many colors can you expect on your 17-inch monitor?

Normally, you'd just have to try it out and hope for the best. But because I care (really, I do), I'm including the following chart, which shows how many colors you get with different amounts of VRAM on different sizes of monitors. It's a $29.95 value — I didn't have it appraised or anything, but I just know it's worth at least that — and I'm giving it to you for free. That's just the kind of guy I am.

For what it's worth, most Macs don't permit more than 1MB of VRAM, and very few go higher than 2MB. So if you're considering buying a larger monitor and you want millions of colors, you'll probably need to buy an additional video board as well.

VRAM	Screen Sizes				
	12-inch	14-inch	17-inch	20-inch	21-inch
256K	256	16	16	NA	NA
512K	thousands	256	256	NA	NA
768K	thousands	thousands	256	NA	NA
1MB	millions	thousands	thousands	256	256
2MB	millions	millions	millions	thousands	thousands
4MB	millions	millions	millions	millions	millions

When everything else fails, buy a board

You can make most kinds of Macs more powerful by adding special pieces of hardware called *boards*. These flat, green planks of electronic stuff fit into slots inside your computer's case. You might also hear them called *cards*. I think that it depends on what part of the country you're from. You know, just like when Easterners say "soda" and Westerners say "pop."

Anyway, just so that you have a vague idea of what I'm talking about, Figure 4-5 shows what a typical video board looks like. Friendly little item, isn't it? The first time I was instructed to handle one of these things, it scared me silly. It looks like something you'd break if you looked at it wrong. But as long as you're reasonably careful — as I spell out shortly — you'll do just fine.

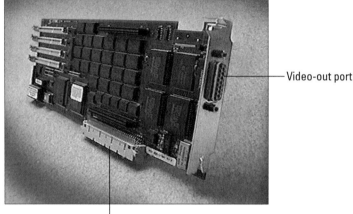

Figure 4-5: A typical video board, longing to be hidden away inside your computer.

— Video-out port

NuBus connector

(In case you're interested, the video board in the figure comes from a company called Radius. Radius makes the best video boards around — a little on the expensive side, but very reliable and very fast. I have yet to be disappointed by one of this company's products. If you're interested in seeing what it has to offer, call 800-227-2795 for the name of a dealer in your area.)

Every board features a connector at the bottom where it hooks into your computer. As things stand now, this connector is called a *NuBus* (pronounced *new bus*) connector. (See "Make way for the new board" if you're hungry for more details.) The board also has a metal strip on one side. In the case of a video board, the metal strip includes a video-out port, as shown in the figure.

Figure 4-6 shows a computer with its lid off, revealing the Mac's strange and bewildering guts. (That's the back of the computer in the bottom-left portion of the figure.) These particular guts happen to belong to a Mac IIci.

The board plugs into the white NuBus slots, labeled in the figure, with the board's metal strip toward the back of the computer. The video-out port on the board has to be able to connect to the monitor cable when the case is closed. So you pop out the corresponding plastic cover plate — they really do pop right out — to reveal an opening in the computer's case. (For dramatic effect, light pours out of the opening in Figure 4-6.) When you put the lid back on, you can plug the monitor into the new video-out port in the back of the computer, which is easily available through the opening.

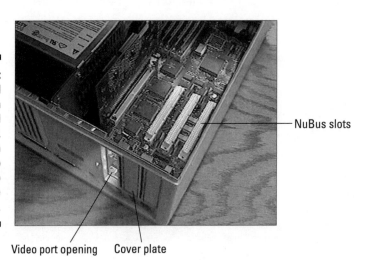

Figure 4-6: A typical Mac shown with its lid peeled off. You can plug a video board into one of the slots.

NuBus slots

Video port opening   Cover plate

- If you decide to insert the board yourself, unplug your Mac before opening it. Believe it or not, many folks don't do this. In fact, some technicians even recommend that you leave the computer plugged in to make sure that the power supply is grounded. But although there aren't many ways to electrocute yourself inside a computer, it is possible to shock yourself good. I know, I've done it. So why risk it?

- Make sure that you are static free before opening the computer case. If you're wearing a wool sweater, take it off. Then touch a piece of grounded metal, preferably something that's plugged in. If your home or office includes metal plates around the light switches, touch one of these. Otherwise, look for a metal knob on a piece of stereo equipment or the metal base of a lamp. If you can't find anything else, open the case and touch the square, metal power supply inside the computer. If you get a little shock, be glad. That means that you've discharged the static electricity.

- Many boards come with little wrist straps that are designed to discharge any static that may build up as you work. Though not absolutely necessary, it's a good precaution to wear it. Wrap one end around your wrist and attach the other to the power supply (the large metal cube inside the computer).

Chapter 4: See All That You Can See **63**

Make way for the new board

The thing that you plug the board into inside your computer is called a *bus slot*. In computer lingo, a *bus* is a pathway through which data is transmitted. But for our purposes, bus is just a word I want to make you familiar with so I can get on with more important things.

Since the Mac II came out more than eight years ago, Macs have used a bus specification called *NuBus*. That's why, when you go to a computer store to buy a video board, the guy at the counter might mutter something about NuBus boards. These boards adhere to the NuBus standard.

Well, by the time you read this, NuBus will be on its way out. Apple is now building a different kind of bus into all new Macs. It's called *PCI* (that's P-C-I, not *picky*). The PCI bus has been around for a while on the PC, but now it's coming over to the Mac. The first Mac to support PCI boards is the Power Mac 9500. More will follow.

The good news is that there are lots of companies out there selling PCI boards, so prices are bound to come down. A board that costs $1,000 today might cost less than half that in a year. That's a pretty significant savings.

The bad news is that the NuBus board in your present Mac won't be compatible with the new Macs. This isn't the end of the world; you can just sell the board along with the computer later on down the line. But it also means that while PCI boards go down in price, NuBus boards will probably stay as expensive as they are now. With time, they'll also get harder to find as manufacturers phase them out. It's the price we pay for progress.

- I can' stress enough, however, that if you don't feel comfortable installing a video board for yourself, it's best to have a technician do the work for you. But at least now you know how the process works and what to expect for your money.

- According to Apple, opening the computer's case and installing a NuBus card does not invalidate the warranty. Just the same, be careful.

Some Macs need special care

Many Macs won't accept standard, run-of-the-mill video boards without special help, and some don't support NuBus or PCI boards at all. For the record, the Macs I'm talking about are the SE/30, IIsi, Color Classic, Centris 610, Quadra 605, 610, or 630, Power Mac 5200 or 6100, and all LCs and Performas. Quite a list, huh? The odd-ball Macs are practically a majority unto themselves.

These Macs support a special kind of bus called a *PDS*. If it helps any, these initials stand for *Processor Director Slot*. Apple provides a $200 adapter that allows a few of these machines — including the IIsi, Centris and Quadra 610, and the Power Mac and Performa 6100 series — to use a NuBus video board.

But the video board must be no longer than 7 inches from metal strip to opposite end. A 12-inch board like the one in Figure 4-5 will not fit. Most video boards sold today are 7-inch boards, but used boards from 1993 or earlier are not. Get out the ruler if you're not sure.

The Quadra 630 is a special case. It requires a petite LC III-type PDS board, which is strangely shaped and highly specialized. A couple of companies sell such a board, but my favorite board is the 1724PD from Micro Conversions in Arlington, Texas, 817-468-9922. The propeller-head name of the board — I personally think that "Speedy Munchkin" has a better ring to it — comes from the fact that it supports 24-bit color on 17-inch monitors. It also handles 256 colors on a 21-inch monitor. This board works inside the Color Classic II, all LCs except the first LC and the LC II, the Quadra 605 and 630, the Mac TV, and most Performas.

The SE/30, LC, LC II, Color Classic, and Performas 400 through 430 are a league unto themselves. The SE/30 takes one kind of board; the others take a special LC variety. The only company that has consistently sold these types of video boards is Focus Enhancements. Call them at 800-538-6000 and ask them about their Lapis boards. (Lapis is a brand name, by the way, not some perplexing new technical term.)

My CD-ROM Won't Play

As I mentioned earlier, most CD-ROMs play just fine on 256-color screens. What I neglected to mention was that some CDs refuse to play at all if your screen is set to more colors. A message appears, telling you to lower the number of colors to 256 and then try again. This doesn't mean you have to remove some VRAM or yank out your video board. You can very easily change the number of colors without even restarting your machine or quitting a program:

1. **Open the Monitors control panel.**

    Choose Apple⇨Control Panels and then double-click on the Monitors icon.

2. **Click on the number 256 in the scrolling list at the top of the control panel.**

    The monitor will flash and redraw. Don't panic, you didn't break anything. This is supposed to happen.

3. **Click on the close box to close the control panel.**

After you finish playing with the CD, be sure to set the Monitors control panel back to the highest color setting. Again, you do this by clicking on an option in the scrolling list.

Chapter 5
What in the World is Going on with AV?

In This Chapter
- All about Apple's best multimedia computers
- Comparing the AV Quadras to the AV Power Macs
- Inserting an AV Technologies card into the PDS slot
- Understanding the difference between computer and television video
- Connecting a VCR to an AV computer
- Improving AV performance
- Adding audio and video stuff to an aging Mac

*I*f you're much more than 25 — years old, that is, not inches high or meters around — the initials *AV* probably conjure up images of those anonymous guys in high school who were in charge of maintaining films, records, and other moldy scraps of media that few people outside the P.E. department seemed to take any interest in. It might call to mind an old, cantankerous projector that made loud, snapping sounds in the middle of a movie until someone stuck a piece of paper in it. And of course, no matter who was in charge of the slide projector, the person always seemed to miss a beep so that, for example, the image of a pale scientist in a white coat holding a lab rat appeared on-screen at the very moment the narration turned to the dangers of heavy petting.

Well, scrap all those mental associations you've harbored these many years. When it comes to the Mac, AV signals an entirely new breed of audio/video gadgetry. AV Macs are on the cutting edge of insanely great multimedia technology, enabling you to manipulate sound and movies in ways that your home entertainment center — no matter how much money you've dumped into it — simply won't allow.

AV Macs let you record videotaped movies to disk, complete with CD-quality, stereo sound. Like text in a word processor, digital movies are fully editable, down to the last pixel in the last frame. After you finish editing the movie by applying special effects, adding musical sound tracks, and generally twisting reality around your little finger, you can play the movies from your Mac and record them back to videotape, or you can integrate them into multimedia presentations. Then again, you might just want to invite unsuspecting guests over to your house, sit them in front of your computer, and say, "Check out what I did!" as you play every digital movie in your collection.

In a broad, general sense, this chapter explains how to set up your Mac to record and play moving images on-screen. But because the AV Macs are the only ones specifically designed to record movies or play them back out to videotape, it makes sense to concentrate my discussions on Apple's AV line. This chapter, therefore, provides some background information to help you sort out the various AV Macs on the market. It also tells you how to hook your AV Mac to a VCR, camcorder, laserdisc player, or even your TV (and suggests reasons why you might want to do that in the first place). I even go that extra mile and tell you how to add AV capabilities to a non-AV Mac.

Like the other chapters in Part I, this chapter doesn't tell you what to do after you get things all hooked together. If you want to find out how to actually use these various components to do a bunch of cool stuff, read Chapter 17.

The Primo Multimedia Macs

If using your computer to create and play movies is one of your primary goals, you should definitely consider one of the AV Macs. The more powerful models actually have the initials *AV* in their names. I discuss these in the "Big AVs on Campus" section, which follows immediately on many of these pages. A slightly less powerful but more affordable group of systems offer no hint of their capabilities in their naming schemes. In fact, they aren't even named consistently. I examine these wonderful machines in the section after next, "The Spunky AV Junior."

Big AVs on campus

Apple's AV push started a couple of years ago with the release of the Centris 660AV and the Quadra 840AV. Soon after, the Centris 660AV was renamed the Quadra 660AV. (Marketing folks do the craziest things.) And a year later, three AV Power Macs — the 6100AV, 7100AV, and 8100AV — joined the fray.

By the time you read this, a few more AV models will undoubtedly become available. Keep an eye out for the Power mac 7500, 8500, and others.

But regardless of their names and numbers, all AV Macs offer the following capabilities:

- ✔ You can record CD-quality sound in full stereo. In many ways, the sound is every bit as good as music recorded with professional sound equipment. I explain exactly what this means in Chapter 12. But I can tell you this right now — whatever you record, it'll sound way better than the Styx and Toto cassettes those AV guys used to listen to in high school.

- ✔ You can also record quarter-screen movies from videotape without purchasing any additional hardware. Whether you want to grab a favorite sequence from last summer's blockbuster epic or edit a home movie from last summer's frenzied vacation, this feature comes in mighty handy.

- ✔ You can even capture a single, full-screen frame from a movie, edit it, and print it out. Considering that one of those Sony video printers — which does the same thing — can run you several hundred bucks, this isn't a bad side benefit.

- ✔ When you finish editing a movie, you can play it and record it back onto videotape. Even though you can record only quarter-screen movies, you can blow them back up to full-screen size during playback by doubling the pixels, as I explain in Chapter 19.

- ✔ Few folks know about this one, but you can turn your AV Mac into an answering machine that logs your messages and lets you listen to them out of order. However, to get up and running, you have to purchase this thing called a GeoPort Telecom Adapter for about $100 and plug it into the modem port — the one with the little phone icon — on the back of the computer.

- ✔ You can make your machine pronounce words, and you can make it respond when you talk to it. Quite honestly, Macintosh speech recognition is really in its infancy right now; if you're serious about trying to teach your Mac to understand vocal commands, you're in for a lot of frustration. But getting your Mac to talk to *you* is easy. Check out Chapter 14 for a taste of the 21st century.

- ✔ Oh, yeah, I almost forgot. All AV Macs include internal CD-ROM drives. This is multimedia computing as it should be.

The spunky AV junior

Another group of Macs offers many of these same AV capabilities, but none of these machines has *AV* in its name. The first among the junior AV set was the Mac TV, released a few months after the first AV Macs hit the shelves. Universally panned and discontinued six months later, this machine paved the way for the much improved Quadra 630 and its knockoffs, the LC 630 and the Performa 630, 635, and so on. The latest addition to the group is the Power Mac 5200 LC, which is a monitor equipped with a fully functioning computer. As with the AV Macs, more models are undoubtedly in the cards.

Even though these junior AV Macs are less expensive than their big brothers, they still pack in some interesting and useful features:

- ✔ A headphone jack, two stereo speakers, and volume controls are built into the front of these machines. This setup makes for an ideal home machine. No more digging around in back of the machine when you want to put on headphones after the kids or visiting in-laws have gone to bed.

- ✔ Though the sound quality isn't quite as good as the standard AV Macs, you can record music and other sounds in stereo.

- ✔ For an extra $250, the computer store will throw in the Apple TV/Video System. The TV half of the system is a cable-ready television tuner. If you have cable TV installed in your home or office, just plug the coaxial cable coming out of your wall into your Mac and change channels. The system can tune in up to 181 channels and scan out inactive stations automatically.

- ✔ You can name channels and then switch channels by choosing one of the names from a menu, as demonstrated in Figure 5-1. You can even ask your computer to remind you a few minutes before a favorite show is about to begin and then play the show for you automatically. It won't exactly help you get work done, but it will help you take a break. Too bad it can't block out the commercials.

- ✔ The second half of the Apple TV/Video System lets you record videos. (Sadly, this is not an option with the Mac TV, which may be one of the reasons it's dead.) As with the AV Macs, you record the movies at quarter-screen size.

- ✔ If you want to play your movies back to videotape, you have to buy a piece of hardware that converts a computer graphics signal to TV video. An example is the $300 Apple Presentation System.

Figure 5-1:
On a Quadra 630 or similar Mac, you can watch TV in a quarter-screen window and even change channels by choosing a channel name from a menu.

- ✔ Internal CD-ROM drives are optional. The Performa 636 doesn't include a drive, for example, while the Performa 636CD does.

- ✔ Each computer includes an infrared sensor up front and a remote control. You can use the remote to change TV channels, play audio CDs, skip tracks, and so on, all without touching the computer. You can even turn the computer on and off.

This chapter is mostly about using full-fledged AV Macs. However, much of the information is also applicable to the junior AV models as well. If you own a Quadra 630 (or one of the other 630 spin-offs) or a Power Mac 5200 LC, read the "Get Out Your VCRs!" section later in this chapter to learn how to hook up a VCR to your computer.

What Makes AV Tick, Whir, and Flicker?

Though their capabilities are the same, the old and new AV computers break into slightly different camps. On one side are the Centris 600AV, Quadra 660AV, and Quadra 840AV, which I'll call the AV Quadras. On the other side are the Power Mac 6100AV, 7100AV, 8100AV, and future models. I'll call these machines the AV Power Macs.

- The sound and video capabilities of the AV Quadras are built into the main logic board. (The *logic board* is the large green slab of chips and transistors that is responsible for most of what the computer does. Some folks call it the *motherboard* because it's the mother of all boards.) This setup means that you cannot buy an AV Quadra without sound or video hardware. It's one package, take it or leave it.

- CD-quality sound is a feature of all Power Macs — whether there's an *AV* in the title or not — as long as there's no *LC* in the title. The Power Mac 5200 LC, for example, is not quite as well equipped in the sound department as the Power Mac 6100.

- The only difference between similarly numbered Power Macs with and without AV is a thing called the AV Technologies card. The Power Mac 7100AV has the AV Technologies card, for example; the Power Mac 7100 does not. This card lets you record and output video.

- If you purchased a Power Mac 6100, 7100, or 8100 without the *AV* in its name or one of the Macs in the Performa 6100 series, you can purchase an AV Technologies card independently for about $480. Stick it in your computer, and you're in business.

Figure 5-2 shows a little diagram of the AV Technologies card that I sketched for your viewing enjoyment. It goes inside the computer's case just like a video board. But rather than fitting into a NuBus or PCI slot, the AV card fits into the PDS slot. (Read the last few pages of Chapter 4 for details on NuBus, PCI, and PDS.)

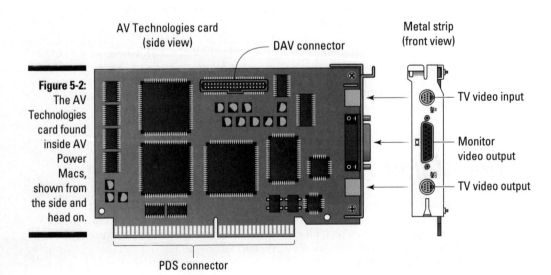

Figure 5-2: The AV Technologies card found inside AV Power Macs, shown from the side and head on.

Chapter 5: What in the World is Going on with AV?

Although each of the current crop of Power Macs differs on the inside, Figure 5-3 shows the innards of the most typical model, the Power Mac 7100. (The back of the computer is on the left side of the figure; you're looking in through the left side of the computer.) I removed all NuBus boards and the AV Technologies card so that you can easily see the slots. The white slots — as always — are NuBus. The skinny tall slot just beyond the last NuBus slot is the lone PDS slot. (Interestingly enough, no Mac has more than one PDS slot.) This slot is where the AV Technologies card hangs out.

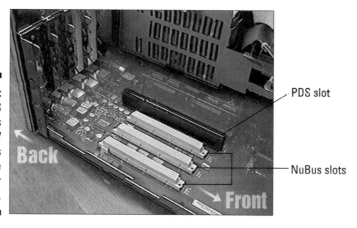

Figure 5-3: The PDS slot holds the AV Technologies card inside a Power Mac.

If you bought a vanilla Power Mac without AV, the PDS slot is occupied by a regular old video board. You have to remove this board before inserting the AV Technologies card in its place. Just press the PDS connector on the card, labeled in Figure 5-2, into the PDS slot in the computer. As always, be sure that you're not harboring static electricity, and don't forget to unplug the computer.

Get Out Your VCRs!

The easiest way to get video images into your AV Mac is to hook up a VCR to the computer. You'll need a VCR with RCA jacks. Typically, these jacks are labeled Line In and Line Out. Use the Line Out jacks to play video out to the computer; use the Line In jacks to record computer movies back to videotape. Most VCRs manufactured in the last five to ten years provide RCA jacks.

The difference between computer video and TV

Computer video is sometimes called *RGB composite video* because red, green, and blue light is mixed together on a pixel-by-pixel basis. The monitor projects colors onto the screen one horizontal line at a time. Though it may seem hard to believe, the monitor manages to completely redraw the screen anywhere from 60 to more than 80 times a second. It's as if your Mac were playing an interactive movie at 60 or more frames per second. Cool, huh?

(Technical types refer to a monitor's redraw rate — called the *scan rate* — in terms of *hertz*, or *Hz* for short. One hertz equals one cycle per second, so a monitor that updates 60 times a second has a scan rate of 60Hz. You don't need to remember this or anything. I just thought that I'd stick it in here in case you needed to look it up in the index for some reason. Outside of this paragraph, the only time I ever say "hertz" is when I'm in pain.)

Television video is different depending on what country you're in. In the U.S., Japan, Korea, Mexico, and some South American and Caribbean countries, the television standard is *NTSC*, which stands for National Television, uh, Somethingarather Committee. Whatever — it doesn't matter, anyway. What matters is that NTSC video measures 640 pixels wide by 480 pixels tall and plays at 30 frames per second (30Hz).

The other big TV standard, PAL, is a favorite throughout nearly all of Europe — including England, Germany, Italy, and all those others — as well as China, Kuwait, Australia, and a few other wacky places. The video image measures 768 by 576 pixels and plays at 25 frames per second.

All AV Macs support both the NTSC and PAL standards, regardless of what country you bought your computer in. However, they don't support the third and far less prevalent standard, SECAM. Most closely associated with France — the country that's always doing it's own thing — SECAM is also used in Russia, Hungary, and some really scary places such as Iran and Iraq.

You can also hook up a camcorder to your computer, as long as it has RCA jacks. Many camcorders have just one set of jacks; you have to flip a switch to determine whether the sound and video signals are going in or out. On many popular Sony camcorders, for example, you can set a switch to either Input or Output. When the switch is set to Output, you can view the movie on your computer screen; when it's set to Input; you can record whatever's happening on your computer onto videotape.

Plug it again, Jack

Whether you're using a VCR or camcorder, here's how the RCA jacks work:

- ✓ The white and red jacks represent the left and right audio jacks, just as they do on a CD-ROM drive. The left jack may alternatively be black.

- If you see a white or black jack but no red jack, you're looking at a mono VCR. The sound won't be quite as good, but what can you do? Sometimes, we must resolve ourselves to work with what we have.

- The yellow jack is for video (not to be confused with yellow jackets, of course, which are stinging members of the wasp family that are rarely found near VCRs).

More sophisticated VCRs and camcorders offer an additional jack labeled S-video. The *S* is for *super,* as in super-duper, not the guy who owns your building. Standard VHS and 8mm decks don't offer S-video jacks, but Super VHS and Hi-8 decks do. Many laserdisc players also offer S-video jacks. It's usually a function of price; if you spent less than $400 for your VCR, you can safely assume that your deck doesn't qualify.

Any S-video deck provides both S-video and yellow RCA jacks. However, there's no reason to use both. Just use the S-video jack along with the white and red audio jacks; you can go ahead and ignore the yellow RCA jack entirely.

What's all this S-video stuff about? The short answer is, S-video is better. The long answer is, well, longer. Serious video people call a video signal that goes through an RCA jack *composite video*. This means that both the *luminance* (how light and dark everything is) and *chrominance* (a fancy word for color) portions of the video signal are all mixed together. As a result, bright colors bleed into each other, and other colors look less sharp. An S-video cable is actually two cables in one, keeping luminance and chrominance entirely separate.

How do I play video into my computer?

When you understand what the various cables floating about your room are for, plugging the VCR into the computer is actually a fairly straightforward process. For example, if you want to play a tape on your VCR and view it on your computer screen, do the following:

1. **Plug the video cable into the Line Out jack on your VCR.**

   If you have an S-video jack and cable, use it. If not, go with the yellow RCA jack.

2. **Plug the other end of the cable into the In video jack on your AV Mac.**

   The video jack is marked with a little camcorder icon (as shown on the metal strip in Figure 5-2).

   The AV Quadras — as well as the Quadra 630 and Power Mac 5200 LC — include both RCA and S-video input jacks. However, the AV Power Macs

74 Part I: Meet Your Awesome Multimedia Mac

include S-video input jacks only. To connect an RCA cable, you have to use one of the gray, six-inch long conversion cables included with your computer.

Be sure to use the conversion cable labeled In. Otherwise, you won't get any signal.

3. **Locate a Y cable with a stereo miniplug at one end and two RCA jacks at the other.**

   If you're playing from a mono VCR, you need a cable with a mono miniplug on one end and a single RCA plug at the other. If you can't remember what a Y cable is or you're itching for those Radio Shack part numbers, read the "Channel-splitting" section of Chapter 3.

4. **Insert the RCA plugs (or plug) from the cable into the audio Line Out jacks on your VCR.**

   Remember, white or black is left, and red is right.

5. **Insert the miniplug end of the cable into the sound-in port on the back of the computer.**

   The sound-in port sports a little microphone icon.

Figure 5-4 shows what the cables look like when hooked up to a Power Mac 7100AV. In this case, the cable hooked up to the AV Technologies card is an S-video cable; the stereo miniplug cable is hooked up to the sound-in port. That's all there is to it.

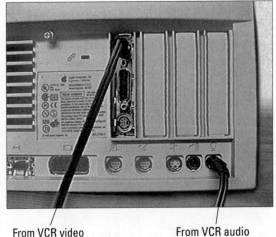

Figure 5-4: The cable hookups required to play a videotape, complete with sound, into an AV Mac.

From VCR video   From VCR audio

By the way, if you have a laserdisc player and you feel like hauling it over to your computer, you can just as easily hook it up as a VCR. Just plug the video and audio cables in as explained for a VCR. Laserdisc players can be especially useful for capturing still frames because you can pause indefinitely without hurting the disc. Players in the $400 to $500 range let you pause low-capacity CAV discs only. More expensive decks lets you pause any disc, including the more common CLV variety.

And how do I send computer signals to the VCR?

If you want to record what you see on your computer screen onto videotape, you take the very same cables mentioned in the preceding section and plug them in differently. (On the AV Power Macs, you have to swap a conversion cable, but that's it.) Here's the complete story:

1. **Plug the video cable into the Line In jack on your VCR.**

    Plug into that S-video jack if you have it; settle for the yellow RCA jack if you don't.

2. **Plug the other end of the cable into the Out video jack on your AV Mac.**

    Again, AV Quadras, 630 models, and the Power Mac 5200 LC offer both RCA and S-video output jacks, while the AV Power Macs provide S-video output jacks only. If you're hankering to plug in an RCA cable, locate the gray conversion cable that came with the computer.

    Be sure to use the conversion cable labeled Out. If you get mixed up and use the In cable, your VCR will record in black and white.

3. **Insert the RCA end of the audio cable into the audio Line In jacks on your VCR.**

    If you're recording to a stereo VCR, you should stick in two RCA plugs. When using a mono VCR, one RCA plug will do it.

4. **Stick the miniplug end of the cable into the sound-out port on the back of the computer.**

    If you read Chapter 3, you may recollect that the sound-out port has a little speaker icon above it. Of course, in order to complete this step, you have to unplug the speakers from the sound-out port. Life is just rampant with these kinds of compromises.

Figure 5-5 shows the back of my Power Mac 7100AV set up to play video and sound out to a VCR.

Figure 5-5: If you want to record stuff from your computer, hook up the cables this-a-way.

To VCR video

To VCR audio

 To see the same thing on your monitor that the VCR sees, you need to make sure that the monitor is hooked up to the Mac's built-in video port. In the case of the AV Power Macs, this means the monitor video port between the two S-video ports on the AV Technologies card. If you have the monitor hooked up to a separate video board or to the so-called AudioVision port included with the AV Power Macs, what you see and what the VCR sees won't jibe.

 To hear what the VCR is recording, you can hook up your speakers to the VCR in a number of ways. If the speakers provide RCA jacks, just hook them up to the audio Line Out jacks on the VCR. If the speakers support a stereo minijack connection only, insert the miniplug into the headphone jack on the VCR.

If the VCR lacks a headphone jack, or if you don't have any speakers, hook up a television to the Line Out jacks on the VCR just as you normally do when watching movies. You can even connect the VCR and TV with a household coaxial cable. This way, you'll be able to see and hear what you're recording on a single device.

Make Your AV Even Better

There's only one problem with AV — it's not wildly powerful. For example, on a Power Mac 7100 or 8100, you can record quarter-screen movies — 320 by 240 pixels — at 15 frames per second. That's one-fourth the size of standard TV and one-half the speed. The result is video recording that's good — sufficient to give you a few thrills and amaze your friends — but not outstanding.

A technology named DAV

But Apple thought ahead. Every full-fledged AV Mac released so far includes something called a *DAV connector*. (DAV stands for *digital audio/video*, but folks just say *Dave*.) This connector allows other companies to develop acceleration hardware to speed up the frame rate and increase the size of recorded movies.

You'll find the DAV connector on the logic board of the Quadra 840 AV or on a special NuBus adapter card in the case of the Quadra 660AV. Either way, the DAV slot is in line with one of the NuBus slots. On the AV Power Macs, the DAV connector resides at the top of the AV Technologies card (and is even labeled back in Figure 5-2).

How to get hitched to DAV

Thus far, only one company creates a DAV card, but it works like a charm. Radius, a vendor with a long history of providing video hardware for the Mac, sells a $1,000 DAV acceleration board called the SpigotPower AV. Not to be overshadowed by the bazillion computer acronyms wafting through the ether, Radius loving calls its DAV board SPAV. It's distinctive, anyway.

Shown at the top of Figure 5-6, the board fits into a NuBus slot. It sports two DAV connectors, one at the base of the card beside the NuBus connector to support the two AV Quadras, and one at the top of the card for the AV Power Macs. (SPAV is not compatible with the Power Mac 6100AV because you can't fit a NuBus board and an AV Technologies card in the 6100 at the same time.)

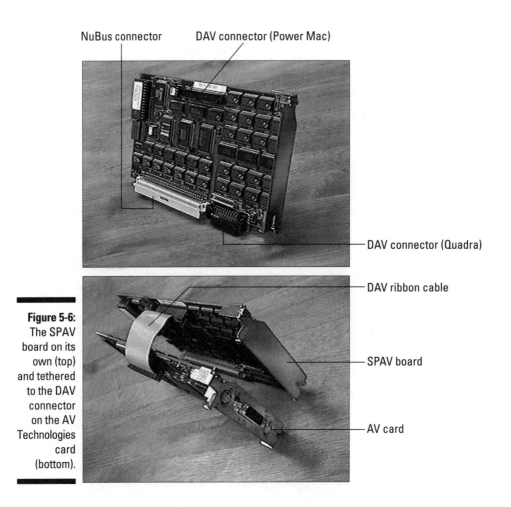

Figure 5-6: The SPAV board on its own (top) and tethered to the DAV connector on the AV Technologies card (bottom).

To fit the SPAV board into an AV Quadra, you just give a push. But in the case of the AV Power Macs, you have to stretch a ribbon cable from the DAV connector on the SPAV board to the DAV connector on the AV Technologies card, as shown in the second example of Figure 5-6.

Generally speaking, you want to fit the SPAV card into the NuBus slot right next to the PDS slot. This way, the ribbon cable can reach both DAV connectors quite easily. However, the Power Mac 7100AV happens to have some weird little capacitors that poke up beside the first NuBus slot and get in the way of the

SPAV's second DAV connector (the one intended for the AV Quadras). Rather than shove the board in there anyway, which is basically what the SPAV manual suggests, you're better off sticking the card into the next NuBus slot over. It's a stretch for the ribbon cable, but it works just fine.

After you get the SPAV installed, you can start recording full-screen movies with as many as 30 frames per second (which is the optimum setting for U.S. television). If you're not satisfied — you demanding creature — Radius already has a successor for the SPAV card in the works. It's called the SpigotPro AV, and it will output video without the help of the AV Technologies card. Of course, it costs more, too. You can reach Radius at 800-227-2795.

Can You Add AV to Your Old Mac?

After reading all this stuff, you're no doubt consumed with AV lust and wishing that you, too, had an AV computer. Your Mac couldn't possibly muster up to the awesome and unyielding multimedia power of AV.

Or could it? Here are some things you should consider before you decide to bag your current machine:

- As I've mentioned more than once, all Macs provide sound-out ports. This means that you can record sound out to videotape regardless of which machine you own.

- Unless you own a Mac without a sound-in port — that is, the Plus, SE, SE/30, Classic, II, IIx, IIcx, IIci, or IIfx — you can record sound from videotape.

- Be sure to use a cable with a mono miniplug if your Mac's sound-out or sound-in capabilities are limited to mono sound. Consult the "Sound Out" and "Sound In" columns in the tables in Chapter 1 to be sure.

- If your Mac lacks a sound-in port, you can purchase an inexpensive mono sound recorder such as the $100 MacRecorder from MacroMedia, 415-252-2000, which is pictured in Figure 5-7. You just plug the MacRecorder into your computer's modem port and then insert a mono miniplug into the Line jack. I've used one of these with my IIci for years.

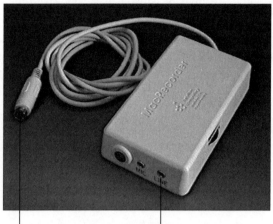

Figure 5-7: This sound-input device lets you record sound with some of the crustiest old Macs.

Plug into modem port   Mono minijack

- A few years ago, a company called SuperMac used to sell a whole line of video-recording boards under the brand name VideoSpigot. Some provided video-in ports only and others offered both video-in and -out capabilities. When new, these boards cost $500 and up; you may be able to locate a used board for a reduced price.

- Since then, Radius gobbled up SuperMac in one of those big computer company mergers and discontinued most of the VideoSpigot boards. Nowadays, Radius sells just one of these boards, the $900 Spigot II Tape. Every bit as capable as Apple's AV Technologies board, the II Tape records and plays quarter-screen movies at 15 or more frames per second.

- If you get a board with no video-output capabilities, you may want to purchase Apple's $300 Presentation System. This is a separate box that plugs into your computer's standard monitor port. You then plug your monitor into the box so that you can still see the on-screen graphics. You can also cable a VCR to the box and record the outgoing graphics onto videotape.

Now, very possibly, none of these options is worth the money to you. After all, it's hard to justify spending $500 to $1,000 to upgrade an old Mac when newer, faster, and better equipped junior AV models are available for about $1,500 to $2,000. Whatever you decide to do, shop around first. Though AV Macs and their junior AV siblings are monstrously cool, you have to decide just how much multimedia you need and whether you're willing to go into hock for it.

Chapter 6
You Can Never Have Enough Digital Closet Space

In This Chapter
- What is RAM?
- How much RAM do you need?
- Measuring digital space
- Purchasing RAM
- Why you need a larger hard drive
- Buying a hard drive
- The three main kinds of removable media

I subscribe to the theory that the innermost workings of your computer — down to the last transistor — can be communicated in very basic terms using real-world analogies. Take the subject of computer memory and hard drive storage, for example. There's a highly technical and, frankly, drop-dead boring topic that has a direct parallel in our everyday lives.

Here's what I mean: You're at a shopping mall, okay? You're looking at the floor-plan directory when you notice, standing next to you, a magic elf dressed in green, terry-cloth jodhpurs and one of those really tall, floppy hats that you see on Dr. Seuss charac . . . what do you mean, this isn't an everyday event? I haven't finished yet. How can you judge until I finish?

All right. So anyway, this elf is no ordinary mall elf. So many elves are kind of aloof and standoffish these days, you know? But this one, well, he seems really interested in your welfare. He offers to take you to any store in the mall and buy you as many clothes as you want. Naturally, you're a little suspect. I mean, it's not like you rescued the guy from a bottle or anything — he was just standing there in the mall. But he convinces you that he's on the up and up and shows you one of his major credit cards to prove it.

So there you are, picking out all this stuff at Neiman Marcus and just heaping it onto an overjoyed clerk. Meanwhile, the elf is patient and even offers a few opinions when you aren't sure which Ralph Lauren unitard to buy. At the end of a hard day of procuring everything that looks even mildly interesting, you're watching the exhausted clerk ring up your 50 or so thousand dollars in merchandise — when the elf hesitates before signing the credit slip.

"Uh, one little catch," he says. Great, you think, he wants something in return. You're just about to offer some choice comment about the horrible things that can happen to lecherous pixies when he continues. "I can't give you this stuff — not even a fabric sample — if you don't have enough closet space to hold it."

Well, of course, that's exactly the attitude that multimedia cops when sizing up the memory and hard disk space available to your computer. Sound, images, movies — they all consume gobs and gobs of digital space.

Think about it — in Chapter 2, you learned that a CD holds 74 minutes of music or 650MB of data. That means that a single minute of CD-quality sound consumes six to seven floppy disks! Even if you lower the quality — as discussed in Chapter 13 — a minute of monophonic sound just barely fits on a single disk. Movies are even worse. A typical, minute-long, full-screen, 30-frame-per-second movie is big enough to fill anywhere from 30 to 50 disks. Suffice it to say, these files can be flat out enormous.

And that's why you need to carefully consider your computer closet space before you go accepting handouts from any multimedia elves, no matter how nattily dressed they may be.

Your Mac Can't Think Straight without Memory

Memory — also known as *RAM* — is a bunch of chips inside your computer. Like hard drives, floppy disks, and CDs, RAM is a kind of storage device. But although your computer has to spin floppy disks, CDs, and hard drives to read the data on them, that's not the case with RAM. RAM has no moving parts — just some electricity zapping through it, which makes it incredibly fast.

Your computer stores active software in RAM so that it can access the program information quickly. Your Mac's system software is in memory, just as is any other program you decide to use, whether it be Microsoft Word, Excel, Photoshop, or whatever. Every time you start a program, most of it goes into RAM. Every time you quit a program, it comes out.

How much RAM is enough?

Having lots of RAM is good for the following reasons:

- ✔ It lets you run many programs at the same time and conveniently switch back and forth between them without quitting one program and starting another, quitting that program and starting a third, and then quitting that program and returning to the first — which gets old almost as fast as this sentence.

- ✔ You can open very large files inside a program. As I mentioned a moment ago, multimedia files can be very large.

- ✔ You can perform complex manipulations to a sound, image, or movie. The computer has to figure out all those calculations in RAM before it writes the results to your hard drive.

- ✔ Lots of RAM makes a program faster because your computer doesn't have to load stuff from the hard drive as often.

Every computer built these days has at least four megabytes (4MB) of RAM. Considering that the system software takes up at least 2MB of that space, 4MB is the absolute bare-bones minimum — enough to run a word processor, and that's about it.

The next step up is 8MB. You need at least 8MB of RAM to run the vast majority of multimedia CDs, so you should consider 8MB the minimum amount for a functioning multimedia computer.

If you can afford it, 16MB of RAM is better. Super-cool games require 16MB of RAM to run smoothly. Key multimedia programs such as Adobe Photoshop and Adobe Premiere need this much RAM. And if you want to record and edit movies, 16MB is the only way to go.

Beyond that, it's up to you. I'd start out with 16MB or 20MB and see how it goes. If you decide to upgrade, you have to do so in fairly large chunks. Generally speaking, the next level up from 20MB is 32MB, and then 64MB.

Part I: Meet Your Awesome Multimedia Mac

Measuring the vast expanses of digital space

You've probably heard folks kick around terms such as *megabytes* or *K* and wondered what they were yacking about. It's very simple, actually. These terms are the units of measure in the digital world.

It all begins with the smallest thing your computer knows, a *bit*. A bit is a single digit that can be 0 or 1. If you ever saw the movie *Tron*, the bit was a hovering shape whose only purpose was to say "Yes" or "No" to Jeff Bridges. It's a *binary*—two-possibility — digit. Say "binary digit" really fast and you get bit (particularly if you're standing next to a mean dog).

When you string eight bits together, you get a *byte*. This term started off as something of a joke, really. *Byte* sounds like the present tense of *bit*, get it? For a while, they even called four bits a *nybble*. But you never hear that one anymore; it was just too silly.

A good way to think of a byte is a number that's 8 digits long and made up entirely of 0s and 1s. Altogether, you can create 2^8, or 256, unique combinations — 00000001, 00000010, 00000011, 00000100, and so on. (Remember from Chapter 4 that 8-bit color means 256 colors on-screen at the same time? Well, you could just as accurately call it 1-byte color.)

As computers grew in power, bytes became so insignificant that no one wanted to be seen with them. So we grouped them into 1,024 bytes (that's 10 bits of bytes) and called them *kilobytes*. Tech-heads started out abbreviating this term *Kbytes*, but these days, we're so sophisticated and blasé, we just say *K*.

When you're sick of kilobytes — and, who isn't? — you multiply those by 1,024 and get *megabytes*. You write a megabyte *MB*, but you say *meg*. Herd 1,024MB together, and they suddenly become a *gigabyte*, which is more than you can fit on a CD. That's *GB* on paper or *gig* in polite conversation. Radically insane power users like to get together and whisper *terabyte* to each other. That's 1,024GB, and they say the whole word — *ter-a-byte* — because that kind of space is in their dreams.

If I only had some RAM

If only the Wizard of Oz had known about RAM, he could have stuffed Scarecrow's head full of it instead of giving him that stupid and useless honorary degree. When it comes your turn to stuff the Scarecrow, don't you make the same mistake.

RAM for desktop Macs comes on little circuit boards called SIMMs. (Believe me, you don't care what it stands for — just say *simms*.) When purchasing SIMMs, you have to consider three things:

- **Size:** SIMMs come in different sizes — 1MB, 4MB, 8MB, 16MB, or 32MB each. At current market prices, you can expect to pay about $40 per megabyte, with discounts if you buy a lot of megabytes at once. More megs mean fewer bucks per meg.

Chapter 6: You Can Never Have Enough Digital Closet Space

- **Speed:** RAM speed is measured in *nanoseconds* (abbreviated *ns*) which are billionths of a second, brief spans of time that you and I hardly notice. SIMMs are rated according to how fast they can write the teeniest smidgen of data. The lower the number, the faster the SIMM. You have to buy a SIMM that's at least fast enough to accommodate your computer. Most new Macs, including the Power Macs, require 80ns SIMMs, but some go faster, to 70 or even 60ns. Your computer dealer can look up your specific model requirements for you.

- **Pins:** In the book *The Wizard of Oz*, the Wizard mixes a concoction that includes pins and needles to insert into the Scarecrow's cranium, thus ensuring that the Scarecrow is "sharp" — a much wiser choice than the honorary degree handed out by the Hollywood-version Wizard. Though not quite so prickly, RAM chips also have *pins*, which are the little feet at the base of the chip. If you bought your computer in the last two years, it takes 72-pin SIMMs. Older machines take 30-pin SIMMs. Only one Mac, the IIfx, requires 64-pin SIMMs. Again, consult your computer dealer about your specific model.

If your computer has only one SIMM slot, as does the Quadra 630, you can purchase a single SIMM. Otherwise, you have to buy at least two and probably four at a time, depending on your kind of computer. See, neighboring sockets inside your computer have to be filled with identical SIMMs. That's just the way it is. If you have a technician install the SIMMs for you, he or she will know what to do.

If you own a PowerBook, you probably have to buy your RAM on larger boards. Many different kinds exist, so be ready to tell your dealer exactly which kind of PowerBook you have.

Space on the Platter

Wow, isn't this topic exciting? I told you it would be, thanks to that analogy up front. Whenever your eyes start to glaze over, just think about that mall elf, and you'll be right back on track.

The next item on our madcap journey into the darkest regions of your computer is *storage*. Memory's best buddy, storage includes floppy disks, hard drives, and other kinds of disks and tapes onto which you can copy your files. Unlike memory, which holds files only temporarily, this kind of storage — which you'll find me collectively referring to as disks — can hold files indefinitely. (Well, at least it does as long as you don't step on it or accidentally set it down for a moment on a powerful magnet.)

When it comes to multimedia, floppy disks are useless because they simply can't hold enough stuff. And while CDs are certainly big enough, you as a user can't copy files to them. That leaves your hard drive as the primary storage device for multimedia files.

Give me space, lots of space

Hard drives come in various shapes and sizes, internal and external. Your computer undoubtedly already has an internal drive. But if the internal drive is any smaller than 500MB, you may want to consider replacing it with a bigger one, or better yet, adding an external drive.

To see how big your internal drive is, double-click on the drive icon in the upper-right corner of your Finder desktop. A window showing the contents of the drive opens, as shown in Figure 6-1. At the top of the window, just below the title bar, you should see a strip that tells the number of items on the drive and two size values. If this information is not visible, choose View⇨By Icon.

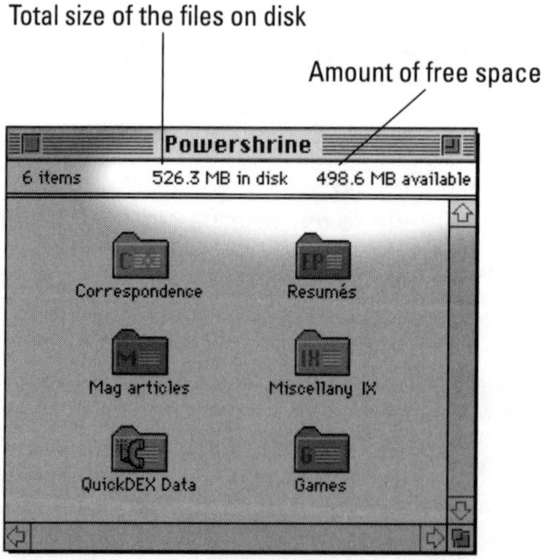

Figure 6-1: Add the two spotlighted values to figure out the size of your hard drive.

The first value tells you the total size of the files on the disk, and the second value tells you how much space on the drive remains empty. Add these two values together, and you get the overall size of the hard drive. In Figure 6-1, for example, 526.3MB + 498.6MB = 1,024.9MB, or approximately 1GB.

Chapter 6: You Can Never Have Enough Digital Closet Space

If you decide to purchase an additional drive, be prepared to spend between 50¢ and $1 per megabyte, which is a heck of a deal compared with RAM. As the size of the drive increases, the cost per MB goes down. For example, a gigabyte hard drive might cost you close to $1,000, whereas a 4GB hard drive might cost only $2,000. Just recently, I saw a 9GB drive for $3,000. What a deal!

With this price structure in mind, it's a good idea to overestimate. If you think you'll need 500MB, buy a 1GB drive. If you think you'll need 1GB, get 2GB. Not only does the extra storage capacity bring down the per MB cost, it gives you room to grow. Like an enormous bookshelf, a huge hard drive seems ostentatiously large at first, but you'll have it filled up in a month.

Tips for buying that new digital parcel

Here are some things to keep in mind when purchasing and using an external hard drive:

- As you do with an external CD-ROM drive, you hook up an external hard drive using a SCSI cable. Make sure that your new drive comes with the necessary cables.

- If you plan on hooking up the drive to a CD drive or other piece of external hardware, ask whether you can get a 50-pin-to-50-pin cable as well. Most drives just come with a 25-pin-to-50-pin cable for hooking the drive directly to the computer.

- Make sure to hook up your drive when the power is off. And set the SCSI-ID number to something that the other drives aren't using. (See "The drive's more important rear end" in Chapter 2 for the full SCSI-ID story.)

- Hard drive speed is measured in two ways. The first is *seek time*, which is how fast your Mac can locate a specific file on the drive, as measured in *milliseconds* (*ms*, millionths of a second). Seek time is important for copying and opening small files.

But when you're recording large sound and movie files, the second speed criteria — *sustainable read and write rate* — is more important. This value refers to how fast the drive can read and write data on disk over a long period of time. A good multimedia drive, such as the Micropolis 4.0AV, provides sustained rates of about 5MB per second. This wonderful drive will keep up with any multimedia activity your computer throws its way.

- System 7.5 includes a system extension called SCSI Manager 4.3, which helps to improve the performance of external hard drives and other SCSI devices on many kinds of Centris, Quadra, and LC 500-series computers. (It is not compatible with the Quadra 630.)

SCSI Manager 4.3 is included in the basic code built into all AV Macs, so the system extension is not needed on these machines. However, if you install System 7.5 from a CD, the system extension is automatically installed, which can actually cause problems. If you own an AV Mac, open the System Folder, open the Extensions folder, locate SCSI Manager 4.3, and throw it away.

✔ Easily my favorite hard drive vendor is APS Technologies, 800-325-6316. This company sells drives from major manufacturers such as Micropolis and Quantum, its salespeople know their stuff, and its products are priced very competitively. It also frequently garners the top honors in *Macworld* magazine's hardware roundups. APS Technologies even sells CD-ROM drives and other storage hardware. Go on, give them a call.

Storage on the Run

As any digital-space enthusiast will tell you, a hard drive isn't the only kind of massive storage hardware out there. The Mac supports lots of different kinds of *removable media*, which is a fancy term for large-capacity disks that you can take out of a drive and hand off to a friend. We're talking floppy disks on anabolic steroids.

Here are the three primary kinds of removable media you might want to investigate:

✔ **SyQuest:** A SyQuest is typically a big disk that measures 5 $^1/_4$ inches across — just like those old DOS floppies — and holds anywhere from 44MB to 200MB of data, depending on which kind of drive you buy. SyQuest drives cost between $300 and $700, while the disks themselves (called *cartridges*) run $40 to $70 apiece. (As you might expect, 44MB drives and disks are at the low end of the price spectrum, while 200MB drives and disks hang out at the high end.)

SyQuest disks also come in smaller, 3 $^1/_2$-inch sizes, which — though faster than their larger cousins — aren't yet as popular. The 3 $^1/_2$-inch disks hold 105MB or 270MB and cost about $70 apiece. The drives cost $500 to $700.

✔ **Magneto-Optical:** If you're looking for really safe storage — every bit as resilient as CDs — go with a magneto-optical drive, also just called an MO. (Wouldn't it be weird if something *wasn't* known by its initials?) MO disks come in two sizes: 3 $^1/_2$-inch, which hold 128MB or 230MB, and 5 $^1/_4$-inch, which hold 650MB to 1.3GB. Drives cost $700 to $3,000; disks cost $30 to $90. Although tough, MOs are also slow. So they're great for backing up movie and sound files, but you don't want to record directly to them.

Chapter 6: You Can Never Have Enough Digital Closet Space

   ✔ **Digital Audio Tape:** That's right, DAT, the tape that was supposed to replace the common cassette for recording music, is more widely used for digital storage. A typical tape costs less than $15 and holds 4GB — yes, that's right, 4 gigabytes — of data. But it's only for backup. Remember that I mentioned that super-fast hard drives can write 5MB per second? Well, a typical $1,000 DAT drive writes more like 15MB per minute.

And now for the recap:

   ✔ SyQuests are fast (though not as fast as a hard drive), moderately sturdy, and rather expensive.

   ✔ MOs are slow, extremely sturdy, and slightly less expensive per MB of storage space.

   ✔ DATs are slow as molasses in the middle of January, moderately sturdy, and very cheap.

And now there's one more option: The newest removable storage device is the Zip drive, which costs $200. Each Zip disk costs $20 (or $15 if you buy them in quantity), measures 3 1/2 inches across, and holds 100MB. Although I have yet to see one of these puppies — hey, give me a break, they just came out — rumor has it that they're about the same speed as MOs. But the Zip drive is significantly less expensive than an MO drive, and the disks are a good value, too. So far, Zips have been selling like hotcakes; only time will tell whether they become a standard.

Regardless of what kind of removable media you decide to purchase (if any), you should always record directly to your hard drive and later copy the file to the disk.

Part II
The Glorious World of Digital Images

The 5th Wave　　　　　By Rich Tennant

"Remember, Charles and Di can be pasted next to anyone but each other, and your Elvis should appear bald and slightly hunched - nice Big Foot, Brad.- Keep your two-headed animals in the shadows and your alien spacecrafts crisp and defined."

In this part . . .

Still images are the first elements of the multimedia triad, which also includes sound and moving video. Chapters 7 through 10 are devoted to computer photographs — where to get 'em, how to keep 'em in line, and how to make 'em bend to your digital will.

For example, using Kodak's Photo CD technology, you can pack up to 100 photographs onto a CD-ROM. Using Apple's QuickTake digital camera, you can snap pictures and send them directly to computer memory. Using a piece of software such as Fetch or PhotoFlash, you can keep your images organized, add captions, and sort through large or small image libraries in a matter of minutes. And with the help of the immensely popular program Photoshop, you can correct the focus and enhance the colors in a photograph that turned out to be less than picture-perfect. Take a peek at how and why digital photography will one day make film all but obsolete.

Chapter 7
Putting Your Photo Albums on CD

In This Chapter
- The amazing benefits of Photo CD
- Taking your photos to a Photo CD vendor
- Arranging your thumbnail sheets in more convenient locations
- Previewing your photos on-screen
- Opening a photograph at full-screen size
- Printing and saving a photo
- Figuring out when a photo was scanned

There are few things as wonderful as a photo album. I can spend hours pouring through one, whether it contains pictures of people I know and love or snapshots of complete strangers who have somehow muddled through life without the sunshine of my presence. Like a good novel, a good album may remind you of events in your own life, or it may let you vicariously experience the lives of others like a time-traveling Peeping Tom. Either way, the pictures provide just enough information to inspire the imagination. All you get is a split-second view, combined on some occasions with the company of a narrating eyewitness. You have to make up the rest.

But wouldn't you know it, photo albums also suffer the same drawbacks as books. They age, for example. The album itself may become tattered or dented; the pictures inside fade over time and may even become damaged from that sticky stuff that seals the plastic covering to the page. Unless your home happens to contain a vast library, photo albums are so enormous that they frequently end up at the bottom of a box in the basement, well out of day-to-day reach. And it's nearly impossible to locate a specific photo unless you're prepared to devote an hour or more to the search.

Kodak's Photo CD technology, which enables you to put images on a CD-ROM, gives you an alternative way to store and view your priceless photographic memories (as well as the not-so-priceless but still entertaining ones). Photo CD offers nearly all the benefits of a traditional photo album and none of the liabilities:

- A CD is much more durable than a photographic print — which is just a piece of paper with a few photographic chemicals sprinkled on it. A hundred years from now, an image on a Photo CD should look every bit as good as it does today. (Notice that I use the word *should* because, obviously, no CD has yet been around that long.)
- CDs take up very little space on your shelves. You can fit 10 to 20 CD cases into the space occupied by a single album.
- It's relatively easy to find an image on a CD. Each Photo CD includes a few sheets of paper with tiny thumbnail versions of each photo. The thumbnails are even numbered according to the way the image files are numbered on disk.

But wait, there's more:

- The type of film you use doesn't matter when the final image is saved as little, colored screen pixels. This means that you can store slides and snapshots together on the same CD. Try to do that with a photo album.
- You can open an image from a Photo CD on your computer and edit it. You can enhance the colors, sharpen the focus, crop out extraneous details, or remove an unwanted photographic interloper.
- You can print the image to a black-and-white or color printer and make absolutely as many copies as you like.
- Though you may not remember the exact day that a photo was shot, you can quickly determine the day it was placed on the CD. In many cases, that's enough to trigger your memory (the memory in your head, that is).

In fact, Photo CD has only three disadvantages. First, it's fairly expensive to put an image on CD — about $2 per photo. Second, you typically have to provide the original photographic negative to get the photo on CD. And third, you have to have a computer with a CD-ROM drive to look at the photos, which may or may not make things tough for Grandma and other less technically-equipped members of the family. So although Photo CD isn't the best means to store each and every photo you shoot, it's a great way to archive your most treasured photos for future electronically-dependent generations to enjoy.

Getting Those Pics on the Discs

Figure 7-1 shows the ingredients in a Photo CD. It comes in its own little case. It's gold, so it looks really important. And the case includes thumbnails of the photos so that you can see what's on the CD without firing up your computer.

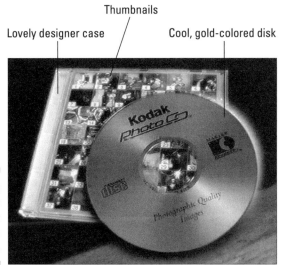

Figure 7-1: What you get when you buy a Photo CD.

A Photo CD holds up to 100 images. A Photo CD merchant can scan photographic negatives, undeveloped film, or 35mm slides onto a CD. If all you have is a photographic print — like the snapshot in an album — you have to pay to have an intermediate negative — or *interneg* — made. This step can cost several dollars per photo.

The CD itself costs $10 to $15. On top of that, you pay a fee for each photo, anywhere from $1 to $3 apiece, depending on how many photos you have scanned at a time and whether you want any fancy enhancements. If you can live without the enhancements — all of which you can do yourself with a program such as Adobe Photoshop — expect to pay about $200 for a Photo CD filled to the gills. (This estimate does not include the cost of developing newly shot rolls of film or creating internegs.)

You can have as many images scanned at a time as you like, and you can use the same CD over and over again. For example, you might walk in one day with a 24-shot roll of film and have the whole thing developed and slapped onto a brand new Photo CD. Two weeks later, you can take in a few 35mm slides that you shot a couple of years ago and have those images tossed on the CD as well. Just don't forget to bring the CD in with you each time you want to add images.

To find a reputable establishment to create your next digital photo album, open the Yellow Pages to "Photo Finishing-Retail" and look at the ads. Most ads provide lists of the services offered, and somewhere in one of those lists, you should find the crucial words "Photo CD."

Keeping Abreast of Your Thumbnails

After you have your images put on CD, the first way to check out your photos is to peruse the thumbnails, which are included on sheets called *proofs*. Each proof holds up to 40 images, so you can conveniently search through many pictures at once. A completely filled Photo CD includes three proof sheets.

The problem is — at least *I* think that it's a problem — most Photo CD vendors just stick all the proofs in the lid of the case. This means that you can generally see the first proof sheet through the front of the lid, but you have to remove the other two proofs to look at them.

Here's what I suggest: Take out the second and third proofs. Then reinsert the second proof sheet into the lid backward, facing the CD, as demonstrated so helpfully in Figure 7-2. This way, you can just open the case to see the second set of thumbnails.

Next, remove the black CD holder from the clear base of the CD case. Four tabs secure the holder in place. Gently twist the base to pop the holder out. (You may want to take out the CD first so that it doesn't fly across the room if the holder pops out a tad quickly.) Then place the third proof sheet under the holder, against the base, so that it faces outward. If the sheet doesn't quite fit, trim a little off the bottom edge using an X-Acto knife, a pair of scissors, or a blunt safety razor. (Don't forget your safety goggles!) After fitting the holder back in place, you'll be able to see the last thumbnails just by turning the case over.

Chapter 7: Putting Your Photo Albums on CD *97*

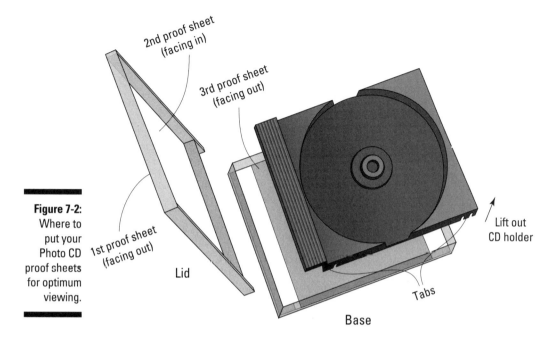

Figure 7-2: Where to put your Photo CD proof sheets for optimum viewing.

Sticking the Photo CD in the Drive

Obviously, to view the images on-screen and edit them, you need to stick the CD in your drive. As long as the Foreign File Access and Apple Photo Access extensions are in your System Folder (as discussed in Chapter 2), the CD mounts on your desktop. It appears on the desktop with some meaningless name like PCD0196 (the initials for Photo CD followed by a serial number). Because you can't modify a CD, you can't change its name either, so I'm afraid that you're stuck with the bizarre name the processing lab gives you.

Double-click on the CD icon to open the disk and view its contents. Two icons, Slide Show and Slide Show Viewer, appear at the top of the window, as you can see in Figure 7-3. Slide Show Viewer is a program that lets you look at thumbnail pictures of your image on-screen. Slide Show is the file that contains the thumbnails.

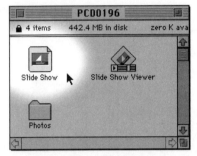

Figure 7-3: The files included on every Photo CD, no matter where you get it.

Take a stroll through your digital album

To use the Slide Show Viewer, do thusly:

1. **Double-click on the Slide Show icon.**

   I spotlighted it in Figure 7-2 just so that you don't go double-clicking on something else. After a fairly lengthy interval of private computer business, a window like the one shown in Figure 7-4 appears. It shows the first image on the CD.

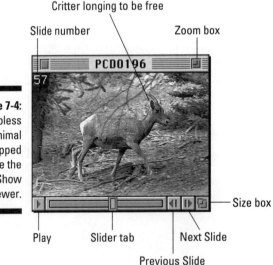

Figure 7-4: A hapless animal trapped inside the Slide Show Viewer.

If you can't get the Slide Show Viewer to run, it's probably because you don't have the QuickTime system extension loaded into your System Folder. This extension is included with Systems 7.1 and 7.5. For more information on QuickTime, bone up on Chapter 16.

Chapter 7: Putting Your Photo Albums on CD

2. **To view the next image on the CD, click on the Next Slide button.**

   Labeled in Figure 7-4, this button advances you from one photograph to the next. The number in the upper-left corner of the image updates to show you which slide you're viewing.

   You can also advance to the next slide by pressing the right-arrow key.

3. **To view the previous image, click on the Previous Slide button.**

   Or press the left-arrow key.

4. **To let Slide Show Viewer do the work, click on the Play button.**

   The program plays the slide show automatically, displaying each photograph on-screen for one full second before advancing to the next one.

   For those who like to memorize keyboard tricks: You can play the slide show by pressing either the Return key or the spacebar.

   When the slide show is playing, the Play button changes to a Pause button. Click on the Pause button to stop advancing the photographs. Or simply press the Return key or the spacebar to pause the slide show.

5. **To skip a bunch of slides, drag the slider tab.**

   This option isn't super useful because you never know exactly where inside the slide show you'll land. But with a little practice, you can get fairly good at skipping to general groups of slides. Then you can scoot around with the Next Slide and Previous Slide buttons (or the right- and left-arrow keys) to view a specific photo.

You can also try out the following tricks inside the Slide Show Viewer:

- Option-click on the Next Slide button to see the last image added to the Photo CD. Option-click on the Previous Slide button to return to the first image.

- To play the photos backward, ⌘-click on the Previous Slide button. The playback may be jerky because the software isn't optimized to play in this direction. (You can also ⌘-click on the Next Slide button to play forward, but what's the point?)

- Press the Control key and hold the mouse button down on either the Next Slide or Previous Slide button to produce a very small slider bar. With Control down, drag the slider to the right or left to play the slide show forward or backward. The farther you drag from the center, the faster the images play. Experiment, and you'll see what I mean.

These controls and keyboard shortcuts are the same as those you encounter when playing a QuickTime digital movie. So prepare yourself to experience that tingly sensation of déjà vu when you read Chapter 16, "A New Kind of Picture Show." So prepare yourself to experience . . . oh, wait, I already said that.

How to get a closer look

The obvious defect with the Slide Show Viewer is that the images are itsy bitsy. They're larger than the printed thumbnails on the proof sheets, but nonetheless dinky. The proper way to address this grave situation is to open the photograph that you want to scrutinize in some other program.

You can increase the size of the window in the Slide Show Viewer program by dragging the standard Macintosh size box in the lower-right corner of the window. Unfortunately, doing so merely increases the size of the pixels without revealing more detail. In other words, don't bother. To return the window to its original size, click on the zoom box in the window's upper-right corner. (Both size box and zoom box are labeled in Figure 7-4.)

You can open an image from a Photo CD with any program that supports the Mac's common picture format, known from hill to dale as *PICT*. These programs include Adobe Photoshop, ClarisWorks, Deneba's Canvas, and even the occasional word processor, such as Microsoft Word.

Here's how to set things up inside the Slide Show Viewer:

1. **Scroll to the photo you want to open.**

    Use the buttons and other controls as I laid out in the previous section.

2. **Choose File⇨Preferences.**

    The Preferences dialog box shown in Figure 7-5 appears.

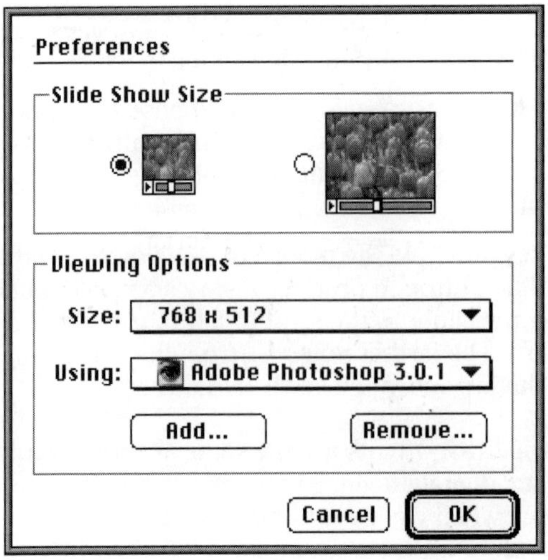

Figure 7-5: Here's where you specify the program that Slide Show Viewer uses to open a specific photo.

3. **Choose the program that you want to use to open the photo from the Using pop-up menu.**

   If this is your first time, the only program in the list will be TeachText or SimpleText, depending on which version of the system software you're running. Apple changed the name of the program between Systems 7.1 (TeachText) and 7.5 (SimpleText).

4. **If you don't want to use TeachText/SimpleText, abandon Step 3 and click on the Add button.**

   You can now add some other program to the pop-up menu. Just locate the program that you want to use on disk and double-click on it (or select it and press the Return key). If you have Photoshop, use it. It's a top-notch program for viewing Photo CD stuff. The program you select is active automatically in the Using pop-up menu.

5. **Select the size at which you want to view the image in the Size pop-up menu.**

   One of the wonders of Photo CD is that each image can be viewed at multiple *resolutions*. The resolution determines how many tiny colored pixels are packed into the image. The Size options list the number of pixels wide by the number of pixels tall. More pixels mean better detail and better clarity. But they also mean more intense computer processing. You need gobs of RAM and hard disk space to open the highest resolution — 3072 × 2048 — and even then, it will be slow going. I recommend that you stick with the default setting, 768 × 512. That's big enough to fill up most of the screen on a 17-inch monitor.

6. **Press Return or click OK to exit the dialog box.**

   Everything is now set up to view the photograph in all its splendor. The Slide Show Viewer saves your preference settings to your System Folder so that you don't ever have to go through those steps again (unless you decide to change your settings). From now on, to open up an image, scroll to it inside the Slide Show Viewer and then just choose Photo⇔View or press the keyboard equivalent, ⌘-E. Your Mac automatically launches the program of your choosing and opens up the photograph. All you have to do is sit back and watch. Figure 7-6 shows the mountain goat photo as it appears when opened in Photoshop. Beautiful, ain't it?

You can also open a photograph in your chosen program by double-clicking on it in the Slide Show Viewer window.

Figure 7-6: Photoshop is the perfect program for opening, editing, and printing your Photo CD images.

Print, edit, have a ball

After you get the image open, you can print as many copies as you like. Just choose File⇨Print (or press ⌘-P), enter the number of copies in the Copies option box, and press Return.

If you manipulate the photograph in Photoshop or some other image editor, you can save the revised photograph to your hard drive. You cannot, however, save your changes back to the Photo CD, because the contents of a CD are locked in stone. (At least, *you* can't change them.) For more information on editing Photo CD images, read Chapter 10. If you're really motivated, you can read an entire book on the subject, *Photoshop 3 For Macs For Dummies*.

When was this photo scanned?

The only trick to figuring out when a specific image was placed on a Photo CD is to find the images in the first place. If you return to the Finder desktop, you'll see that the Photo CD contains a folder called Photos. Open that folder by double-clicking on it. Herein, you'll see five more folders, each named according to image size. Open any one of these folders; it doesn't matter which one.

Inside this folder are the photograph files, numbered 001 through 100. Select the number that corresponds to the photograph you're curious about — consult the thumbnails on the proof sheets if you're not sure which number goes with which photo — and choose File⇨Get Info (or press ⌘-I). The Info window appears, sporting two dates, Created and Modified, which are identical. This date is the date that the image was scanned.

Chapter 8
Taking Computer Pictures

In This Chapter
- Getting acquainted with cameras that shoot digital pictures
- Comparing digital cameras to Photo CD
- Taking a look at the QuickTake 150 and Digital Camera 40
- Using the QuickTake
- Shooting still photos with a camcorder

Snapping pictures and scanning them to Photo CD is all very well and groovy — the best thing going in the world of digital imaging and all that — but it isn't a perfect solution, is it? It costs a fair amount of money, so it's not the kind of thing you're liable to do more than a few times a year. It requires a week or so of turnaround time, which means that you have to plan a little in advance. And it isn't altogether convenient — you have to gather a bunch of pictures together and find a place to scan them. Aren't computers supposed to eliminate this kind of bone-grinding drudgery?

What's a better solution? Well, if you're the kind of person who wakes up in the middle of the night with big ideas — "Feed the tuna mayonnaise!" and the like — then the super-charged synapses in that amazing brain of yours are undoubtedly firing at top speed. "Why don't they just get rid of the middleman?" Sure, it's a revolutionary concept, but that doesn't stop your hyperkinetic imagination. "Why don't they make a camera," you sputter, wiping the sweat from your intense thoughts off your brow, "that shoots pictures directly to disk?!"

You are a genius. It's as if you read my mind or something. Or maybe you just read the last issue of *Macworld* magazine. In any case, making a camera that shoots pictures to disk is exactly what Apple, Kodak, and a bunch of other folks have done. These companies sell *digital cameras* that let you shoot pictures right to disk, RAM, or what have you. There's no film, no processing, no scanning, no fuss. Just point, click, and plug into your computer.

Unfortunately, this technology is kind of in its infancy right now. In fact, you'll find only two basic kinds of digital cameras:

- **Mondo-expensive gizmos that cost more than most of us pay for a new car:** Unless you make your living from photography — and I mean *quite* a living — there's no way in heck you'd be caught dead breathing on one of these things. But, I have to admit, they shoot nice pictures.

- **Less-expensive cameras priced to sell under $1,000:** Okay, so we're not exactly talking bargain-basement prices. And the cameras in this price range don't exactly take what I'd call awesome pictures, either. But you can get adequate, full-screen photos out of them at a moment's notice. And because you don't have to worry about film or development costs, your only maintenance expense is batteries.

One day in the not-so-distant future, digital cameras will be both inexpensive and high quality. Some prediction, huh? Well, here's a better one: In about 10 years, your local supermarket will no longer offer film-development services, because the market will have dried up. Think I'm nuts? Well, then, tell me this, Mr. or Ms. Smartypants. When's the last time you shot a roll of Super 8? Just as we use camcorders instead of movie cameras today, we'll all be packing digital cameras in the next century.

Don't these far-flung predictions just give you the chills? Maybe I should hire myself out to late-night infomercials as the next Nostradamus.

Shooting Computerized Polaroids

A few years back, Polaroid cameras were all the rage. Everybody who was anybody owned one, despite the thing's considerable drawbacks. Polaroid cameras were expensive, they didn't offer any focus or zoom controls, they required specialized and costly film, and the picture quality was cheesy at best. Yet folks were willing to accept the imperfections and pay the higher price in order to get immediate results.

Any digital camera under $1,000 is nothing more than a modern Polaroid:

- The least expensive color digital camera, Apple's QuickTake 150, sells for about $750. That ain't hay, as they say where I come from. (Actually, I don't know anyone who says that, but it was the only rustic expression I could come up with on such short notice.) In fact, you could buy a couple of Polaroid cameras for that money.

- You aren't likely to find focus or zoom options at this price point. Optically speaking, the QuickTake is the equivalent of a $10 disposable camera.
- Okay, so you don't need special film. But you do need a computer to view the pictures, so that rules out long trips unless you have a PowerBook handy. And you'll do well to throw a few batteries in the glove compartment just to be safe.
- The picture quality is okay, but it's nothing compared with Photo CD.
- But here comes the good news: You can shoot a picture, copy it to your hard drive, edit it, and print it in less than 10 minutes.

The quickest shooter in the West

Just to prove how fast these babies are, I went out about 20 minutes ago and shot a "roll" of photos with my QuickTake 150. Figure 8-1 shows two full-screen photos that I snapped this very morning.

Figure 8-1: A couple of the sights within minutes of my office, as captured with the QuickTake 150 and slapped on disk in record time.

For the record, *full-screen* means 640 × 480 pixels, the size of a screen on a 14-inch monitor. Another term you might hear bandied about is *quarter-screen*, which means 320 × 240 pixels, or one-fourth the space on a 14-inch screen.

Considering that I spent about 10 minutes roaming downtown Boulder, Colorado, snapping randomly at anything that didn't need to sign a model release, the images in Figure 8-1 don't look half bad. In fact, if I were in your shoes, I might say something like, "Dang, these Hush Puppies are big." No, wait, I'd say,

"These photos look all right to me. In fact, they look every bit as good as that silly mountain goat from Figure 7-6."

Ah ha, that's where you're wrong. Scaled down in Figure 8-1, the images look fine. But if I were to blow them up, you'd see just how cruddy they can be. Figure 8-2 is a case in point. In the figure, I enlarged a detail of one of the QuickTake images and similarly enlarged a detail from the Photo CD goat. At this size, you can plainly see great, hurky jaggies developing in the QuickTake image. Meanwhile, the goat looks a little grainy, but that's from the original film, not the image file itself. The Photo CD image contains up to 20 times as many pixels as the QuickTake image. The color clarity is much better as well.

Figure 8-2:
A comparison of QuickTake (left) and Photo CD (right) photos enlarged by 300 percent.

The moral of the story is, digital cameras are great for shooting small photos that you want to plop into a newsletter or a presentation. But don't expect the photos to look good at enlarged sizes. You wouldn't want to print one across a full page, for example. It would look about as good as it does in Figure 8-2.

Who needs a digital camera?

Unless you have ready supplies of cash and you like to spend it recklessly, you probably don't want to buy one of these things for vacation photos. (Actually, I once took a QuickTake and a PowerBook on a cruise to the Bahamas. But I'm a geek, and I had the camera on loan. So you don't want to use me as a model.)

But in corporate life, a digital camera can come in very handy. For example, my wife works with a team of realtors, so a digital camera fits right in. She sends a guy out to shoot a few listings, prints them out, and starts faxing the pictures to other realtors. There's even been talk of distributing the photos electronically. Maybe it'll bring in business, may be it won't. But it's definitely cool.

Comparing a Couple of Cameras

At the time I write this, only two digital cameras cost less than $1,000 and are worth a hill of beans. The first is the QuickTake, discussed earlier, and the other is Kodak's Digital Camera 40. The latter is better, but the former is less expensive. Here's how things shake down:

- The QuickTake 150 costs $750. The Digital Camera 40 retails for $995.

- Both cameras can take only so many pictures before they're full. When the camera is full, you copy the photos to your hard drive, clear the camera, and take some more pictures. The QuickTake can snap up to 16 full-screen images, 32 quarter-screen images, or some combination of the two. The Kodak model can hold 48 large images — 756 × 504 pixels, which is 20 percent larger than full-screen — and 99 small images — 378 × 256 pixels.

- Both cameras have fixed-focus lenses. This setup means that the cameras don't provide auto-focusing, and you can't adjust the focus manually, either. As long as you stand at least four feet away from what you're shooting, the picture is in focus; get any closer, and the image is fuzzy.

- The QuickTake does include a snap-on close-up lens for shooting photos from 8 to 14 inches away. It's cheesy and hard to get on and off, but what the hey, it works. Figure 8-3 shows a couple of in-the-thick-of-it pictures shot with the close-up lens.

Figure 8-3: A couple of pictures of some cold flowers shot with the QuickTake's close-up lens.

- Not to be outdone, the Digital Camera 40 supports standard video lenses, including zoom, wide-angle, and close-up lenses. But you have to buy the lenses separately.

- Both cameras include built-in flashes that light anything from four to nine feet away. If the subject is any farther away than that, it's in the dark. You can let the camera decide when to flash automatically or force the flash in case your subject happens to be in a shadow.

- You know those automatic timers that let you press the shutter release and then run around and get in the frame before the picture is actually snapped? Both cameras have 'em.

- You can screw either camera onto a tripod.

- Apple's toll-free phone number is 800-776-2333. Kodak's is 800-235-6325.

Snapping Philmless Fotos

Figure 8-4 shows a few pictures of the QuickTake 150, showing both back and front views. (The leather grip costs extra.) As you do with any camera, you look through the viewfinder, point the camera at the desired object, and press the shutter release. A control panel next to the viewfinder tells you how many photos you've shot so far, how many are left, and other pertinent information. You can force the flash, set the auto-timer, and change the image size by pressing those round buttons around the control panel.

Chapter 8: Taking Computer Pictures   *109*

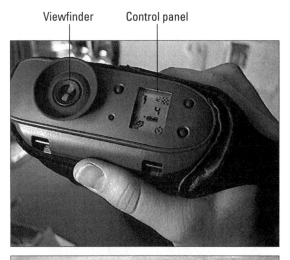

Viewfinder   Control panel

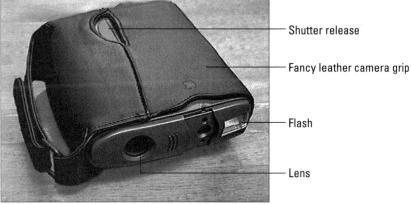

Shutter release

Fancy leather camera grip

Flash

Lens

Figure 8-4: The diminutive and lightweight QuickTake viewed from its best angles.

Regardless of what kind of digital camera you use, always shoot your photos at the largest image size possible. Even if you plan to use the image at a smaller size — say, in an on-screen presentation — you're better off cropping it and reducing it inside Photoshop instead of shooting it small in the first place. Larger images provide better picture quality and increased flexibility.

After you finish snapping your pics, you hook up the camera to your Mac's modem port. Software provided with the camera lets you mount it on your desktop, just as if it were a disk, as shown in Figure 8-5. You can then open the camera by double-clicking on its icon. Your photos appear as separate little image files, each named according to the date it was shot. You can select the files, copy them to your hard drive, and open them inside Photoshop or some other program.

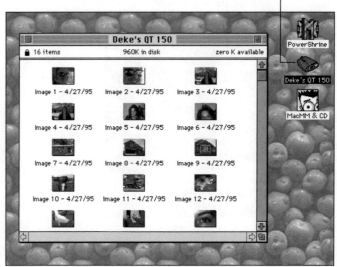

Figure 8-5:
You can mount the QuickTake camera, open it up, and copy the image files to your hard drive.

 Like camcorders, digital cameras need batteries to give them power. The QuickTake uses three AA batteries, the same kind used by just about every portable gadget. Apple claims that the batteries should hang in there for about 200 photos, assuming that you use the flash 50 percent of the time; I've shot more than 300 pictures with the same batteries. Still, over the course of a year, you can count on sucking the life out of lots of batteries. If you shoot 50 pictures a week, for example, you'll go through 36 batteries a year. I recommend that you go out and buy one of those big packs of AA cells and stock them away in a fridge for safekeeping.

Turning Your Camcorder into a Digital Camera

Obviously, I think that digital cameras are a pretty swell idea. In fact, I was hoping to lay my hands on one the moment I started on this book. I wanted to use it to shoot the various products that I discuss throughout these humble pages. Unfortunately, thanks to a variety of circumstances that I won't bore you with, I didn't get a camera until the day I started writing this chapter.

Chapter 8: Taking Computer Pictures 111

Until then, I had to improvise. I could have shot the photos with a 35mm camera and had them scanned to Photo CD, but I didn't have the time. So I came up with a solution that was inexpensive and fast.

I used a camcorder. Here's how:

1. Every time I wanted to shoot something for the book, I took out my Sony Hi8 video camera, set it on top of a tripod, and filmed the subject for 10 to 20 seconds. At 30 frames per second, that's the equivalent of several hundred pictures, which is more than enough to get at least one good shot.

2. I slapped the tape into a VCR that I have hooked up to the AV Technologies card in my Power Mac 7100. (If you read Chapter 5, you may recall my discussion of this very topic in the section titled "Get Out Your VCRs!")

3. I rewound the tape to the beginning of the segment, played the segment, and recorded it to disk using Adobe Premiere. I explain how this process works in Chapter 17.

4. I viewed each frame until I found one I liked. Then I saved that frame to a separate file on disk. This process is explained in the "Grabbing a still image" section of Chapter 17.

5. Inside Photoshop, I opened the frame and edited it. Read Chapter 10 to learn more about Photoshop.

For example, I shot both of the photos shown back in Figure 8-4 with a camcorder. Even after the QuickTake arrived, I couldn't use the camera to shoot a picture of itself — not without a complex system of fun-house mirrors, anyway. So I held the camcorder in one hand and filmed a picture of the QuickTake in the other. (Yes, I'm proud to say, that is my thumb. And here you thought it belonged to a professional hand model.)

In the name of a frank and honest comparison, Figure 8-6 shows details from both a QuickTake picture and a video frame enlarged by 300 percent. The digital image is less grainy and offers better looking lines. The video image, on the other hand, is riddled with lots of random pixels. Still, the two images aren't wildly different, and both hold up pretty well when you print them at small sizes.

So if you have an AV Mac (or one of the junior AV models I discussed in Chapter 5) and you already own a camcorder, you can shoot digital pictures quickly and conveniently without spending another dime.

Figure 8-6: Enlarged details from a QuickTake photo (left) and a frame captured from a Hi8 videotape (right).

Chapter 9
Keeping Track of Your Images (and Other Media)

In This Chapter

- Putting together on-screen catalogs of digital photos
- Using two cataloging programs: PhotoFlash and Fetch
- Viewing and editing an image in the catalog
- Adding captions and keywords
- Searching a catalog for images
- Understanding file formats

With a little effort, you can assemble a sizable collection of digital images in a short period of time. I, for example, have already shot several hundred photos with my QuickTake in the last few days. I don't have to pay for the film, so why should I use discretion?

But after you fill a SyQuest cartridge or two, it's easy to forget what the heck you shot and where you put the photos. I've managed to sock away many disks full of digital photos that are several years old now, and with the exception of a few favorites, I have only a vague idea of what kind of images populate my collection.

When you reach this point — notice that it's not a question of *if*, because you will undoubtedly be knee-deep in digital photos one day — you'll be in the market for a cataloging program such as Apple's PhotoFlash (included gratis with the QuickTake camera) or Adobe's Fetch. Both programs let you assemble folders full of images in on-screen directories so that you can browse through sheets of thumbnails and quickly find a desired image. You can also create a caption for a photo, search for images according to caption text or filename, and view any photo in the catalog at full size.

GOSSIP

Fetch goes a few steps farther by letting you add sounds and movies to a catalog as well as images. Heck, you can even add a word-processing file or two. We're talking about a full-fledged multimedia way station.

If you don't buy the QuickTake camera, PhotoFlash costs $130. Fetch runs $150 retail. If you don't own either of these programs and you don't feel like parting with the cash just because I said, "Gee whizickers, these products are nifty" — although I'd think that would be enough reason for most folks — I recommend that you go ahead and read this chapter to see whether a cataloging program might be of use to you.

Creating an On-Screen Image Album in PhotoFlash

To create a catalog of images inside either PhotoFlash or Fetch, you have to make a new catalog and add images to it. Here's how it works inside PhotoFlash:

1. Choose File⇨New.

Or press ⌘-N. PhotoFlash asks whether you want to create a catalog or an image. Just press Return to create a catalog. An empty catalog full of gray picture-holders appears on-screen, as shown in Figure 9-1.

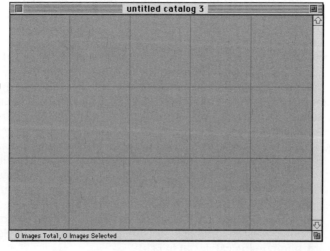

Figure 9-1: A new PhotoFlash catalog, ready and waiting for your images. Exciting, ain't it?

2. **Choose File▷Add to Catalog.**

   A standard Open dialog box appears, allowing you to locate the images you want to add.

3. **Select the file or folder full of files you want to add and click on the Add button.**

   The dialog box remains open after you click on Add. A little message at the bottom of the dialog box tells you that the file or folder will be added. You can keep locating more files and folders and clicking on the Add button to add them to the catalog. In Figure 9-2, for example, I've added a total of one folder and four files.

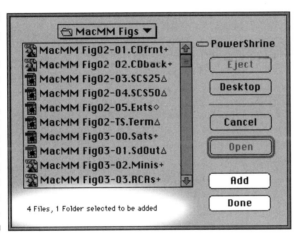

Figure 9-2: When you add images to a catalog in PhotoFlash, the dialog box stays up on-screen until you click on the Done button.

4. **When you finish adding files and folders, click on the Done button.**

   PhotoFlash gets to work adding the images to the catalog. This process may take a minute or so. When the program finishes, the image thumbnails appear in the picture holders. PhotoFlash tells you the number of images in the catalog in the lower-left corner of the window, as you can see in Figure 9-3.

Part II: The Glorious World of Digital Images

Figure 9-3:
A new catalog full of images.

5. **Save the catalog to disk.**

    To do this, choose File⇨Save or press ⌘-S. Then name the file and specify its location on disk. You don't have to save the catalog in the same folder or even on the same disk as the images. Just save it any old place that's convenient.

6. **To add more images to the catalog, repeat Steps 2 through 5.**

Amassing Your Digital Imagery in Fetch

In Fetch, the principle is the same, but the actual steps differ a little. The following steps tell all:

1. **In Fetch, choose File⇨New or press ⌘-N.**

    If any window is open in the program, the New command appears gray. Close all the windows and try again.

2. **Name the new catalog file, select a location on disk, and press Return.**

    Fetch displays a Find dialog box. It's kind of confusing to be presented with a Find option when there's nothing to find. Luckily, you can just ignore the dialog box for now.

3. **Choose Admin⇨Add/Update Items.**

    Or press ⌘-E. A big dialog box with about 5,000 strange options comes up. The options let you change how the images are interpreted, but the default settings are perfectly acceptable. Just press Return or click on Continue to move on. A standard Open dialog box appears.

Chapter 9: Keeping Track of Your Images (and Other Media)   117

If you make some changes and then freak out because you're sure that you've botched things, just click on the Cancel button or press ⌘-period. Then press ⌘-E to redisplay the big dialog box with the original settings intact.

4. Select the file and click on the Open button to add the file to the catalog.

If you want to add an entire folder full of images, select a file inside the folder you want to add and then click on the Folder button. Either way, Fetch displays a Modification Status window that shows you each image as it is added to the catalog (see Figure 9-4). When all the images are added, you are sent back to the big, complicated dialog box first mentioned in Step 3.

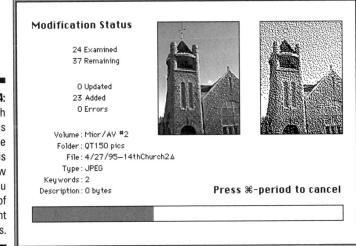

Figure 9-4: As Fetch adds images to the catalog, this window keeps you abreast of current events.

5. If you still have more images to add, press Return or click on Continue and then repeat Step 4.

6. When you finish adding images, click on the Done button or press Enter.

7. Click on the Find All button inside the Find dialog box.

Or just press Return. Fetch displays a window filled with thumbnails, much like the one shown back in Figure 9-3.

Unlike PhotoFlash, Fetch automatically saves the catalog to disk, so you don't need to choose File⇨Save. In fact, there is no Save command. No matter what you do, you'll never lose any work.

Playing with Your Catalog

When skimming the family photo album, you have four basic options: open the album, turn the page, look at the picture, and close the album. Undoubtedly, if you sat down and thought about it for a while, you could come up with some less conventional options — set the album on fire, dip it in hot chocolate, teach it some basic tricks like "sit" and "play dead" — but most of us prefer the tried-and-true open, turn, look, and close.

An on-screen album is not nearly so limited. Here are but a few of the things you can do, all within the confines of common sense and public decency:

- To view an image at full size, double-click on it. The image appears in a separate window, as shown in Figure 9-5.

Figure 9-5: To view the misty crane at full size in Fetch, I simply double-clicked on its thumbnail.

Chapter 9: Keeping Track of Your Images (and Other Media)

- In PhotoFlash, you can modify an image by rotating it, cropping it, sharpening the focus, changing the brightness and contrast, and all the other stuff I explain in the next chapter.
- After editing an image in PhotoFlash, you can save it to disk using a different name or file format. I explain more about file formats in the following section, "Figuring Out Files and Files of Formats."
- Fetch is strictly a cataloging program. If you want to edit the image, you have to open it inside a different program, such as Photoshop. To do so, choose Item⇨Edit Original (or press ⌘-G). If Fetch can't find the program to open the image, it asks you to tell it which program you want to use.

- To remove an image from the catalog, click on it and press Delete. This step does not delete the image from disk, so pressing Delete is entirely safe. If worse comes to worst, you can always restore the image to the catalog by using File⇨Add to Catalog in PhotoFlash or Admin⇨Add/Update Items in Fetch.
- You can add a descriptive caption to an image for future reference. In PhotoFlash, choose File⇨Get Info (or press ⌘-I). Then type away. When you're finished, click on the close box. PhotoFlash saves the caption with the original image.
- In Fetch, you can add a caption by choosing Edit⇨Description (⌘-U). After you enter the caption, press Enter or click on Done. Unlike PhotoFlash, Fetch saves the caption as part of the catalog, so you can create different captions in different catalogs for a single image.
- In Fetch, you can also add *keywords* for searching. If I add the keyword *Horse* to every photo that contains a horse, for example, I can later locate those pictures simply by searching for *Horse*. To add a keyword or two, choose Edit⇨Keywords or press ⌘-Y. After each keyword, press Return. When you finish, press Enter.
- To search for images in PhotoFlash, choose commands from the Search menu. You can search by caption text or filename. You can also search for visual similarities, though the commands that are supposed to do this don't work worth a hill of beans. (You can use the mouse to draw a microscopic sketch of the image you want to find, for example, and watch as PhotoFlash, not surprisingly, comes up with no match.) In any case, PhotoFlash highlights all the found images and even transfers them to a separate catalog if you ask nicely.
- In Fetch, choose Search⇨Find or press ⌘-F. You can search by multiple keywords, filename, disk, and file format. Fetch hides all thumbnails that do not match the search criteria.

- To display all images in a Fetch catalog, choose Search⇨All or press ⌘-quote.

- If you want to be able to examine your thumbnails without opening the catalog or even turning on your computer, you can print out sheets of thumbnails. Both PhotoFlash and Fetch let you print all thumbnails, only those thumbnails found in the search, or full-size images.

Figuring Out Files and Files of Formats

One of the great things about both PhotoFlash and Fetch is that they support lots and lots of file formats. This means that no matter where your photo comes from, either of these programs can probably open it.

File formats are different ways of storing the various colored pixels inside a digital image on disk. Formats are designed to ensure that many programs can open a single file. The only problem is that there are so many formats that most folks have no idea which one to use and what the different formats mean. That's why I'm here to help out.

The most common image formats on the Mac are as follows:

- **PICT:** PICT (pronounced *pict*) was Apple's original graphic format for the Macintosh computer and has been around as long as the Mac. Not surprisingly, more Macintosh programs support this format than any other. Many programs let you save PICT files with JPEG compression, which I discuss in the paragraph after next.

- **TIFF:** PICT may be the most common format on the Mac, but when you consider all those other computers out there — including Windows-based PCs — TIFF is the most popular of them all. TIFF (pronounced *tiff*) was designed especially for digital photographs, so you can't go wrong with it. In fact, it's better than PICT.

- **JPEG:** JPEG (pronounced *jay-peg*) is a special file format that *compresses* a file so that it takes up less room on disk. JPEG actually throws away colors and redraws details, so you have to be careful if you use it. If presented with a Quality option when saving a JPEG image, always select the highest setting — Maximum or Excellent.

- **EPS:** EPS (pronounced *E-P-S*) and its cousin, DCS, are professional-level file formats that aren't worth knowing about unless you plan to print your images on high-quality, mondo-expensive imagesetters. Both formats are perfectly acceptable, but they result in large files that take up a lots of room on disk.

- **Photoshop:** This format is a specialized file format used by Adobe Photoshop. But because Photoshop (the program) is so popular, many other programs let you open Photoshop files without first converting them to TIFF, JPEG, or something else. (Photoshop saves to TIFF, JPEG, and other formats as well, so just because you edited an image in Photoshop doesn't mean that it's saved in the Photoshop format.)

- **Photo CD:** As discussed in Chapter 7, this file format is used to save images on Photo CD disks. As things stand now, no program can save images as Photo CD files, but many can open them.

Both Fetch and PhotoFlash let you open images saved in any of these formats. Fetch also opens images saved in the RIFF format, which is used in the amazing image-creation program Fractal Design Painter. And, as I alluded to at the beginning of the chapter, Fetch lets you open many of the sound and movie file formats that I discuss in future chapters.

In addition, Fetch can open GIF images, which generally come from on-line services — such as CompuServe or America Online — or the Internet. But the GIF format saves only 256 colors, and in my book, any format that trashes 65,000 colors for every one it keeps is pretty lame.

Because PhotoFlash lets you edit images, it also enables you to save the results of your editing to any of the file formats in the preceding list except Photo CD. The ability to convert an image into another format can come in handy. For example, if you want to use a Photo CD image in a program that doesn't support the Photo CD format, you can open the image up in PhotoFlash and save it in one of the other formats, such as TIFF or PICT. Really, it's no sweat.

You can also convert images to different formats using Photoshop. To find out more information about Photoshop, just turn the page and keep reading.

The 5th Wave   By Rich Tennant

ATTEMPTING TO SAVE MONEY ON FAMILY PHOTOS, THE DILBRANTS SCAN THEIR NEWBORN INTO A PHOTO IMAGING PROGRAM WITH PLANS OF JUST DITHERING THE CHILD INTO ADOLESCENCE.

Nope! She must have moved again! Run the scanner down her once more.

Chapter 10
Playing with Pictures

In This Chapter
- How to edit photographs on the Mac
- Using Photoshop, the most popular image editor around
- Rotating a skewed photo
- Cropping away extraneous background junk
- Bringing your image into sharp focus
- Correcting brightness and contrast

When it comes to photography, most of us are rank amateurs. Even if you're more adept than my mom — who, though an amazing person in many respects, can't take a picture without cutting off someone's head — I'm willing to bet that you occasionally turn out a photo that's fuzzy, skewed, or several shades less colorful than you had hoped. Sure, these flawed snapshots remind you of grand times gone by, so you gotta love 'em. But wouldn't it be refreshing if they all looked exactly the way you wanted them to?

That's the beauty of an image editing program such as Photoshop from Adobe, 415-961-4400. You can open a digital photograph and make it look much better than it did in real life. You can sharpen the focus and enhance the colors — two operations that will improve the image dramatically. Or you can go all out and turn the photo into an inspired piece of surrealism, without any regard for reality whatsoever.

Now, Photoshop isn't the only image editor on the planet. Though readily available, it is quite expensive — you'll pay about $500 through a mail-order company or at your local computer store. If that sounds like more than your particular market will bear, here are a few other choices:

- New users may want to consider the $150 Color It! from MicroFrontier, 515-270-8109.
- If you want to apply wild effects and add some artistic touches, look to the $500 Painter from Fractal Design, 408-688-8800.

- And if you don't like either of those options, you can try the $400 PixelPaint Pro from Pixel Resources, 404-449-4947.
- Heck, you can even edit images with Apple's PhotoFlash, as I mentioned in Chapter 9.

Just the same, Photoshop is generally the best and certainly the most popular image editor on the planet. So I concentrate solely on it in this chapter. Luckily, many of the functions that I discuss — cropping, rotating, and focus- and color-correcting — work very similarly in PixelPaint and PhotoFlash and virtually the same in Color It! (which even uses most of the same keyboard shortcuts).

If you just want to play with Photoshop, many Kinko's and other photocopy centers that offer self-service Macs have Photoshop available for customer use. You can go in and rent the machine by the hour.

Er, I should fess up and admit that I sort of have this thing going with Photoshop. I have written, well, *three* books on the topic. This might strike you as a bit excessive on my part, but Photoshop is just that kind of terrific program. "S'wonderful," as they say in the song. Anyway, if you want to learn more about Photoshop, *Photoshop 3 For Macs For Dummies* will probably serve you best. It's a quick read and packed with straightforward info. Critics are calling it the feel-good manual of the year.

Just What Can Photoshop Do?

As a bit of a teaser, I've prepared some figures to show you just what you can do to a digital image if you really try. In Figure 10-1, for example, I start off with one of my typically inept photographs. The first image in the figure is soft on focus, low on contrast, and lopsided to boot. I'm tempted to fault my QuickTake camera, but it's a poor carpenter who blames his tools, eh? So rather than cursing the image, I might as well just fix it up in Photoshop.

Chapter 10: Playing with Pictures 125

Figure 10-1: A terrifically entertaining storage shed before (left) and after (right) I gave it the once-over-lightly in Photoshop.

The corrected image on the right side of Figure 10-1 is the result of three common operations in Photoshop. I rotated the image to make it upright, I sharpened the focus to give it crisper edges, and I corrected the contrast to throw a little light on the subject. The result is a Grade A busted up, rusted, completely abandoned metal shed out in the middle of nowhere, every bit as magnificent and grand as Mother Nature intended it to be.

But you don't have to stop there. As Figure 10-2 demonstrates, you can go quite a bit further. In the first example, I administered a series of special effects to specific image elements. Most prominent among these are the relief effect I applied to the shed and the marblelike cloud texture in the sky.

Figure 10-2: The infamous storage shed of Dracula (left) and an even scarier scene (right) manufactured by Photoshop.

In the second example, I combined the shed image with three other photos. I pasted a brick walkway into the sky above the shed; I inserted the marquee from the local courthouse into the shed's entrance; and I topped it all off with my own grinning mug. Truly a sight to behold.

I won't be getting into special effects in this chapter — for that, you'll have to look to *Photoshop 3 For Macs For Dummies* or some other title, preferably bearing my name. However, I will show you how to correct your photos so that they look every bit as good as they did in real life and possibly even better.

Stilt the Tilt

It's not easy to take a picture that's exactly straight up and down. In some cases, you don't have any frame of reference for what is straight and what's not. Other times, you're not on a balanced surface when you're taking the shot. And who's to say that the subject of your photo is straight in the first place?

Figure 10-3 is a good example. I mean, what in the world are you supposed to do when shooting the Tower of Pisa? The thing isn't leaning, it's falling on its side. So do you align the camera with the ground or with the tower? Quite the photographic nuisance, I call it.

Figure 10-3: This notorious subject is forever in need of straightening.

Putting the image on the up and up

To straighten an image, you have to rotate it. Photoshop offers a small collection of rotation commands, all under the Image⇨Rotate submenu:

- **180°:** This command turns the image upside-down. It's rarely useful unless you're trying to empty the photograph's pockets.

- **90° CW:** This command rotates the image one quarter-turn clockwise, so that the top of the image topples over to the right.

- **90° CCW:** Choose this command to rotate the image one quarter-turn counterclockwise (to the left). This command is especially useful for righting tall Photo CD images. Because Photo CD images are invariably wider than they are tall, tall images are laid on their sides. In fact, this was true of the tower image when I first opened it. One application of Image⇨Rotate⇨90° CCW, and everything was hunky dory.

- **Arbitrary:** Choose Image⇨Rotate⇨Arbitrary to rotate the image by a numerical amount. You just enter the number of degrees you want to rotate the image into an option box and select either the CW or CCW radio button to rotate the image clockwise or counterclockwise. Remember, 360 degrees represents a full-circle turn.

- **Free:** Before choosing this command, you have to select part of the image. For example, to select the tower, I dragged around it with the rectangular marquee tool, labeled in Figure 10-4. After choosing Image⇨Rotate⇨Free, you drag one of the four corner handles around the selection. You can keep dragging until you get it just right. Then click inside the selection with the gavel cursor, spotlighted in Figure 10-4.

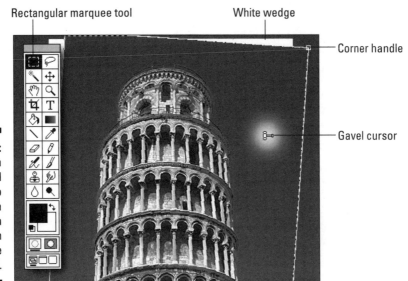

Figure 10-4: Click with the gavel icon to complete a rotation begun with the Free command.

To prevent those white wedges from showing up around the edges of a rotated selection — you can see a couple of wedges in Figure 10-4 — you must *float* the selection before applying Image⇨Rotate⇨Free. Choose Select⇨Float (or press ⌘-J) after selecting the image. Photoshop creates a copy of the selection and keeps it hovering above the surface of the original. Now you can feel free to rotate away.

Making the tower go straight

When you apply any command in the Image⇨Rotate submenu, Photoshop has to recalculate the colors of the image pixels to come up with the newly rotated image. The 180°, 90° CW, and 90° CCW commands merely shift pixels around, so they don't do any permanent damage. For example, after choosing 90° CW, you can choose 90° CCW to arrive right back at the original.

When you use the Arbitrary and Free commands, however, Photoshop has to invent totally new pixels. This means that these commands slightly degrade the image: Each application of Arbitrary or Free makes the image fuzzier and fuzzier. So if the first application of the command doesn't quite do the trick, choose Undo and try again from scratch; don't simply apply the command two or three times in a row.

Here's what I mean. Say, for example, that I want to rotate the esteemed landmark from Pisa. Because I want to rotate the entire tower, the best command is Image⇨Rotate⇨Arbitrary, which doesn't require that I first select the image. But short of taping a protractor to the screen, how am I supposed to know how many degrees to rotate the darned thing? Here's how:

1. **I chose Image⇨Rotate⇨Arbitrary and entered 12 into the Angle option box.**

   For some reason, I had it in my head that the Tower of Pisa was leaning at a 12-degree angle. So I reckoned that I might as well give it a shot.

2. **I selected the CW radio button and pressed Return.**

   Obviously, the thing needed to be rotated clockwise. But the result, shown in the first example of Figure 10-5, was no good. I rotated the tower way too far. That kind of shock can ruin historic structures.

3. **I chose Edit⇨Undo.**

   Actually, I pressed ⌘-Z, the universal shortcut for the Undo command. Time to try again.

4. **I chose Image⇨Rotate⇨Arbitrary, entered 8, and pressed Return.**

   Another stab in the dark. And just as wrong. The result was another excessive rotation.

5. **I repeated Step 3.**

   I've probably repeated Step 3 several thousand times in my life.

6. **Again, I chose the Arbitrary command, but this time I entered 4 and pressed Return.**

   That did it. As you can see in the right example of Figure 10-5, the tower is now corrected and once again open for business.

Figure 10-5: The results of rotating the tower 12 degrees (left) and 4 degrees (right).

Clip Away the Excess Gunkage

Earlier, I mentioned that you can get rid of the white wedges around a rotated image by first floating it. But that only works if you first select the image, which you don't typically do when applying Image⇨Rotate⇨Arbitrary. So how do I clean up the second image in Figure 10-5? Why, by cropping, naturally.

To *crop* an image is to cut away its edges. It's a great way to focus in on an image by throwing away the extraneous background junk and keeping only the most important stuff. Professional photographers crop just about every single photo they shoot, so why should you be an exception?

To crop an image in Photoshop, you use the crop tool, labeled in Figure 10-6. Select the tool and drag around the area you want to retain. If you don't get it right the first time, no sweat. You can drag the corner handles until you surround the desired area perfectly. Then click inside the cropping boundary with the scissors cursor.

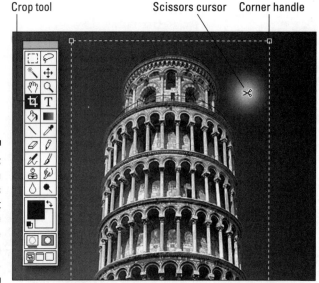

Figure 10-6: Click with the scissors cursor to get rid of the stuff outside the cropping boundary.

You can rotate and crop an image in a single operation. After dragging with the crop tool to surround the general area that you want to retain, Option-drag a corner handle to rotate the cropping boundary. Cool, huh? From here on out, you can drag the corner handle to change the size of the cropping boundary or Option-drag to further rotate it. After you click inside the boundary with the scissors cursor, Photoshop rotates the boundary so that it's straight up and down.

You can also move the cropping boundary around by ⌘-dragging on a corner handle. Try it out!

Sharpen the Focus

After you finish rotating and copping your image, you'll probably want to sharpen the focus a tiny bit. Sharpening is one of Photoshop's most powerful and most intricate functions.

If a photograph is a big blurry mess to begin with, you're not going to be able to generate detail out of thin blue air inside Photoshop. The commands under the Filter⇨Sharpen submenu are designed to create nice, crisp edges where soft edges existed before. But you have to have some kind of edges to start with.

Figure 10-7 shows what I'm talking about. The first image contains lots of detail, but the transitions between lights and darks are too subtle. The second example shows the photo after I sharpened the focus inside Photoshop. The program didn't add any detail — it's not *that* smart — it just enhanced the detail that was already there.

The Filter⇨Sharpen submenu offers several commands, but as fortune would have it, only one of them — Unsharp Mask — is worth your time. The others — Sharpen, Sharpen Edges, and Sharpen More — are easy to use but deliver get-by results. If you want to sharpen with style, you have to go with Unsharp Mask.

Figure 10-7: A scenic dome before sharpening in Photoshop (left) and after (right).

Choose Filter⇨Sharpen⇨Unsharp Mask to display the dialog box shown in Figure 10-8. It may look complicated, but when you boil it down into its elements, it becomes the picture of simplicity.

- **Preview box:** The box at the top of the dialog box shows a preview of the photograph sharpened according to the values in the option boxes. You can preview a different section by clicking outside the dialog box on some other portion of the image.

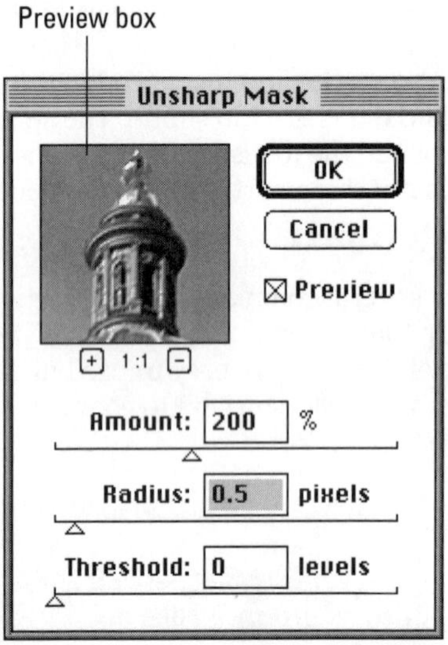

Figure 10-8: Keep an eye on the preview box to see how different Amount and Radius values will affect your image.

- **Preview:** When the Preview check box is on, Photoshop applies the effect in the main image window so that you can see exactly how your sharpened image will look. If this big preview is slowing things down, by all means turn off the check box. The preview box still shows you how the effect will look, even when the Preview check box is off.
- **Amount:** How much sharpening do you want to apply? If you want to sharpen the image just a little, enter a value under 100 percent. If you want to sharpen it a lot, enter a value of 100 percent or more, all the way up to 500 percent.
- **Radius:** Here's where you tell Photoshop the width of the edges that you want to sharpen. If the edges are pretty smooth, a value of 0.5 or 1.0 should do it. If the image contains lots of rough edges and loose pixels — like a photo shot with a QuickTake camera — raise the Radius to 2.0 or more.
- **Threshold:** This option is a dumb one. It enables you to sharpen some edges while leaving others blurry, which looks really weird. Leave it set to 0.

To give you an idea of how the Amount and Radius values work, I applied several different settings to the top of the dome in Figure 10-9. The first number in each label is the Amount value; the second number is the Radius value. Notice that higher Amount values produce crisper edges, while higher Radius value result in thicker edges.

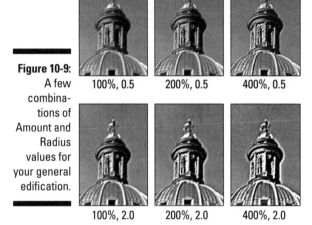

Figure 10-9: A few combinations of Amount and Radius values for your general edification.

In case you're curious, I used an Amount value of 300 percent and a Radius of 0.5 to sharpen the second image back in Figure 10-7. I like my edges crisp and razor thin.

Breathe New Life into Dead Colors

The final common problem with digital photographs is color balance. Most images are too dark and low on contrast, as the first example in Figure 10-10 demonstrates. But don't despair. Even a bad digital photo contains several million colors; all you need to do is redistribute the colors so that the image looks better, as in the second example in the figure.

Figure 10-10: A typical photograph before (left) and after (right) adjusting the brightness and contrast.

A lot of new Photoshop users try to use Image➪Adjust➪Brightness/Contrast to adjust brightness and contrast. Oh, the folly of it! Sure, the Brightness/Contrast command ought to improve brightness and contrast, but in truth, it just mucks things up. Heed my words, Dear Reader, and steer clear of it.

Taking colors to new levels

The better command for correcting brightness and contrast is Image➪Adjust➪Levels, or ⌘-L for short. This command brings up the Levels dialog box, shown in Figure 10-11. It's a complicated dialog box, full of technical-looking options that don't make a lick of sense at first glance. That's why most new users run screaming from this feature.

Luckily, I'm here to ease you in slowly. In Figure 10-11, for example, I've grayed out everything that isn't absolutely essential to adjusting brightness and contrast. All that's left is the birthmark in the center of the dialog box, the three slider triangles underneath it, the Auto button, and the Preview check box.

- **The birthmark:** The strange shape in the middle of the Levels dialog box is called a *histogram*. The histogram graphs all the colors in the image, ranging from black on the left side to white on the right. In Figure 10-11, most of the color in my image is concentrated on the black end, as is invariably the way with an overly dark image.

- **The black triangle:** This triangle controls the darkness of the darkest colors in the image. Drag the black triangle to the right to make more pixels black.

Chapter 10: Playing with Pictures

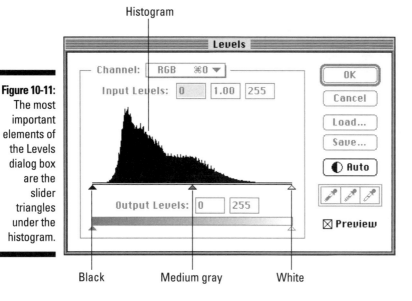

Figure 10-11: The most important elements of the Levels dialog box are the slider triangles under the histogram.

- ✓ **The medium gray triangle:** Use this triangle to control the lightness or darkness of medium gray pixels. As I'll demonstrate in a moment, this control is perhaps the most important option in the Levels dialog box. Drag the triangle to the left to lighten the image; drag it to the right to darken the image.

- ✓ **The white triangle:** This triangle enables you to control the lightness of the lightest colors in the image. Drag the triangle left to make more pixels white.

- ✓ **The Auto button:** Click on this button to automatically set the black and white slider triangles to their optimal settings.

- ✓ **The Preview check box:** When turned on, this check box ensures that you can see the results of your color-jumbling inside the image window. When the check box is off, Photoshop applies your edits to the entire screen, which can be both confusing and inaccurate — a rather bad combination if you ask me.

Doing the color correction five-step

Knowing the functions of the bizarre options in the Levels dialog box is all very well and good, but if I were you, I'd be more concerned with how I'm supposed to use them. Here's how to enhance the contrast of an image and bump up the brightness in a few, easy steps.

1. **Choose Image➪Adjust➪Levels.**

   Or make life easier and just press ⌘-L.

2. **Make sure that the Preview check box is turned on.**

   This way, you can see the effects of your color manipulations inside the image window.

3. **To fix the contrast, click on the Auto button.**

   If you're working on a black-and-white image, Photoshop automatically adjusts the placement of the black and white slider triangles. In a color image, the program stretches the histogram out to fill the gamut from black to white. Either way, the result is an automatic improvement in the contrast between colors in the photo.

4. **To adjust the brightness, drag the medium gray triangle.**

   Most likely, you'll want to lighten the image by dragging the triangle to the left. Pretend that the histogram is an animal that you're trying to balance on the gray triangle. The animal's mass should be evenly distributed on the left and right sides.

5. **When you're happy with the results, press Return.**

   You're done.

Pretty easy, huh? It may look like a tough dialog box, but deep down inside, it's a softy.

Part III
Teaching Your Mac to Sing, Record, and Speak

The 5th Wave   By Rich Tennant

"Now when someone rings my doorbell, the current goes to a scanner that digitizes the audio impulses and sends the image to the Mac where it's converted to a Tiff file. The image is then animated, compressed, and sent via high-speed modem to an automated phone service that sends an e-mail message back to tell me someone was at my door about 40 minutes ago."

In this part . . .

The Mac is the only personal computer ever made that was able to sound off the day it was born. It spoke at its first press conference, it's been recording for the last five years, and it has always remained one step ahead of the crowd.

Chapters 11 through 14 explain the myriad ways that your computer can make noise and record it. From playing audio CDs to recording sounds with inexpensive microphones to speaking in one of 22 tongues, your Mac makes a more interesting aural companion than most of the people in your car pool.

So plug in those speakers, plug in the mike, and prepare to turn your Mac into the smartest jukebox this side of Robby the Robot. Man, is your stereo ever going to be jealous when it gets a load of this.

Chapter 11
Listening to Your Audio CDs

In This Chapter
- ▶ Making sure that your external CD-ROM drive is ready to go
- ▶ Setting up your internal drive so that you can hear music CDs
- ▶ Using the old CD Remote desk accessory
- ▶ Entering CD and track titles
- ▶ Using the new AppleCD Audio Player
- ▶ Programming the order in which tracks play
- ▶ Quickly discovering the length of a song
- ▶ Figuring out why your sound occasionally cuts out

*I*don't know what kind of job you have — sorry, the crack statisticians at Top-Secret Dummies Headquarters haven't quite finished tabulating that particular information yet — but I'm willing to guess that there are times when you could stand a little music in your work-a-day routine. If your computer is equipped with CD-ROM drive and speakers (as explained in Chapters 2 and 3, respectively), and your drive doesn't have some boring computer CD spinning around inside it, you could be listening to your favorite audio CD right this second. This chapter explains how.

Hear the Music

If you have an external CD-ROM drive, and the drive is hooked up to speakers or to a stereo system via the RCA ports in the back of the drive (as explained in the "What about my external CD-ROM drive?" section of Chapter 3), you can skip this section. Just make sure that your speakers or stereo are turned on, and you're ready to listen to your audio CDs.

If you have an internal CD-ROM drive, however, you need to tell your Mac that you want to listen to it. You accomplish this using the Sound control panel, as explained in the following steps.

Part III: Teaching Your Mac to Sing, Record, and Speak

You don't have to perform these steps if you own a Centris 610 or 650 or a Quadra 610, 650, or 800. These machines are set up to automatically play audio CDs through the speakers, as long as no microphone is plugged into the sound-in port. If you own one of these machines, disconnect any mike that you may have hooked up and skip to the next section.

1. **First, quit any program that locks the sound options of your Mac.**

   For example, if you're watching a videotape with the Video Monitor program, go ahead and quit. If you're writing a letter in Microsoft Word, however, don't worry about it.

2. **Choose the Control Panels command from the Apple menu and double-click on the Sound control panel icon to open it.**

   If you are running System 7.5, you can choose Apple➪Control Panel➪Sound.

3. **Select Sound In from the pop-up menu in the upper-left corner of the control panel.**

   Figure 11-1 shows what I mean. After you select Sound In, you'll see a rather sparse set of options that let you record sounds into your computer. As you'll see, you can also use these options to play audio CDs.

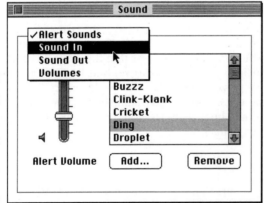

Figure 11-1: Select the Sound In option to get to the CD sound options.

If you are using System 7.01 or older, your version of the Sound control panel will look different than the one shown in Figure 11-1. To follow these steps, you need to upgrade to Version 8 of the Sound control panel or install System 7.1 or 7.5.

4. **If you have some additional sound equipment hooked up to your computer, click on the Built-in icon.**

   This icon is found in the Choose a Source for Recording list. It ensures that you're controlling the sound input capabilities of your Mac, not some other piece of hardware. If Built-in is the only icon in the list, you can skip this step.

5. **Click on the Options button to display the Input Source dialog box.**

   The Input Source dialog box appears, as shown in Figure 11-2. (If the Options button is dimmed, your machine does not contain an internal CD-ROM drive.)

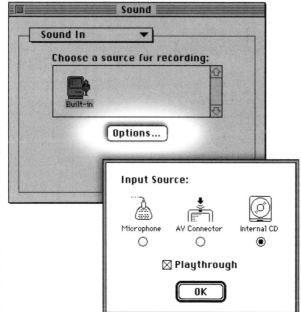

Figure 11-2: Click on the Options button, select the Internal CD radio button, and turn on the Playthrough check box.

6. **Select the Internal CD radio button.**

   This tells your Mac, "Hey, I'm in a CD-listening mood."

7. **Make sure that the Playthrough option is checked.**

   If it's not, select it now. The Playthrough check box tells your Mac that you want to listen to the CD while you record from it. Now, you and I know that you don't really want to record a darn thing. But if you don't select Playthrough, you won't be able to hear a music CD whether you're recording it or not.

Part III: Teaching Your Mac to Sing, Record, and Speak

On all machines except the AV Macs and Power Mac models, this option is both dimmed and selected, preventing you from deselecting it. These Macs are automatically set up to play CDs through the speakers after you complete Step 6.

8. Press the Return key.

The Input Source dialog box closes.

9. Select Volumes from the pop-up menu in the upper-left corner of the control panel.

You'll find at least one slider bar, labeled Built-in. Power Macs also include a Built-in Headphones slider, as shown in Figure 11-3. If you own an AudioVision monitor, or if your computer permits TV input, you may come across a few other sliders as well. The more, the murkier, as I always say.

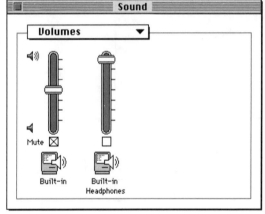

Figure 11-3: Here's one of the places you can control the volume of the sound blaring out of your speakers.

If the Volumes option is not available, you do not have Sound Manager 3 installed in the Extensions folder in your System Folder. Sound Manager is included with System 7.5 and many CD-ROM titles (especially games). Luckily, you don't need it to play audio CDs. For now, just skip to Step 11.

10. Drag the Built-in slider all the way up to the maximum volume.

This step assumes that you have only one slider. If you own a Power Mac, however, you should raise the Built-in Headphones slider instead because this slider specifically controls the speakers. If you have an AudioVision monitor, use the AudioVision Speakers slider. Or if you just want to be safe, raise all the sliders. (If a slider doesn't respond to your changes, it's not active; don't worry about it.)

Chapter 11: Listening to Your Audio CDs

Whatever the slider, maxing out the volume allows you to better control the sound levels from the CD Remote or CD Audio Player program — as you'll learn shortly — and from your speakers.

11. **Select Alert Sounds from the pop-up menu in the upper-left corner of the control panel.**

    The options you see now control the volume of error beeps. You don't want those error beeps drilling through your head, so you may want to make them a little softer.

12. **Lower the Alert Volume slider until the beep sounds right.**

    I usually set it somewhere between the second and third tick mark from the bottom.

13. **Close the Sound control panel.**

    Click on the close box on the left side of the title bar. You are now officially ready to go.

If you're using a Power Mac or Performa 6100 but you haven't yet upgraded to System 7.5, the Sound control panel settings may reset every time you reboot your computer. This means that you have to repeat the preceding steps every time you want to listen to a CD. You can call Apple or comb the on-line services for a thing called System Update 3.0, which corrects the problem, but the simplest solution is to install System 7.5.

By the way, if folks tell you that you need to change the Sound Out options in the Sound control panel to get the best sound possible, don't believe them. Unlike multimedia CDs, audio CDs always play at top-notch sound quality, no matter how you set the Sound Out options.

Spin the Silver Platters

Depending on which version of the system software you have, the software you use to play CDs differs slightly. Scratch that — it differs a lot. Before System 7.5, Apple used to ship the CD Remote program, shown in Figure 11-4. Looking at its white type mired in a sea of blackness, you might be tempted to describe the interface as austere, or perhaps unfriendly. But I prefer to call it b'ugly.

System 7.5 introduced the prettier AppleCD Audio Player, on view in Figure 11-5. This interface features soft shadows and three-dimensional buttons with natural highlighting. In fact, Apple introduced the AppleCD Audio Player with a fair amount of fanfare, saying that it represents the shape of system interfaces to come. Not bad.

Figure 11-4:
The unattractive CD Remote program.

Figure 11-5:
The stunning AppleCD Audio Player.

Even though CD Remote is tragically homely, I favor both it and AppleCD Audio Player with discussions throughout the remainder of this chapter.

By the way, CD Remote and AppleCD Audio Player are not the only CD-playing programs out there. Many CD-ROM drives shipped with player programs because, for a while, Apple didn't provide any. For the most part, these non-Apple programs work like CD Remote.

Before you can use any program to play an audio CD, you must get the CD to mount on your desktop. Generally, this process is merely a matter of inserting the CD into the drive. If your Mac refuses to recognize a music CD, however, it's probably because you're missing a system extension or two. Read the "CD Software Stuff" section in Chapter 2 for more information.

Take My CD Remote, Please

CD Remote is a desk accessory, so you start it by choosing its name from the Apple menu. Assuming that you have an audio CD loaded into your CD-ROM drive, you can use the various buttons inside CD Remote as follows:

- **Stop, Play, Pause:** These buttons stop, play, and pause the CD. No surprises there. The Pause button keeps the CD set to the last point you played it at; Stop sends the CD back to the beginning. After pausing a CD, you can click on Pause again to play it.

- The area below the Stop, Play, and Pause buttons may look like a button, but it isn't. It shows you the track being played (or paused) and the amount of the track that has been played so far, in minutes.

- **Track:** Click on the Track buttons to move to the next track or the previous one, just as on a standard stereo CD player.

- **Scan:** To fast-forward or fast-reverse through a track, press one of the Scan buttons. You'll hear a mess of notes fly by, which may or may not sound better than the track played at the normal speed.

- **Audio Channels:** These buttons let you play just the left or right channel of the CD. Click on either button to turn that channel off or on. When one channel is off, the remaining channel plays through both speakers.

- **Repeat:** Click on the first Repeat button — the one that looks like an arrow — to switch between the single-play mode and the repeat-this-CD-over-and-over mode. Just to make sure that we're all clear, the right-pointing arrow plays the CD once; the looping arrow plays the disk repeatedly. Click on the button to switch back and forth between the two.

If you want to record the first track of a CD, you may find it helpful to turn on the repeat mode and skip to the last track. This gives you time to switch to your recording software and set things up properly. For example, say you want to record the song "She" from the billion-sold-in-Europe album *Music by Candlelight,* from that pan-flute-playing madman, Zamfir. "She" is the first song, so even if you're mighty fast on the draw, it'll take a couple of seconds to start the CD playing, switch to SoundEdit 16 or some other sound recorder, and click on the Record button. This means that you'll miss the first few ethereal refrains from the ancient harmonica that has mesmerized so many on late-night commercials. The solution is to skip to the last song on the album, "Adagio 8," fast-forward until you have about 15 seconds of the song to go, switch to SoundEdit, and poise yourself to begin recording. When you hear the last lilting notes of "Adagio 8," you're ready to spring into action.

- **AB:** The second Repeat button, labeled AB, is a little trickier and a whole lot less useful. It lets you repeat a specified segment of a track. Click on the button to change it to an *A*. Click on the A to set the beginning of the segment you want to repeat. The button changes to a *B*. Click on the B to set the end point. The segment then repeats *ad nauseum* until you go bonkers. I'm listening to a repeating segment right now, so I can empathize. Click again to put an end to the repeating and return to the AB button. Ah, doesn't that feel good?

- **Program:** When set to On, this button plays checked tracks only. Don't know what checked tracks are? I'll tell you in a second.

- **Shuffle:** Click on the button to listen to tracks in a random order. Leave everything to pure chance, you reckless creature, you.

  If both Program and Shuffle are set to On, you hear the checked tracks in random order. Personally, this is my favorite way to listen.

- **Time:** Click on this button to change the way the track time appears above the Scan buttons. You can switch between elapsed time and time remaining. Whoopee.

- **Eject:** Click on this button to unmount the CD and eject it from the drive. If you changed the names of songs or added some checks — as I explain shortly — CD Remote asks whether you want to save the changes.

- **Volume:** Drag this slider back and forth to change the volume of sound blasting through your roaring speakers. Drag to the right to make things louder; drag left to make things quieter.

If you click in the zoom box in the upper-right corner of the CD Remote window — labeled in Figure 11-6 — the window opens up to reveal a list of song titles — also shown in the figure. The first time you play a CD, the tracks have generic titles. After you label them, however, CD Remote remembers the labels for all time.

Here are the many things you can do:

- Select the Disc Title area and enter the name of the CD. You'll probably want to enter both musician and album title because CD Remote does not offer separate areas for the two. For example, I entered "Abba — Ring Ring" as befits this classic recording.

- After changing the name of the disk, press the Return key to highlight the first track title. Then enter the first track name and press Return to continue on to the next track, and so on. You'll have the whole darn thing labeled in no time.

Chapter 11: Listening to Your Audio CDs 147

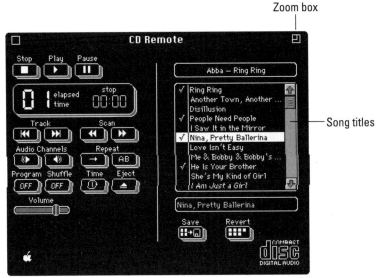

Figure 11-6: Click in the zoom box to display a list of song titles.

- Click in front of track names to turn check marks on and off. These check marks indicate songs that will play when the Program button is set to On. This function is essential when playing Abba albums. Nobody should submit themselves to bad Abba songs; the good ones are bad enough. "Nina, pretty ballerina, now she is the queen of the dancing floor, this is the moment she's waited for, just like Cinderella!" See how awful the best can be?

- Double-click on a track name to listen to the track.

- Click on the Save button to save all titles and check marks. The next time you insert the disk, CD Remote recognizes it — based on the length and number of the tracks — and brings up the saved title information. (In case you're curious, CD Remote saves titles and check marks to a file called CD Remote Programs in the Preferences folder inside the System Folder.)

- Click on the Revert button to restore the last-saved titles and check marks. You can't undo a mistake in CD Remote by pressing ⌘-Z, so the Restore button is often your only choice.

One last note: CD Remote requires that a system extension called CD Remote INIT is inside the Extensions folder inside your System Folder. If the system extension is missing, you will not be able to use this wondrous program. Just thought you might like to know.

The Just Plain Better CD Audio Player

The AppleCD Audio Player is not only better looking, it's more functional, easier to use, and supplies lots of shortcuts. Please, do not darken its door with disco.

As you do with the CD Remote desk accessory, you start the CD Audio Player by choosing it from the Apple menu. Because most of the buttons aren't labeled on-screen, I've taken the liberty of labeling them in Figure 11-7. Here's how the main buttons work:

- **Play and pause:** To play the CD, click on the play button. The button changes to two vertical bars that symbolize that abstract concept, pause. Click on this button to pause the CD.

  You can also press the Enter key or the spacebar to play or pause. This shortcut and all others work only when the CD Audio Player is in the foreground (in front of other programs).

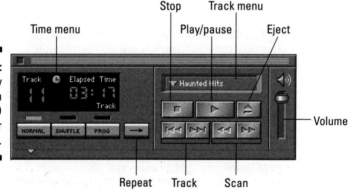

Figure 11-7: The many buttons in the AppleCD Audio Player window.

- **Stop:** Click on the stop button to stop the CD and return to the beginning. You can also press Delete.

- **Eject:** Click on this button or press ⌘-E to unmount the CD and send it flying out of the drive like a killer projectile. Well, actually, it's not quite that exciting. It just kind of scoots out.

- **Track:** Click on these buttons to go to the previous or next track.

  You can also switch tracks by pressing the left or right arrow keys.

- **Scan:** To go backward or forward inside a track, use these buttons.

- **Volume:** Raise the slider to raise the volume. Nudge the slider down to decrease the volume.

Better yet, press the up and down arrow keys. It takes 16 presses to get from the quietest level to the loudest. And if you're really in a hurry to change the volume — the second Mom and Dad walk out the door, for example — press and hold an arrow key.

- **Normal, Shuffle, and Prog:** Only one of these buttons can be active at a time. Click on Normal to play the songs in their normal order. Click on Shuffle to play the songs randomly. And click on Prog to play your favorite songs in their programmed order, as I describe shortly.

The great thing about the Shuffle function is that it plays each song only once, without randomly repeating some song seven times. If you don't like an order, just click on Shuffle again to re-randomize things.

- **Repeat:** When this button appears as a right-pointing arrow, the CD plays once. When the arrow loops, the CD plays until your computer breaks. Click on the button to switch between the two modes.
- **Time menu:** Click and hold on the little clock icon to display a pop-up menu that changes the time display. You can select from the time elapsed or remaining for a track or the time elapsed or remaining for the entire CD.
- **Track menu:** Click and hold on the CD title above the play button to display a pop-up menu of track names. Select a track name to skip to that track.

Naming the tracks

To reveal the track names, click on the triangular expand button, labeled in Figure 11-8. If you can't see all the tracks, you can drag the size box to display more. You can then select and rename the CD and track titles as you see fit. There is no need to save the titles; CD Audio Player saves them automatically to a file called AppleCD Audio Player Prefs in the Preferences folder inside the System Folder.

While naming tracks, you can press either the Return or Tab key to advance from one track to the next. To highlight the previous track, press Shift-Return or Shift-Tab.

Customizing the album

When you click on the Prog button, the track titles split into two columns, as demonstrated in Figure 11-9. At this point, you can specify exactly which tracks you want to play and in which order. You can even play tracks multiple times.

Figure 11-8: Click on the expand button to show all the track names.

- Initially, the right column — which represents the programmed tracks — is empty. To add a track to the programmed list, drag it from the left column and drop it in place in the right. As you drag, a little arrowhead shows you where the track will be inserted.
- To play a track more than once, drag it over to the right column multiple times.
- To change the order of a track, drag it up or down in the right column.
- To delete a track from the programmed list, drag it from the right column and drop it back in the left column or outside the CD Audio Player window.

As shown in Figure 11-9, the track pop-up menu even changes to reflect the programmed titles. If a track hasn't been programmed, it doesn't appear in the menu.

Chapter 11: Listening to Your Audio CDs   *151*

Figure 11-9: When the Prog button is active, you can drag track names in and out of the programmed list.

You can't change the CD or track names in the Prog mode. You have to first click on the Normal or Shuffle button.

Fooling around with the options

When you're using the AppleCD Audio Player, the menu bar contains the standard File and Edit menus. But it also contains an Options menu. The commands in this menu let you change the way the CD Audio Player looks and which channels play.

- **Window Color:** Choose the color that you want to apply to the background of the CD Audio Player window. Dark Gray, Green, and Magenta are the only tolerable colors, in my humble opinion, but there's no accounting for tastes, yours or mine.

- **Indicator Color:** These options control the colors of the track and time numbers.

Part III: Teaching Your Mac to Sing, Record, and Speak

- **Sound:** If you want to play a single channel through both speakers, choose Left Channel Only or Right Channel Only.

- **Startup CD Drive:** If you have more than one CD-ROM drive, you can set one to be the primary drive for listening to music CDs by choosing its SCSI ID number from this submenu.

How Long's that Song?

I don't know about you, but every once in a while, I like to record some of the best songs from my various music CDs to cassette tape. Unfortunately, not all CDs list how long the tracks are.

I guess that I should deliver some pompous warning about how you should only record from CDs that you own. But, frankly, I don't care what you record. I don't advocate it, mind you, but pirating is a personal choice. Let your conscience — however depraved — be your guide.

To discover the length of any track without opening any software, double-click on the CD icon at the Finder desktop. A window appears, showing all the tracks, labeled Track 1, Track 2, and so on. Select the track in question and choose File➪Get Info (or press ⌘-I). The length of the track appears in the Comments box, as shown in Figure 11-10.

Figure 11-10: Choose the Get Info command to find out the length of any track.

Chapter 11: Listening to Your Audio CDs

To discover the length of the entire album, select the CD icon on the desktop and choose Get Info or press ⌘-I. The Comments box now contains a total time message.

My Sound is Cutting Out!

When listening to a classical album or one of those nature samplers that you can purchase for $10 a four-pack at Price Club, you may notice an irritating phenomenon. The music cuts out. In the middle of some soft flute solo or jungle-cat growl, the sound simply disappears.

The culprit isn't your Mac, it's your speakers. As I mentioned in the "More criteria for the savvy shopper" section in Chapter 3, you have speakers that automatically turn off when the volume level is low. This conserves power and prolongs the speakers' life, but it's also incredibly distracting.

The only way to combat the problem is to maximize all volume settings from your Mac. As mentioned in Step 10 at the beginning of this chapter, make sure that the sliders in the Volumes area of the Sounds control panel are pumped up all the way. Also raise the volume slider in the CD Remote or AppleCD Audio Player to its maximum setting.

While you're busy maxing out all those other sliders, don't forget to set the Alert Volume slider in the Alert Sounds area of the Sound control panel very low. Otherwise the error beeps will make your ears bleed.

For this point on, regulate all volumes by adjusting the knobs on the speakers. This strategy may not solve the problem entirely, but it's the best solution short of buying a new set of speakers.

Chapter 12
Recording Sounds for Fun and Profit

In This Chapter
- Understanding the benefits of recording digital sounds
- Predicting a possible future of top-40 music on disk
- Using internal and external microphones
- Recording from an external CD-ROM drive
- Telling your Mac what you want to record
- Recording a new alert sound
- Renaming, copying, and deleting sounds
- Creating a startup sound
- Playing a sound as a scale in ResEdit
- Adding a voice message to a letter

The cassette tape is a study in technological irony. Here it is, the most popular medium for recording sound, and yet it's fairly awful. Just think about all the problems you've had with cassette tapes over the years. They all stretch to varying degrees; a few twist, mangle, or break; and I don't know about you, but I've had a couple of cassettes warp into unplayable shapes after I abandoned them in the car all summer.

But even if tapes were absolutely impervious to damage, they would still pale in comparison to other sound media. Every cassette — even the deluxe, high-bias, chromium-oxide variety — is plagued by tape hiss. (Sure, Dolby noise reduction helps, but it also distorts the sound and muffles some of your more soprano tones, hardly an ideal solution.) Much of this hiss can be blamed on the thinness of the tape. The narrow width and slow playback speed permit relatively little magnetic information to be recorded or played at a time. In fact, you can get much better sound from a hi-fi videotape than the highest grade cassette, almost exclusively by virtue of the difference in tape thickness.

If you own a hi-fi VCR and you happen to have it hooked up to a stereo system, give it a try. Record some music from a CD onto both a cassette and a videotape and then play the two. You'll be amazed at how much better the videotape sounds.

But cassettes are compact and cheap. They're a lot handier than videotapes, which tend to be large, so you aren't likely to stick one in a Walkman or play it in your car. And other recordable media — DAT, MiniDiscs, and so on — cost upwards of $10 a pop and show no signs of dropping in price. So the question is, what on earth will once and for all overthrow the cassette and assume its rightful place as the next consumer-grade sound-recording medium?

As with so many of life's riddles, the answer resides in your computer. Here's an astoundingly capable machine that can record any sound to disk. These disks will never stretch or twist, and they'll only break if you step on them or give them a karate chop or two (though, I must admit, they still might melt in the sun). Because the recording is digital, you don't get any hiss, and the disk copy is every bit as good as the original. No matter how many duplicates you make, there's absolutely no reduction in quality.

The problem is that sound takes up a ton of room on disk. A floppy disk barely holds anything, and, as things stand now, higher-capacity storage options aren't much better. The $15 Zip disk I mentioned in Chapter 6, for example, can hold about ten minutes of CD-quality stereo sound — too much money for too little music. However, it's only a matter of time until larger, cheaper storage options are available.

Imagine in the not-so-distant future sticking a $5 disk into your home computer and copying a few hundred choice song files from an electronic subscription service. You'll be charged for each song that you copy, but once you have a song on disk, you can make as many reproductions as you like, every one absolutely identical to the original. An entire disk full of songs — perhaps three or four hours' worth — will copy in a matter of seconds. A few moments later, you can pop the disk in your car computer and listen to it over the course of several commutes. Unfortunately, this kind of media-independent sound format will render your present cassettes and CDs as useless as your old 8-tracks and LPs. I'm afraid that progress simply has no place for old technology.

While you're waiting for this amazing future to become the mundane present, you can record some of the more precious sounds in your life to disk right now. You may not have enough storage space to record more than a few minutes of sound, and you won't be able to play them in your car unless you dub them back to a cassette, but they'll be absolutely impervious to the ravages of time.

Think about it. One day when you're very old, you'll play a crystal clear sound from the 1990s for your granddaughter. "But Gramps," she'll say, "you didn't have ProtoSound/128" — or whatever they'll call the darn thing — "back in the old days, did you?" You'll just smile and assure her that, although your rustic era was not blessed with that particular format, you've simply never been the kind who waits for progress to catch up with you.

Bonding with Your Microphone

Every Mac that includes a sound-in port lets you record sounds from a microphone. However, just to keep you on your toes, not all Macs come with mikes, and different Mac models require different kinds of mikes. Some Macs even include internal microphones, built right into the case of the computer or monitor. The only constant is that all mikes currently sold by Apple — whether internal or external — are monophonic.

If you own an older Mac — including the Plus, SE, SE/30, II, IIx, IIcx, IIci, IIfx, and Classic — your computer doesn't provide a sound-in port, so you can't hook up a microphone. You need to purchase a MacRecorder (discussed in Chapter 5) or some other recording hardware that plugs into the modem port.

Mike in the box

Many Macs include internal microphones built right into the casing of the computer — among them, PowerBooks released in the last three years, including the 160, 180, and 500 series, as well as the Duos. PowerBook mikes are located at the top of the keyboard.

A few desktop models, including the Color Classic, the LC and Performa 500 series, and the Power Mac 5200 LC, also offer built-in mikes. In each case, the mike looks like a pin prick just above the built-in monitor.

Apple even built an internal mike into its AudioVision monitor. As shown in Figure 12-1, the monitor includes speakers and other controls. The microphone is positioned along the top of the monitor. The second image in the figure shows a low-flying bird's-eye view of the microphone from the rear.

Some older PowerBooks have a tendency to pick up sounds from the computer because the mike is located so close to the hard drive and disk drive. So you may want to purchase an external mike if you own one of these computers. The internal mikes in the PowerBooks 520 and 540 and the desktop models, however, are positioned sufficiently far from your computer's noisy innards that they record your voice with almost no interference.

Built-in mike

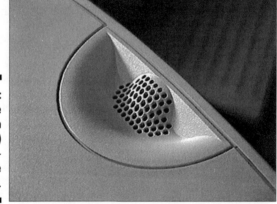

Figure 12-1: The AudioVision monitor (top) and its built-in mike (bottom).

I should also mention that all internal mikes do a good job of picking up sounds from a few feet away. In other words, you don't have to shove your face into the microphone; you can remain seated comfortably and be heard just fine.

The nasty exception rears its head in the case of the AudioVision monitor. If you combine this monitor with the Quadra 630 (or one of the other members of the 630 series), you have to put your mouth right next to the mike, and even then, the sound quality is awful. So for Pete's sake, if you own a 630, don't get an AudioVision monitor. And if you already bought both, unplug the monitor from the computer's sound-in port and plug in a standard mike instead.

Which mike is right for your Mac?

Apple sells two kinds of external microphones, the Apple Microphone and the PlainTalk Microphone. Figure 12-2 shows the Apple Microphone at top and the PlainTalk puppy on the bottom.

The $20 Apple Microphone looks like a little circle with a hole in it. The one in the figure is dark gray to match the PowerBooks, but it comes in light gray as well. The $30 PlainTalk mike looks like a tea bag, except that it's hard and plastic and there's absolutely no way to stuff herbs into it.

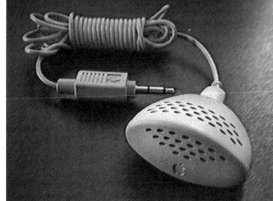

Figure 12-2: Apple sells just two mikes, the Apple Microphone (top) and the PlainTalk microphone (bottom).

- The PlainTalk mike is compatible only with a handful of recent Macs, including the LC and Performa 475, 476, and 500 series; the Quadra 605; the Quadra, LC, and Performa 630 series; the Performa 6100 series; and all AV Macs and Power Macs.
- All other Macs — except the PowerBooks 520 and 540 — use the Apple Microphone.
- The 500 series PowerBooks require stereo mikes, which Apple doesn't sell. You have to either buy a stereo mike from a stereo equipment store or satisfy yourself with the internal mike.

If you're at all unsure about what kind of mike your Mac takes, you can easily figure out the answer if you can lay your hands on a PlainTalk mike. The miniplug on the PlainTalk mike is longer than the one on the Apple Microphone, thus preventing it from fitting into many machines. If the PlainTalk fits, great. If not, you need the Apple Microphone.

The PlainTalk microphone was designed for voice recognition, which requires very good sound quality. Therefore, it provides something called a *line-level signal*, just like the sound carried by a standard audio cable (as discussed in Chapter 3). The Apple Microphone provides a lower quality, *mike-level signal*, which isn't nearly as clean and crisp as its line-level cousin.

When using the PlainTalk mike, be sure to plug it in all the way. Don't force it, but be sure to stick it in the jack nice and snug. That extra length at the end of the miniplug allows the mike to access the power it needs to amplify the signal. If you don't plug it in properly, you won't get any amplification, so your recordings will be overly soft and wheezing with hiss.

Recording from That Crazy External CD-ROM Drive

If you want to record sounds from an internal CD-ROM drive, no problem. Because the sound is processed inside the computer, there's absolutely no hardware to hook up. You don't even have to go to all the work of plugging in a mike.

However, if you want to record from an external CD-ROM drive, you have to cable the RCA ports on the back of the drive to the sound-in port on the back of your computer. All you need to do this is a Y cable that has two RCA plugs at one end and a miniplug at the other end. If your Mac records only mono sounds, you need a Y cable with a mono miniplug. If your Mac supports stereo input, buy a Y cable with a stereo miniplug. See the "Sound In" column in the tables in Chapter 1 to decide whether your Mac supports mono or stereo recording. For more information on Y cables in general, read the "Channel-splitting" section in Chapter 3.

This same technique works for recording sounds from cassette tape decks, standard CD players, and other stereo equipment as well. If you want to record some wacky TV sounds, cable the audio outputs from a VCR to your Mac's sound-in port. You never know, you might even be able to hook up an 8-track tape player if you try hard enough.

Setting Up a Recording Session

If you're recording on an old Mac without an internal CD-ROM drive, you can only record from one source, the sound-in port. This means that you don't have to bother with any fancy setup options.

If you own a machine produced in the last three years — particularly if it includes an internal CD-ROM drive or special AV capabilities — you need to engage in a little exploratory preparation. The only exception is if you own a Centris or Quadra 610, 650, or 800. These models record from whatever is plugged into the sound-in port. Only if the sound-in port is empty does the Mac record from the internal CD-ROM drive.

Just to be safe, follow these steps, which explain how to specify a recording source in the Sound control panel. If the Options button is dimmed or nonexistent in Step 3, you can close the Sound control panel and skip to the next section, secure in the knowledge that you're all ready to go.

1. **Choose Apple⇨Control Panels⇨Sound.**

   If choosing the Control Panels command doesn't display a submenu, go ahead and choose the command and then double-click on the Sound icon. Either way, you open the Sound control panel.

2. **Select the Sound In option from the pop-up menu in the upper-left corner of the control panel.**

   If the Built-in icon is not selected, click on it.

   By the way, this step assumes that you're using System 7.1 or 7.5. If you're using and older version, it's high time to upgrade.

3. Click on the Options button.

You may be able to bail at this point. If the Options button is not available, your Mac determines the recording source automatically based on whether or not something is plugged into the sound-in port. You can skip ahead to Step 6.

On the other hand, if the Options button is in working condition, click on it to display the Input Source dialog box, shown in Figure 12-3.

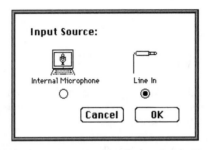
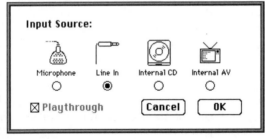
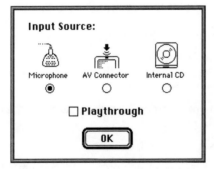

Figure 12-3: The Input Source options available to three typical Macs — a PowerBook 540 (top), a Quadra 630 (middle), and a Power Mac 7100 (bottom).

4. **Select the radio button that corresponds to the device you want to record from.**

   If you want to record from the mike, select Internal Microphone or just plain Microphone. To record from the internal CD-ROM drive, select Internal CD.

   The optimal choice isn't quite so obvious if you have an external CD-ROM drive or a piece of stereo equipment hooked up to the sound-in port. If your Mac offers a Line In option, as in the first and second dialog boxes in Figure 12-3, select that option. On such Macs, the Microphone option is frequently designed for unamplified mike-level signals and distorts other sounds.

   If your Mac supports the PlainTalk mike, however, there may be no Line In option, as in the third dialog box in the figure. The Microphone option supports all line-level signals, whether generated by a mike or an external piece of stereo equipment.

5. **Do what you gotta do to the Playthrough check box.**

   When recording your voice with a mike, it's best to turn the check box off to avoid feedback. Otherwise, turn it on so that you can hear what you're recording through the speakers.

   If the Playthrough check box is dimmed and turned on, it means that your Mac will automatically play sounds through the speakers. This happens with some machines when you select the Internal CD radio button.

   Many of these same machines, however, do not let you hear sounds from external CD-ROM drives and other equipment hooked up to the sound-in port. The Playthrough option might be dimmed and turned off when you select the Line In option, or there might not be a Playthrough option at all. If either turns out to be the case, you can plug a pair of headphones into the front of the external CD-ROM drive and listen to the music that way. After you record the music to disk, you can play the sound over your computer's speakers.

6. **Close the Sound control panel.**

   Click on the close box on the left side of the title bar.

Creating That Perfect Error Beep

Ready to record something? After all this time, I should think so. Your Mac is all set up to record *alert sounds*, which are those special beeps, buzzes, and boings that go off when you do something wrong. You can make that sound be absolutely anything you want.

Part III: Teaching Your Mac to Sing, Record, and Speak

Can you burp on cue? That would make a good alert sound. Can you whistle, snap, or make noises with your armpits? Perhaps you're wearing some musical jewelry. There must be a million sounds out there waiting to be your perfect error beep.

Here's how to record your own personal alert sound with a microphone.

1. **Open the Sound control panel.**

    The control panel contains a list of prerecorded alert sounds.

2. **Click on the Add button.**

    A little sound recording window pops up, as shown in Figure 12-4.

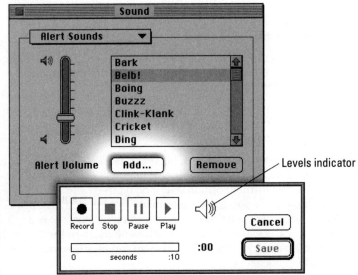

Figure 12-4: Click on the Add button to display this wonderfully compact sound recording window.

3. **Test the recording levels.**

    Say a few words into the mike. "These pretzels are making me thirsty" or some other "Seinfeld" line will do just fine. The speaker to the right of the Play button is the levels indicator. Curved lines appear to the right of the speaker to demonstrate the sound levels. The louder the noise, the more curved lines you see. Anything up to four curved lines is fine, but if you get a fifth, straight line, you're too loud. Start with the mike close to your mouth and move it away until you get to the point where the dreaded straight line never appears.

Chapter 12: Recording Sounds for Fun and Profit

4. **Click on the Record button.**

   You are now recording.

5. **Hurry up and make an obnoxious sound.**

   Anything will do. You can always re-record your sound if you don't like it. Keep an eye on the levels indicator. And remember, the maximum recording time is 10 seconds.

6. **Click on the Stop button to stop recording.**

   You can also simply click on the Record button again.

7. **Click on the Play button.**

   The Sound control panel plays back your recording in all its splendor.

8. **If you like the sound, click on the Save button to save it to the System file.**

   Or just press the Return key.

   If you don't like the sound, you can record a new one by clicking on the Record button or abort the recording session by clicking on Cancel.

9. **Enter a name for your sound and press the Return key.**

   The sound appears in the list with the other alert sounds. Click on it to play it again and again.

10. **Use the Alert Volume slider to set the volume for your new alert sound.**

    Drag up to increase the volume; drag down to make it softer.

11. **Close the Sound control panel.**

    Or you can stick around a while and record more sounds.

Sound advice

Alert sounds are like political sound bites — the briefer the better. Though you can record anything up to ten seconds long, you'll have the best luck if you keep it under a second. A ten-second sound may seem cool the first time you play it, but imagine having to sit on your hands for ten seconds every time you make a mistake while working on your computer. Believe me, it'll drive you nuts.

Here's some more stuff to keep in mind while recording alert sounds:

- Hold the mike as far away from the mouse as possible. If you get too close, you'll pick up the sounds of yourself clicking on the Record and Stop buttons. (When recording from an internal PowerBook mike, you pick up the clicks regardless of what you do, which is yet another reason to buy an Apple Microphone.)

- Start making noise the exact same moment that you click on the Record button. And keep making noise until you click on Stop. You don't want any delay at the beginning or end of the sound.

- I failed to explain in the steps a fourth recording button, Pause. This button lets you temporarily pause the recording, allowing you to add more sounds later. For example, try this: While saying a long "*aaaaaa*," click on Record and then Pause. Now say "*eeeeee*" and click on Pause twice in a row. Then say "*r r r r r r*" and click on Pause twice again. Finally, click on Stop. When you play the sound back, you get an *aa-ee-rr* noise that's very bizarre, even though it came out of your throat.

- To record a sound from a music CD, you need to start playing the CD in place of Step 3. Use the CD Remote or AppleCD Audio Player desk accessory, as explained in the previous chapter. You'll probably want to turn the volume up all the way in the CD player program because the volume affects the recording level. Experiment for the best results. When you get to the section you like, click on the Record button. Click on Stop to end the recording and press Return to save it. Before you can hear the new alert sound distinctly, you need to switch to the CD player program and pause the CD.

- To test out your sound after you record it — while still in the Sound control panel — click on the Add button. Then click outside of the little recording window. Your Mac won't let you switch to a different program while the recording window is up, so it will beep at you with your new sound. Click on the Cancel button once you've amused yourself sufficiently.

- You can't rename sounds in the Sound control panel. But you can after you close the control panel. Open the System Folder and double-click on the System file icon to open it and display a window full of alert sounds, as shown in Figure 12-5. Click on the filename you want to change and move your cursor away from it. The filename becomes highlighted, just like any other file on the Finder desktop. Enter a new name and press Return.

- If you want to listen to a sound in the System file, just double-click on it.

- If you want to keep a special sound around for quick access, you can copy it to a spot outside the System file. Just Option-drag a sound name from the System window onto an empty portion of the desktop to duplicate it. Then move the sound file into any folder you like or leave it out on the desktop. Now you can double-click on the file and listen to it any time you like.

- If you like a sound so much that you want to hear it every time your machine starts up, place it inside the Startup Items folder in the System folder. Again, however, you should stick with short sounds because your Mac won't let you do anything as long as the sound is playing.

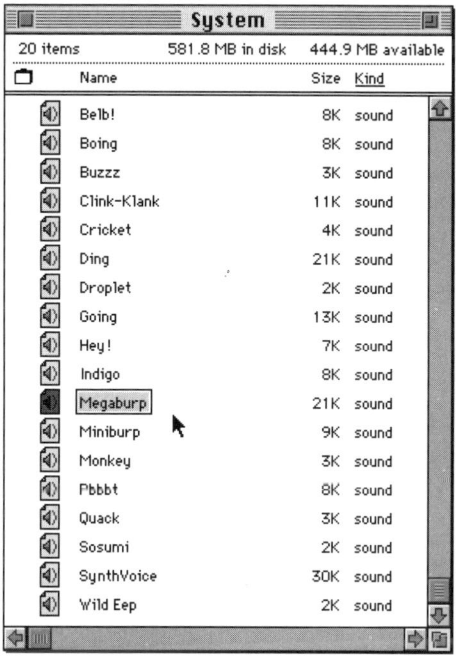

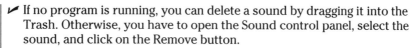

Figure 12-5: Here I am in the act of renaming the alert sound "Megaburp." I think I'll call it "Mightyburp" instead.

- If no program is running, you can delete a sound by dragging it into the Trash. Otherwise, you have to open the Sound control panel, select the sound, and click on the Remove button.

- Don't forget to close the System file when you're finished renaming, playing, and copying sounds. You're less likely to hurt the System if it's not lying around open to the world.

How to play an alert scale

If you have an Apple program called ResEdit lying around, you can perform a fun little trick. Look for Version 2.1 or higher. Apple gives away ResEdit for free over on-line services, which you can access by modem. You may also have a friend who has the program. Don't worry if you can't find ResEdit, though — you're not missing anything important. These steps are just for laughs:

1. **Duplicate the System file.**

    Select the System file at the Finder desktop and Option-drag it outside of the System Folder. This step creates a duplicate of the System so that you don't mess up the original in ResEdit.

2. **Start ResEdit.**

   Locate the program icon and double-click on it.

3. **Open the duplicate System file on the desktop.**

   Press ⌘-O, ⌘-D. Then enter **sys** to select the System file and press Return to open it. A window full of bizarre icons appears on-screen.

4. **Locate the Snd icon — which looks like a speaker — and double-click on it.**

   Another window appears, containing all the alert sounds, as shown in the middle of Figure 12-6.

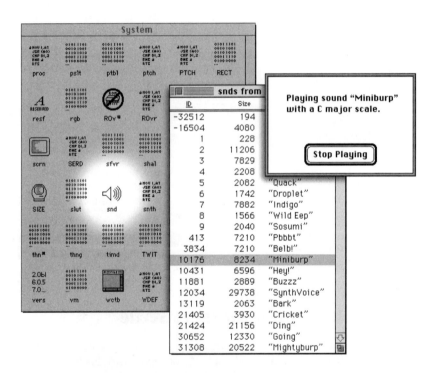

Figure 12-6: Opening a sound and playing it as a C-major scale inside ResEdit is one of the Mac's most important productivity features.

5. **Click on a sound name to select it.**

   I selected Miniburp, which is slightly shorter and more polite than Mightyburp. If you don't have any burp sounds handy, try Indigo.

6. **Choose Snd⇨Try Scale with Sound.**

   ResEdit plays the sound as a C-major scale.

7. **When you're done, quit ResEdit.**

   Press ⌘-Q.

8. **Drag the duplicate System on the desktop into the Trash.**

   And choose Special⇨Empty Trash. If a message appears asking whether you really want to bag the System, press Return to respond in the affirmative.

   Be sure to perform this last step. There's no sense in having extra System files floating around. It can confuse your computer, which would be no laughing matter.

Teaching Your Files to Speak

The Sound control panel isn't the only software that lets you record sound. Thanks to the Mac's long history of sound capabilities, sound recording has managed to work its way into all kinds of programs.

- Both Microsoft Word and WordPerfect let you record sounds for inclusion in letters. This feature, of course, assumes that you'll be sharing the letter with someone as a file on disk. (Actually, my technical editor tells me that if you're super high-tech, Xerox has a method for encoding sound and other digitized info on paper for faxing. You can then use another machine to read the sound and play it. Amazing.)

- If you have an electronic mail system such as CE Software's QuickMail set up on your computers at work, you can record a sound and shoot it off to a buddy a few cubicles down. "What are you doing for lunch?", "Meet you at the candy machine", and "Who could use a Slurpee?" are some sure-fire winners.

- If you're interested in sound effects and editing, you can record sounds inside a dedicated sound manipulation program such as MacroMedia's SoundEdit 16. I discuss this program in a modicum of detail in the next chapter.

- You can record music inside Adobe Premiere to add it to a digital movie. I explain digital movies, Premiere, and other related stuff in Chapters 17 and 18.

Take Microsoft Word as an example. In Word, you can add a *voice annotation,* which is a little bit of sound that other folks can listen to on their Macs. Say that you wanted to say "Hi, what's up?" to a hipster grandmother who also owns a Mac. You could add the bit of sound to a letter you've typed up in Word, copy the letter to a floppy disk, and put it in a disk mailer for prompt delivery. When the elder relative opens the file, she can play the sound merely by double-clicking on an icon.

In order to record sounds in Word, you must have included the Voice Annotation module when you first installed Word on your hard drive. If you neglected to install this module and you have the original Microsoft Word disks handy, you can rerun the Setup program from the first disk and install Voice Annotation any old time you like.

Here's how to create a personal voice message inside Word 6:

1. **Start Word and open a letter.**

   Or create a new file and type a letter from scratch. It's up to you.

2. **Click on some spot in the letter.**

   It doesn't matter where. You can move the voice annotation around later.

3. **Choose Insert⇨Annotation.**

   Word splits the window in two and inserts your initials inside brackets. (Word gets your initials from way back when you entered your name when installing the program. If you're using someone else's machine or — gad — someone else's software, you'll get someone else's initials.) The bottom portion of the window sports a little button that looks like that hideous creature, the cassette tape, as shown in Figure 12-7.

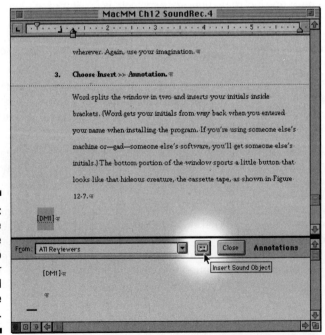

Figure 12-7: Click on the cassette button to record your personal voice message.

4. **Click on the cassette button.**

    Word starts up the Voice Annotation program. A few seconds later, a little recording window appears, just like the one shown back in Figure 12-4.

5. **Click on Record to start recording the sound.**

    Then speak into the mike.

6. **When you're finished, click on Stop.**
7. **Click on the Save button to insert the sound into your Word file.**

    Word quits the Voice Annotation module and returns you to your file, which now contains a little speaker icon.

8. **Drag the little speaker icon from the bottom portion of the window into the main letter area.**

    You may have to drag the I-beam cursor over the icon to select it. Position your cursor over the speaker until the cursor changes to an arrow. Then drag away.

    This step can be a little tricky, but it's worth the effort because it makes it easier for Grandma to find the sound. If you didn't take this step, Grandma would have to open the Annotation area just to find the speaker icon. She wouldn't even know you inserted a sound in the file if you didn't tell her.

9. **Click on the Close button at the top of the Annotation area.**

    It's the one immediately to the right of the cassette button. The window returns to its normal appearance.

10. **Double-click on the speaker icon to play the sound.**

    Keen, huh?

If you decide that you want to delete the sound, drag over it to select it and then press Delete. Note that the sound icon doesn't appear highlighted after you select it, but it's selected just the same. It's weird, but Word's weird, so what do you expect?

Chapter 13
Editing Sounds Like a Pro

In This Chapter

▶ Scouting for inexpensive sound editing programs
▶ Using SoundEdit 16, a popular sound editing program
▶ Understanding resolution and sampling rate
▶ Recording mono and stereo sounds
▶ Making sense of a sound wave
▶ Editing sounds and applying special effects
▶ Mixing voice with music
▶ Editing an alert sound in the System file
▶ Copying a sound from a program and pasting it in the System file

Sounds are a lot like images. They both appeal to our senses, they're both integral links in the great multimedia chain, and they can both be manufactured by turning transistors on a computer chip on and off. But the number-one similarity between sounds and images is their absolute transience and changeability. Frankly, there's no sense in taking a picture or recording a sound to disk unless you're going to edit it. As with images, few sounds are born perfect, but they can be made perfect inside the fluid and forever modifiable world of the computer.

In this chapter, I explore the most popular sound editing program for the Mac, SoundEdit 16 from Macromedia, 415-252-2000. I explain how to record sounds inside the program — both in mono and stereo — how to access sounds from inside the System file and other files and how to edit sounds by deleting words, mixing words with music, and applying special effects. For those on a budget, I also offer some less-expensive, shareware alternatives to SoundEdit 16.

Editing Sound for Pennies on the Dollar

As with all categories of software covered in this book, SoundEdit 16 isn't the only fish in the sea. It is ideally suited to casual users, combining a straightforward interface with lots of great capabilities, but it's also fairly expensive, running about $380 retail.

If you'd like to get a feel for sound editors before you invest in one, you may want to try out one of the shareware or freeware programs available from online services such as America Online or CompuServe. These programs aren't quite as well-equipped as SoundEdit, but they do allow you to perform many of the techniques that I describe in this chapter.

Incidentally, the term *shareware* means that you can use the program without paying for it for a few weeks, but if you like it and intend to continue using it in the foreseeable future, you are on your honor to pay a modest fee to the programmer (usually around $15). *Freeware* is just that — totally free. Cool, huh?

The one problem with shareware and freeware programs is that they are typically written by independent programmers who, though bright, industrious, and extremely capable, may not be in the programming game for the long haul. If the programmer gets a more demanding job, decides to change professions, or graduates from high school — many shareware programmers are in their teens — the program may suddenly become orphaned, meaning that a program that works for you today may not work for you tomorrow.

With the understanding that what is here today may be gone tomorrow, here are a few interesting programs to consider:

- SoundEffects from Alberto Ricci is currently the most stalwart shareware sound editor, costing a mere $15 for those good souls who respectfully pay their fees (and plaguing those who don't with relentless guilt, bad fortune, and even head lice). This program provides most of the functions found in SoundEdit but lacks a smidgen of the polish. For example, the present version lacks a working Undo command.

- Sound Sculptor from Jeff Smith is half sound editor and half sound creator. Like an electronic synthesizer, the $20 shareware program actually lets you concoct your own sounds.

- Dale Veeneman's SoundHandle handles only low-quality, mono sounds, but it's freeware, so what can you lose?

- Ah, yes, but the freeware SoundBuilder from Ken Arthur provides a moderate collection of sound effects *and* supports stereo, so you might want to look at it instead.

- Sound Editor from David Veldhuizen is yet another piece of freeware that is more limited in scope but comes with thorough documentation.

Most of these programs have come out in the last year. Undoubtedly, there are lots and lots of other programs from years gone by and there will be many more in years to come. So don't cast a jaundiced eye on a program just because I don't happen to mention it in this list. In fact, if I were you, I'd greedily snap up any ol' sound program and give it the once-around-the-block.

Grasping the Semantics of Cybernetic Sound

The first benefit to a specialized program such as SoundEdit or one of the software/freeware titles is that you can record sounds of just about any length. The sounds can be several seconds or several minutes long. I've even created sounds that are more than an hour in length (though, as I mentioned in Chapter 12, such sound files take up a prohibitive amount of disk space).

Another benefit is that you can control the sound quality and specify whether the sound is monophonic or stereo. You can also label portions of your sound and save the sound file to disk for later use.

Inside every sound bite is a bunch of bits

Before you start recording, you need to tell SoundEdit just how good you want your sounds to be. Your first reaction might be, "I want the highest quality possible, please," but that isn't always the best choice. A stereo, CD-quality sound file takes up eight times as much space on disk as the same sound file recorded in low-quality mono sound. That's a difference worth considering.

Sound quality is measured in terms of two attributes: *resolution* and *sampling rate*. See, your Mac emulates sound by playing a continuous stream of very short blips, each one differing slightly in *amplitude*, or what we humans call volume. Each of these blips is called a *sample*. The number of blips played per second is the sampling rate, and the number of volumes available to each blip is the resolution.

(What may seem to be missing here is any discussion of pitch. In fact, if it weren't for the fact that you trust me implicitly, you might think that I have my facts mixed up and that it makes more sense for each blip to differ in pitch rather than volume. But pitch is actually created by the periodic increase and decrease in blip volume, as I explain further in the upcoming section "Reading the sound wave.")

Like the resolution of color screen images, sound resolution is measured in bits. You can select from two resolutions, 8-bit and 16-bit. An 8-bit blip can be one of 256 volumes, just as an 8-bit image pixel can be one of 256 colors. A 16-bit blip can take its pick from thousands of volumes, just as a 16-bit image contains thousands of colors.

This may make you think that 8-bit sounds are softer and 16-bit sounds are louder. But it's not the range of volumes that are at issue — both 8-bit and 16-bit blips can be equally soft or loud — but rather the variations in volume available. By way of an example, Figure 13-1 shows three possible versions of the same sound represented as graphs. The resolutions are imaginary, but the first contains only eight volumes, the second contains 32, and the third contains an infinite number. You can see how fewer volumes per blip lead to more jagged graphs, while more volumes make the graph smoother.

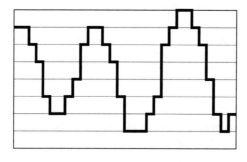

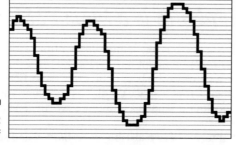

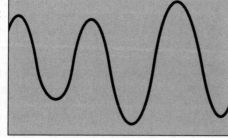

Figure 13-1: Graphs of the same sound recorded at three imaginary resolutions, the lowest at top and the highest at bottom.

The practical upshot of all this gobbledygook is that 8-bit audio sounds noisier than 16-bit. In fact, the difference is roughly the same as that between sounds played on a small, AM transistor radio with a little static thrown in and on a clear, resonant, FM stereo system.

Blips per second

If you happen to be in a theorizing mood, you might speculate that because a videotape plays movies by showing a new frame 30 times per second, a digital sound probably blips away at about the same speed. But because each blip is such a small fragment of sound — one that, on its own, doesn't sound like anything — it takes *way* more blips to fool your ears than it takes frames to fool your eyes. Several thousand blips per second, in fact.

Therefore, sampling rate is measured in *kilohertz*, abbreviated *kHz*, which means "thousand times a second." The two typical sampling rates at which you record sounds on the Mac are 22.050 kHz and 44.100 kHz, better known with their decimals lopped off as 22 kHz and 44 kHz. (Although you can choose other sampling rates, these two are the most common.) Like a higher resolution, a higher sampling rate also results in smoother sound.

Yes, well, very nice, but so what?

Now that I've taken you through this tortuous explanation of stuff you never wanted to know, your first reaction might be, "So what? What do I do with this technical stuff?" The following items tell the practical half of the story.

- ✔ Audio CDs play 16-bit, 44 kHz stereo sound. Hence, this particular combination of settings is called *CD-quality sound*.

- ✔ All machines with internal CD-ROMs can play music CDs at the highest quality, but few can record it. In fact, only the AV Macs, Power Macs, Performa 6100 series, and the PowerBook 500 series can presently record 16-bit, 44 kHz stereo sound.

- ✔ The Quadra 630 and the other junior AV Macs record 8-bit, 22 kHz stereo sound. Nearly all the other Macs are limited to 8-bit, 22 kHz mono recording.

- ✔ In other words, if you're working on anything but an AV Mac, Power Mac, Performa 6100 series, or PowerBook 500 series, you'll have to accept 8-bit, 22 kHz sound. Feel free to skip to the next section.

Even if you own one of the better sound machines, you'll want to be selective with your use of high-end sound. CD-quality sound is overkill except when you're recording stereo music. Here are some recommendations:

- ✔ 8-bit, 22 kHz sound is usually good enough for recording voice sounds. You'll generally want to use these settings when recording with a mike.

- ✔ If the sound includes voice and music mixed together, or if you simply want higher quality voices, you can bump the sound up to 16-bit, 22 kHz.

- There's no sense in pairing 8-bit resolution with a 44 kHz sampling rate. Because 8-bit provides so few volumes to choose from, increasing the sampling rate often has the effect of simply repeating the same blips that you get with the lower sampling rate. 16-bit, 22 kHz sound takes up the same amount of room on disk as 8-bit, 44 kHz sound, but it sounds much better.

- Only when recording music directly from a CD should you bother with 16-bit, 44 kHz. Your recording will sound every bit as good as the CD.

For the record, 16-bit sound consumes exactly twice as much disk space as 8-bit; 44 kHz takes up twice as much as 22 kHz; and stereo takes up twice as much as mono. Just so you know what you're in for, I've prepared Table 13-1, which tells you how much disk space a minute of sound takes up at each setting.

Table 13-1	How Your Sound Measures Up on Disk		
Channels	Resolution	Sampling Rate	Size of One-Minute File
Mono	8-bit	22 kHz	1.3MB
Stereo	8-bit	22 kHz	2.5MB
Mono	16-bit	22 kHz	2.5MB
Stereo	16-bit	22 kHz	5.0MB
Mono	16-bit	44 kHz	5.0MB
Stereo	16-bit	44 kHz	10.1MB

Recording in Style

In many respects, recording a sound in SoundEdit 16 is just like recording an alert sound in the Sound control panel. You click on a Record button to start recording, and you click on Stop to stop. But with resolution, sampling rate, and the many other considerations you have to worry about, you do have to prepare a little differently, as explained in the following sections.

Recording monophonic stuff

SoundEdit gets a little persnickety when recording stereo sound, so I'll start things off by explaining how to record mono sounds.

Chapter 13: Editing Sounds Like a Pro

1. **Create a new file.**

   SoundEdit does this automatically when you start the program, but if you want to record a second sound or if you accidentally closed the first window, choose File⇨New or press ⌘-N.

2. **Choose Sound⇨Recording Options and select a source.**

   The Recording Options command brings up the Input Source dialog box, as shown back in Figure 12-3. Select the desired source for your recording, turn on the Playthrough check box if you want to hear the sound as you record it (leave the option off when recording from a mike), and click on OK to move on.

3. **Choose Sound⇨Sound Format and select a sampling rate and resolution.**

   Choosing the Sound Format command or pressing ⌘-I displays the dialog box shown in Figure 13-2. Select the desired sampling rate from the Rate pop-up menu. As you can see in the figure, SoundEdit offers a lot of rates, but only the few marked with the microphone icon are supported by your computer. Select either 22.050 kHz or 44.100 kHz.

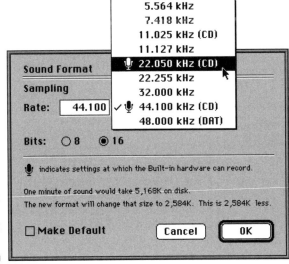

Figure 13-2: Select one of the options that has a mike icon next to it.

Select the desired Bits radio button — for 8-bit or 16-bit sound — and press Return to exit the dialog box.

4. **Get your source ready.**

   If you're recording from a mike, pick it up. If you want to record a CD, start it playing with the CD Remote or AppleCD Audio Player program. Be sure to set the volume on the CD player to its absolutely highest setting.

5. **Inside SoundEdit, click on the input level test button (labeled in Figure 13-3) and test the levels.**

   If you're using a mike, say a few words into it. Otherwise, just observe. A green bar jumps around inside the input level meter to show the loudness of the source, whether it's your voice or the CD. If some red appears occasionally on the right side of the meter, the source volume is too high. Pull the mike away from your face slightly or reduce the volume inside the CD Remote or AppleCD Audio Player program.

   Much to its detriment, SoundEdit offers no levels control, so you have to change the volume of the source directly. It's inconvenient — in fact, this is probably SoundEdit's number-one flaw — but that's just the way it is.

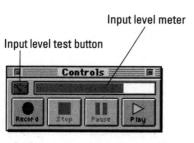

Figure 13-3: Set your sound level so that the green bar in the input level meter jumps as far to the right as possible without turning red.

6. **When you're ready to record, click on the Record button.**

   Or press ⌘-R.

7. **Click on Stop when you're done.**

   Or press ⌘-R again. SoundEdit takes a few moments to calculate the new sound and then displays it inside the window, as shown in Figure 13-4.

Chapter 13: Editing Sounds Like a Pro   181

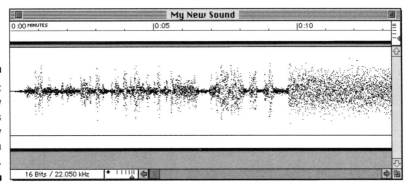

Figure 13-4: The new sound looks like a spray of random pixels.

8. **Save the sound to disk.**

    Choose File⇨Save or press ⌘-S. Enter a name for the new sound and select a destination on disk.

You can play your newly recorded sound by clicking on the Play button or by simply pressing the spacebar.

Reading the sound wave

After you record a sound, the SoundEdit window probably looks like somebody took a can of spray paint to it. But the window actually contains a precise graph of your sound that starts on the far left side of the window and continues off to the right. It just looks like a bunch of random dots because the graph is tightly packed together.

I'll show you what I mean. By dragging the slider triangle that's just to the left of the horizontal scroll bar — labeled in Figure 13-5 — you can zoom in and out on your sound graph. Drag to the left to zoom in; drag to the right to zoom out.

In Figure 13-5, I've zoomed in quite a bit. The entire length of sound in the window now takes up about one-tenth of a second. Now you can see the graph for what it really is — a continuous horizontal line that wiggles up and down across the center of the window. This, my friend, is the *sound wave*.

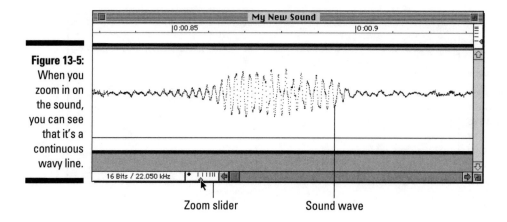

Figure 13-5:
When you zoom in on the sound, you can see that it's a continuous wavy line.

- Zoom slider
- Sound wave

 ✔ When the sound wave is flat, there is no sound — in other words, a flat portion of a wave indicates silence.

 ✔ The higher and lower the sound wave wiggles, the louder the sound. In Figure 13-5, for example, the sound starts soft, gets loud, and then softens again. In case you're curious, that loud lump is the vowel *a* spoken at the end of a word in a voice recording.

 ✔ The pace at which the line wiggles indicates the pitch of the sound. High-pitched sounds wiggle — or more correctly, *vibrate* — very quickly. Low-pitched sounds vibrate slowly. The lump in Figure 13-5 is a tenor male voice.

For the sake of comparison, Figure 13-6 shows the very *a* from Figure 13-5 electronically lowered half an octave. See how the sound wave vibrates more slowly? The vowel sound that took up half the window in Figure 13-5 spreads across the entire window in Figure 13-6.

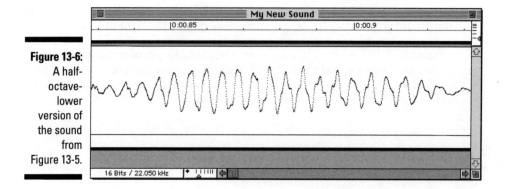

Figure 13-6:
A half-octave-lower version of the sound from Figure 13-5.

Recording two channels at a time

Recording stereo sound in SoundEdit 16 involves a few more preparatory steps as well as a couple of finishing touches. The following steps tell how it's done.

You can perform these steps only if your Mac supports stereo recording and you're recording from a stereo source, such as a CD. Consult the "Sound In" columns in the infamous Tables 1-1 and 1-2 to find out whether your machine can handle these steps.

1. **Create a new file.**

    You always have to do this. Got to have an empty receptacle for your sound, don't you know.

2. **Choose Sound⇨Add Track or press ⌘-T.**

    This command creates a new track inside your new file. Tracks hold the channels in SoundEdit 16. You have to have two tracks to hold the stereo sound: one track for the left channel and one for the right.

3. **Check the Recording Options and Sound Format commands.**

    Make sure that you're happy with the source, resolution, and sampling rate settings. See Steps 2 and 3 of the "Recording monophonic stuff" section earlier in this chapter if you forget how these work.

4. **Choose Edit⇨Select All or press ⌘-A.**

    After you create the second track in Step 2, SoundEdit activates the new track and deactivates the top track. Unfortunately, regardless of how many tracks are available, SoundEdit records sound to a track only if it is active. This means that you have to activate both the top and bottom tracks to get stereo sound. The Select All command does this.

5. **Prime your source and test the levels.**

    See Steps 4 and 5 of the "Recording monophonic stuff" section for full descriptions.

6. **Click on the Record button to start the recording, and click on Stop when you're finished.**

    You end up with two tracks of random dots (which you, of course, keenly recognize as tightly packed sound waves).

    The problem is, SoundEdit doesn't know which track is which. It thinks that it's supposed to play both tracks to both speakers at the same time. Bad, program, bad. You have to set it right.

7. **Choose View⇨Display Options.**

    This command brings up the dialog box shown in Figure 13-7.

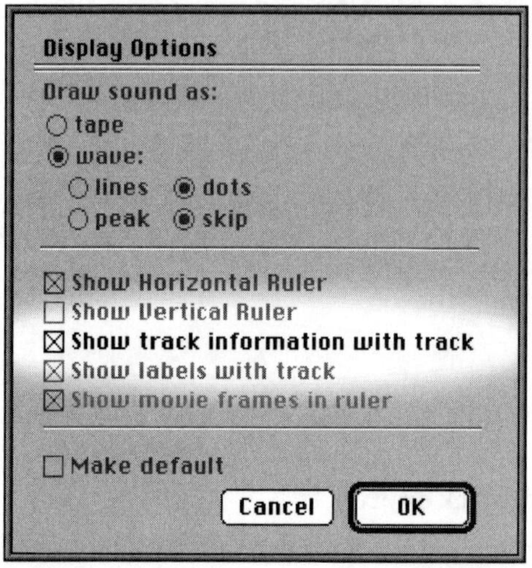

Figure 13-7: Select this check box so that you can specify which track plays through which speaker.

Display Options

Draw sound as:
○ tape
● wave:
  ○ lines ● dots
  ○ peak   ● skip

☒ Show Horizontal Ruler
☐ Show Vertical Ruler
☒ **Show track information with track**
☒ Show labels with track
☒ Show movie frames in ruler

☐ Make default

[Cancel] [OK]

8. **Select the Show Track Information with Track check box.**

   It's the third check box down — the one that's spotlighted in the figure. This check box displays options that let you associate each track with a left or right channel. After you select it, press Return to get out of the Display Options dialog box.

   A horizontal information bar appears above each track, as shown in Figure 13-8. The most important options are the channel pop-up menu, which controls the speaker that each track plays through, and the track name option box, which lets you name the track.

9. **For each track, choose the proper speaker icon from the channel pop-up menu.**

   The current version of SoundEdit 16 — Version 1.0.1 — automatically records the right channel into the top track and the left channel into the bottom track. But to ensure that you hear the sound played back properly, you have to select the appropriate speaker icons. So I chose the right speaker icon from the top pop-up menu, as you can see in Figure 13-8, and the left speaker icon from the bottom pop-up menu.

10. **Name each track according to the channel that it represents.**

    Select the contents of the top track name option box and enter **Right Channel.** Then press Tab and name the bottom track **Left Channel.**

Chapter 13: Editing Sounds Like a Pro   185

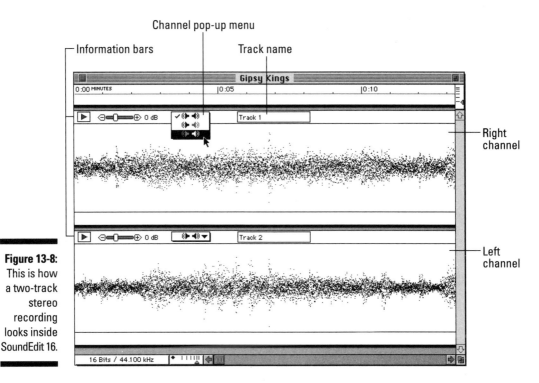

Figure 13-8: This is how a two-track stereo recording looks inside SoundEdit 16.

11. Shift-click on the Play button to play both tracks simultaneously.

Or just press Shift-spacebar. The top track plays through the right speaker and the bottom track plays through the left, creating true stereo sound.

12. Save the sound file to disk.

Just choose File⇨Save or press ⌘-S.

It is possible to record stereo sound without going through all these steps — theoretically, that is. If no track is active, SoundEdit 16 automatically creates two channels for stereo recording. The best way to make sure that no track is active is to make sure that there is no track. After creating a new file, choose Sound⇨Delete Track or press ⌘-D. Then record away. As long as your Mac supports stereo recording, SoundEdit records two tracks of stereo sound.

The problem with this method is that SoundEdit records in stereo even if your source is mono. If you're recording your voice with a monophonic PlainTalk mike, for example, SoundEdit still goes ahead and records the single channel twice, which wastes valuable disk space. Unless you know for certain that your source is stereo — as with most music recordings made in the last 20 years — record a single track only.

It's also worth noting that SoundEdit 16 1.0.1 switches the left and right channels when it automatically records stereo sound. Quite a bug! To remedy the problem, you need to select different speaker icons and rename the tracks as described in Steps 9 and 10 above.

In other words, even though the 12-step process I outlined may seem long and tedious, it's the best way to go.

Wreaking Havoc on Your Sounds

Now that you've recorded some source material, it's high time you started bending and shaping it to meet your peculiar requirements. Sound editing is nothing new — I myself used to labor in the back of a college radio station splicing reel-to-reel tape and mixing in music on a console as large as a dining table — but SoundEdit and programs like it bring a new level of flexibility and accuracy. You can edit at any point without any audible sign of the edit ever having taken place (provided that you're careful enough). And there's no chance of slicing your finger with a razor blade. It's just another of the miraculous wonders that come with living in a digital world.

Here are just a few ways you can edit sounds in SoundEdit 16:

- Select a section of the sound by dragging across it. The selected sound wave becomes highlighted, just like text in a word processor.
- To select a portion of both tracks in a stereo recording, click at the beginning of the area you want to select in one track and then Shift-click at the end of the area you want to select in the other track.
- Click on the Play button or press the spacebar to play the selected portion of the sound.
- Few of us can read a sound wave just by looking at it. So after you select an area and play it, you may want to take a moment and label it for future reference. To do this, choose Edit⇨Make Label (or press ⌘-L). Then enter your label name and press Return. The label appears below the selected sound, as shown in Figure 13-9.

Chapter 13: Editing Sounds Like a Pro   187

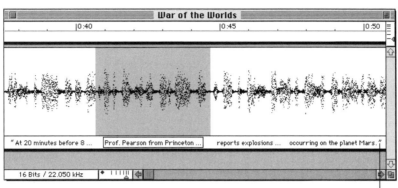

Figure 13-9: A labeled version of the classic 1938 radio broadcast of "The War of the Worlds."

Label bar

- After you label a selection, you can easily reselect the area simply by clicking on its name in the label bar.

- To delete a selected area of sound, just press the Delete key.

- Be sure to play the selection before deleting it, listening with special attention to the beginning and end to make sure that you haven't selected too much sound or too little. After pressing Delete, select the area around the deleted sound and play it, too, so that you can preview any glitches that may be created by your edit. If it doesn't sound just right, choose Edit⇨Undo or press ⌘-Z to reinstate the deleted sound. Then reselect the sound and try again.

- If you're having problems making an edit sound right, magnify the sound wave by dragging the zoom slider. You can then take a closer look at the sound and gain more exacting control over your selection.

- If you want to switch around the order of some recorded dialog, first select the sound you want to reposition and remove it by choosing Edit⇨Cut or pressing ⌘-X. Determine the exact point where you want to insert the sound by selecting and playing. Then click at that point to set the insertion marker. Finally, paste the sound into place by choosing Edit⇨Paste or pressing ⌘-V.

- To apply a special effect to some sound, select it and choose a command from the Effects menu. You can add echoes, make the sound reverberate as if it were recorded in a stadium, raise or lower the pitch, fade it in or out, and so on. You can even play it backwards, great for deciphering those "Paul is dead" messages on your old Beatles CDs.

- To mix sounds together, you have to first to place them in different tracks. Suppose that you want to add some music to a voice recording. Click in the empty area below the last track to deselect all sounds. Then record the music that you want to mix. SoundEdit automatically creates one or two new tracks to hold the music, depending on whether your Mac records in mono or stereo. Then press Shift-spacebar to play voice and music together.

- Any time your sound file contains multiple tracks, you can edit each track independently of the others. You can even offset one track with respect to the others by Option-dragging it. This feature is especially useful when you want the music to begin at a specific point or want one voice to fade in just as another is fading out.

Messing about with the System's Innards

Another great use for SoundEdit (and other sound programs) is to refine sounds that you've recorded inside other programs. You can even open sounds from inside the System file — while the System is running, no less. Suppose that you recorded a sound using your PowerBook's built-in mike, and you can hear where you clicked the trackball button to stop recording the sound. No problem. You can easily delete the click inside SoundEdit.

Lifting a sound right out of the System

The steps that you are about to read walk you through the process of opening a sound from inside the System, refining it, and saving it again. Editing anything from the System file is tricky work because the System is such an integral part of your Mac. Though there's very little chance that anything can go wrong, it always pays to be careful and follow the steps exactly as I've laid them out:

1. **Choose File➪Open**

    Or press ⌘-O.

2. **Inside the Open dialog box, select the Resource Files option from the Show pop-up menu.**

    Figure 13-10 shows me doing just that. This option enables you to open *sound resources* — which are little bits of audio code — from inside programs.

Chapter 13: Editing Sounds Like a Pro

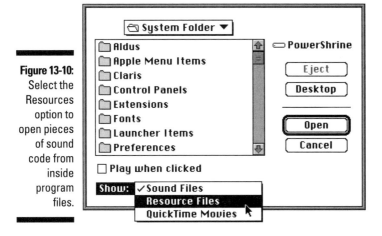

Figure 13-10: Select the Resources option to open pieces of sound code from inside program files.

3. **Locate the System file inside the System Folder.**

   When you find it, double-click on it to open it. The System Resources window appears, listing every sound resource found inside your System file, much as in Figure 13-11.

Figure 13-11: The System sounds ready for editing.

4. Select the Preview Play Resource When Selected check box.

In English, this option means that when you click on a sound name, SoundEdit will play it.

5. After you select the option you want to edit, click on the Edit button or press Return.

Or you can just double-click on the sound. This step opens the sound inside a new editing window.

6. Edit the sound as desired.

Some sounds are weird and may not be altogether editable. You can't even open Simple Beep, for example, because it isn't a recorded sound. Others are downright idiosyncratic. Just to be sure, play the sound after you open it. If it sounds different than it did when you clicked on it in the System Resources window, leave the sound unmolested and close the file.

7. After you're done, save the sound.

You can do this in two ways. If you want to replace the sound in the System file with the edited sound, just choose File⇨Save (or press ⌘-S) and the close the sound file. That's it, you're done. You can skip the rest of the steps.

However, if you want to retain the unedited sound and save the new sound with a different name, choose File⇨Save As to display the Save dialog box, shown in Figure 13-12. Then keep reading.

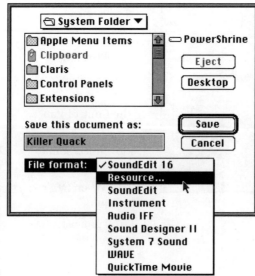

Figure 13-12: Enter the name and then select the Resource option.

Chapter 13: Editing Sounds Like a Pro

8. **Enter the name for your new sound in the option box.**

   In the figure, for example, I entered *Killer Quack*.

9. **Select the Resource option from the File Format pop-up menu.**

   This very act is dramatized in Figure 13-12. Immediately thereafter, another dialog box appears, asking you in which file you want to save the resource.

10. **Select the System file and click on the Save button.**

    SoundEdit saves the sound resource inside the System file. The new sound appears inside System Resources window.

Pilfering sounds from other programs

Many programs in addition to the System file contain special sound resources. SoundEdit lets you open and edit resources from inside Fetch, QuarkXPress, HyperCard, FreeHand, ResEdit, and any number of other programs. You can even open SoundEdit 16 itself to discover two sounds, a bark and the ding of a small bell.

If you like one of these sounds, you can copy it and paste it into the System file. In fact, these next steps explain how to usurp one of my all-time favorite sounds, which hides inside Version 8.0.3 of the Sound control panel. It's totally great.

1. **Press ⌘-O.**

   Or choose File⇨Open.

2. **Select the Resource Files option from the Show pop-up menu.**

   This step is always a must if you want to open a sound resource from inside a program.

3. **Locate the Sound control panel inside the Control Panels folder in the System Folder.**

   Then double-click on it to open it. A window titled Sound Resources appears. It lists just one sound, which has no name.

4. **Make sure that the Preview Play Resource When Selected check box is selected and then click on the untitled sound.**

   To say that it sounds like a beleaguered troll groaning "Waauuuoogh!" would be nothing more than a rough approximation of this unique audio experience.

5. **Copy the selected sound.**

   Choose Edit➪Copy or press ⌘-C.

6. **Click on the System Resources window to bring it to front.**

   I'm assuming that the System file is open from the previous set of steps. If not, open it by performing Steps 1 through 3 of the preceding section.

7. **Paste the copied sound.**

   You do this by choosing Edit➪Paste or pressing ⌘-V. The new sound is titled *Untitled Resource* with a number, which is an unacceptable predicament that the next step seeks to remedy.

8. **Click on the Info button at the top of the System Resources window.**

   Figure 13-11 sports this button if you'd like to check it out. The button brings up a dialog box that lets you rename the sound.

9. **Enter the name of your choice into the Name option box.**

   Be creative. This is a most excellent sound. Then click on the OK button or press Return.

Now you have this splendid example of the Mac's awesome audio prowess available to you as an alert sound for all time. Oh happy day.

But don't stop there. Feel free to prowl about and inspect the contents of every program, control panel, and system extension on your hard disk. Multimedia CDs also contain lots of great sounds. I mean, honestly, does life get any more fun than this?

Chapter 14
Conversing with Your Computer

In This Chapter
- ▶ Teaching your computer to speak
- ▶ Installing Speech Manager and MacinTalk Pro
- ▶ Converting text to talk in SimpleText
- ▶ Using the high-quality voices of Agnes, Bruce, and Victoria
- ▶ Getting acquainted with the other voices
- ▶ Using the singing voices
- ▶ Hearing the time and error messages with SmartVoice
- ▶ Playing copied sounds with QuicKeys

*O*ne of the more recent rages in multimedia computing is voice recognition. You speak to your computer, and it willingly obeys your every instruction, just like a high-priced machine ought to. No more searching through menus for lost commands; no more two-handed keyboard equivalents that would challenge the most seasoned Twister-playing contortionist; no more aching wrists from repeating the same darn mouse movement 100 times in a row. You just wag your tongue, and things start to leap around on the screen.

Sounds dreamy, huh? The only problem is, voice recognition is still pretty rough. You can *theoretically* train a handful of Macs to respond to voice commands by installing special software called PlainTalk (just like the tea-bag-shaped mike I discussed in Chapter 12). But the software is difficult to use, it's awful at interpreting accents, and it consumes a whopping 2.5MB of RAM space, greatly impairing your ability to get work done in other programs unless your Mac's memory supply is well up in the double digits. And speech recognition works only on machines that can record 16-bit, 44 kHz sound — that is, the AV Macs, Power Macs, Performa 6100 series, and PowerBook 500 series. No offense, mind you, but to a Mac that's limited to the more common 8-bit, 22 kHz sound, you sound like you're talking with your mouth full of marbles.

But although your Mac may be a cruddy listener, it's a surprisingly gifted speaker. Included with System 7.5 is software that allows your computer to say just about anything that you care to type on-screen. This software can read regular English with very few mistakes and in a wide variety of voices. It even inflects downward at the end of a sentence or upward when it comes across a question mark. And, unlike the digital sound files I discussed in Chapters 12 and 13, the text files that your computer reads take up almost no space on disk.

No two ways about it: Synthesized speech is one of your Mac's most amazing and least publicized multimedia capabilities. Once you hear your computer talk, you realize that it won't be long until you and it begin to engage in some really deep and meaningful conversations. You know, like Hal and his pesky human sidekicks in *2001: A Space Odyssey*. I say, let the bonding begin.

How to Install Your Computer's Vocal Cords

Though you may very well have System 7.5 running on your machine, the chances of your having already installed the PlainTalk voice recognition and speech software is roughly the same as that of your having been born with a prehensile tail. The folks over at Apple did such a splendid job of hiding PlainTalk that even the most curious users will never find it. I guess they suspected that the voice recognition half of the software wasn't liable to be a rousing success.

Whatever Apple's reasoning, I thought that I'd take a brief moment to explain how to locate and install the speech half of PlainTalk:

1. **Insert your original System 7.5 CD.**

    If you don't have System 7.5 on a CD, you may be able to find a floppy disk that's labeled *PlainTalk*. If you own an AV Mac, the PlainTalk installer is tucked away on your hard drive (unless you threw it away). In any case, stick whatever you think is your best bet in the CD-ROM or floppy disk drive and try out the next couple of steps.

2. **Choose File⇨Find at the Finder desktop (or press ⌘-F).**

    The Find File dialog box appears.

3. **Enter *PlainTalk* and press Return.**

    If a message appears telling you that no items were found, you can consider upgrading to System 7.5. At about $100, it's well worth the price. Or you can download the PlainTalk software from an on-line service such as CompuServe. If you don't like either of those suggestions, you can purchase SmartVoice, a $50 piece of software from Quality Computers,

Chapter 14: Conversing with Your Computer

800-777-3642. The program includes PlainTalk for no extra charge. It also happens to be a valuable piece of software in its own right, as I discuss in the "Some Ways to Put Speech to Practical Use" section later in this chapter.

If the Find command locates a PlainTalk file or two, look for the PlainTalk Installer program. Under System 7.1 or earlier, you may have to press ⌘-G a few times before you locate the Installer file. Under System 7.5, it should appear in the Items Found list.

4. Double-click on the PlainTalk Installer icon to start the program.

A window appears welcoming you to the Speech Installer. Press Return to move on.

5. Select Custom Install from the pop-up menu in the upper-left corner of the Install Speech dialog box.

You see the options shown in Figure 14-1.

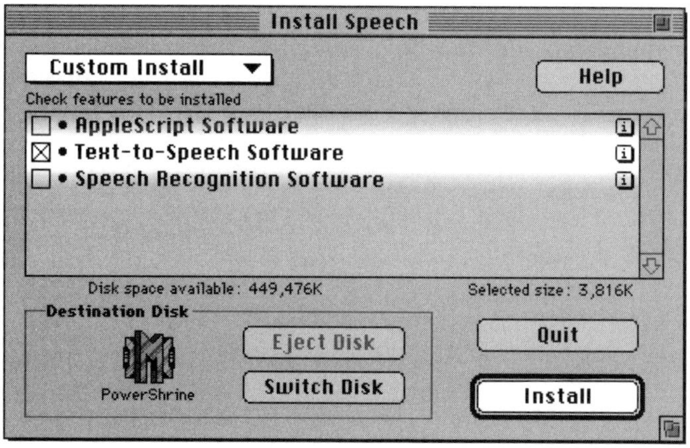

Figure 14-1: Check the Text-to-Speech Software option to endow your computer with instant communication skills.

6. Select the Text-to-Speech Software check box.

Leave the other two check boxes turned off, as in the figure.

7. Click on the Install button.

That's all there is to it. After a few minutes of waiting for the software to install, the installation program asks you to restart your machine. Click on the Restart button to give your permission.

For the record, you just finished installing a variety of files, none of which is named PlainTalk. You installed two system extensions, Speech Manager and MacinTalk Pro, as well as a folder full of synthesized voices. Altogether, this stuff takes up 700K of space in RAM, less than a third as much as the PlainTalk voice recognition software, but quite a bit nonetheless. If you decide later that you want to free up the RAM, remove Speech Manager from the Extensions folder inside the System Folder and restart your computer (by choosing Special⇨Restart).

MacinTalk Pro requires a Macintosh LC or better — which includes just about every machine made in the last four years. If you own one of the incompatible machines — Plus, SE, Classic, or PowerBook 100 — you can run a less powerful speech synthesizer called MacinTalk 2. Though not included with System 7.5, MacinTalk 2 ships with SmartVoice.

Computer's First Words

To make your computer talk, you need a speech-compatible piece of software, such as Apple's SimpleText. Designed as a bare-bones word processor, SimpleText's primary purpose is to let you check out those ReadMe files that come with just about every piece of software made these days. You know, the files that contain late-breaking news and instructions that didn't make it into the printed documentation.

Well, anyway, the mild-mannered SimpleText offers a second, more amazing capability that virtually no one knows about. After your computer is properly armed with its wondrous speech capabilities, SimpleText can turn written text into sound, as explained in the following steps.

SimpleText is the successor to TeachText, Apple's old, bare-bones word processor. The two programs are very similar except that TeachText doesn't let you convert speech to text. You need the not-so-simple SimpleText to accomplish this deed.

1. **Start the SimpleText program.**

    After you find SimpleText on your hard drive — you may have to use File⇨Find (⌘-F) to locate the program — double-click on it to start it up. After a few seconds, a blank document appears on-screen.

2. **Enter some text that you want your computer to say.**

    I might suggest "Greetings, benign master. I am your eager electronic slave, ready and willing to do your bidding." There is actually a point to this silly sentence, so go ahead and enter it.

3. Choose a style of synthesized voice from the Sound⇨Voice submenu.

You can choose from 22 options, all shown in Figure 14-2.

Figure 14-2: Choose your favorite voice from this submenu.

4. Choose Sound⇨Speak All.

Or press ⌘-H. Your Mac miraculously pronounces the words. Too bad you can't make it bow and scrape while it's at it.

Assuming that you spelled everything correctly, the computer's pronunciation is amazing. Its only slip-up — depending on which voice you selected — may be the word *benign*, which the computer may say with a short *i* as in *begin*. I explain this mistake and why it occurs with some voices and not with others in the next section.

Some voices are smarter than others

Most of the voices in the Sound⇨Voices submenu are small sound files that merely change the pitch and general tone of the voice. The intonation and pronunciation are determined by MacinTalk Pro.

Three voices, however, are smarter. Agnes, Bruce, and Victoria take up much more room on disk — about 800K apiece versus about 10K for the other voices — but they are much smarter as well. Each of these smart voices, for example, knows how to properly say the word *benign*.

Want a really good demonstration? All right, enter the following text, just as it's written:

> Having misplaced his glasses, Dr. Brian O'Brian asked his assistant, "I cannot read this report. Will you read it?" The report documented an acute sclerotic liver condition. The liver in question belonged to a Mrs. Myrtle McDermott from Maple Dr.

Now choose any other voice besides Agnes, Bruce, or Victoria, and press ⌘-H to ask your Mac to speak the text. Though the dumb voice does pretty well — especially compared with non-Macintosh speech synthesizers — it makes five obvious mistakes:

- It says *Brian* right, but pronounces *O'Brian* as *O-Bree-an*.
- The voice says the second *read* as *red*.
- Though it manages to utter *acute sclerotic liver* without any problem — I think most humans might stumble on that one — it says the second *liver* with a long *i*, as in *live-er*. Weird.
- The voice doesn't recognize the name *McDermott*, so it says *M-C-Dermott*, as if Myrtle were a rapper.
- The patient seems to live at a place called *Maple D-R*. Though the voice can pronounce *Dr.* as *Doctor*, it doesn't know what to do with the initials when they fall at the end of a sentence.

Now choose Agnes, Bruce, or Victoria and try again. *O'Brian, read, liver*, and *drive* all come through with flying colors. *McDermott* is still something of a problem, but at least the voice says *M'Dermott* instead of *M-C-Dermott*.

Now, I don't mean to imply that the smart voices are perfect. You can just as easily confuse them as the other voices. If you do come across a word or two that the voice can't pronounce, spell it out phonetically. For example, any voice can pronounce the text if you write it out like this (with changes in bold):

> Having misplaced his glasses, Dr. Brian **O Brian** asked his assistant, "I cannot read this report. Will you **reed** it?" The report documented an acute sclerotic liver condition. The **livver** in question belonged to a Mrs. Myrtle **Mick Dermott** from Maple **Drive**.

In fact, if you're short on disk space, you may want to toss Agnes, Bruce, and Victoria in the trash. They are indeed smarter, but it doesn't take much work to make the dumber voices speak correctly.

Meet the cast

So much for Agnes, Bruce, and Victoria, the smart voices. What about the dumb voices? Because there are so many of them and some of them are so unusual, I thought I'd give you a brief rundown on these unique personalities, along with some sample phrases to try out:

- **Albert:** This guy sounds like he's on his last legs. Try pairing him with the sentence "Gosh, I sure could use a nap."

- **Bad News:** This is one of the five singing voices. Type "Your report is over due way over due time to invent an excuse a good excuse," with no punctuation except a period at the end. (The dumb voices can't pronounce *overdue* properly, so you have to make it two separate words.)

  Wait, late-breaking news: My editor tells me that the kid-tested silly lyrics for this song are, "Pray for the dead, and the dead will pray for you. This is because they have nothing else to do." You choose.

- **Bahh:** It's the electronic Scrooge. Try "Forget it, Tiny Tim, there'll be no Christmas duck for you."

- **Bells:** The second singing voice rings like the bells of Big Ben.

- **Boing:** This voice plays in little bounces. I recommend "You kids will love this new sensational toy."

- **Bubbles:** This voice seems to be underwater, especially when it says, "Excuse me, have you seen my snorkel?"

- **Cellos:** This is the third singing voice, perfect for 26-syllable phrases such as, "Have you seen my rubber ball where'd it go down the hall if you see my rubber ball please give it back to me." Again, avoid all punctuation except the final period.

- **Deranged:** Definitely a strange character. It might say something like "I promise, if you let me out of this straitjacket, I'll be good."

- **Fred, Kathy, and Ralph:** Normal, well-adjusted male and female voices. How dull.

- **Good News:** Yes, it's the fourth singing voice. This one is designed for uninterrupted 22-syllable phrases such as "Hey where is my wallet I'd swore I brought it please loan me ten dollars and I'll pay you soon."

- **Hysterical:** I can't tell whether this character is hilariously happy or overly distraught. The voice chortles or sobs after every syllable. "Good gravy, I never saw such a sight" is a statement that could go either way.

- **Junior and Princess:** You can use the voices of two little kids: Junior, the boy, and Princess, the girl. They say things like "I want a bike" and "Why do I have to?" quite well.

- **Pipe Organ:** This is the last singing voice and the one with the longest song — 37 syllables. You can make it say, "The creature rose from the brackish lake I knew right then I'd made a mistake I ran for it but it ran too and followed me into the burger palace" if you can't come up with something more clever.

- **Trinoids:** This one gives you three voices talking in a continuous monotone. It's just the thing for statements such as "Take us to your leader or we'll fry you with our Clotvorian trismebulators." I love how these voices aren't the least bit phased by nonsense words.

- **Whisper:** This voice whispers, as in "Let go of my trachea."

- **Zarvox:** I believe this fellow is the king of the Trinoids, which is why he sounds right at home saying, "Get back here, you Trinoids, and finish your homework."

Speaking tips

As you get acquainted with the whole MacinTalk Pro gang, you'll want to keep the following facts in mind:

- None of the voices can exclaim, so there's no audible difference between a period and an exclamation point. The question mark is the only punctuation that has a different effect on inflection than a period.

- If you just want to listen to a few words, select the words and choose Sound⇨Speak Selection or press ⌘-H.

- To make the computer shut its trap, choose Sound⇨Stop Speaking or press ⌘-period.

- The musical voices start over every time they reach any punctuation, whether it's a period, comma, or question mark. Also, these voices don't inflect up on questions. So for the best results, don't use punctuation at all. Instead, enter your text in phrases, with each phrase on a separate line to make it visually distinguishable from the others.

Some Ways to Put Speech to Practical Use

Okay, so playing around with a bunch of simulated voices is a great way to waste the day, but the novelty wears off pretty fast. Is there any practical reason to own a talking computer?

Well, that depends. Because most programs don't offer special support for speech functions, your Mac is likely to spend most of its time silent. Unless, that is, you're willing to invest in some rather specialized software. For $50, Quality Computer's SmartVoice makes your Mac speak up under a variety of circumstances, many of which are useful indeed.

Getting your computer to tell you every little thing

The SmartVoice package includes seven different speaking programs. The following list explains these programs in order of practicality:

- ClockTalk makes your Mac tell you the time on the hour, every half hour, or every 15 minutes. It can even sneak up on you and share the time randomly. Or you can set things up so that you just press some keys to hear the time. Being constantly on the verge of missing the Fed Ex drop-off deadline myself, I find this feature very helpful.

- ExcuseMe is a system extension that reads the contents of alert boxes. If your printer is out of paper or you don't have enough memory to start another program, you hear about it as well as see the message on-screen. (This function works with so-called "notification" messages only. Because many messages don't fall into this camp, only a few get read by ExcuseMe. Quality Computers is working on an update that will handle more messages.)

- SayIt will speak selected text in just about any program. With SayIt running in the background, you can select some text in Microsoft Word, for example, and press a series of keys to make your Mac say the text aloud. This feature is great for proofreading text — though *you* may miss mistakes as you read, your Mac won't. In fact, if your Mac gets it right, the text must be perfect.

- Greetings shares a welcoming message and tells you the date and time every time you fire up your computer.

- CalcTalk is a talking calculator. Though it may not be the kind of program you use on a daily basis, it provides a small glimpse of what the future might be like for talking programs.

- SpeechLab lets you fool around with voices by modifying the pitch, speed, and modulation (which is the variation in inflection). You can even save a message spoken by Agnes, Bruce, or Victoria to disk and share it with someone whose Mac isn't blessed with speech.

- Eliza is an artificial intelligence program that emulates a psychologist. It asks you a question, you answer it, it responds with a comment or question, and so on. Most of the program's reactions are absolute non sequiturs, but it's mildly interesting for a simulated shrink.

Getting a rise out of a few keys

Another program that can make the Mac talk is the $140 QuicKeys 3 from CE Software, 515-221-1801. QuicKeys lets you define special shortcuts to launch programs, choose commands, and so on. You can also assign a shortcut that makes the Mac talk.

Inside QuicKeys, choose Define⇨Extensions⇨System Tools⇨Speak Ease — as demonstrated in Figure 14-3 — to create a speech shortcut. After selecting the voice you want your computer to use, you can enter the text you want it to say. Or you can set up a shortcut that speaks aloud any text that's in the Clipboard, which is a more useful feature. It enables you to select some text inside any program, copy it by choosing Edit⇨Copy, and then press a keyboard shortcut to hear the sound.

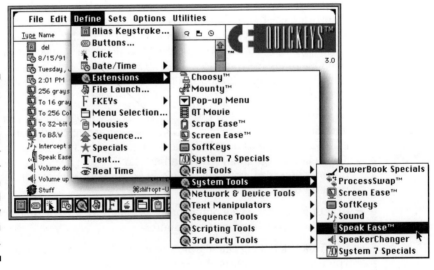

Figure 14-3: With QuicKeys, you can make your computer talk inside any old program by pushing a few keys.

Many programs have independent Clipboards that they don't share with the system until you switch programs. For example, after copying text in Microsoft Word, you might have to switch to Photoshop before you can play the text using your QuicKeys shortcut.

I'm So Glad You've Had This Time Together

I don't know about you, but after experimenting with all these different ways to speak with my computer, I feel — I don't know — kind of closer to it. I mean, it's not like I'm tempted to invite it over for dinner or anything, but I think that we've developed a little bit of sympathy for one another. Perhaps it will behave a little better in the future, and perhaps I'll be less likely to beat it with a mallet the next time it refuses to start up. We've opened up lines of communication, you know. I hope — oh, gosh I'm sorry, I'm starting to get all weepy here — I *sincerely* hope that you have as well. Best of luck with your new-found friend.

Part IV
Hollywood in a Box

In this part...

When it comes to sound technology, the PC is behind the Mac. But in the area of moving video, the PC is dreadfully behind. Ever since the demise of the Commodore Amiga, the Mac has taken over as the personal computer of choice in professional TV news departments and video editing studios. Much of what you see on TV has passed through a souped-up Mac.

You may not be able to turn your Mac into a state-of-the-art video editing powerhouse — not unless you have $20,000 to $50,000 burning a hole in your pocket — but you can play videos on-screen and edit them in a program such as Premiere. And if you have the right kind of Mac — that is, an AV or junior AV model — you can even watch TV on your monitor and record stuff from videotape onto disk. Full-motion video is the most exciting thing happening on personal computers today, and the Mac is the computer that's leading the way.

Chapter 15
TV Meets Monitor

In This Chapter
- Playing TV on your computer — and why it's such a gas
- Hooking up a coaxial cable to your junior AV
- Using the Apple Video Player
- Removing inactive and unwanted channels
- Naming channels by network or call letters
- Locking channels and assigning a password
- Automatically watching your favorite programs
- Displaying closed captioning
- Capturing a still frame from a video
- Watching TV on an AV machine
- Figuring out what's wrong if you can't see video or hear sound

You, yes *you*, may be able to watch television on your computer screen. All you need is an AV Mac, a junior AV model, or some other Mac with a special video board installed (as explained in the "Can You Add AV to Your Old Mac?" section of Chapter 5). Why miss out on your favorite TV show, the latest breaking news, or that new Pampers commercial you've been so interested in seeing when it could be right there, nestled amongst the five zillion others things brewing on your monitor?

Now, right away, some of you skeptical types are thinking, "Why in the name of End-of-the-Year Close-out Sale-athons would I want to see TV on my computer screen?" Well, I'll tell you why:

- You can update those boring financial records in Microsoft Excel while keeping an eye on VH1 in the background. Why listen to the radio when you can have your music with full-motion video?

- If you're the kind of person who calls up an on-line service such as America Online or CompuServe and reads the news section, stop it this second. Think of the money you're wasting. Turn off your modem and turn on CNN's "Headline News" on-screen.

- ✓ Ever watched one of those education channels — MEU or JCN — that are dedicated to teaching the masses how to use their computers? (If you do and you're truly unlucky, you may happen upon my grinning face.) Well, what better way to learn how to use a computer program than to follow along on your Mac? It's like watching Julia Child while working in the kitchen — a match made in 21st-century heaven.

- ✓ Why be satisfied with playing a CD-ROM game that has incredibly state-of-the-art graphics when you could also be watching "Ren and Stimpy" on a second monitor? Come on, there's no such thing as too much simultaneous entertainment!

The best thing about monitoring a TV signal is that it takes almost no effort on the part of your computer. The television images can play away at the full 30 frames per second (or 25 outside the U.S.) without having any impact whatsoever on the performance of other software. Likewise, you can save and open files, play sounds and digital movies, and perform complex operations in any number of computer programs without missing a beat in the TV show.

The Couch Potato's Dream Machine

The junior AV machines — which, as you may recall, include the Power Mac 5200 LC and any machine with a 630 in its name — turn TV watching into an art form. As long as your junior AV model is equipped with the $250 Apple TV/Video System (as explained in the "The Spunky AV Junior" section of Chapter 5), you can try out all the stuff I explain in this chapter.

If you're at all unsure of whether or not your junior AV is ready for prime time — TV, that is — take a look (or a feel) at the back of your machine and see whether a big, fat coaxial jack is jutting out the top of it, as shown in Figure 15-1. This jack is the same kind that's found on modern television sets. Just plug in your TV cable or an antenna with a coaxial converter, and you're in business.

I should also mention that all cable TV-ready Macs come with remote controls. You point the remote at the little infrared sensor on the front of the computer, as illustrated in Figure 15-2. You can use the remote to turn on the computer, adjust the volume, change channels, and do all those other things that remote controls are so good at. You can even shut your Mac down. Too bad every Mac doesn't have one.

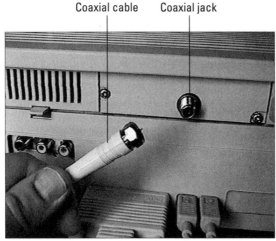

Figure 15-1: The rear side of a Quadra 630 equipped with a TV/Video System for watching TV.

Figure 15-2: Point the remote control at the dark red rectangle on the front of the computer.

My favorite thing about the remote is that it affects the TV functions even when the TV software — Apple Video Player — is running in the background. Suppose that you're writing thank you notes in Word while the Video Player is playing away in the background. A commercial comes on and you want to change channels. Without the remote, you'd have to switch to the Video Player program and fiddle about. But with the remote, you can press a button while remaining inside Word. Will these modern miracles never cease?

Part IV: Hollywood in a Box

The four buttons at the bottom of the remote control — Stop/Eject, Rev, Play/Pause, and Fwd — affect the playing of audio CDs in the internal CD-ROM drive. These buttons have no influence over on-screen TV.

Getting to TV-watching headquarters

To watch TV, choose Apple Video Player from the Apple menu. (Although Apple installs the Video Player on the hard drives of all junior AV machines, it won't run unless you have the proper TV/Video System hardware.) The Video window, shown in Figure 15-3, appears.

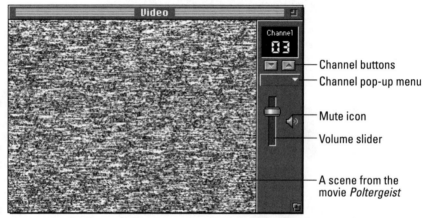

Figure 15-3: The Apple Video Player program set to a bad channel.

You can also start the Video Player program by pressing Option-Tab or pressing the TV/Mac button on the right side of the remote control.

When you first start the program, you may get nothing but static, as Figure 15-3 makes apparent. The static just means that the software is set to a channel that's unavailable in your neck of the woods. As it does with a TV, changing the channel quickly remedies this problem.

The small collection of controls along the right side of the Video window work as follows:

✓ **Channel buttons:** Click on these icons to skip from one channel to the next. You can also use the Channel buttons on the remote control.

Better yet, press the right- and left-arrow keys to advance one channel up or down. You can also type the number of the channel you want to watch. (If you want the channel to change a little quicker, press Return after entering the number.)

If you still can't get anything but static after changing channels, you need to choose Setup⇨Channel Setup, as explained in the next section.

- **Channel pop-up menu:** After you name your favorite channels, you can choose them from this pop-up menu. But until you add some names — as I explain in the "Fine-tuning the setup" section later in this chapter — the pop-up menu isn't even visible.

- **Mute icon:** Click on the little speaker to shut off the TV sound — a great feature for those occasional times when you need to devote a smidgen of concentration to your work. You can also press the Mute button on the remote. Neither the icon nor the button affects other sounds, such as those from audio CDs or computer-generated beeps.

The keyboard equivalent for the mute function is ⌘-M.

- **Volume slider:** To raise or lower the volume, you can drag the slider or use the Volume buttons on the remote.

The most convenient way to change the volume, however, is to press the up- and down-arrow keys.

Introducing the Video Player to the neighborhood

When hooking up a new cable-ready TV, one of the first things you do is make the set scan for active channels in your neighborhood. The same holds true for a cable-ready Mac. Whether you sprung for cable in your home or office or you're using an antenna to glean your entertainment from the ether, it's important to let the Video Player take a quick look around.

1. **Choose Setup⇨Channel Setup.**

    The dialog box shown in Figure 15-4 appears.

2. **Select the appropriate option from the Connection pop-up menu.**

    As shown in the lower-left corner of Figure 15-4, the pop-up menu offers three options. If you're using rabbit ears, select Antenna. Otherwise, select Cable. (I'll get to HRC Cable in a moment.)

3. **Click on the Auto Add button.**

    Video Player takes a few moments and scans through all the channels it can find. If you're using an antenna, the program searches channels 2 through 69. Otherwise, it looks at channels 1 through 125. In either case, the software removes a channel whenever it can't find an active signal.

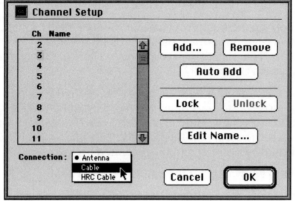

Figure 15-4: Select a source for your TV signal and click on the Auto Add button to acquaint the Video Player program with its immediate surroundings.

   4. **After Video Player completes its scan, consult the list on the left side of the dialog box.**

   Every channel in the list should be a bona fide, active channel.

   If you're hooked up to cable TV and the list doesn't contain any channels above 13, select HRC Cable from the Connection pop-up menu and repeat Step 3.

   5. **Press Return or click on the OK button to exit the dialog box.**

From this point on, clicking on the channel buttons in the Video window or pressing the right- and left-arrow keys advances from one active channel to the next, skipping the channels that were removed from the list in the scanning process.

Fine-tuning the setup

You don't have to accept the list of channels that the Video Player program automatically picks out for you. Come on, this is a computer — you can modify the list of channels as you see fit. You can delete channels that you positively can't stand or add channels that you think are missing. You can also name stations and later select them from a pop-up menu — a feature that even $1,000 TVs don't offer.

To perform any of these channel modifications, choose Setup⇨Channel Setup again. Then try out the following buttons:

Chapter 15: TV Meets Monitor 213

- **Remove:** To delete an undesirable channel — say, for example, a public access channel that seems to always be playing heavy metal music while displaying the equivalent of on-screen want ads — select the channel from the list and click on the Remove button.

  You can select multiple channels inside any list in the Video Player by Shift-dragging down the list or Shift-clicking on specific numbers.

- **Add:** I don't know about you, but my cable vendor offers a free weekend of The Disney Channel about once a month. No doubt it works wonders on the younger crowd. I and my lovely wife don't have kids, however, so I've never subscribed to this channel. But I like to keep it open just in case it happens to be on.

  To add Disney or some other presently dormant channel, click on the Add button. A list of inactive channels appears in a list. Select the channel you want to add and press Return.

- **Edit Name:** Named channels appear in the pop-up menu in the Video window. Therefore, you should name the channels that you think you'll watch most often.

  To do so, select a channel and click on the Edit Name button or just double-click on the channel number. Enter the name of the channel in the Name option box. Then press Return. The name now appears in the Name column of the channel list.

After you exit the Channel Setup dialog box, you can select a channel name from the pop-up menu in the Video window. Clicking on the channel buttons or pressing the right- and left-arrow keys cycles through all the channels except the ones you removed. If you decide later that you want to check out a removed station, just type the channel number using the keyboard.

Protecting impressionable minds

If you want to prevent the kids from watching some of life's more risqué entertainment, or if you're tired of your husband watching those sorority-house-massacre movies that run in continuous loops on the USA network, you can lock out a channel so that it's accessible by password only. Here's how:

1. **Choose Setup⇨Channel Setup.**

   We revisit familiar haunts.

2. **Select the offending channel (or channels) from the list.**

   By way of example, I've selected the USA network in Figure 15-5. But the channel does not have to be named.

Part IV: Hollywood in a Box

Figure 15-5: Select the channel you want to lock and click on the Lock button.

3. **Click on the Lock button.**

   A little lock icon appears next to the channel in the list.

4. **Press the Return key.**

   So far, all you've done is make Video Player question you when you select the locked channel. To access the channel, all folks have to do is click on an OK button, and they're in like Flynn. If you want to lock out the channel good and proper, you have to assign a password.

5. **Choose Setup⇨Set Channel Password.**

   The dialog box shown in Figure 15-6 appears.

Figure 15-6: Use these options to specify a password and provide your future self with a clue.

6. **Enter the password in the Password option box.**

   If you think that you may have problems remembering the password down the line, enter a hint of some kind into the Clue option box. Be careful, though. The same clue that helps you remember your password can help others figure it out. (You may not want to enter a clue such as "The cat's name," for example.)

7. **Press Return to save the password.**

You're done. From now on, you have to enter the password whenever you want to watch the forbidden channel, enter the Channel Setup dialog box, or change the password. If you entered a clue in Step 6, it will be there to help you out. Incidentally, it doesn't matter whether you use capital or lowercase letters when you enter your password.

If you forget the password entirely and not even the clue seems to be of much help, you can remove the Apple Video Player Prefs file from the Preferences folder inside the System Folder. (Doing so also gets rids of the channel names and inactive channels.) I label this information with the warning icon because if you can do it, so can the kids. You may want to copy the file to a safe place by Option-dragging it to a different folder at the Finder desktop. This way, if the kids delete the file, at least you can reinstate it.

Other Stuff You Can Do with a Computerized TV

So far, I've given you a taste of how the junior AVs provide specialized control over TV watching. But that's just the tip of the iceberg. Junior AV Macs can do all sorts of things that conventional TVs never imagined in their minuscule conventional-TV brains. Nearly every one of the following techniques is possible only on a *computerized* TV:

- Press Tab to switch back and forth between the channel you're watching now and the last channel you watched. Press Return to display the channel name and time, in case you forget what the heck channel you're watching. (All right, all right, so you can perform both of these tricks on a regular TV set. I'm just warming up.)

- Choose commands from the Windows menu to change the size of the TV window. Your choices are Largest Size (⌘-3), which makes the TV image fill an entire 14-inch monitor; Normal Size (⌘-2), which displays the conventional quarter-size screen; and Smallest Size (⌘-1), which makes the TV image very small indeed. You can also choose Windows➪Other Size to enter your own wacky window size.

- You can switch the window between the current size and the full-screen size by pressing the Display button on the remote control.

- A junior AV Mac is so smart that it can remind you to watch a favorite show on a regular or one-time basis. To specify a show, choose Setup➪TV Reminders. Then click on the Add button to display the dialog box shown in Figure 15-7. You can enter the name of the show, select the day and time, enter the channel, and specify how often you want to watch it.

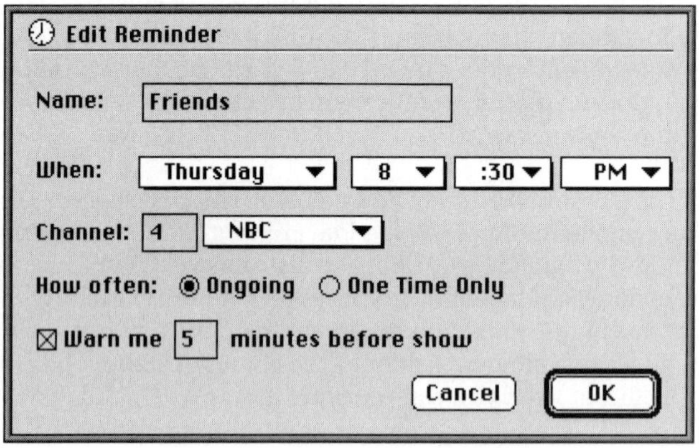

Figure 15-7: What other TV automatically turns on when your favorite show is about to start?

Select the Warn Me check box if you want your Mac to give you a heads-up a few minutes before the show starts.

From that point on, a message appears on-screen when it's time for the show to begin. The Video Player program doesn't have to be running, but the computer does have to be on. If you want to watch the show, just press Return.

- Choose Windows➪Show Controls Window (or press ⌘-4) to display the Controls palette, which is chock full of video and sound controls.

- Click on the TV screen icon along the left side of the Controls palette to access Brightness, Sharpness, and Tint sliders that let you adjust the picture quality. Click on the speaker icon to switch between stereo and mono sound as well as to adjust the balance and tone. These controls are shown in Figure 15-8.

- The TV panel offers three Video Source buttons, which determine what kind of signal you're watching. When TV is selected, you're seeing the cable or antenna broadcast signal coming in through the coaxial jack. Select Video or S-Video only if you have a VCR hooked up to the RCA input

Chapter 15: TV Meets Monitor **217**

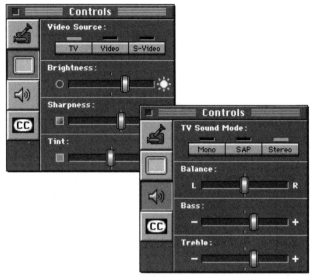

Figure 15-8:
The Video Player program provides all the sound and picture options associated with high-end TVs.

jacks, as explained in Chapter 5. You cannot change channels when watching a videotape.

- The sound panel contains an SAP button, which warrants additional explanation. Short for *Second Audio Program,* the SAP button brings to life a second soundtrack, generally a foreign language translation or a description service for the visually impaired. (Most channels don't offer SAP, and when they do, the nature of the broadcast varies.)

- Click on the CC icon along the left side of the Channels palette to turn on closed captioning for the hearing impaired. Generally, you'll want to select the CC 1 button; CC 2 is reserved for a second language. In Figure 15-9, I've turned on closed captioning for a scene from *It's a Wonderful Life*. Little notes flank the text to show that we're reading lyrics.

- You can select one of the two Text buttons in the closed captioning panel to display broadcast schedules on some channels. This service is very rare, but if it gets more popular in the future, your Mac is prepared.

- The Video Player window does not offer a close box in its upper-left corner. To quit the program, either choose File⇨Quit, press ⌘-Q, or press the keyboard equivalent that starts Video Player, Option-Tab. And if none of those options appeals to you, you can press the TV/Mac button on the Remote.

Figure 15-9:
When you see notes in closed captioning, be sure to sing along.

The Video Player program not only offers options for watching TV, but also for recording it. I discuss this topic in greater detail in Chapter 17. But because I hate to see you wait that long for this tempting information, I'll dole out a few morsels right now:

- Click on the camcorder icon in the Controls palette to display the options shown in Figure 15-10. Click on the Freeze button to stop the video on a single frame. (The sound will continue playing away.) Click on the Save button to save the frame as a PICT image on disk.

Figure 15-10:
These options let you capture bits and pieces of television shows and store them on disk.

- Click again on the Freeze button to turn off the freeze-frame function and continue viewing full-motion TV.
- You can also grab a single frame by choosing Edit⇨Copy Video Display or pressing ⌘-C. This command transfers the frame to the Clipboard without freezing the video. You can then switch to an image editing program such

as Photoshop, create a new document, and paste the frame into the document. (Photoshop automatically sizes the new document to fit the contents of the Clipboard, so you can just press ⌘-N, Return, and ⌘-V to capture the frame.) Then you can save the image in TIFF, JPEG, or any format you like.

✔ To record several frames from a TV broadcast, click on the Record button. This topic is a big one — it takes all of Chapters 16 and 17 to discuss fully.

How to Watch TV on the Big AV

Viewing a television signal on an AV machine or a Mac with video hardware is not nearly as sophisticated as it is on the junior AVs. In fact, by comparison, it's almost embarrassingly primitive. But you can still do it, so take heart.

The first thing you need to know is that there's no TV tuner, which means that you can't change channels from the computer. If you want to watch TV, you have to hook the coaxial cable up to a cable-ready VCR and then hook the VCR to the Mac using RCA cables, as discussed in the "How do I play video into my computer?" section of Chapter 5. You then use the VCR to change channels.

To view the TV image on-screen, locate and start up the Video Monitor program, included with all AV Macs. A single Monitor window appears on-screen. Assuming that the VCR is on, you see the video in this window.

For the best results with a Centris or Quadra AV, you should have a monitor hooked up to the Mac's built-in video port. If you're using a Power Mac, the monitor should be connected to the AV card (the one featured so prominently back in Figures 5-2 and 5-4). If you're using more than one monitor, drag the Monitor window to the screen that's connected to the built-in video or AV card. The video will play more smoothly this way.

Beyond the functions related directly to changing channels, Video Monitor does a pretty good job of keeping up with the junior AV's Apple Video Player program. Here's some general advice on using Video Monitor:

✔ If the VCR is on and you can't see anything in the Monitor window, it may be because the VCR is set to display the line signal. Put a tape in the machine and play it. If a picture appears on-screen, consult your VCR manual to see how to view regular TV channels.

✔ If a picture still doesn't appear, it's probably because you have the VCR hooked up to the computer using an S-video cable rather than an RCA cable. To let the Video Monitor program in on this fact, choose Monitor➪Video Settings to display the Video dialog box shown in Figure 15-11. Select S-Video from the Input pop-up menu. Full-motion video should suddenly appear in the preview on the right side of the dialog box.

Part IV: Hollywood in a Box

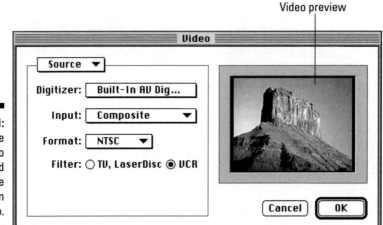

Figure 15-11: Use these options to locate and stabilize the on-screen video.

- If you can see a picture but it's all discolored and jiggly, choose Monitor⇨Video Settings and select TV, LaserDisc from the Filter radio buttons. This option properly filters the TV signal. (If that doesn't help, you're probably trying to watch a premium channel that you haven't paid for. Sorry, your Mac is not a descrambler.)

- If you can't hear any sound, choose Monitor⇨Sound Settings to display the Sound dialog box shown in Figure 15-12. Select Microphone from the Input pop-up menu to play the sound coming in through the sound-in jack. And select On from the Speaker pop-up menu. (Volume and Gain have no effect.)

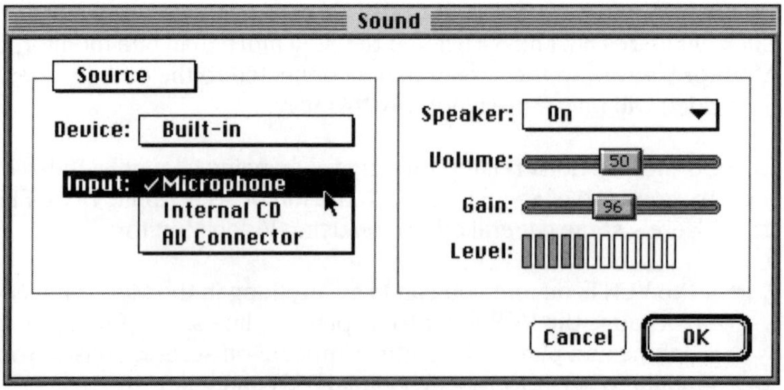

Figure 15-12: Check the settings in the Sound dialog box if you can't hear any sound.

Chapter 15: TV Meets Monitor   221

- Choose Monitor⇨Mute or press ⌘-M to mute the sound so that you can concentrate.

- You can change the size of the video window by choosing Full Size (⌘-1), Half Size (⌘-2), and Quarter Size (⌘-4) from the Monitor menu. (Half Size results in a quarter-screen image — half as wide and half as tall equals one-fourth the area. Similarly, Quarter Size delivers a $1/16$-screen image.)

- To grab a particularly lovely frame, choose Edit⇨Copy or press ⌘-C. (The computer may take a half second or so to react, so you have to be pretty quick on the draw to get a good picture.) By default, the Video Monitor program saves the frame to disk as a PICT file. You'll find the file on the Finder desktop; it'll be named PICT followed by a number.

- If you'd rather copy the frame to the Clipboard so that you can paste it into Photoshop or some other image editor, choose File⇨Preferences and select the Clipboard radio button.

- If your other programs behave strangely while Video Monitor is running in the background, you may want to close the Monitor window and see whether that helps. For example, when the Monitor window is active, you may find that the cursor in Photoshop flickers, even if the VCR is turned off.

- To redisplay the Monitor window, just choose File⇨Open or press ⌘-O.

- To quit Video Monitor, choose File⇨Quit or press ⌘-Q.

Chapter 16
A New Kind of Picture Show

In This Chapter
▶ Understanding QuickTime
▶ Acquiring movies and player programs
▶ Watching QuickTime movies
▶ Playing movies backward and at different speeds
▶ What's new in the world of virtual reality

The Mac is nothing if not innovative. You can always bet that you're getting gobs of new technology first on the Mac, especially in the multimedia department. The problem is, some of this technology comes so early that it's almost premature. Though Apple intends to make a big splash with it, and the computer press gobbles it up, most of us are sitting around thinking, "So what?" Simply put, unless you live this stuff day in and day out, the new technology just doesn't make all that much sense.

Take QuickTime, for example. When Apple first came out with this groundbreaking technology in 1991, computer pundits, program developers, and industry wags were bustling with enthusiasm over the idea. Here was a breakthrough that allowed folks to play digital movies directly from disk. QuickTime saved each movie frame as a separate image file and then played them in sequence to create simulated movement, just like traditional film or videotape.

Meanwhile, the rest of us noticed two things: the movies were laughably small, and they were jerky to boot, like some kind of minuscule Claymation movies. Because the technology was new and the computers of the day weren't particularly powerful, the standard size for a QuickTime movie was a mere 160 pixels wide × 120 pixels tall, or 2 inches × $1^1/_2$ inches on a typical computer screen, as witnessed by the microscopic Figure 16-1. And QuickTime movies played at 10 frames per second. It was a sorry combination that left most folks speechless with apathy.

Figure 16-1: The first QuickTime movies were a feast for the eyes of gnats.

But Apple kept assuring any and all skeptics that its little David of a technology would one day grow up to be a Goliath. And, for all practical purposes, that's exactly what has happened. The typical QuickTime movie has grown fourfold, to 320 × 240 pixels (quarter-screen), as shown in Figure 16-2. And most machines made in the last two years can play quarter-screen movies at the full 30 frames per second.

Figure 16-2: Though still relatively petite, your average, everyday QuickTime movie fills one quarter of a 14-inch screen.

But the most amazing aspect of QuickTime is its effect on the multimedia industry. Virtually every Macintosh CD-ROM title produced these days includes QuickTime movies, as do many CDs for Microsoft Windows. Simply put, QuickTime makes multimedia as we know it possible .

The QuickTime Collection

QuickTime hangs out in the Extensions folder inside your System Folder. The most recent incarnation of QuickTime, Version 2.0, includes as many as four system extensions, as shown in Figure 16-3. All the extensions are compatible with any version of System 7. They work as follows:

- **QuickTime:** This extension is the essential program for viewing and — as you'll learn in the next chapter — recording QuickTime movies. It takes up more than its fair share of space on disk and in memory — more than 1MB — but it's worth it.

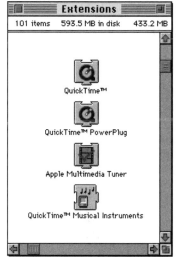

Figure 16-3: The QuickTime gang of four.

- **QuickTime PowerPlug:** If you own a machine with a PowerPC chip — Power Mac, Performa 6100, and so on — you also have to have the PowerPlug extension to make QuickTime run. It consumes another 650K in memory, but what are you going to do?

- **Apple Multimedia Tuner:** No program is perfect, and QuickTime 2.0 is no exception. But rather than releasing a rehabilitated version of QuickTime, Apple decided to release this little fix-it extension instead. Not all Macs need the Multimedia Tuner. But because the extension is smart enough to load into memory only if your computer will benefit from it, I advise that you go ahead and install it if you don't already have it.

✔ **QuickTime Musical Instruments:** In most cases, you don't need this extension. And if a CD-ROM title does need it — as is the case with HyperBole Studios' interactive game Quantum Gate — the CD will install it for you. In case you're curious, this extension contains a bunch of instrument samples so that your Mac can play musical scores called MIDI (pronounced *middy*) files.

All system extensions except for Apple Multimedia Tuner are included with System 7.5. If you're using an older version of the system, never fear; the QuickTime extensions are about as scarce as flies at a rodeo. QuickTime, QuickTime PowerPlug, and Multimedia Tuner are all included with just about every CD-ROM title you can buy these days.

Where to Find Movies and a Program to Play Them

In the next chapter, I explain how to record your own QuickTime movies. But if recording isn't your bag, you can find absolutely thousands of QuickTime movies floating around out there. You can use a modem to download QuickTime movies from America Online, CompuServe, and other on-line services. Or you can purchase CDs of movies, such as QuickTime: The CD from Sumeria, 415-904-0800, which includes two disks of award-winning movies from the International QuickTime Film Festival. Apple even includes a few movies on its System 7.5 CD-ROM. (Choose File⇨Find or press ⌘-F at the Finder desktop and search for a folder called Movies.)

To play a QuickTime movie, you need a QuickTime player program. Apple includes a program called MoviePlayer on the System 7.5 CD. QuickTime: The CD and other CD-ROM collections also include player programs. If you can't locate one of those, scout about on an on-line service for Popcorn or EasyPlay. Popcorn is a piece of freeware from Aladdin Systems, and EasyPlay is a $20 shareware program from Michael O'Connor.

Or just use SimpleText, the little word processor that Apple includes with System 7.5. In addition to converting words into computer voices (as discussed in Chapter 14), it opens and plays QuickTime movies. Sadly, you cannot open QuickTime movies in SimpleText's predecessor, TeachText.

You can also play a QuickTime movie without any program at all. To do this, name the movie Startup Movie (be sure to include the space between the two words) and put it inside your System Folder. Then restart your Mac. The movie now will play every time you boot up your computer. To stop it from doing so, either remove it from the System Folder or rename it.

Chapter 16: A New Kind of Picture Show **227**

Take a Crack at the QuickTime Projector

Whatever player program you use, it offers a familiar set of basic options. When you open a movie, the standard QuickTime window appears, as shown in Figure 16-4. It offers these amazing controls:

- **Volume slider:** Click and hold on the speaker icon to display the volume slider, which allows you to adjust the loudness of the movie. If the movie doesn't include sound, the speaker icon is absent.

  You can also press the up- and down-arrow keys to adjust the volume from the keyboard. However, you'll get the best results if you leave the volume slider set to the maximum level and fine-tune the volume of the speakers instead.

  As if that's not enough, you can Option-click on the speaker icon to mute the sound. Option-click again to bring back the sound.

- **Play/pause:** When the movie is stopped, the button next to the speaker looks like an arrow. Click on the button to play the movie. The button changes to a pause button with two vertical lines, as in Figure 16-4. Click on this button to pause the movie.

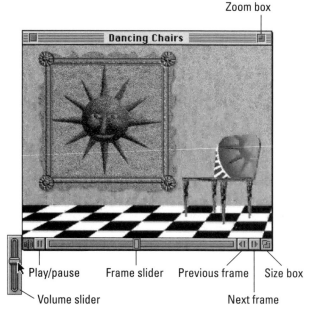

Figure 16-4: A frame from the film *Dancing Chairs* by Go Fukusaki and Yoko Kikukawa from QuickTime: The CD.

TIP

Press the spacebar or Return to play or pause a movie from the keyboard. Or double-click inside the movie itself.

If the movie looks a little jerky, it's probably because the player program is dropping frames. See, in order to maintain the correct speed, the program may slough off a frame here and there in the name of expediency. If you would rather see each and every frame than play the movie at the correct speed, Option-click on the play button or press Option-spacebar or Option-Return.

✓ **Frame slider:** Drag the slider tab to move quickly from one point in the movie to another. For the best results, pause the movie before dragging the tab.

✓ **Previous/next frame:** Click on the previous frame button to go one frame back. Click on the next frame button to . . . you don't really need me to tell you this, do you?

TIP

All right, here's the stuff you couldn't figure out for yourself: Press the left- and right-arrow keys to go one frame backward or forward. Option-click on the previous frame button (or press Option-left arrow) to go to the first frame in the movie; Option-click on the next frame button (or press Option-right arrow) to go to the last.

But that's not all. You can also ⌘-click on the previous frame button or press ⌘-left arrow to play the movie backward. (If you don't like that method, try Shift-double-clicking inside the movie.) Even the sound plays backward. Don't expect the movie to play smoothly, however; reading previous frames from disk is not one of QuickTime's strong suits.

Put away that checkbook, there's still more! Press Control and drag on either the previous or next frame button to display a tiny speed slider, as shown in Figure 16-5. Drag the slider tab to the left to play the movie forward; drag right to play it backward. Dragging farther from the center increases the speed. But remember, you have to hold the mouse button down for the movie to play smoothly. If you release it without returning the slider tab to its center position, the movie becomes a jerky mess until you pause it and start it up again.

✓ **Size box:** *Don't* drag the size box to change the size of the frame. If you want to view the movie at a larger or smaller size, Option-drag it. This way, the frame snaps to a size that is twice as large or twice as small, which ensures much smoother playback than some random resizing. (Then again, if you think that it's fun to look at a tall skinny movie or a short fat one, release the Option key and drag away.)

✓ **Zoom box:** After you grow weary of resizing the movie, you can click in the zoom box to restore the movie to its original and proper size.

Figure 16-5: Control-drag on the previous or next frame button to access the top-secret speed slider.

If you look back at Figure 7-4, you'll notice that the Photo CD preview window supplied by the Slide Show Viewer program is a standard QuickTime window. In fact, QuickTime is instrumental to Apple's handling of Photo CDs. It just goes to show how QuickTime influences almost all aspects of multimedia on the Mac.

QuickTime Movies on a CD-ROM

As I mentioned earlier, most multimedia CDs include QuickTime movies. However, the movies are usually integrated into the interactive production. Sometimes, you can display the standard QuickTime controls by clicking on a Controls button or the like. But more often than not, the movie plays automatically without permitting you to display the controls.

If you want to pause a movie or advance from one frame to the next, you may be able to take advantage of the keyboard shortcuts I mentioned in the preceding section. As an experiment, try pressing the spacebar to see whether that pauses the movie. (I recommend the spacebar over the Return key because Return may activate some other function in the interactive production.) Just press the spacebar once and wait; don't get impatient and press it several times in a row.

If the spacebar doesn't work, try clicking inside the movie. Your click may pause the movie, or it may skip the movie entirely. Some CDs also let you skip a movie by pressing the Escape key. It varies from one CD-ROM to the next, so you'll have to experiment.

To make the movies on a CD-ROM play more smoothly — or at least as smoothly as possible — check out Chapter 20, "Ten Ways to Make Your CD-ROMs Perform Like Champs." This chapter provides a wealth of wisdom for making CDs sing.

QuickTime's Virtual World

Every once in a while, I like to throw in a paragraph or two whose only purpose is to show how intensely groovy the Mac is. Well, this whole section is like that. It won't help you use your computer any better. If you're looking for that, skip to the next chapter. But this section will give you a small insight into what's going on behind the scenes of the best of all possible multimedia computers.

What I'm talking about is QuickTime VR, as in *virtual reality*. QuickTime VR is a smidgen of extra technology built into QuickTime that lets you wander around inside an imaginary environment. As you look up, turn around, or look down, the screen image pans smoothly, almost as if you were really there.

The first multimedia CD-ROM to exploit QuickTime VR is Star Trek: The Next Generation Interactive Technical Manual from Simon and Schuster Interactive, 212-698-7000. This CD lets you wander around the USS Enterprise — well, actually, you walk around the sets from the TV show. You can go aboard the bridge, inside sick bay, among the tables and behind the bar of Ten Forward, and so on.

After you arrive in a room, you can pan the screen by dragging with the cursor. Figure 16-6 finds me dragging about inside the transporter room. As you can see, I am afforded a smooth, seamless pan of the transporter and surrounding milieu. I can turn around a full 360 degrees. I can also drag up to look at the ceiling and drag down to look at the floor — as I spin about, no less.

To create these very realistic conditions, the developers of the Interactive Technical Manual shot a series of overlapping still pictures in complete circles from various points on the sets. QuickTime VR then distorts these pictures and stitches them together to create virtual environments. No special panoramic lenses are required during the photographing; everything is accomplished digitally, inside the computer.

In fact, amazing as it may seem, every one of the views from Figure 16-6 is an amalgam of two or more photos blended together. Notice the distortion of the transporter pad as I look to one side of it or the other? This distortion heightens the realism of the scene, simulating the effect of peripheral vision.

You can see what a few of the original photographs look like without the digital stitching and distorting by turning off QuickTime VR. You do this by pressing and holding the Shift key when starting up the Interactive Technical Manual. In the transporter room, the result is one still image from each of three perspectives. Hardly the same all-encompassing experience.

Chapter 16: A New Kind of Picture Show   231

What can I say? The future is here. It's virtual reality without the goggles. Okay, so you can't pick up virtual items and fling them about virtual rooms with your $100,000, grip-sensing gloves, but that's just a matter of time. A few lines of code, and you'll never have to leave your house again.

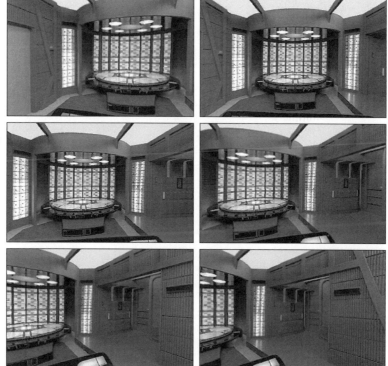

Figure 16-6: Thanks to QuickTime VR, I can view every nook and cranny of the transporter room from the "Star Trek: The Next Generation" TV series.

Chapter 17
Recording Your Own QuickTime Movies to Disk

In This Chapter
- Checking that your VCR is hooked up properly
- Reducing the number of colors visible on-screen
- Recording a QuickTime movie in 24 easy steps
- Selecting the appropriate compression option
- Setting the frame rate and frame quality
- Adjusting the sound levels and changing the frame size
- Capturing a single frame
- Using two live cameras, the QuickCam and FlexCam

You can play a QuickTime movie on virtually any Macintosh computer. But recording your own QuickTime movies requires special hardware. As explained in Chapter 5, you need an AV Mac, a junior AV, or a video-input board.

If your Mac isn't equipped with any of this stuff, you can record live movies using a little $200 digital camera called QuickCam from Connectix. It records black-and-white movies only, but you can use it with low-end computers such as the LC and Mac II series. I discuss the QuickCam later in this chapter.

Another little item to keep in mind is that QuickTime movies eat disk space with a ravenous appetite known only to army ants and teenagers. It's no joke — digital movies make sound files look puny. Although it's impossible to exactly nail down how much space a QuickTime movie consumes, the ballpark figure for a quarter-screen (320 by 240-pixel) movie recorded at 15 frames per second is anywhere from 20MB to 100MB per minute. And that's not including sound, which adds on another 1MB to 10MB per minute, as I explained back in Table 13-1.

The important point is, it takes a pretty pumped up computer system with lots of RAM and hard disk space to handle QuickTime movie recording. But if you have the necessary hardware, you're ready to enter some very exciting territory. After you record a movie to disk, you can make as many copies as you want without degrading the quality. You can edit and combine scenes with amazing accuracy. And you can back up the movie to a SyQuest cartridge or other removable media, where it will be much safer than on videotape.

Checking Your P's and Q's

QuickTime recording is a fairly involved topic. It's not all that difficult, mind you, but it involves a lot of messing about with options and a fair amount of experimenting. So it's important that all your hardware is properly in place. Take a moment to scan this last-minute checklist before you jump into the fray:

- ✔ You have wired an RCA or S-video cable from the video jack of your VCR, camcorder, or laserdisc player into the video-in jack on the back of your Mac. See the "How do I play video into my computer?" section of Chapter 5 for an explanation.

- ✔ If you want to record sound along with your video, you have connected the audio RCA jack(s) from the video player to the sound-in minijack on the back of your Mac. See Steps 3 through 5 of that same "How do I play video into my computer?" section for details.

- ✔ For the best results, your monitor is plugged into the video socket built into your computer. In the case of the AV Power Macs, the monitor should be plugged into the computer video port on the AV card. (You can have additional monitors hooked up to NuBus boards or to the Power Mac's AudioVision port, but at least one monitor should be plugged into the built-in port.)

- ✔ You have sufficient space available on your hard drive. Open some folder on the hard drive and look at the space-available number in the upper-right corner of the window. (If necessary, choose View➪By Icon.) This value should be at least 50MB. If it's less than that, it's time to do some housecleaning and delete some files from the hard drive.

- ✔ Your VCR, camcorder, or laserdisc player is plugged in — to the wall, that is, so that it can access that magical ingredient, electricity. It's also helpful to turn the video player on and stick a videotape or laserdisc into it.

As long as all these connections are in place, you're ready to record. From here on out, mercifully, everything is in the hands of software.

Bringing Big Movies to the Small Screen

Of the many video recording programs orbiting about the Macintosh stratosphere, your best bet is FusionRecorder or Adobe Premiere. FusionRecorder is convenient because it's included on the hard drives of all AV Macs. Premiere, however, is the accepted standard, just as Photoshop is the standard for still images and SoundEdit 16 is the standard for sound. Premiere also has a habit of producing slightly better recordings.

Luckily, the recording features provided by the two programs are nearly identical. So although I concentrate my attentions on the more commonly available FusionRecorder, you can easily translate my instructions to Premiere if you decide to use that software instead.

Flying your colors at half mast

AV Macs are a bit eccentric when it comes to displaying live video. In order to see what you're recording — which is roughly as helpful as keeping your eyes open while driving — you have to redo the number of colors visible on-screen. For example, if you can set your monitor to display millions of colors, you need to ratchet it down to thousands. If your monitor maxes out at thousands, I'm afraid you'll have to turn it down to 256 colors.

If you're curious why this is the case — and there's no reason you need to be — it's because your AV Mac is actually trying to display two kinds of images at once: regular old computer images and incoming video stuff. To make this happen, the computer splits its VRAM in two, devoting half to each kind of images. Half the VRAM means half the bits, and half the bits means way fewer colors.

To change the number of colors, walk this way:

1. **Open the Monitors control panel.**

   The Monitors control panel appears, as in Figure 17-1.

2. **If you have only one monitor hooked up to your Mac, skip this step.**

   If you're lucky enough to own two or more monitors, you see an icon for each in the central portion of the control panel window. Click on the icon that corresponds to the monitor plugged into the built-in video port. (If you aren't sure which icon is which, click and hold on the Identify button. Big numbers appear on your screens; these numbers match the icon numbers.)

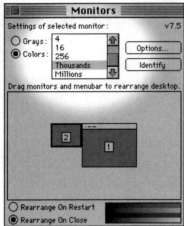

Figure 17-1: For QuickTime movie recording, you have to reduce your on-screen colors to one setting below the maximum.

3. **Scroll down the list at the top of the control panel (if you can) to check out the maximum number of colors your monitor can display.**

   In Figure 17-1, the maximum number is Millions. On a Centris 660AV, Quadra 660AV, or Power Mac 6100AV, the number is probably Thousands, in which case, you can't scroll.

4. **Click on the second-highest value in the list.**

   In my case, I select Thousands. If Thousands is your maximum, click on 256.

5. **Close the control panel.**

The good news is that even though you can only see the incoming video in 8-bit or 16-bit color, your Mac records QuickTime movies in millions of colors. And, as explained in Chapter 19, you can play back the movies at the maximum number of colors available.

Making a recording

After you start FusionRecorder, you see a smallish window with Rec and Stop buttons at the top. This window is the record window. If you play a videotape, the video displays inside the window, as demonstrated in Figure 17-2.

If you're using Premiere, click on the Presentation — 320 × 240 option in the New Project Presets dialog box that automatically appears and then press Return. Next, choose File⇨Capture⇨Movie Capture or press the F10 key. (If a message appears asking to deactivate AppleTalk, just hit the Return key.) The Movie Capture window appears, sporting a big Record button at the top. Again, you can see the incoming video in the center of the window.

Chapter 17: Recording Your Own QuickTime Movies to Disk 237

Figure 17-2: The record window displays the video signal.

If you don't see the incoming video but instead get a message complaining about the "Built-In Digitizer," you didn't set your monitor to the correct number of colors as I instructed in the preceding section. Go back and try again. If the record window is black when you play a videotape, read Step 4 of the following steps before you panic. And don't worry about the sound until you get to Steps 14 and 15.

Here's how to record a QuickTime movie inside FusionRecorder. Though the process is identical in Premiere, some of the command names are slightly different, as I note throughout. Now, I warn you, these steps are lengthy — in fact, there are 24 steps in all — but they aren't difficult to accomplish if you have the patience.

1. **Start playing the videotape or laserdisc.**

    Don't worry about whether you're playing the part of the tape you want to record. For the moment, you just need some incoming video to make sure that everything's working.

2. **Choose Record⇨Video Settings.**

    In Premiere, choose Movie Capture⇨Video Input. In either program, the response is the Video dialog box shown in Figure 17-3.

3. **Select the Source option from the pop-up menu in the top-left corner of the dialog box.**

    You now see the options shown in Figure 17-3.

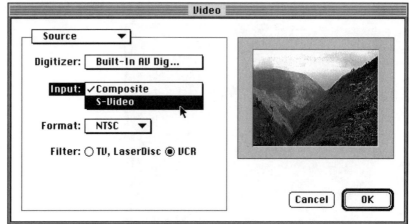

Figure 17-3:
Use the Source options to locate that pesky video signal.

4. **Select the appropriate option from the Input pop-up menu.**

   If you hooked up the video jacks on your VCR and computer using an RCA cable, select the Composite option. If you're using an S-video cable, select the S-Video option. When you get it right, you should see the incoming video on the right side of the dialog box.

   If you don't see any video, the VCR isn't connected properly. Check to see whether your connections match those recommended in Chapter 5.

5. **If you're playing a laserdisc, select the TV, LaserDisc radio button.**

   If you're playing a videotape, leave the VCR option selected.

6. **Select the Compression option from the upper-left pop-up menu in the Video dialog box.**

   This step takes you to the options shown in Figure 17-4.

7. **Select the Video or Component Video option from the Compressor pop-up menu.**

   In technical circles, the options in the Compressor pop-up menu are known as *codecs* (pronounced *ko-decks*), which is short for *compression/decompression*. These compression options permit FusionRecorder or Premiere to save disk space by throwing away colors, much like the JPEG compression I discussed in Chapter 9. While a quarter-screen frame would normally consume exactly 225K of disk space, a compressed version of that frame might take up 50K or even less. Compression degrades the quality of the image slightly, but when it's used in moderation, the tradeoff is more than satisfactory.

Chapter 17: Recording Your Own QuickTime Movies to Disk   *239*

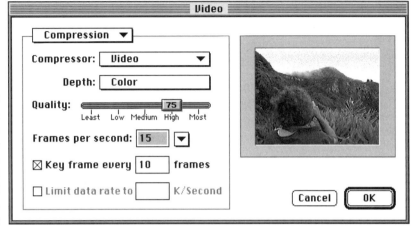

Figure 17-4:
These options help determine how good the final movie looks.

The Video compression option is ideally suited to recording movies from videotape over an RCA cable. If the VCR and Mac are connected by an S-video cable, select the Component Video option instead.

If you are using SPAV or some other special digital video board, use the compression option recommended by the manual that came with your hardware. This setting is *very* important because SPAV and other boards accelerate their particular brands of frame compression to create better-looking movies.

8. If you own a Power Mac, change the Frames Per Second value to 15.

This frame rate is about the best any Mac can achieve when recording. If you own a Centris, Quadra, or a junior AV model, lower the value to 10. Or just select the Best option from the pop-up menu and let FusionRecorder or Premiere figure things out.

My advice here assumes that you aren't using additional hardware, such as the SPAV board I recommended in the "How to get hitched to DAV" section in Chapter 5. If — quite contrary to my assumptions — you *are* using additional hardware, you may be able to get much better frame rates. The SPAV board, for example, is easily able to record 15 frames per second on any machine and 30 frames per second on the AV Power Macs.

9. Set the Quality slider to High.

The Quality setting determines how much compression (from Step 7) is applied. Higher Quality settings mean less compression. The default Quality setting of Medium is a little too low in my opinion. High looks much better while continuing to save space on disk.

10. **Press the Return key.**

    So much for that dialog box.

11. **If you don't want to record sound with your video, choose Record⇔Turn Sound Off.**

    In Premiere, choose Movie Capture⇔Sound Off so that the command has a check mark next to it. Then skip to Step 21.

    If you continue to hear the sound after turning it off, don't worry about it. From your computer's perspective, sound recording and sound playthrough are entirely independent. As long as the computer doesn't record the sound, that's all that counts.

    Choose this command again inside either program to turn the sound back on. Or, if you want to go ahead and record sound, skip this step entirely.

12. **If you do want to record sound, choose Record⇔Sound Settings now.**

    In Premiere, choose Movie Capture⇔Sound Input.

13. **Select Source from the pop-up menu in the upper-left corner.**

    The marvelous options shown in Figure 17-5 appear.

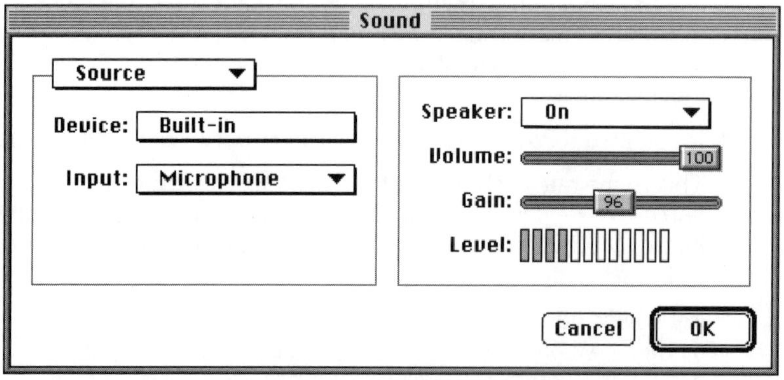

Figure 17-5: Use the Source options to determine where the sound is coming from.

14. **Select Microphone from the Input pop-up menu.**

    This option records sound from the source plugged into the sound-in port. You could alternatively record music from an internal CD, but you're better off recording music separately and mixing it in with the original movie soundtrack.

15. **Select On from the Speaker pop-up menu on the right side of the dialog box.**

Chapter 17: Recording Your Own QuickTime Movies to Disk

You should now be able to hear your videotape. (Again, if you can't, you have some wiring problems. Consult Chapter 5.)

16. Adjust the Gain slider to change the recording level.

Adjust the slider so that the third bar from the right in the Level meter flashes red only occasionally. Higher recording levels are generally better, but if you get two red bars or more, you're liable to encounter distortion. The idea is to strike a happy medium.

17. Select the Sample option from the upper-left pop-up menu.

Now you see the options that are so accurately mirrored in Figure 17-6.

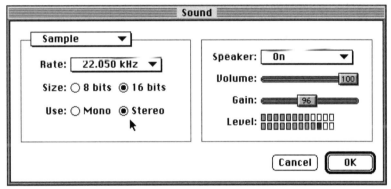

Figure 17-6: These options let you control the quality and file size of your sound track.

18. To record stereo sound, select the Stereo radio button.

The Level meter splits in two to show the sound levels of the left and right channels. If necessary, readjust the Gain value.

If the two halves of the Level meter seem to bounce along in perfect unison, the videotape is probably recorded in mono. (Most camcorders record mono sound.) If this is the case, save space on disk as well as wear and tear on your computer's delicate psyche by selecting the Mono radio button.

19. Change the Rate and Size values as you see fit.

On junior AV Macs, you're stuck with 8-bit, 22 kHz sound. But on standard AVs, you can go as high as CD-quality, 16-bit, 44 kHz. My advice is to settle for 16-bit, 22 kHz when recording from videotape.

20. Press Return to close the Sound dialog box.

The Compression option in the pop-up menu in the Sound dialog box allows you to lower the quality of your soundtrack and thereby save room on disk. It's applicable to 8-bit, 22 kHz mono sound only, and the results are absolutely horrible. Don't do it.

21. **Select the size of the movie you want to record by choosing an option from Record⇨Record Window Size.**

    Choose the Half Size option to record 320 × 240-pixel movies. You can record smaller movies, but you won't be able to record larger ones without additional hardware (again, such as SPAV).

    You can specify what size movie you want to record in Premiere by choosing Movie Capture⇨Recording Settings. Or, to record a 320 × 240-pixel movie, don't do anything; the default size is 320 × 240.

22. **Stop the videotape or pause the laserdisc.**

    Then rewind to a spot that's a minute or so before where you want to start recording, and start playing the tape or disc again.

23. **Click on the Rec button (or Record in Premiere) to start recording.**

    Click a few seconds before you see the first frames you want to capture to give yourself some margin. Better to record too much than too little.

24. **Click on the Stop button to stop recording.**

    In Premiere, click anywhere. If Premiere doesn't seem to notice your click, click again. Keep clicking until the darn thing stops.

    Unless you have a secondary hard drive just for recording QuickTime movies, you probably won't be able to record much more than a minute at a time before you run out of disk space. I told you that these things were disk pigs.

In FusionRecorder, the new movie appears in a standard QuickTime window. In Premiere, the window looks quite different, though it offers many of the same controls (and then some). You can play and pause the movie in either program by pressing the spacebar.

Be sure to save your movie to disk. The recording program automatically saves in the QuickTime format. So all you have to do is choose File⇨Save, enter a name, and press Return.

Grabbing a still image

After recording a digital movie, you can easily copy a single frame and paste it into Photoshop or some other image editing program. As you may recall from the "Turning Your Camcorder into a Digital Camera" section of Chapter 8, I used this technique to create all the pictures of the various products in this book (including the QuickCam and FlexCam cameras in Figures 17-7 and 17-9).

The first step is to record a movie at full-screen resolution, 640 × 480 pixels. Now, no machine can handle full-screen movies at a reasonable frame rate (not without special hardware, anyway). But who cares if FusionRecorder or Premiere misses a few frames — all you want is one frame. And obviously, there's no need to record sound.

After you record the movie, find the frame you want to copy. Look carefully: Many of the frames will look jiggly — that is, one horizontal strip of pixels will appear slightly out of sync with the next. This effect is called *interlacing*.

On TV, every other horizontal line is displayed in a group. First you see the odd lines from frame 1, followed by the even lines from frame 1, followed by the odd lines from frame 2, and so on. Each set of odd and even lines is called a *field*. If there is a lot of change between two fields in the same frame, the image looks terrible.

After you locate a good frame that doesn't look interlaced, you need to grab it. In Premiere, doing so is very easy. Choose File⇨Export⇨Frame as PICT to save the frame as a PICT file. Then open the PICT file inside Photoshop. No sweat.

In FusionRecorder, the process is a little more involved, but not much. Start off by finding your favorite frame. Then Shift-click on the next frame button (or press Shift-right arrow) to select the favorite frame and move to the next one. A sliver of a black line appears in the frame slider to show that the frame is selected. Next, choose Edit⇨Copy (⌘-C). This copies the favorite frame to the Clipboard. Finally, switch to Photoshop, choose File⇨New (⌘-N) to create a new image, and choose Edit⇨Paste (⌘-V) to paste the copied frame.

Picking Up the Pace

In theory, when you record a digital movie from videotape, you're simply making a conversion from one medium to another. You're saying, "Take these video frames from the tape and put them on disk. And be snappy about it."

Unfortunately, it takes time to write data to disk. In Photoshop, for example, you'd be very happy to see the program take no more than two or three seconds to save a small image to disk. But when you're recording a QuickTime movie, your computer has to be able to process several images per second. It's quite a feat.

Although it may come as no surprise that your Mac has problems recording each and every frame you ask it to, you can take some steps to improve its performance. The following are a few suggestions for making your computer record movies more smoothly and more accurately:

- Turn off all extensions and control panels except the essentials. Obviously, anything that has the words *QuickTime* or *Sound* in it has to remain on. But you don't need a bunch of extra stuff, including virus extensions (such as SAM), screen savers (After Dark), shortcut utilities (QuicKeys), general system customizers (Now Utilities), and type managers (ATM). You can turn these programs off using Extensions Manager or remove them from the Extensions and Control Panels folders in your System Folder. Then restart your computer. The advice of a local computer guru might be helpful.

- If you're on a network, turn off file sharing. You do this by opening the Sharing Setup control panel and clicking on the Stop button under File Sharing.

- If you're connected to a networked or PostScript printer, turn off AppleTalk. Choose the Chooser desk accessory from the Apple menu and select Inactive from the two AppleTalk radio buttons. (You don't have to worry about this step in Premiere because that program temporarily turns off AppleTalk automatically when you click on the Movie Capture button.)

- Quit all other programs and assign as much memory as you can to FusionRecorder or Premiere. After quitting all programs, choose About This Macintosh from the Apple menu. Note the Largest Unused Block value and close the dialog box. Then select FusionRecorder or Premiere and choose File➪Get Info (or press ⌘-I). Subtract about 1,000K from the Largest Unused Block value you noted a minute ago and enter the result in the Preferred Size option box. (This 1,000K margin gives the system software room to grow and shrink.) Then close the Info dialog box and start up the program.

- Ask the QuickTime recording program to compress the movie after it gets done recording it. This way, the program doesn't have to perform two jobs at once, which results in better movies. In FusionRecorder, choose Record➪Record Preferences and select the Post Compress check box. In Premiere, choose Movie Capture➪Recording Settings and select Post-Compress Video. The program takes much longer to display the movie on-screen after you finish recording it — several minutes, in some cases — but it's worth it.

Buying a Live Video Camera

If you intend to shoot lots and lots of videos around the office and you're willing to pay for convenience, there's nothing like a live video camera that sends moving images right to your disk. For a few hundred bucks, you can purchase a direct link from reality into your computer. No messing around with camcorders and VCRs, no scrounging for extra videotapes. In a fraction of a second, the physical world falls down a digital rabbit hole and lands smack dab in a pile of bits and bytes.

The least expensive, least demanding, and all-around dinkiest digital camera is the QuickCam from Connectix, 800-950-5880. Figure 17-7 offers a look at this $200 bit of technology. Slightly smaller than a tennis ball, the QuickCam lets you record quarter-screen, 15 frame-per-second, black-and-white movies. As you can see in Figure 17-8, it captures just 16 shades of gray — that's black, white, and 14 others — which is about a million times fewer than you can achieve with an AV machine. But when you consider that the QuickCam is less expensive than the cheapest digital still camera, I'd say that it amounts to something of a bargain.

Figure 17-7: How I see the QuickCam.

Figure 17-8: How the QuickCam sees me.

The QuickCam plugs into the modem port of just about any Mac. (Only the Plus, SE, Classic, and PowerBook 100 are incompatible.) Those little holes you can see on the left and right sides of the camera in Figure 17-7 represent an 8-bit, mono microphone. You can pivot the camera inside its triangular base, which fits tidily on a monitor or other out-of-the-way surface, or you can screw it onto a conventional tripod. And it comes with all the software needed to shoot movies, record sound, and capture still images. The quality isn't anything to write home about, but if all you're looking for is small, black-and-white movies, the QuickCam delivers like a champ.

The other live camera option, the $395 FlexCam from VideoLabs, 612-988-0055, isn't a digital camera at all. It's more of a stationary video camera. Just as you do with a camcorder, you have to have special hardware — such as that included with an AV or junior AV Macs — to convert the moving images to pixels.

Shown in Figure 17-9, the FlexCam is a lens perched atop a flexible, 15-inch neck that you can bend and twist in just about any direction you want. Like a VCR, the FlexCam provides an RCA video cable that you plug into the back of your AV computer. It also includes a stereo microphone along with left and right RCA audio cables. (The fourth cable you can see in the figure plugs into the power supply.) Unfortunately, the FlexCam doesn't include a Y cable with a stereo miniplug so that you can plug the audio into the sound-in jack on your Mac. The Y cable is not expensive, but it's no fun to have to go out and buy one when you're itching to start using your new camera.

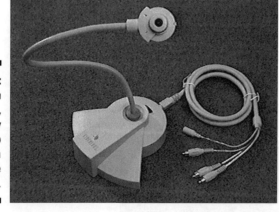

Figure 17-9: The FlexCam is a flexible, stationary video camera without the videotape.

After you get the FlexCam connections squared away, however, the camera's a dream. It doesn't require any software; you just plug and play. You can record movies with FusionRecorder, Premiere, or any other QuickTime recording program. It performs well in low-light situations, and you can manually adjust the focus by spinning an outer ring. Figure 17-10 demonstrates — perhaps too clearly — the range of the cameras focus capabilities. In the lower image, you can easily make out individual hairs, weird skin imperfections, and fetching eyeball veins. If you look very closely, you can even make out the rim of my contact lens.

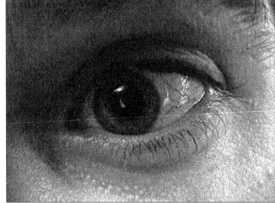

Figure 17-10: Proof of the old adage that authors should be read and not seen.

So, as a recap: The QuickCam is for folks with low-end Macs who don't want to miss out on the miracles of QuickTime movie recording. The FlexCam is for owners of full-fledged multimedia machines who value unlimited colors, stereo audio, and precise focus capabilities. Both cameras are remarkably inexpensive, far more competitively priced than their still-image cousins. Color me impressed.

Chapter 18
Cutting Room Meets Special Effects Factory

In This Chapter
- Using Adobe Premiere
- Making sense of the Construction Window
- Cutting your movies into independent scenes
- Deleting clips without mercy or remorse
- Fading the sound track in and out
- Experimenting with special effects
- Assigning and editing transition effects
- Previewing a portion of your project
- Saving the final edited version as a QuickTime movie

*I*f you own a camcorder — and you haven't gone and lost interest in the thing — you've undoubtedly amassed hours and hours of footage on videotape. Though I'm sure that there are many happy moments stocked away inside your collection, I'm willing to bet that much of the footage is awful. Mixed in with the good shots are lots of unfocused zooms, erratic pans, and pictures of people twiddling their thumbs — all of which are even more boring to watch than they were to experience. And who can forget those special times when you unwittingly left the camera on for minutes at a time, filming your feet and those of absolute strangers as you bustled along some legendary boulevard?

Well, if you don't like to watch this stuff, imagine how your friends, distant family members, and (heaven forbid) colleagues feel. Look at them, stifling yawns as you fast-forward through the boring stuff. Admire their pasted-on smiles as you explain what you were trying to film inside a dimly lit room or what you would have shot if only you hadn't stopped recording when you meant to start. These people aren't relaxing, they're knocking themselves out to be polite.

If you want to return the favor, edit without mercy. Record very little of the footage to disk and then hack it to pieces. You may also want to change the order of events, create transitions between scenes, and apply special effects.

You can then export the finished piece back to videotape — as discussed in the next chapter — or leave it on disk so that you can show it to folks in digestible chunks. (After all, if you go to videotape, you may feel tempted to fill the entire two hours of your tape.)

In this chapter, I take a look at Adobe Premiere, which is — dare I say? — the premier movie editing program on the Mac. Like Photoshop, the program is expensive — $800 retail. And it requires lots of free hard drive space; you need at least 200MB. Because QuickTime movies are so gall-darn enormous, you may find yourself looking for more disk space pretty quickly.

Unfortunately, you won't find many alternatives to Premiere. The only other affordable QuickTime editors are VideoFusion from Radius, 800-227-2795, and VideoShop from Avid, 800-949-2843. Both products cost $400. Of the two, I prefer VideoFusion, which happens to be the basis for the FusionRecorder program that I discussed in Chapter 17.

Even more unfortunately, Premiere, VideoFusion, and VideoShop aren't very similar in structure, so you won't be able to take the specific Premiere techniques I discuss here and apply them in one of the other two programs. The good news, however, is that the general capabilities of the programs *are* similar. You can delete frames, add transition effects, and divide and restructure a movie in any of them. So look upon this virtuous chapter as a specific discussion of Premiere and a general overview of QuickTime movie editors. You'll be glad you did.

Premiere Just Wants to Be Understood

Premiere is not an easy program to get to first base with. Although it eventually makes sense, its first few moves are enough to make you shriek and hold your hands up to your face — if not with quite the same gut-wrenching anguish portrayed by that poor blighter in Edvard Munch's *The Scream*, then at least with the same hapless goofiness as pantomimed by millionaire urchin Macaulay Culkin in *Home Alone*. I mean to say, you might feel a trifle baffled.

Whereas you may expect to be able to open a movie and start editing away, in much the same way that you open and edit a still image in Photoshop or a sound in SoundEdit 16, Premiere requires a different approach. You start by creating a new *project*, which is an empty vessel into which you put the movies you want to edit. It's as if you have 10 videotapes full of stuff and you want to record the best clips from those videos onto a new videotape. The project is that new videotape.

Still a little unclear? Well, permit me to be of service. Here are some steps to carry you through the thick of things:

Chapter 18: Cutting Room Meets Special Effects Factory 251

1. **Start Premiere.**

   Just double-click on its icon at the Finder desktop. You didn't need my help for that, of course. I only included this step because of what Premiere does in return. After taking the usual time to load its billion or so bits of data into RAM, it greets you with the bewildering items shown in Figure 18-1. This sort of greeting is enough to make the heartiest souls close their eyes and press ⌘-Q.

   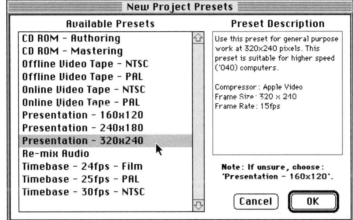

   Figure 18-1: Premiere wants to know what kind of movie you want to create.

2. **Select the Presentation — 320 × 240 option from the left list.**

   This instruction assumes that you want to edit quarter-screen movies. If you recorded your movies at a smaller size, select Presentation — 240 × 180 or Presentation — 160 × 120.

   You can find out the size of a movie by using the Movie Analysis function. First, cancel out of the dialog box pictured in Figure 18-1. Then click on the Movie Analysis button in the Commands palette (or press the shortcut key, F13). Find the movie in question on disk and double-click on it to open it. After the Analysis window appears, scroll to the bottom. You'll see an item such as Frame size = 320 × 240. This items tells you the width and height of the movie. After you note the size, close the Analysis window and press ⌘-N (or choose File➪New➪New Project) to return to the dialog box in Figure 18-1.

3. **Press Return to create the new project.**

   The main window for your new project doesn't look much like anything. It lists the items inside your project, and because you haven't had time to put anything in the project yet, the window is empty. Meanwhile, Premiere also displays a few palettes, including Commands, Transitions, and, the most important one, Construction Window. This last palette is where all the editing takes place.

4. **Choose File⇨Import⇨File (or press ⌘-I) to add a QuickTime movie to the project.**

   Locate the movie you want to add on disk and double-click on it. The movie appears in the Project window, as shown in Figure 18-2. You see a thumbnail of the first frame in the movie. If the movie contains sound, an orange bar appears below the thumbnail. The name column lists the name of the movie, the length in minutes and seconds, the width and height, and sound info.

   To import several movies at once, choose File⇨Import⇨Multiple. Inside the Import dialog box, double-click on each movie you want to add. Then click on the Done button.

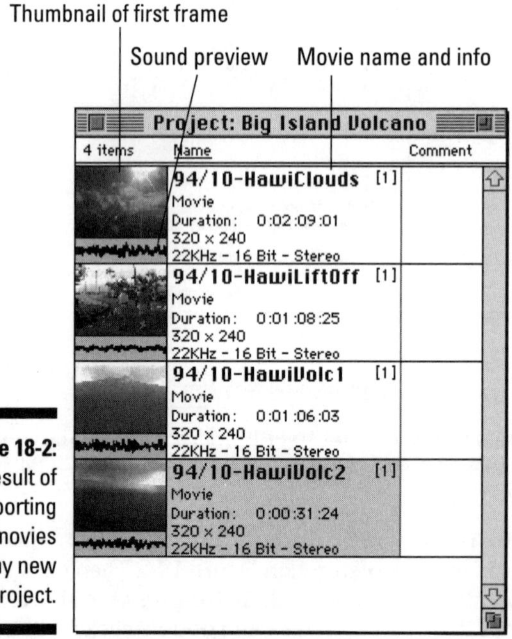

Figure 18-2: The result of importing four movies into my new project.

5. **To edit a movie, you need to drag it from the Project window and drop it into the Construction Window palette.**

   Drop the movie into the top row. As shown in Figure 18-3, the top row fills with little thumbnails, representing frames in the movie. The top row, labeled A on the right side of the Construction Window, is the first track, which is equivalent to a scene in the movie. Row B is the second track. The idea is to fade from the top track to the bottom and then from the bottom back to the top, and so on, moving from one scene in the movie to the next.

   If the movie contains sound, its sound track automatically drops into the A track in the Audio section of the Construction window. As with the Video section, you have an A track and a B track. The two tracks don't represent stereo sound as they do in SoundEdit 16. Each track can contain stereo or mono sound; having two tracks merely allows you to blend them together.

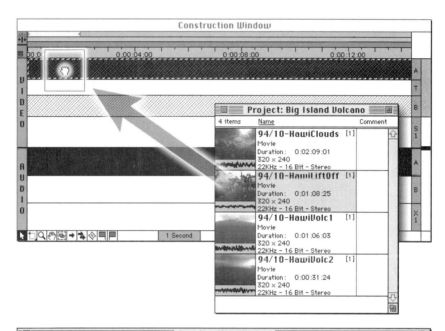

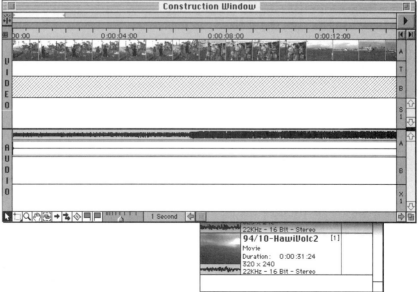

Figure 18-3: Drag a movie from the Project window (top) and drop it into the Construction Window (bottom), where you can edit it.

The T track in the Video section is for transition effects, which enable you to fade from one scene to the other, as explained later in this chapter. The S1 Video Track and the X1 Audio track enable you to superimpose additional video and audio tracks. For example, you might create layered video effects — you know, like words floating over the sky — using track S1 and create background music in track X1.

6. Save your project to disk.

Choose File⇨Save or press ⌘-S. Believe me, you do not want to spend a lot of time on a project in Premiere and then lose your work because of a crash or dumb mistake. Remember to save, save, save.

Now that you have a movie nestled comfortably inside the Construction Window, you can go in about 20 different directions. You can splice the movie, delete portions of it, move it to a different track, create transitions between scenes, apply special effects, add more movies, and so on. Rather than step you through these options — which could very well take us the next 25 pages — I explain each one on its own in the following sections.

First, Carve Up Your Scenes

The first thing you should do with the movie you dropped into the Construction Window is slice and dice it into its independent scenes. These scenes — which Premiere calls *clips* — can last anywhere from a few seconds to a minute or more. The length doesn't matter. What does matter is that you decide exactly where you want the action to begin and where you want it to end. You have absolute control, so you may as well take advantage of it.

Before you cut the movie, you may want to make the thumbnails in the Construction Window bigger and more numerous so that you can better see what you're doing:

- To increase the size of the thumbnails, choose Windows⇨Construction Window Options (or press ⌘-1). Inside the resulting dialog box, select the largest Icon Size radio button and then press Return.

- By default, you only see one thumbnail for every second of movie. That's not very precise. To see more of the frames, select the zoom tool — which looks like a magnifying glass — in the lower-left corner of the Construction Window or press the Z key. Then position the cursor over the thumbnails and click. Now you see one frame for every half-second of action. Keep clicking with the tool to zoom in further.

To cut a movie in two, you slice it with a razor. Not a real one, mind you — tests have shown that real razors are bad for the screen — but the razor tool in the lower-left corner of the Construction Window (labeled in Figure 18-4). Here's how to create an exact slice:

1. **Select the razor tool.**

   Or press R to select the tool from the keyboard.

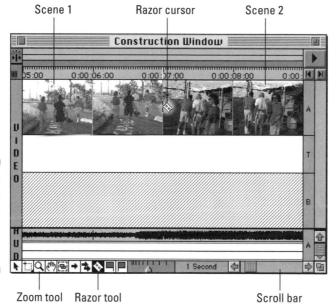

Figure 18-4: Use the razor tool to slice a movie into two clips.

2. **Scroll to the place where you want to make your cut.**

   Use the horizontal scroll bar in the lower-right corner of the window (also labeled in Figure 18-4).

3. **Click between the two thumbnails that represent the end of one scene and the beginning of another.**

   The movie splits in two, just as if you had sliced a piece of film with a real razor blade. What was once one movie in the Project window turns into two. The two movies both share the same name, but one has a little 1 in brackets next to it, and the other has a little 2.

4. **Using the arrow tool, drag the second clip to track B in the Construction Window.**

   You can select the arrow tool, if it isn't already selected, by pressing the A (for arrow) or S (for selection) key.

   When you drag the video to track B, the sound for that clip moves to track B as well. With the second scene in the second track, you can adjust the two clips without having one bump shoulders with the other. Trust me, it's better this way.

5. **To get the cut just right, double-click on the first clip.**

   The Clip window, which is Premiere's pumped-up version of the QuickTime movie window, appears, as shown in Figure 18-5. You can play the movie, advance one frame at a time, and do lots of other things in this window.

Figure 18-5: To go to the cut at the end of the first clip, select the Out option from the Goto pop-up menu.

6. **Select Out from the Goto pop-up menu.**

   Or just press the O key. This option takes you to the end of the clip, the point at which you cut the movie with the razor tool. The word Out even appears in the upper-right corner of the frame.

   The thing is, the movie keeps going on beyond this point. Even though you went and razored the film right in twain, the entire movie remains available inside the Clip window. Cool.

7. **Press the right- and left-arrow keys to find the exact spot at which you want the clip to end.**

   You see, all you have so far is an approximate cut. You probably couldn't see every frame inside the Construction Window — unless you zoomed *way* in — so your cut landed within a range of frames. To get it right on, you need to find the exact frame that represents the end of the scene (not the beginning of the next one).

8. **Click on the Out button.**

   This step repositions the end of the cut. Click in the close box or press ⌘-W to close the Clip window and return to the Construction Window.

Chapter 18: Cutting Room Meets Special Effects Factory

9. **Double-click on the second clip in the Construction Window.**

    Again, this brings up the Clip window, but for the second clip in the movie. You automatically come to the In point.

10. **Press the right- and left-arrow keys to find the exact beginning of the scene.**

    As with the Out point assigned by Premiere, the In point falls within a range of frames but is not exact. Look for the exact frame that starts the scene.

11. **Click on the In button.**

    This sets the In point right where you want it. Press ⌘-W to close the Clip window.

Now you're cutting scenes like a pro. You simply can't achieve this kind of control when recording from one consumer-quality VCR to another. Premiere brings home all the precision of traditional film splicing, plus a whole lot more, as you'll discover in the very next section.

What to Do with All Those Clips

As you slice and dice your movie into a bunch of individual clips, alternate each clip to the opposite track. For example, if the first clip starts off in track A and the second is in track B, as I suggested in the previous section, put the third clip in track A, the fourth in track B, the fifth in track A, and so on. This system makes it easier to keep the clips separate as you work on them. You can always move them around later.

After you get a handful of clips put together, here are some things to try out:

- If you decide that you don't want a clip — as you undoubtedly will throughout your spree of merciless editing — select the clip and press Delete.
- Ah ha, but that only deletes the video. The sound remains behind. If you want to delete both sound and video, press Shift-Delete.
- Ah ha, ha-ha-ha, but both Delete and Shift-Delete merely remove the clip in the Construction Window. The clip remains available in the Project window just in case you want it back. To delete the clip completely, select it in the Project window and delete it.
- You can move a clip left or right in a track by dragging it. Both video and sound move together.

- To move the sound independently of the video, select it with the arrow tool and press the left- or right-arrow key. Pressing either arrow key moves the sound one frame, which is a great way to fix voices if they don't sync with lip movements. Press Shift with the left- or right-arrow key to move the sound in five-frame increments.

- If you prefer to drag the video or sound track independently rather than nudge it from the keyboard, you have to switch tools. Click on the range select tool (immediately to the right of the arrow) or select it by pressing E. Then click on the track to select it. Now you can drag away.

- When video and sound don't align as they were originally recorded, little red arrowheads appear on the left sides of the clips. To realign video or sound, click and hold on the respective arrowhead. The cursor changes to a red arrow, and a one-line pop-up menu appears, showing the number of seconds and frames that the video and sound are off. Select this option to shift video or sound back into exact alignment.

- You may have noticed a horizontal line underneath every sound track in the Audio tracks. This line lets you fade sounds in and out. The line represents the volume of the sound. By default, the volume is set to a constant medium. At each end of the line is a point. You can move this point up or down to increase or decrease the volume. You can also add points by clicking on the line. In Figure 18-6, I've clicked to create two points inside the line, and I've dragged the outermost points all the way down. The result is a sound track that fades in, levels off, and then fades out.

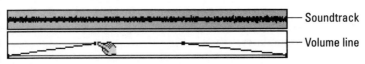

Figure 18-6: Add points to the volume line and drag the points up and down to create fade-ins and fade-outs.

- To apply a special effect to a selected clip, choose Clip➪Filters or press ⌘-F. Inside the Filters dialog box, double-click on an effect listed on the left to apply it to the clip. You can add as many filtering effects as you like. Available effects include focus- and color-correcting, distortions, cropping, and a whole mess of other stuff.

- You can also bring up the Filters dialog box by pressing the Option key and clicking and holding on the clip in the Construction Window. A pop-up menu with a single option, Filters, appears. Select the option, and away you go.

- Each effect in the Filters dialog box works differently, and some are rather complex. If you get overwhelmed, you can always click on the Cancel button to return to the Construction Window without harming a single frame.

Fade to Bob, Alone by the Marigolds

Premiere enables you to create two basic kinds of transitions between clips. You can opt for a *clean cut*, which means that one clip merely starts where the other one ends. To do this, drag the clip in one track until its left edge snaps into alignment with the right edge of the clip in the other track. That's all there is to it.

But if you want to fade one clip into the other, you have to work a little harder. Premiere provides more than 60 different kinds of fades, which are known from Hollywood to Gotham as *transition effects*. Here's how you can assign one of these amazing fades:

1. **Adjust the clips so that they slightly overlap each other.**

    For example, in Figure 18-7, the clip in track A ends at the eight-second mark, while the one in track B begins at four seconds. That's a four-second overlap.

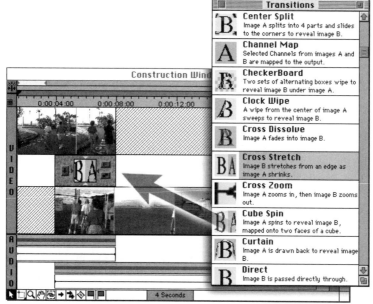

Figure 18-7: Drag an effect from the Transitions palette into track T to create a fade between two clips.

2. **If the Transitions palette is not already open, open it.**

    You do this by choosing Windows➪Transitions or pressing ⌘-6.

3. **Decide which transition effect you want to use.**

   Scroll down the list. For your viewing enjoyment, Premiere presents you with an animated preview that features the letter *A* fading to a letter *B*. The *A* represents the contents of track A, while the *B* represents a half-pound of boneless chicken . . . wait, no, I seem to have scrawled a few grocery items on my Premiere notes. Let's see, it says here that the *A* represents, uh, a head of lettuce. Yes, of course, that's it. Sorry about the confusion.

4. **Drag the desired effect from the Transitions palette and drop it into track T.**

   The T track resides between A and B. The effect automatically starts at the beginning of the second track and ends at the end of the first, as shown in Figure 18-7.

If you take a close look at the transition marker inside track T, you can see a few controls. So you don't sue me for eye strain, I've expanded and labeled the marker in Figure 18-8. Here's how the controls work:

- **Track selector:** The arrow indicates whether the transition is going from track A to track B (pointing down), or from track B to track A (pointing up). When you insert the transition effect, Premiere automatically sets the transition in the right direction. But if you later change the order of tracks, you may also have to change the direction of the transition. To do so, click on the track selector icon.

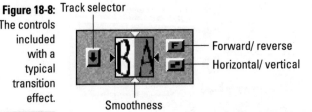

Figure 18-8: The controls included with a typical transition effect.

- **Forward/reverse:** To play the transition in reverse, click on this icon to change it from an *F* to an *R*. For example, with the cube effect shown in the figure, track B enters from the left when the effect is played forward. If you reverse the effect, track B enters from the right. To change the R back to an F, just click.

- **Smoothness:** Click on this icon to select between three degrees of smoothness — that is, how carefully the pixels in the different tracks are blended during the transition. The default setting, jagged, takes the least amount of time to calculate when saving and previewing. But if you think that the effect is too jagged, you may want to select one of the smoother, slower settings.

✓ **Horizontal/vertical:** Not all transitions offer these tiny little arrowheads around the effect icon. But when available, the arrowheads let you spin the effect in a different direction. For example, if you were to click on the white arrows, track B would spin in from the top or the bottom of the screen (depending on the setting of the forward/reverse control).

Prelude to a Movie

To view how a transition effect looks when applied to your particular clips, you have to preview a portion of the project. In other words, you actually play that portion of the movie. It takes a few minutes for Premiere to calculate all the frames, but it's the only way to see what's what.

You specify the portion of the project you want to preview using the *work area bar*, which is that yellow horizontal strip just below the Construction Window title bar, as shown in Figure 18-9. If you don't see any yellow strip in your Construction Window, double-click inside the gray strip below the title bar. Premiere relocates the work area bar to your neck of the woods.

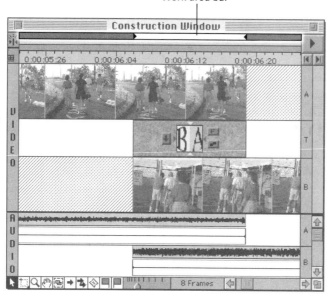

Figure 18-9: Use the work area bar to specify which portion of your project you want to check out.

The work area bar is flanked by two red arrowheads. Drag the arrowheads to determine the length of the bar. In Figure 18-9, I resized the bar so that it fits exactly over the transition effect. This permits me to preview the transition and its effect on the tracks without suffering through the rest of the movie.

After you stretch the bar according to your needs, choose Project⇨Preview or, better yet, just press Return. Premiere tells you that it has to think about things for a few minutes. If you need to go to the bathroom, now's a good time.

When you come back, Premiere should be ready to show you your movie. As you can see in Figure 18-10, the preview appears in a plain window without any QuickTime controls. (The image shown here, incidentally, is a frame from the Cube Spin transition effect, with track B entering from the left.)

Figure 18-10: Previewing the work area of your project is as easy as pressing Return.

If you miss the preview or simply want to look at it again, press Return again. Because Premiere stores the preview in RAM, it doesn't have to regenerate it. It can replay the preview almost instantaneously.

When you finish viewing the effect, you can modify it and play the preview again. (You don't need to close the Preview window in the meantime.) As long as you continue to preview the same section of your project, Premiere takes less time to generate the preview the second time around because it only has to recalculate the changed frames.

Show Time

After you get your project arranged just the way you like it, it's time to make it into a QuickTime movie. That way, you can play it inside other programs or include it with multimedia presentations. You can also play the QuickTime movie at top speed for recording to videotape, as discussed in the next chapter.

1. **Save your project.**

    You should be doing this all along, but it's always a good idea to save before doing anything major. It's usually the major stuff that crashes your Mac, don't you know.

2. **Resize the work area bar to cover the portion of the project that you want to make into a movie.**

    If you want to make the entire project into a movie, skip this step.

3. **Choose Make⇨Movie or press ⌘-K.**

    Premiere greets you with a standard Save dialog box so that you can explain where on disk and under what name you'd like to save the movie. At the bottom of the dialog box are two buttons, Output Options and Compression.

4. **Enter a name for the movie and specify a location.**

    Do what you do whenever you save a file to disk.

5. **Click on the Output Options button.**

    The fun-filled, lunatic of a dialog box shown in Figure 18-11 frolics onto the screen.

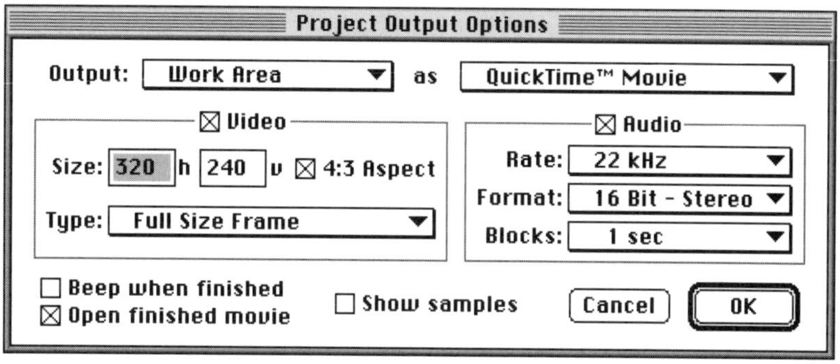

Figure 18-11: Don't you wish you had to deal with this many complex options every time you saved a file to disk?

6. **If you want to make a movie of the work area only, select Work Area from the Output pop-up menu.**

   To make the entire project into a movie, select Entire Project instead.

7. **Select QuickTime Movie from the second pop-up menu.**

   The QuickTime Composite option, which is the default setting, recalculates only those frames that have changed from the original movies in your project. However, the compression option that you'll be using later in these steps, Cinepak, rewrites all frames to produce the best playback speeds. So QuickTime Movie, which saves everything from scratch, is the better choice here.

8. **Check the two Size values under the Video check box to make sure that the frame size is correct.**

   The Size values should conform to the size of the QuickTime movies that you imported into the Premier project. If they're not right, change them. (You can ignore the other Video options.)

9. **Confirm the settings of the Rate and Format pop-up menus under the Audio check box.**

   Unless you're using 8-bit, 22 kHz mono sound, you need to change these settings. In Figure 18-11, for example, I selected 16-bit, 22 kHz stereo sound.

10. **Ignore all the other options and press Return.**

    Welcome back to the Save dialog box.

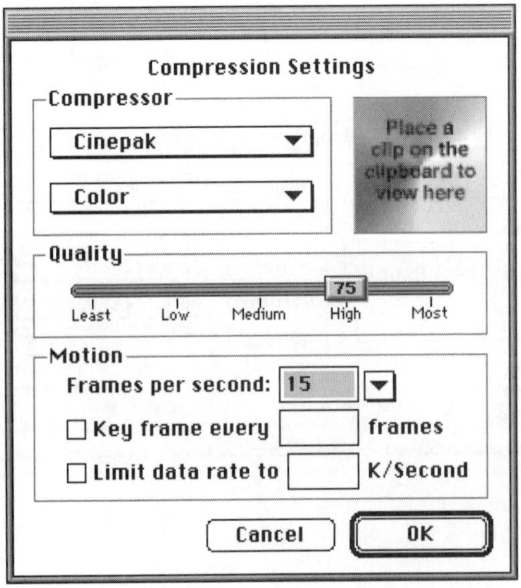

Figure 18-12: Cinepak is the perfect compression setting for playing back movies on any Mac.

Chapter 18: Cutting Room Meets Special Effects Factory 265

11. **Click on the Compression button.**

    The Compression Settings dialog box shown in the esteemed Figure 18-12 appears.

12. **Select the Cinepak option from the first Compressor pop-up menu.**

    Pronounced like *cinema* except with a *pack* instead of a *ma*, Cinepak is an amazing compression option. It takes forever to save your work, so you have to abandon your machine for a while, but it provides excellent playback capabilities. After a movie is saved to Cinepak, you can play it on just about any Mac. In fact, virtually all CD-ROM vendors save their movies in Cinepak. For maximum flexibility, you should, too.

    In Chapter 17, I recommended that you save your newly recorded movies using the Video or Component Video codec (compression option), and that advice still stands. Both of these codecs are good in-between compressors, allowing you to save movies relatively quickly and with little loss in quality. Though Cinepak movies play fast, they don't hold up well if you try to edit them. Cinepak is an end-of-the-line codec.

13. **Adjust the Quality slider as desired.**

    Use the rainbow-colored preview in the upper-right corner to gauge how much damage the compression does. Remember, lower Quality means a smaller file on disk, but it also means an uglier file.

    If you copied a frame to the Clipboard before choosing Make➪Movie, the frame appears in the upper-right corner of the dialog box in place of the rainbow preview. However, I personally find the rainbow preview more useful.

14. **Ignore the other options and press the Return key twice.**

    Premiere closes the Compression Settings dialog box and saves the movie to disk.

As I mentioned earlier, the Cinepak compression option takes a long time to work its magic — a *very* long time. You can count on several minutes per every minute in the movie, depending on the speed of your Mac. Although you can run other programs and let Premiere make the movie in the background, I would play it safe and let Premiere work away unhampered. Go do something that doesn't involve a computer for a half hour or so. You could use the break.

Chapter 19
Sending Your Movies Back to Videotape

In This Chapter
▶ Using a television as a monitor
▶ Fixing things when your video totally disappears
▶ Underscanning versus overscanning
▶ Playing a movie at full-screen size with MoviePlay
▶ Printing a movie to videotape with Premiere

If I weren't quite so verbose, I could have summed up a few of the chapters in this book in single sentences. Instead of writing Chapter 3, I could have just said, "Buy a pair of speakers and plug them in." In place of Chapter 7, I could have written the sentence "Take your pictures into a Photo CD lab and ask someone who appears to work there what's up." But you know me — I start writing, and I just can't shut up.

This chapter is another case in point. I could just write, "Turn on your VCR, play your QuickTime movie, and record it to videotape," and we could all get on with our lives that much quicker. In fact, if *Reader's Digest* ever decides to condense this book — and it's a safe bet they won't — that sentence is all that will be left of this chapter.

But then again, if I decided to go the *Reader's Digest* route, think of all your burning questions that would go unanswered:

✔ How do I get the QuickTime movie to go out the RCA jacks so that my VCR can record it?

✔ How do I make the movie fill the screen so that I don't record a bunch of desktop garbage?

✔ Is there any way to set up a delay so that I have time to start my VCR recording before the action begins?

- Where can I get some of those color bars that those professional movie guys always seem to use?
- What is overscanning and underscanning? I've never even heard these terms before, but I've just got to know what they mean.

It is out of respect for your questions that I write the remainder of this chapter. Thank golly there are still some unabridged compendiums of knowledge like this one to make the world a more straightforward place in which to live.

On a serious note — B flat has always seemed like the buttoned-down type to me — you need special hardware to play video from your computer out to a VCR. AV Macs comes with this hardware built in. If you own a junior AV Mac, however, you have to buy additional hardware, such as the Apple Presentation System, to convert the computer RGB signal to NTSC TV. Some products from other vendors, such as the Spigot II Tape from Radius, also offer video-output capabilities. Read the last section in Chapter 5, "Can You Add AV to Your Old Mac?" for the complete story.

How to Send Video Out to Your VCR

When you play a movie out to videotape, you can't see the movie on your computer monitor. That's because AV Macs let you display computer video signals on a monitor *or* a television device, but not both. The video signal either goes through the computer video jack to the monitor or through the RCA and S-video jacks to the VCR.

The upshot of this is that you need a VCR to record the QuickTime movie and a TV to see what the heck you're doing. If you have a second monitor hooked up to your computer, you can make do with a small monitor, like one of those little Sony gadgets, because you can read the menu bars and small text on the second monitor. But otherwise, you need a full-sized TV. Don't simply hook up a camcorder to your Mac, for example, and try to monitor the proceedings through the viewfinder. Trying to read menu names on a tiny screen like that is very near impossible.

Assuming that you have a VCR and TV on hand, here's what you do:

1. **Hook up your VCR to the AV Mac as instructed in the "And how do I send computer signals to the VCR?" section of Chapter 5.**

    Cable the video-output jack on the Mac to the video-input jack on your VCR. Then hook the sound-out jack on the Mac to the sound-in jacks on the video deck using a Y cable (assuming that the VCR records in stereo).

Chapter 19: Sending Your Movies Back to Videotape

2. **Attach the TV to the VCR.**

   You can connect the VCR to the TV using a coaxial cable and then watch the computer signal on channel 3. Or, if your TV supports RCA inputs — as is true of most $300 and up TVs made in recent years — cable the video- and sound-output jacks on the VCR to the input jacks on the TV. If all else fails, consult the manual that came with your TV.

3. **Turn on the VCR and TV.**

   Don't worry if all you see on the TV is a lot of black. You haven't sent the computer signal out to the TV yet, so there's nothing to see. In fact, black is a good sign; it shows that you aren't picking up TV signals instead.

4. **Open the Monitors control panel.**

   You do this by choosing the Control Panels command from the Apple menu and double-clicking on the Monitors icon. Or you may be able to choose Apple⇨Control Panels⇨Monitors.

5. **Click on the screen icon in the center of the control panel window.**

   If there is more than one icon — indicating that you have more than one monitor — select the one that represents the screen hooked up to the built-in video port on your AV Centris or Quadra or the video port on the AV card in your Power Mac.

6. **Click on the Options button.**

   Or just double-click on the screen icon. Either of these actions displays the Built-In AV Video dialog box, shown in Figure 19-1.

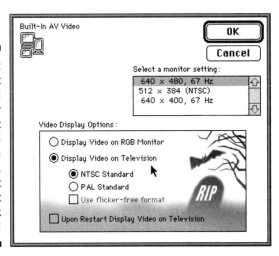

Figure 19-1: AV Macs let you send computer graphics out to an RGB monitor or a television. Just don't select that last check box!

270   Part IV: Hollywood in a Box

7. **Make sure that the 640 × 480 option is selected in the Select a Monitor Setting list.**

   If you use a 14-inch monitor, this option is definitely selected, so you can skip this step. But if you're using a 17-inch screen or larger, you have to select the lower resolution.

   After you do so, press Return or click on OK to switch the resolution. If the resolution doesn't change right away, restart your Mac. However, if the screen resolution does change, go ahead and click on the Options button again and continue through the steps.

   (If you did have to restart your Mac, just redisplay the Monitors control panel, click on the Options button, and proceed to the next step.)

8. **Select the Display Video on Television radio button.**

   By default, the NTSC Standard option becomes selected. This option makes the computer signal compatible with U.S. televisions. If you want to record your video for a friend in Finland or one of those other European places, however, select the PAL Standard option.

   To record a PAL signal, you need a PAL-compatible VCR and a PAL-compatible TV. Needless to say, these machines aren't very popular on this side of the Atlantic. (Well, you can find them in Brazil, but that's still a long drive.)

   Whatever you do, do *not* — I repeat, don't *even* — select the Upon Restart Display Video on Television check box. This dangerous option tells your Mac to send the computer video out to the TV from now on, even after you restart the computer. The thing is, if something goes wrong and you lose the video signal, restarting the computer is your only solution. And because you told the computer to display the signal on your TV, all you get is that same empty screen as before. There ought to be a skull-and-crossbones drinking poison against a backdrop of nuclear silos next to this option. Stay away!

9. **Press Return or click on OK.**

   The dialog box closes, and a message appears to warn you that if you go through with this action, the computer screen display will transfer to the television and your monitor will go black. This is a very important warning. If you only have one monitor and you do not have a TV hooked up to your computer, you will no longer be able to see anything that's going on with your computer.

10. **If you're sure that everything is ready to go, click on the Switch button.**

    If you want to recheck your connections — or if you just thought it'd be interesting to follow along with these steps even though you don't have a TV hooked up — now is a good time to click on the Cancel button.

The computer screen display switches over to the TV, and the monitor goes black. You are now ready to send your movies out to videotape.

If both TV and monitor go black, something isn't hooked up correctly. Check your connections and try to find out where you went wrong. If you really get desperate, call the neighborhood computer whiz for help.

In the meantime, to get the computer image back over to the monitor, you have to restart your Mac. Press the restart button on the front or side of your computer — the one with a little left-facing arrowhead on it. If you don't have a restart button, press ⌘ and Ctrl along with the power button in the upper-left corner of your keyboard. Your computer will restart with the computer image back on the monitor.

If that doesn't work — possibly because you selected the Upon Restart Display Video on Television check box — restart your Mac again and immediately press and hold the ⌘, Option, P, and R keys. Keep holding all four keys until the computer repeats the startup tone a second time. The screen will also flash. This technique resets all hardware settings to their factory defaults. (The *P* and *R,* incidentally, stand for *Parameter Ram,* or PRAM. This method of restarting your computer is called *zapping the PRAM.*)

Where's My Menu Bar?

One of the key differences between computer monitors and TVs is that monitors show you the whole picture, and TVs don't. TVs crop the picture so that it looks better.

A television draws a picture on the screen in a series of horizontal lines called *scan lines.* The scan lines at the top and bottom of the signal frequently get garbled during transmission or recording. (That's why you may see skewed details and weird static at the top and bottom of the QuickTime movies you record.) Your TV doesn't want you to get your nose out of joint when watching your favorite shows, so it simply chops away some of the detail around the edges. The entire picture is still there, mind you, it's just that your TV doesn't show it all.

To make matters more interesting, different TVs chop off different amounts of the picture. Suppose that you display an image of a big letter *A.* On one TV, that *A* may be exactly centered. On another, it may be an inch up and to the left. In comparison to the standards that monitors have to meet, TVs get away with murder.

What all this means to you is that the menu bar may totally disappear into the nether regions at the top of the TV screen. Luckily, you can fix this problem by making the computer picture smaller on the TV. If you bring up the Monitors control panel again and click on the Options button, you display a list of Select a Monitor Setting options. Click on the 512 × 384 (NTSC) option. This option reduces the size of the computer image by 20 percent, which is a technique called *underscanning*. Click on OK, and your menu bars come inside the confines of the TV screen.

The problem is, when recording a QuickTime movie to videotape, you want to fill the entire 640 × 480-pixel area again. Otherwise, you'll be able to see all that garbage at the top and bottom of the movie when watching the videotape, and the frame may not be centered on the TV screen. So right before you start playing your movie, be sure to click on the Options button in the Monitors control panel again and select the 640 × 480, 67 Hz option. This setting projects the computer images at the highest TV resolution, which is known to broadcast types as *overscanning*.

How to Fill the Screen with Movie

The simplest way to play a movie and record it to tape is to use a QuickTime movie player program. The best one for this purpose is MoviePlay, which Apple includes with the AV Macs. Unlike the similarly named MoviePlayer — which Apple also includes with AV Macs — MoviePlay without the *er* hides the menu bar when you blow a movie up to full-screen size.

If you only have one monitor hooked up to your computer, here's how to play a movie in MoviePlay:

1. **Start the MoviePlay program and open the QuickTime movie you want to record to videotape.**

    Use File⇨Open or ⌘-O, as always.

2. **Choose Movie⇨Screen Size or press ⌘-4.**

    This step doubles the width and height of a quarter-screen movie so that it fills the TV screen. MoviePlay hides the menu bar and all QuickTime controls. (If you are playing a smaller movie, the image still fills the screen, but MoviePlay has to triple or quadruple the width and height of the images, so the movie may not play as smoothly.)

3. **Get your VCR ready to record.**

    Press the Pause and Rec buttons or do whatever you have to do with your VCR when you want to put it in the almost-ready-to-record mode.

    You need to perform the next two steps in rapid-fire succession, so get ready.

Chapter 19: Sending Your Movies Back to Videotape

4. **Start the VCR recording.**

   Every consumer VCR has about a full-second delay from the time you press the Rec button until the heads lock down on the tape and begin recording. So after you press the Rec button or turn off Pause, perform Step 5 very quickly.

5. **Press the spacebar on your keyboard.**

   As you may recall, pressing the spacebar plays the QuickTime movie. Because the play button is hidden, the spacebar (or Return key) is your only option.

6. **A few seconds after the movie stops playing, pause the recording.**

   Instead of immediately pausing the recording when you see the last scene of your movie, I recommend waiting a moment to give yourself some slack. MoviePlay hangs on the last frame, so you can get a clean shot of the frame for a few seconds. Then you can rewind the videotape, play it to the exact edit spot, and get ready to record the next movie with the knowledge that even if the tape slips as much as a second, you'll see a paused frame between movies rather than static.

I Was Told We'd See Color Bars

The problem with MoviePlay and the other freeware QuickTime players that you may find is that they really aren't set up for recording movies to videotape. You can't add a bit of black, silent video to the beginning or end of your movie so that viewers will have some sort of warning before your first scene appears — a technique called *laying down black* in the professional video biz. If you own two monitors, you can't specify which monitor you want to play the movie on. Nary a color bar is to be seen. And the way the program blows the movie up to full-screen size is pretty clumsy.

Enter Premiere, that wonderful QuickTime editing program that can also play movies to tape like a champ. Using Premiere, you can do every one of the things that I mentioned in the previous paragraph. Here's how:

1. **Inside Premiere, open up the movie you want to record.**

   "No open, no play," as Bob Marley used to sing. Of course, that was before he got mad at his girlfriend and changed the lyrics.

2. **If you have more than one monitor, drag the movie onto the TV screen.**

   The movie has to be positioned on the screen on which you want to play it.

3. **Choose File⇨Export⇨Print to Video or press ⌘-M.**

   The dialog box shown in Figure 19-2 appears.

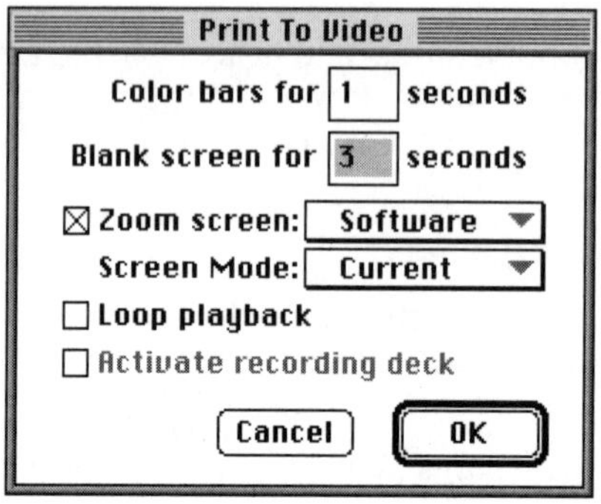

Figure 19-2: Premiere lets you control every aspect of playing a movie and recording it to videotape.

4. **If you want to display color bars, enter the number of seconds you want them to appear on-screen into the first option box.**

   Color bars help you make sure that the tape is sound and that the color settings on your TV are accurate. You may want to record color bars at the beginning of the videotape and at the end for reference.

5. **To add a bit of black screen before and after the movie, enter the duration of the blackness into the second option box.**

   Premiere calls the option Blank Screen, but you really get a black screen.

6. **Select the Zoom Screen check box.**

   This option blows up the movie to fill the screen.

7. **If you want to make a recording of the movie playing over and over again, select the Loop Playback check box.**

   This option is great if you want to record an advertisement video for an exhibition or some other event where crowds will meander past your wares. Premiere plays the movie continuously until you click the mouse button to cancel it.

8. **Get your VCR ready to record.**

   Do what you have to do.

9. **Press the Return key.**

   The Print To Video dialog box closes, and Premiere starts doing its stuff.

10. **Start the VCR recording.**

    First Premiere plays the color bars, then the black screen, then the movie, and then the black screen again.

11. **After Premiere finishes displaying the final black screen, pause the VCR.**

    If something goes wrong and you want to interrupt the movie, just press ⌘-period, the universal Macintosh keyboard equivalent for cancel.

Part V
The Part of Tens

In this part...

Every *...For Dummies* book has a Part of Tens. It's a tradition as rich with heritage as, well, anything else that's been around for five years. The Part of Tens generally contains special tips and tricks lifted from other chapters — quick, humorous information that you can digest quickly and effortlessly.

But I've bucked the trend a little bit. Rather than cover all the various aspects of multimedia in this part, I'm concentrating on what is perhaps the most exciting single multimedia topic, CD-ROMs. Chapter 20, for example, explains the top ten tips for getting the most out of your CDs.

But it's the four lists of top ten CD-ROMs in Chapters 21 through 24 that I think you'll find most interesting. IDG's Suki Gear and I called more than 50 CD-ROM vendors and rounded up more than 300 CDs in less than two months. That was hard, but looking at every one of the CDs and picking the winners to include in my top ten lists was even harder. I haven't been out to a movie or watched more than two or three minutes of TV at a time since the first CD-ROM arrived. Aside from one novel I'm reading, CDs have become my only form of entertainment. It may sound like I'm complaining, but I'm really bragging. I haven't missed TV for a second. I can state without hesitation that if every other form of entertainment besides books and CD-ROMs completely disappeared, we would be none the poorer. The sheer volume of information available on CD-ROM today is staggering. The information that will be available in ten years defies imagination.

So stop buying those videotapes and save up your money for the drop-dead amazing CDs I cover in these chapters. Interactive multimedia CD-ROMs have realized only the smallest fraction of their potential, and yet they're already the best thing going.

Chapter 20
Ten Ways to Make Your CD-ROMs Perform Like Champs

In This Chapter

- ▶ Install QuickTime and its cronies once and never again
- ▶ Turn off file sharing, virtual memory, and Ram Doubler
- ▶ Give HyperCard Player more memory
- ▶ Copy the main program file to your hard drive
- ▶ Set the video to Thousands
- ▶ Click to skip the introductory movie
- ▶ Don't go clicking like a madman
- ▶ Move the cursor away from the movie
- ▶ Press ⌘-Q to skip the closing credits
- ▶ What to do when all else fails

Multimedia CD-ROMs are funny creatures. The best of them are fun, informative, intuitive, and downright addictive. But in return, they pretty much want to monopolize your Mac. Very few CD-ROM titles are willing to share memory, processing time, or screen space with other programs. Most don't even let you access the menu bar. Once you're inside the program, it becomes your little world.

As long as the CD is intent on taking over your Mac whether you like it or not, you may as well give the computer over willingly. That way, your little world will run faster and with fewer hiccups.

Most of the tips in this chapter explain how to make your computer a cushier place for your CD to function. But I also throw in a few tips to help you enjoy your titles more and skip the parts you don't like. Not every tip applies to every CD you'll ever use. But after spending countless hours browsing through 300 CDs, I can assure you that the ideas here apply to most titles and are well worth trying out.

Install QuickTime and Its Cronies Once and Never Again

Just about every CD wants to install QuickTime, Multimedia Tuner, and Sound Manager onto your computer. The CD needs these system extensions to play movies and sound, and it's afraid that your Mac may not be properly equipped.

But after you install these extensions the first time, there's no sense in installing them over and over again. It takes time, and you have to restart your computer. What a bother.

- Most CDs have two separate installers, one for the CD program itself and the other for QuickTime et al. In this case, obviously, you just run the program installer.
- Other CDs have just one installer for all files. For these CDs, select the Custom option inside the Installer program and ask to install the CD program only.
- Still other CDs require that you copy everything manually to your hard drive during installation. When you install these CDs, just copy the program, not the other stuff.

Turn off File Sharing, Virtual Memory, and RAM Doubler

Remember the tips I shared for making QuickTime movies record more smoothly in the "Picking Up the Pace" section of Chapter 17? Well, the first three tips make multimedia CDs perform better as well. Turn off AppleTalk, file sharing, and all unnecessary system extensions and control panels. Turn off Virtual Memory inside the Memory control panel, too. And if you're using RAM Doubler from Connectix, remove it from your Extensions folder. Then restart your Mac by choosing Special⇨Restart.

Give HyperCard Player More Memory

Every Mac sold in the last few years includes HyperCard Player on the hard drive. A few CDs — particularly those from Voyager, 800-446-2001, and Multicom, 800-850-7272 — require the HyperCard Player to work. (Voyager consistently includes HyperCard Player on its disks just in case you trashed your copy; Multicom does not.)

To get the best performance out of such CDs, you need to assign HyperCard Player as much RAM as you can. At the Finder desktop, choose About This Macintosh from the Apple menu and note the size of the Largest Unused Block value. Then select the HyperCard Player icon on disk, press ⌘-I to display the Info dialog box, and enter about 1,000K less than the Largest Unused Block value into the Preferred Size option box.

Copy the Main Program File to Your Hard Drive

If the CD's setup instructions tell you to copy the program file to your hard drive, just drag the program directly from the CD window onto the desktop. Because the CD is locked, a message appears explaining that you can't move the file and asking you whether you want to copy it. Press Return to answer in the affirmative.

Next, assign the program as much RAM as you can, exactly as I suggested for the HyperCard Player program in the preceding section of this chapter. If the Info dialog box doesn't have a Preferred Size check box, no problem. The file is either a HyperCard document or an alias of a file on the CD. In either case, don't worry about changing the RAM value.

Not all CDs require you to copy the main program to the hard disk, and some CDs won't work correctly if you do. Follow the directions included with the CD.

Set the Video to Thousands

Many Macs can display 16 million colors, but most of these colors are lost on multimedia CDs, which are designed for either 32,000 colors or a mere 256. In fact, 24-bit color can actually make your CDs perform worse because the system has to calculate all those extra colors, whether they get used or not.

Before running the CD program, open the Monitors control panel and set the number of colors to Thousands. If you start the program and it complains that it doesn't want to run with more than 256 colors, revisit the Monitors control panel and select 256.

Some multimedia programs are smart enough to automatically set the number of colors to 256. However, most of these same programs neglect to reset the colors to the original number when you quit. If you notice that your Finder icons are appearing less colorful than they normally do — or worse yet, that they appear gray — open the Monitors control panel, select the Colors radio button, and rest the number of colors to Thousands or Millions.

Click to Skip the Introductory Movie

Many of the best CDs play an introductory movie after you start the program. These introductions help acclimate you to the multimedia experience and explain what the CD is all about.

A few such CDs make note of the fact that you've seen the movie in a preferences file in your System Folder so that you don't have to watch the movie every time you start up the program. But, alas, most don't. You can either grin or bear it — and search for that special something that makes the intro a treat, even on the umpteenth viewing — or you can tell the intro to cease and desist.

- Some programs respond to a click.
- Others require you to press the Escape key (in the top left corner of the keyboard).
- Some CDs put on the brakes only if you press ⌘-period. Be careful using this trick, however; pressing ⌘-period makes some programs quit. Stupid but true.

If none of these techniques works, sit back and enjoy the show. Or send the CD back and demand a refund. It depends on whether you're in a fightin' mood.

Don't Go Clicking Like a Madman

All CDs are slow to some extent or another. Some are especially slow to react to your instructions. You may click on a button, for example, and wait several seconds for some sign of life on-screen. Assuming that you've followed all my suggestions so far and you're using a double-speed CD-ROM drive (as explained in Chapter 2), you are witnessing the CD's peak performance. It's just slow.

The reason I touch upon this delicate subject is that many people — especially kids — have a tendency to click compulsively when they don't get an immediate response. I can't tell you how many time's I've heard new CD users remark, "What's this half-witted thing's problem?" while clicking wildly, like a woodpecker after a particularly scrumptious bug.

The problem with this all-too-human reaction is that most programs record your every click. If you click five times in a row, the program tries like heck to perform five operations, even if it takes till next Tuesday. Meanwhile, you continue to mount up more clicks as the program flashes away on-screen.

Here's the better method:

1. **Click once.**
2. **Wait patiently.**

As you wait, take a look at the CD-ROM drive. If the little activity light comes on, or if you can hear the CD spinning around, you know that the program is working on your request.

Move the Cursor away from the Movie

Most multimedia CDs include QuickTime movies. Different programs require you to play these movies in different ways, possibly by clicking on a button or clicking on the movie itself.

In any case, the movie might start playing around the same on-screen location where your cursor is positioned. If it does, two things happen. First, your cursor slightly blocks the view of the movie. Second, the cursor flashes. Because the movie is updating the screen 15 or 30 times a second in the background, the computer updates the cursor along with it, creating a distracting strobe effect.

The solution? Just move the cursor off to a neutral area of the screen where the movie isn't playing. Sounds obvious, huh? Well, it's funny, but few folks seem to figure this one out on their own. Most people say something like, "What is it with this blinking cursor? I sure wish that I could make it stop," search around through the manual for a little while, and decide that the CD has gone haywire.

Press ⌘-Q to Skip the Closing Credits

In many ways, multimedia CDs are the movies of the future. And, like movies, they have credits at the end. After you click on the Quit button or do whatever you have to do to exit the program, the CD displays a list of every person who worked on the production team, offered advice to the production team, or sneezed in the team's general direction.

Luckily, as you can at a movie, you can usually walk out on the credits. Just press ⌘-Q. If that doesn't work, click, press Escape, or press ⌘-period. You will be returned to the Finder desktop.

What to Do When All Else Fails

When something doesn't work, everyone's first inclination is to blame the hardware. Either the computer is busted, the drive is broken, or the CD is defective. Well, I can't vouch for your computer, but I can say a word about the reliability of CDs. Of all the CDs I looked at, nearly every one was fine. About five wouldn't work because they were designed exclusively for Windows, and a couple were quirky about working with external CD-ROM drives. But only one CD was truly flawed. It had a glob of dark ink on the underside of the disk, perhaps from being stacked on another CD before the ink was dry. But even then, I was eventually able to dilute the ink — by rubbing window cleaner on it — and play the CD.

My point is, the CDs usually aren't to blame when something bad happens. If you can't get the CD to mount on your desktop, make sure that all six CD-ROM extensions are available in the Extensions folder in your System Folder (as laid out in the "CD Software Stuff" section of Chapter 2). If they are there, make sure that the box that the CD came in makes some mention of the word *Macintosh*. The box may say something about Windows, but if it doesn't say Macintosh as well, that's a bad sign. (The initials *MPC,* by the way, stand for *Multimedia PC* and have nothing to do with the Mac.)

If you have the extensions and the box mentions the Mac, listen to your CD-ROM drive. Is it making weird, scraping noises, like a large man walking on gravel? If so, it may be having *tracking* problems, meaning that it can't find the first spiral of data on the CD. This happens to CD-ROM drives and stereo CD players alike.

To fix the problem, eject the CD by pressing the eject button on the outside of the case. Remove the CD from the drive and — if applicable — from the caddy. Check the bottom of the CD for smudges and dirt, clean it if necessary, put the CD back in the caddy or drive, and try again. If that doesn't work, patiently repeat the process.

If it *still* doesn't work after about 10 tries, you may have to take your CD-ROM drive in for repairs. But believe me, that's a last resort. I have an audio CD player my wife bought me more than 10 years ago, and it can't track worth a darn. And yet, through our patience and perseverance, it continues to keep us entertained. Sooner or later, we always manage to get the CD to spin and those tunes to come flying out the speakers.

Chapter 21
Top Ten CDs — Interactive Coffee-Table Books

In This Chapter
- Material World: A Global Family Portrait
- American Visions: 20th Century Art from the Roy R. Neuberger Collection
- OceanLife: Volumes 2 through 4
- For All Mankind
- Passage to Vietnam
- The Complete Maus: A Survivor's Tale
- 4 Paws of Crab
- Seven Days in August: Unfold the Drama of the Cold War
- Oceans Below
- Comic Book Confidential
- The Next-Best Ten

You know that you've settled down when you own a coffee table. Granted, you're not quite as settled as the folks who own ottomans and vibrating recliners, but you're well on your way. And you know that you've joined the ranks of middle America when you begin to accumulate big, full-color coffee-table books. For there is nothing quite so decadent as a book that contains a few enormous pages adorned with thoroughly inked, glossy photographs, is too large to fit on a shelf, consumes vast acreage of furniture real estate, and sits around unopened 364 days out of the year. If the coffee-table book isn't a sign of our culture, I don't know what is.

Well, in relatively short order, we Americans will have to use some other means to define ourselves. CD-ROM spells the death of coffee-table books in capital letters as large as the books themselves. Some of the most successful CD titles around today already outclass their coffee-table-bound counterparts. These

CDs provide exceptional pictures, brilliant color throughout, and little snippets of explanatory text. They also offer the usual advantages that CDs have over books, such as sound, video, and interactivity. You can visit absolutely any point in the CD at the click of a button, so there's no chance that a rowdy guest will manhandle the precious pages of your hulking tome.

In fact, these CDs rank as my favorites among favorites. They don't try to take on too much information — as many educational CDs do — thus permitting you to explore the subject in minute detail. They favor sound, video, and still images over text, just as all CDs ought to. (On-screen text is much harder on the eyes and more difficult to read than printed text.) And you are never at the mercy of the CD the way you are with some games. If you tire of exploring one avenue, you can quickly switch to another, all the while setting your own pace.

Will future coffee tables include CD holders? Or better yet, will they include retractable screens so that you can explore the CD without venturing from the comfort of your vibrating recliner? It's too early to tell, but one thing's for sure: You can stop spending $50 a shot for those massive books and start spending your extra $50 on CDs.

Material World: A Global Family Portrait

I just love Charles Kuralt. Listening to his voice triggers immediate relaxation, like I'm waking up to "Sunday Morning." So it's no surprise that one of my favorite CDs features the venerable Kuralt as narrator.

Material World: A Global Family Portrait explains the lives of 30 families from different corners of the world by examining their material possessions — the everyday belongings that we've been taught bear no relevance to the way we think and live. But Kuralt argues otherwise: "From the elements of the material world, we can paint a portrait more intimate and revealing than any view from space." Our stuff defines us, and we in turn define the world.

Your view of each family begins with a picture of family members and belongings amassed outside their home, whether in the alley, on the roof, in the front yard, out in the fields, or, in the case of the Abdullas from Kuwait, over the range of a city block (see Figure 21-1). You can explore each family in detail, in terms of what they own, what they want, and where they come from. The fact that Father Saif Abdulla comes from an expansive family of 29 children, for example, is explained in part by the fact that his father had four wives. Mother Zainab was blessed with a mere 15 siblings; her father had to make do with three wives.

Figure 21-1: The many possessions of the wealthiest family on the CD, the Abdullas of Kuwait.

The CD presents fascinating stories of people living in both extreme and modest circumstances, stories made more poignant by expert photographs, first-hand accounts from photojournalists, and personal details written in the families' own words. I've spent hours with this title and fully intend to spend hours more.

Material World: A Global Family Portrait, StarPress Multimedia, 800-782-7944, 415-274-8383. Estimated street price: $40.

American Visions: 20th Century Art from the Roy R. Neuberger Collection

A few CDs enable you to wander through on-screen art museums, but none provides such an artistic environment in which to do so as American Visions: 20th Century Art from the Roy R. Neuberger Collection. This title immerses you in 20th-century American art, allowing you to view photographs of the artists, read written critiques, and watch movies of the artists describing their personal philosophies and their opinions of their contemporaries. The videos are often accompanied by the music that inspired the artists, including some very solid 20th-century jazz. But best of all, you can access all elements starting from a central work of art, as demonstrated in Figure 21-2.

Figure 21-2: A painting by "impure abstractionist" Stuart Davis (center), a video interview (upper left), and a list of links to additional information about the man (right).

American Visions is a journey through the Neuberger Museum of Art on the campus of the State University of New York. The museum's 1,000-piece collection was amassed privately by millionaire collector Roy Neuberger. Motivated by the story of Van Gogh — who may have failed to sell a single painting during his lifetime but whose paintings now routinely sell at auction for several million dollars — Neuberger decided to devote a sizable chunk of his fortune to purchasing the works of living artists.

The CD includes 200 pieces of art — both paintings and sculpture — from 129 artists, ranging from the celebrated (Jackson Pollack, Georgia O'Keefe) to the obscure (lots of names you wouldn't recognize). You can browse through works according to artist, school, or date. Videos show related paintings as well as 360-degree revolving views of each featured piece of sculpture. American Visions provides a genuine feel for the art, both as it appears today and in the context of the time at which it was created. Quite honestly, the software is more interesting than most real museums I've visited.

So if you love modern art — or if you think you hate it — this eye-opening, ear-pleasing CD can't help but educate and inspire. And if you have a 24-bit monitor, leave the screen set to Millions of colors and prepare yourself for some knockout images.

American Visions: 20th Century Art from the Roy R. Neuberger Collection, Eden Interactive, 800-743-3360, 415-241-1450. Estimated street price: $70.

OceanLife: Volumes 2 through 4

Sumeria's OceanLife series currently offers four volumes, and a fifth is on the way. I've never seen the first volume — the company tells me that the series improved greatly between Volumes 1 and 2 — but I can attest to the fact that the second through fourth volumes are absolutely incredible, filled to the gills with more than three hours apiece of stunning underwater video.

Volumes 2, 3, and 4 document fish native to Micronesia, Hawaii, and Australia's Great Barrier Reef, respectively. (The upcoming Volume 5 will cover the Caribbean.) Volumes 2 and 4 are two-CD sets, while Volume 3 has just one CD. Each volume covers hundreds of species of fish through text and habitat maps (both shown in Figure 21-3), aerial photographs, anatomical diagrams, and lots and lots of narrated videos. If it's a fish and it's managed to swim its way into the Pacific ocean, you'll probably find it on one of these CDs.

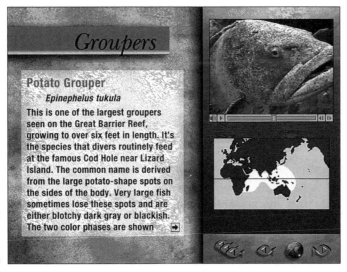

Figure 21-3: Information about the largest of the groupers in the world's largest coral formation, the Great Barrier Reef.

(Actually, I just wrote that because I liked the way it sounded. Sumeria claims that each CD looks at less than 20 percent of the species that exist in any one region. But that's still an awful lot of fish, enough to make OceanLife "the most complete multimedia-based reference series on marine life in the world," as the company fairly boasts.)

As avid snorkelers and scuba wannabes, my wife and I were absolutely agog over these CDs. It took every bit of strength we could muster to resist the temptation to bag this book (and my wife's job) and summon our travel agent posthaste. I can't imagine a better gift for the underwater enthusiast on your shopping list.

OceanLife 2: Micronesia; OceanLife 3: Hawaii; OceanLife 4: The Great Barrier Reef; Sumeria, 415-904-0800. List price: $50 per title.

For All Mankind

This is the first of nine CDs that I'm recommending from a company called Voyager, which is absolutely at the forefront of CD-ROM development for the Mac. If I had to sum up all the reviews in this book into a single sentence, my advice would be: Call Voyager, request a catalog, and buy the first thing that interests you. StarPress, Sumeria, Broderbund, and other companies manage a consistently high level of quality, but they can't keep up with Voyager's quantity and variety. The company isn't without the occasional flop — its People Magazine CD, for example, is more trite than tacky — but it manages to easily outpace the competition, including Microsoft (from which I recommend six titles).

One thing you should know about Voyager: It doesn't publish its technical support number. In fact, the present documentation doesn't include *any* number for Voyager. Handy, huh? But the problem is easily solved. If you run into difficulties, just call 914-591-5500 and ask for tech support.

For All Mankind is an expanded version of the award-winning documentary about the Apollo missions to the moon. Directed and compiled by Al Reinert (screenwriter for the new Tom Hanks film *Apollo 18*), the movie *For All Mankind* made a splash a few years back when it was released exclusively on laserdisc with no plans for distribution on videotape. The lowly videotape, we must surmise, couldn't handle all that unbridled coolness.

Well, the film is indeed wonderful, blending breathtaking footage with the frank reflections and home-spun philosophy of the men who flew the missions. The CD features the entire film as a single QuickTime movie. Though the movie is recorded at quarter-screen, you can magnify its size to full-screen, which is acceptable for viewing at a distance. The 16-bit stereo sound track — featuring music by Brian Eno — is arguably every bit as good as on the laserdisc version. And if you hook the computer to a Dolby Surround Sound receiver, you get the full home-theater treatment. (Only one other CD-ROM I know of goes to these audio extremes.)

The movie is flanked by a descriptive transcript. You can advance through the film by turning pages in the transcript, something you can't do with any other medium. You can also click on the names of the astronauts and other speakers to discover additional information about them, as shown in Figure 21-4.

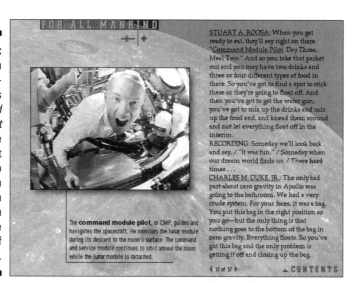

Figure 21-4: I clicked on the underlined words *Command Module Pilot* in the upper-right corner to see an explanation of the term at the bottom of the screen.

In addition to the movie, For All Mankind includes text descriptions of every manned Apollo mission along with information about each of the astronauts. You'll also find essays, animation, and annotated graphics on such topics as John F. Kennedy, the Saturn rocket, and the lunar landing module. This is easily the most comprehensive and awe-inspiring space CD-ROM around. If you have a powerful computer, it is a genuine feast for your eyes and ears.

For All Mankind, Voyager, 800-446-2001, 914-591-5500. List price: $40.

Passage to Vietnam

When you think coffee-table book, you very likely call to mind the popular *Day in the Life* series, in which troops of photographers descend upon some portion of the world and photograph it from every possible angle at every time of day. Passage to Vietnam is a CD version of one of these books. Created by Rick Smolan, the originator of *Day in the Life* and the popular From Alice to Ocean CD-ROM, Passage to Vietnam merges photographs, video, and traditional Vietnamese music to create a virtually seamless media amalgam. If you like *Day in the Life*, you're going to fall head-over-heels for this CD.

The basic framework of the CD is a series of photographs taken over the course of a single week around and about Vietnam in Spring 1994. Though the display is limited to 8-bit color — my only complaint with the title — the color and composition of the photographs are wonderful, and you can generally look beyond the dithered pixels. A diffused information symbol blinks away to alert you to captions and credits. A film canister and speaker indicate video and sound, respectively. Your main method for navigating is a cube — shown in the lower-right corner of Figure 21-5 — which alternatively allows you to access help, other groups of photos, and maps. The interface is at once understated and highly intuitive, a refreshing change from some of the in-your-face interfaces that have been popping up lately in all kinds of programs.

Figure 21-5: One of the 350 photographs from Passage to Vietnam, with information displayed.

The clever blending of action and imagery is evident at the beginning of each new section of photographs (which the CD calls "passages"). The shrunken person of Rick Smolan addresses you from a bridge, from inside a dark tunnel, and from a beach outside a window. You also visit with the chief picture editors from *Newsweek* and *Time* — two of the snootiest characters you'll meet inside any CD — who quibble from tiny chairs perched in front of a massive light box. Other CDs that try to integrate movies with still backgrounds in this way have problems with pixels dancing around the edges of the movies. But the special effects in Passage to Vietnam look perfect to the most trained eyes (including mine).

You can set the CD to play automatically if you haven't changed to a new image in a while. Although I sometimes found it difficult or impossible to interrupt the introduction and special-effects movies, the CD is fascinating to watch if you're willing to sit back and let it take over. All in all, this may be the most impressively designed CD I've seen. Because I found the other topics in the top ten list more interesting, this CD wasn't my favorite in this category, but it wasn't far short, and it may well be your first choice.

Passage to Vietnam, Against All Odds Productions, 415-331-6300. List price: $40 ($70 with the actual coffee-table book).

The Complete Maus: A Survivor's Tale

Cartoonist Art Spiegelman won the Pulitzer Prize for his two-volume *Maus* memoirs. Based on his father's first-hand experiences as a Jew living and surviving in Nazi Germany, the comic books depict the Jews as mice and the Nazis as cats. If this sounds like an over-simplification of the roles of victim and victimizer — in comic book form, no less — then you probably haven't read this painfully personal and stirring account of the Holocaust.

You see the world turn upside-down through the eyes of Spiegelman's father, Vladek, and learn how these events have left present-day Vladek severe and judgmental. You also gain insights into the real-life relationship between father and son, not only though the comic book, but also through QuickTime interviews with both Vladek and Art Spiegelman.

The CD-ROM captures not only the comic book itself — including every page from both *Maus* books — but also the process involved in creating *Maus*. Spiegelman shows how he researched the books, from his taped interviews with Vladek to his reordering of random memories into a linear history. He also discusses how he traveled to Poland and Auschwitz in an effort to retrace some of his father's steps. If that's not enough, you can view the author's abundant sketches, compiled for a show at the Museum of Modern Art.

Spiegelman did not always relegate himself to drawing exactly inside rectangular panels; in many cases, the artwork fills the entire page, meaning that some of the artwork gets cut off on a 14-inch screen. You can scroll with a hand cursor to see more of a page, as shown in Figure 21-6. Or, if you have a larger monitor, you can run a special version of the program that lets you see the entire page all at once.

In the introduction, Spiegelman complains that he couldn't fit as much information on the CD as he had hoped. This may have been a good thing — artists sometimes operate more effectively inside limits, even arbitrary ones. But I wonder why it didn't occur to him or the creators of the CD to simply include a second disk. I would have liked more multimedia — including voice and sound dramatizations of the book — but I nonetheless consider this CD a valuable part of my collection.

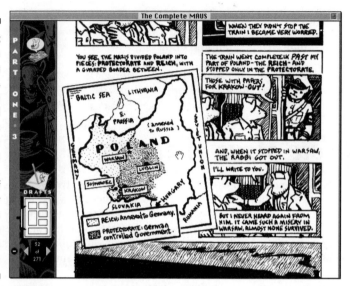

Figure 21-6: If you have a 14-inch monitor, you'll have to scroll through the pages in The Complete Maus. Owners of larger monitors can see whole pages at a time.

The Complete Maus: A Survivor's Tale, Voyager, 800-446-2001, 914-591-5500. List price: $50.

Four Paws of Crab

It's hard to say just what Four Paws of Crab is. Part Thai cookbook, part glossary of Oriental foods (as in Figure 21-7), part analysis of American and Thai cultures, part book of poetry, this CD is about as quirky, whimsical, and utterly unique as they get.

It all started with a Thai cook named Bird and his American friend Nora, who met as exchange students and then later decided to switch places and live in the other's home country. You find out how hard it was for each of the students to adapt. One of Bird's main motivations for visiting the U.S., for example, was to explore its native cuisine. But as he discovers, Americans have no native food — unless you count fast food — but rather subsist on a combination of foods from other countries. I guess we feed from the melting pot. Nora, too, encounters culture shock: In Thailand, for instance, your left hand and your feet are off-limits. If you want to pick something up or hand it to someone, use your right hand or suffer Thai scorn.

Figure 21-7: If you've ever wanted to know the healing properties of Chinese celery, this CD is the place to find out.

The cookbook section of the CD is excellent. In addition to Bird's many recipes, it includes videos of Bird demonstrating how to perform various hard-to-explain cooking techniques. (I had no idea how many steps are involved in producing a glass of that yummy Thai iced coffee.) My wife is an accomplished cook — or so my tummy tells me — and this was the only cooking CD she considered worth recommending.

Four Paws of Crab is a delightful CD packed with practical recipes, engaging commentary, and insightful tidbits of wisdom. I suppose that it won't appeal to all tastes, but if you want to learn more about Thai cooking, I can't imagine a better place to look.

Four Paws of Crab, Live Oak Multimedia, 800-454-7557, 510-654-7480. List price: $45.

Seven Days in August: Unfold the Drama of the Cold War

Seven Days in August: Unfold the Drama of the Cold War is a lively retelling of the events surrounding the construction of the Berlin Wall. It was a time, you are told, when the world's superpowers were creeping close to nuclear war. The CD looks at one week — August 10-16, 1961 — during which the wall was built, and one day — November 20, 1989 — when the wall was largely destroyed.

The CD is broken up into six sections, as indicated by the columns of buttons on the main screen in Figure 21-8. One section explains the frightening experiences of the people who lived through the crisis in the divided German city. Another tells about the citizens of utopian Berlin, Wisconsin, who seemed to have had nothing more stressful on their agendas than to attend the county fair and listen to John Philip Sousa marches in the park.

Figure 21-8: The main screen of Seven Days in August provides direct access to every one of the CD's features.

In a roundtable panel of talking heads, the likes of Strobe Talbott and Daniel Schorr mull over the historic ramifications of the Wall and discuss which high-ranking public officials were poised in what place when. You can also read text biographies of important figures such as Erich Honecker and Nikita Khrushchev or treat yourself to a daily slice of Americana. Here's where things go from serious to light-hearted. The "duck and cover" section, which gives instructions on how one was supposed to survive a nuclear explosion, is especially amusing; for example, the wisdom of the day said that if you wash your hair immediately after exposure to a nuclear explosion, you'll feel better right quick. When you're weary of pondering the possibilities of atomic annihilation, you can play The First Lady of Fashion games, in which you select festive outfits for Jackie Kennedy to wear on outings and to special social events. It's stupid, but funny.

One of the oldest CDs I recommend (it was made way back in the prehistoric days of 1993), Seven Days in August is told entirely in slide shows, with audio throughout but with no video. And the navigation controls are a little rough, preventing you from replaying a small section of audio. Yet the CD still holds up very well. It continues to be both enjoyable and informative, proving that good content, execution, and organization can withstand the tides of shifting technology.

Chapter 21: Top Ten CDs — Interactive Coffee-Table Books **295**

Seven Days in August: Unfold the Drama of the Cold War, Time Warner Interactive Group, 800-482-3766, 818-955-9999. List price: $60.

Comic Book Confidential

Like For All Mankind, Voyager's Comic Book Confidential is based on a documentary of the same name. Included as a single, quarter-screen QuickTime movie, the film *Comic Book Confidential* introduces you to more than 20 comic book artists and writers, including such pioneers in the craft as Harvey Kurtzman, Jack Kirby, and Linda Barry. The movie traces the origin of comic books in America, the comics scare of the 1950s, and the resulting formation of the voluntary Comics Code, which put a temporary end to some of the more gruesome magazines.

Unlike For All Mankind, this CD doesn't include a transcript beside the movie. But it has lots of other good stuff. In addition to written biographies of each of the artists interviewed in the film (plus Paul Mavrides, who appears only in the opening sequence), the disk includes sample comic pages, usually featuring stories in their entirety. You can navigate to specific biographies, comic pages, or points in the movie using the Artists Index, which appears in Figure 21-9.

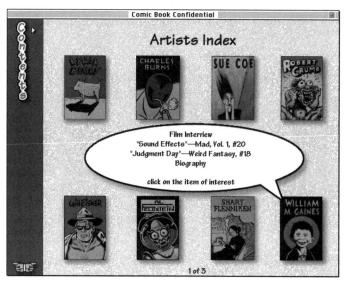

Figure 21-9: You can use the Artists Index to skip to interviews in the movie, view samples of an artist's work, and read a biography.

You can double the size of the movie to fill the screen. And just in case you've ever been curious, the CD lays out every one of the 41 provisions in the Comics Code, including harsh words on "ghouls, cannibalism, and werewolfism" and sharp advice against the "exaggeration of any physical qualities." Suffice it to say that if you don't like comics, you won't like this disk. But if you're a fan of today's graphic novels or yesterday's tattered funnies, prepare to be delighted.

Comic Book Confidential, Voyager, 800-446-2001, 914-591-5500. List price: $50.

Oceans Below

All right, so I'm going overboard on the underwater CDs. So what? If the CD is good, I say recommend it regardless of content. Actually, this CD is quite different from Sumeria's OceanLife. Rather than identifying fish and so on, it lets you join a couple of dive experts in a series of sea-floor explorations. You can select from the Red Sea, Galapagos Islands, Sea of Cortez, and 14 other dive sites.

The construction of the CD is very straightforward. You select a dive site, check out the people and places on land, fling yourself off the side of the boat, look around underwater, and return to the surface. The CD contains 200 QuickTime videos that capture life both above and below water. The videos don't match those in OceanLife for color and quality, but every one of them is accompanied by friendly narration. My only objection is that I get tired of viewing the underwater scenes through a mask, as shown in Figure 21-10.

Figure 21-10: Located in the South Pacific, Truk Lagoon is filled with sunken Japanese ships that now serve as coral reefs.

This is a fun family CD, of equal interest to adults and their fidgety offspring. While you check out the videos, for example, your son or daughter can search for the buried treasure that's socked away at most of the dive sites. If you're looking for a beginning guide to scuba diving or merely trying to find a CD to enjoy with the kids, give Oceans Below a try.

Oceans Below, The Software Toolworks, 800-234-3088, 415-883-3000. List price: $50.

The Next-Best Ten

It hurts my heart to have to say yea to some CDs and nay to others. Worse yet, you — being the independent-minded type you are — may very well disagree with a couple of my top-ten picks. So in the name of fairness and sportsmanship, I've thrown in the following list of ten more titles that are worthy of high praise but aren't quite as over-the-top great as the ones I've mentioned so far:

- **Street Atlas USA,** DeLorme Mapping, 800-227-1656, 207-865-1234. Estimated street price: $80. Okay, so Street Atlas USA doesn't have any sound or video. But it claims to show maps of every street in every city in the United States that existed before 1993. You can even search by zip code, street name, and house number. The scrolling was a little cumbersome, but I was amazed by the accuracy.

- **Small Blue Planet: The Real Picture Atlas** and **Small Blue Planet: The Cities Below,** Now What Software, 415-885-3432. List price: $60 and $50, respectively. If you want a true multimedia atlas, the Small Blue Planet series offers the best on this or any other planet. Both CDs are filled with actual satellite photographs of the earth's surface; one features the entire world, and the other shows cities inside the U.S. The Real Picture Atlas even plays greetings in 70 different languages. Navigating around the maps is harder than it should be, but the images are out of this world (yuk yuk).

- **The Big Green Disc,** Media Design Interactive, UK: 44-1252-737630. Estimated street price: $40. This British CD explains every environmental threat under the sun in helpful and stunning detail. Though it takes its job a tad seriously — billing itself as "The Interactive Guide to Saving the World" — it packs in splendid graphics, a wealth of video interviews, and narration throughout.

- **Warplanes,** Maris Multimedia, 800-762-2189, 317-579-0400. Estimated street price: $50. Okay, I admit, I don't have even the slightest interest in warplanes. But if you think that they're pretty spiffy, this CD is for you. It includes amazing 3-D graphics, authentic flight simulators, and more statistics than you normally associate with baseball.

- **Sports Illustrated Multimedia Almanac,** StarPress Multimedia, 800-782-7944, 415-274-8383. Estimated street price: $50. Ask anyone who knows me, and they'll tell you that I don't know the first thing about sports. (Don't like sports, don't like warplanes — what's my problem?) And yet I enjoyed this CD. It includes great coverage of World Cup and Olympics stuff, as well as the usual deluge of football and basketball info. But it relies too heavily on text, and it needs a search function.

- **The Martial Arts Explorer,** Future Vision Multimedia, 800-472-8777, 914-426-0400. List price: $50. For some reason, Kung Fu stuff *does* interest me, probably because it's ancient, mysterious, and shrouded in weirdness. The Martial Arts Explorer examines the history, techniques, and weapons of jujitsu, tae kwon do, karate, and nine other Oriental studies. Some of the overviews need narration, but the interface is surprisingly clever, and the on-line help — which features a woman in a kimono spraying cleaner on the QuickTime windows while explaining the buttons — is the kind of model that other CDs should follow.

- **Clinton: Portrait of Victory,** Time Warner Interactive Group, 800-482-3766, 818-955-9999. List price: $40. Photojournalist P.F. Bentley talked Bill Clinton into letting him hang around the 1992 presidential campaign and shoot rolls and rolls of insightful and candid black-and-white photographs. Bentley trailed this and only this campaign for a full year; it was just his luck that he backed a winner. The acceptance speech videos are out of place, but the campaign photos are wonderful.

- **Cinemania '95,** Microsoft, 800-228-6270, 206-882-8080. List price: $60. Cinemania is a compendium of movie reviews from Leonard Maltin, Roger Ebert, Ephraim Katz, and Pauline Kael, with a few — *too* few — still images and video snippets thrown in. You can create custom lists of movies you're interested in seeing and even discover titles that might interest you according to subject. It's a fine resource, but I wish it weren't so heavy on the text and so light on the media.

- **Woodstock: 25th Anniversary CD-ROM,** Time Warner Interactive Group, 800-482-3766, 818-955-9999. List price: $60. I personally identify more with Generation X than the Boomers, but I was eventually won over by this CD. Richie Havens' rendition of "Freedom" is fantastic, and you have to love the story of the enterprising Good Humor Man. But the CD is limited to 8-bit sound, and my biggest question still goes unanswered: What in heck was the '50s retro group Sha Na Na doing there?

- **Space: A Visual History of Manned Spaceflight,** Sumeria, 415-904-0800. List price: $50. This CD blends videos about the manned space expeditions — mostly Apollo and space shuttle missions — with good scientific explanations and a bit of news about future shuttle voyages. The search function needs to be faster, and the menu bar doesn't cooperate on large monitors. But if you're the kind of person who would rather spend your tax dollars on the final frontier than just about anything else (hey, that's me!), then add this CD to your collection.

Chapter 22
Top Ten CDs — Educational Resources

• •

In This Chapter
▶ The First Emperor of China
▶ The Crucible
▶ A.D.A.M.
▶ The Cartoon History of the Universe
▶ How Animals Move
▶ Microsoft Exploration Series
▶ The Rosetta Stone Language Library
▶ Exploring Ancient Cities
▶ Macbeth
▶ Learn to Speak Series
▶ The Next-Best Ten

• •

When you think of educational resource CDs, you probably think of encyclopedias. After all, a CD can hold about 300,000 pages of text — more than ten, 30-volume sets of hard-bound books. It's amazing, really. Think about all the shelf space you can save by trashing those dusty, old encyclopedias and buying a wafer-thin CD-ROM.

But although all that raw storage space is very well and good, the real beauty of an interactive multimedia CD is that it offers the potential for new ways to learn. If you are new to a subject, the CD can play a sound and video introduction. When you don't know where to go next, the CD can suggest a few tried-and-true routes. Instead of dead text on a page, a CD can provide live *hypertext* that takes you to related topics, glossary definitions, or multimedia elements when you click on it. A CD can read text to you in many different languages; it can show you several different interpretations of a single event; it can quiz everyone who finishes a single lesson with entirely different sets of questions. It doesn't eliminate the need for a real-life teacher, but it has the capacity to overshadow every other learning vehicle devised so far, including the book you're holding now.

Altogether, I estimate that the top ten CDs and the ten additional finalists that I recommend in this chapter hold one entire brain of information. If you wanted to learn everything contained in these CDs, you'd have to throw all the stuff you currently know in the trash and start from scratch. (Don't ask me how I know this. It would take me days to show you. You should see these formulas I devised. I had to carry 1 several times, and there were a couple of fractions involved.)

Anyway, the good news is, you don't have to stuff your brain with this junk. When it's on CD-ROM, it's on permanent storage. You can go back and visit your information any time you like. These aren't just educational resources, these are educational reserves.

The First Emperor of China

The best CD-ROMs lift you out of your chair and transfer you to a different time and place. None does it quite so well as The First Emperor of China. This amazing CD recounts the life and times of Qin Shi Huang Di (that's *chin sh-wan dee*), the founder of the Chinese imperial system that lasted for more than 2,000 years, until 1911. The CD tells the story of how the emperor assumed the throne of the state of Qin as a young man and unified all other Chinese states under the Qin Dynasty. He also completed the Great Wall, which marked the northern border of Qin.

But most fascinating is the emperor's legacy — a fantastic underground tomb covering three acres and filled with more than 6,000 terra-cotta warriors and horses. Discovered in 1974 by peasants digging a well, these remarkably preserved, life-sized figures face east, protecting the entombed emperor. The army consists of officers, foot soldiers, archers — all clad in distinct uniforms and armor — as well as horses and even war chariots.

The CD shows the original archaeological team retrieving the first figures, amazed by how much they had discovered within a few square yards and little knowing how many more yards they had to go. You learn just about everything there is to know about the Qin Dynasty through maps, time lines, videos, and glossaries. Each video includes a complete transcript of the audio track — which you can play in either English or Chinese. If you click on underlined words in the transcript (see Figure 22-1), you're taken to a glossary that defines the terms.

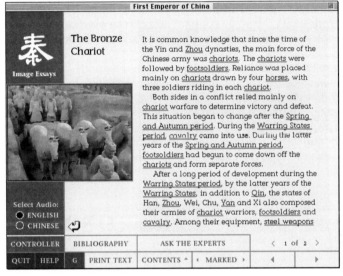

Figure 22-1: The underlined words in the movie transcript are linked to the glossary.

This CD is an incredible wellspring of knowledge. It's well-organized and exhaustively thorough, and the multimedia elements are excellently integrated — you can even switch to a map or timeline as the video continues to play. The First Emperor of China is an amazing journey into archaeology and Chinese imperial history.

The First Emperor of China, Voyager, 800-446-2001, 914-591-5500. List price: $50.

The Crucible

Playwright Arthur Miller wrote *The Crucible* — the play about the Salem witch trials that just about every high school kid has to read — as a protest against the House Un-American Activities Committee hearings provoked by Senator Joseph McCarthy in the 1950s. In a series of videos, Miller describes his involvement in the hearings, relating how he refused to cooperate in what he considered to be an undemocratic abuse of power. In searching afterward for a creative outlet for his frustration, he decided to use one witch trial as a metaphor for the other.

The CD includes a complete text version of the four-act play, with additional descriptive material and added scenes. You can click on unfamiliar words such as *Goody* or strange phrases such as *do you begrudge my bed, Uncle?* to discover their meanings. Though the entire play is not presented in video, you can view a dress rehearsal of the climax in Act III and pore over interviews with the actors who portrayed the parts for London's Youth Theatre of the Young Vic.

You'll also find a wealth of interviews and commentaries by Miller, such as the one shown in Figure 22-2, many of which were filmed especially for the CD. Another area documents the HUAC hearings and the subsequent Hollywood blacklisting. But my favorite section explores the politics of Salem Village and Salem Town in 17th-century Massachusetts. It shows how geography, political disputes, and greed played a role in the accusations. For a deeper understanding, you can examine the events of 1692, when the hangings and crushings took place.

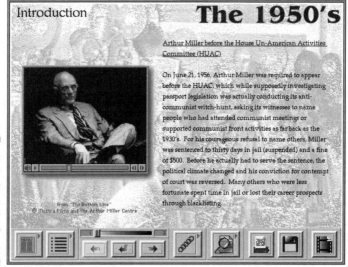

Figure 22-2: Arthur Miller candidly explains his reasons for writing *The Crucible*.

Though this CD is heavily dependent upon text, it contains more than enough supporting material and background information to make it stand out from other scholarly CDs. Where else are you likely to find the writings of noted historians and even highly critical reviews of the play itself bundled together with one of the most important works of American drama produced in the last 50 years? This is truly a landmark CD, one that I wish had existed when I was in 10th grade.

The Crucible, Penguin USA, 212-366-2000. List price: $65.

A.D.A.M.

A.D.A.M. stands for Animated Dissection of Anatomy for Medicine, and EVE stands for the Electronic Viewing Environment, which is your computer. But you can just call husband Adam and wife Eve the happy anatomical couple. They never wear anything but fig leaves — and they can even take those off if you're not squeamish — and they've been known to strip down to their endocrine systems without a moment's hesitation. But gosh darn it, they're fun, they're educational, and you just have to love them.

A.D.A.M. Software sells two wonderful CDs that ought to be in the homes of all families who are interested in staying up to date on the composition of the human body. A.D.A.M.: The Inside Story takes you on a tour of male and female anatomy, while Nine Month Miracle explains how to have a baby and how the little duffer develops. Both are examples of educational multimedia at its best, mixing animation, movies, narration, graphics, dictionaries of terms, and a few games with style and humor, all of which makes for a delightful learning experience.

Both CDs begin with peel-away anatomy illustrations that work something like those acetate pages of frog entrails in school science books. The difference is that you can look at more than 50 layers of human organs, muscles, and tissues, from a cutaway view of the bones to the protective coating of subcutaneous fat that we all wish we had less of. In The Inside Story, you can view narrated animations of all kinds of bodily functions, including breathing, choking, and snoring. Or you can switch to the Family Scrapbook, which takes you on in-depth tours of our inner workings, including the cardiovascular system, illustrated in Figure 22-3.

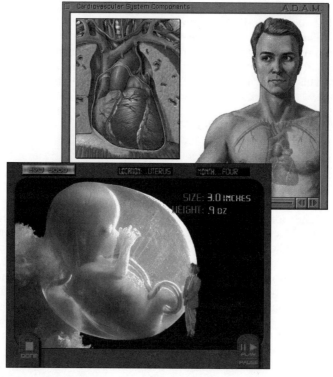

Figure 22-3: Revealing screens from A.D.A.M.: The Inside Story and Nine Month Miracle.

In Nine Month Miracle, you can find detailed information about every month of pregnancy, including very impressive and helpful photographs from inside the womb (also shown in Figure 22-3). There's also a special Child's View of Pregnancy section, which tells what it's like to get a new sister. Both Inside Story and Nine Month Miracle require lots of horsepower to work their magic, so you have to sit through quite a bit of automated program switching in order to explore the CDs, but the end result is definitely worth it.

A.D.A.M.: The Inside Story and *Nine Month Miracle*, A.D.A.M. Software, 800-755-2326, 404-980-0888. Estimated street price: $50 per title.

The Cartoon History of the Universe

Some would argue that this title belongs in Chapter 21 with the other comic books or in Chapter 23 with the entertainment CDs. But although it's true that The Cartoon History of the Universe is a comic book, it's also one heck of an educational resource. It explains, in humorous and sometimes lurid detail, the history of life from the Big Bang to Alexander the Great. Lifted from Larry Gonick's seven-volume comic book of the same name, this interactive lesson in history is so vast that it consumes two CDs.

The main body of The Cartoon History is the enormous comic book itself. As shown in Figure 22-4, the book is presented in basic page form. Each page was scanned from the original black-and-white drawings and then electronically colored. Realizing that this wasn't enough, the programmers assigned voices to every one of the several hundred characters in the book and animated each panel. The fellow in the lower-left corner of Figure 22-4, for example, saws into the table around his knees and then enters the next panel from stage left. The navigation controls are superb, allowing you to assign bookmarks to favorite pages. You can even double-click on entries in an index to find information about a specific topic.

Figure 22-4: A page of historical importance from the action-packed pages of The Cartoon History of the Universe.

As if that weren't enough, The Cartoon History includes several games, all based on places and events in history and mythology. You can play the Maze of the Minotaur, which you learn was created by King Minos of Crete to avenge the death of his son, and The Pyramid of Cheops, which, a quiz explains, was built in 20 years by paid servants. The games include puzzles and realistic 3-D graphics, making them much more interesting than the usually insipid games included with other educational CDs.

Make no mistake about it: Though this CD is thoroughly enjoyable entertainment, there is plenty of knowledge to be gained here. The Cartoon History of the Universe tells it like it was in terms that a Philistine could understand. Sounds like *History For Dummies*, huh?

The Cartoon History of the Universe, Putnam New Media, 212-995-2200. Estimated street price: $40.

How Animals Move

Created as a joint venture between Maris Multimedia and the Discovery Channel, How Animals Move is a vast examination of the ways in which our fellow creatures get around. Now, you may think that this would be a fairly small topic — rabbits hop, snakes slither, birds fly, that sort of thing — but in fact, the way that animals locomote is as varied as the way they look, eat, and procreate. This CD lets you explore the topic superficially or with plenty of detail to spare. It's the kind of title you'll enjoy using again and again.

How Animals Move allows the uninitiated to start off with guided tours that break styles of movement into nine categories, such as gliding, burrowing, and swimming. (You and I would fit into the "walking and running" section.) Within each style, you can investigate variations. For example, you learn that all swimming animals "drive water backward to propel themselves forward," but that different animals accomplish this in different ways. A frog is equipped with the equivalent of oars that use the force of drag, whereas a turtle has hydrofoils that use the force of lift. An octopus seems to be the best outfitted, relying on jet propulsion. You ultimately see every conceivable swimming device, from the quivering cilia of a comb jelly to the horizontal tail flukes of whales.

If the guided tours provide depth, the rest of the CD is bottomless. After locating the Gliding section, you can consult the Soaring subsection, shown in Figure 22-5, where you can view the difference between kestrels and sea-going gannets. These portions of the CD are not narrated, but they provide repeating videos that can play over and over in virtually seamless loops so that you can get a good, long look at the creature in motion.

Chapter 22: Top Ten CDs — Educational Resources

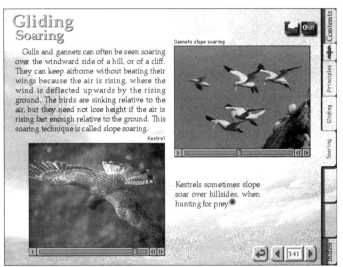

Figure 22-5: Through the use of looping videos, How Animals Move provides you with detailed and lengthy views of hundreds of animals in motion.

If this CD has a problem, it's that it has a tendency to get a little too detailed. Is it safe to assume, for example, that most folks will want to know about the Reynolds number, which measures the fluid flow around a moving body based on body length, speed, fluid density, and viscosity? I'm all for it — the more information the better — but some folks may find it all a bit overwhelming. Still, if you don't like a page, you can skip it (just as you might skip a page in this book if you were absolutely out of your gourd). If you measure your CDs by the old saying "the more the merrier," then How Animals Move is merry indeed.

How Animals Move, Maris Multimedia, 800-762-2189, 317-579-0400. Estimated street price: $50.

Microsoft Exploration Series

Microsoft produces a four-part Exploration Series, three parts of which — Musical Instruments, Dinosaurs, and Dangerous Creatures — are presently available for the Mac. Each of the CDs is sold separately, but they share a common structure. So if you become familiar with Dinosaurs, for example, you'll have no problem adapting to Musical Instruments later on down the line. These are family titles that are sure to appeal to the kids, but they are packed with information that will amaze and educate adults as well.

Because the contents of the CDs are so varied, allow me to take a moment out from my normal reviewer's banter and describe each title on its own:

- If I could buy only one of these CDs, it would be Musical Instruments. This software documents a dizzying assortment of instruments around the world, from the Veracruz Harp to the Burmese Saung-Gauk (both a couple of wacky stringed gizmos). The CD allows you to access the instruments according to country, family, or musical style. Or you can simply leaf through them alphabetically. You can listen to a brief snippet of one instrument when viewing several instruments together or settle down with a single instrument and hear a longer song. The CD also provides pictures and pronunciation throughout.

- Dinosaurs are as obvious a subject for CD-ROMs as they are for books, movies, and anything else you'd like to see sell through the roof. In fact, there must be ten dinosaur CDs out right now, and that's very likely an underestimate. But none are such a pleasure as this one. Microsoft Dinosaurs groups the prehistoric creatures by geography, chronology, biology, and every other which way. You can roam around to your heart's content, either on your own or in a narrated tour. As shown in Figure 22-6, you can even view animated movies — the same ones featured in the four-part "Dinosaurs" TV series on PBS.

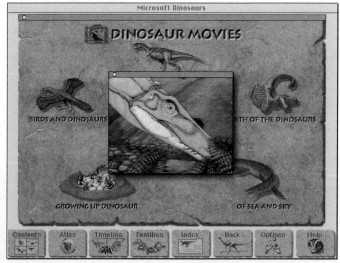

Figure 22-6: Who says there were no videos during the age of dinosaurs?

- Dangerous Creatures is a lot like Dinosaurs, except that these animals are alive now and ready to eat you up. (Actually, most of these animals are more endangered than dangerous, something Microsoft acknowledges only occasionally inside the CD.) The CD abounds with sounds and pictures of predators. You can learn what they use for weapons, where they live, and what fellow critters they eat.

What I like most about these CDs is the nonlinear way they're organized. When watching a movie about baboons in Dangerous Creatures, for example, a button suggests that you move along to cobras next. A few clicks later, you're trying to match predator with prey. You can hop from one spot to another without any idea of where you're going or what comes next, or you can proceed down the straight-and-narrow path and find out information on a specific topic. Each CD is a pleasure to peruse.

Microsoft Musical Instruments, Microsoft Dinosaurs, Microsoft Dangerous Creatures, Microsoft, 800-228-6270, 206-882-8080. List price: $60 per title.

The Rosetta Stone Language Library

I really wish that the whole world spoke English. I don't necessarily think that English is the greatest language or anything, it's just that I'd rather not have to ever worry about learning a second language while I'm still having such a hard time mastering this first one. But folks in other countries insist upon speaking in their native tongues, darn their hides, so occasionally, even idiots like me have to make an effort.

Now, I won't say that The Rosetta Stone Language Library series makes learning languages fun, because "learning languages" and "fun" just don't belong in the same sentence. "Learning languages" and "pain," you bet, but never "fun." And yet, I was definitely intrigued by these CDs. They employ an experiential learning system, something that would be entirely impossible in any medium other than CD-ROM. Rather than telling you that the Russian word for *donkey* is *borscht* (or whatever it is), the CDs teach you a second language in the same way that you learned the first: by exposing you to words and images and letting you establish the links.

Here's a basic example of how it works. The CD says the Russian word for *car*. You see four images on-screen and randomly click on the one that you think is right. After four clicks, you're bound to eventually figure it out. The CD then says another word, and because you've now ruled out car, you select from one of the three remaining images. Pretty soon, you're through with those images and ready to move on to new ones. Next, you hear the word for *cat,* and you repeat the process. A couple of screens later, the CD says *cat* and *car* together. As long as you vaguely recall one word or the other, you know to click on the picture of the cat and car, as in Figure 22-7. I really, truly am stupid when it comes to languages — after four years of French, my entire vocabulary consists of *oui* and *ici* — and yet I got *cat* and *car* and lots of other combinations right on the first try. I don't know any Russian except what I've heard in submarine movies, and yet I scored surprisingly well.

Figure 22-7: If I ever need to say "cat" and "car" in Russian, I'm all set.

After a few hours of using this software, I'm not quite fluent in Russian yet, but I'm a big fan. Fairfield Language Technologies, the company behind the series, claims that its customers include the U.S. State Department along with other governmental agencies and competing language vendor Berlitz, so I'm not alone. Still, my guess is that this is a better long-term learning tool than a cramming tool. You're not going to find out how to say "Hello" and "Where's the bathroom" for your next business trip without a lot of searching around. Verb conjugations and other fine points of the language may also escape you (though I should mention that the phrases get much more extensive than *cat* and *car* as you go along). However, as a beginning learning tool, this strikes me as a tremendous solution.

By the way, the 92-chapter, single-language systems, called the Level Ia series, cost several hundred dollars. If you just want to give The Rosetta Stone method a try, buy the PowerPac, which includes lessons in English, Spanish, French, German, and Russian and costs considerably less.

The Rosetta Stone Language Library, Fairfield Language Technologies, 800-788-0822, 703-432-6166. List price: $100 for PowerPac, $400 for each Level Ia CD.

Exploring Ancient Cities

This creative venture from *Scientific American* magazine and Sumeria examines four lost cities from antiquity: the Middle American Teotihuacán; Petra, in present day Jordan; the Roman town of Pompeii; and the Minoan Palaces on the Mediterranean island of Crete. The CD offers city maps, countless pictures of the ruins, slide shows, videos, and an essay about each site taken from the pages of *Scientific American* and read by poet Rod McKuen. Other than the fact that McKuen sounds like he's battling a severe case of laryngitis, it's a wonderful mix.

For each city, you're encouraged to begin with narrated slide shows that last between 20 and 35 minutes apiece. There are also shorter slide shows about the architecture and artwork from the various cultures, though these are not narrated. You can cancel any slide show by simply clicking. You can then revisit the cities and view the text of the essay, as shown in Figure 22-8. If the name of a site or monument is underlined, clicking on the word brings up a photograph. You can zoom photos to full-screen size by clicking on them. Some photos allow you to enter slide shows. The reconstructed city maps are well rendered and fully labeled.

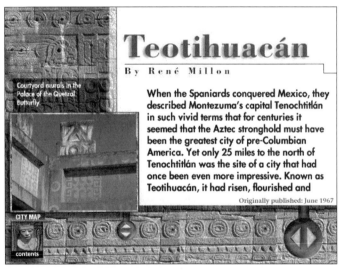

Figure 22-8: From this deceptively straightforward screen, you can access all the information that the CD has to offer about the ancient city of Teotihuacán.

Having visited Pompeii about five years ago, I found it a joy to revisit the city from my living room and learn about other cities that I absolutely crave to visit in the future. The added benefits of an attractive and straightforward interface plus well-written and informative essays made the experience that much more fun. I was a little disappointed that you can't pause a narration and pick it up again at a certain point; you can either listen to it all the way through or start it over again from the beginning. But the CD's benefits easily outweigh this small oversight. My wife was sufficiently impressed to remark, "This is what a CD should be," and she's not one to make such remarks lightly.

Exploring Ancient Cities, Sumeria, 415-904-0800. List price: $50.

Macbeth

I get so sick of *Hamlet* sometimes. You always hear some actor going on about how it's the part everyone dreams of playing. The play within the play is forever the inspiration for some horrid movie within a movie in some unwatchable film. And it seems like every other Shakespeare quote you hear — "To be or not to be," "Something is rotten in the state of Denmark," "Brevity is the soul of wit" — comes from *Hamlet*. Sure, *Hamlet* has implied incest, deep questions of mortality, and a persistent ghost tormenting the hero, but enough is enough. I'd rather watch *Macbeth,* with its undertones of witchcraft, obsessive and evil ambitions, and a good, strong female lead. And besides, you have to admit that Scots are way cooler than Danes.

So it is with a glad smile that I tell you that Voyager, rather than starting off with the obvious Shakespearean tragedy, has gone for the gusto and released an interactive *Macbeth,* complete with an annotated script, more essays than you'll ever read, and a few entertaining surprises. For example, you can listen to members of the Royal Shakespeare Company act out the play in its entirety by simply clicking on a line in the script. You can also view scenes from three film versions of the play by genius directors Roman Polanski, Akira Kurosawa, and my fave among faves, Orson Welles. And if you're itching to try your hand at Lady Macbeth or the Thane of Cawdor himself, you can play Macbeth Karaoke, as shown in Figure 22-9. A trained actor plays one part, and you flub your way through the other.

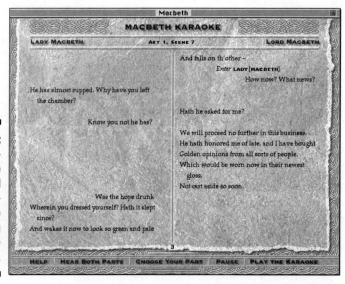

Figure 22-9: Shakespearean karaoke will undoubtedly be the next big thing in dive bars.

The only downside of this remarkable CD is the number of elements you start amassing on-screen. To navigate efficiently, you need to make the toolbox visible, thereby covering a fair portion of the text. And the annotations fill another window, which blocks out still more. On a 14-inch monitor, you'll probably start to feel pretty irritable pretty fast. But on a 17-inch monitor or larger, things loosen up considerably. So Shakespeare buffs take note: Buy a larger monitor and then screw your courage to the sticking-place for an experience of most sacrilegious murder through the fog and filthy air that surrounds great Glamis, worthy Cawdor, and more than a few noble thanes.

Macbeth, Voyager, 800-446-2001, 914-591-5500. List price: $50.

Learn to Speak Spanish

Did I mention that I hate learning languages? Yet here I am recommending a second foreign language CD. Either I'm a masochist, or these CDs are really something special. Well, for the sake of argument, let's assume the latter. Learn to Speak Spanish 5.0 is the newest upgrade in HyperGlot's Learn to Speak series. This two-CD set contains 30 chapters, and I'm talking meaty chapters. These CDs take a more conventional approach than The Rosetta Stone series, but much to their credit, they provide ample opportunity to hammer the lessons home over and over again.

Each chapter begins with a vocabulary lesson. You click on a word in a list, and speakers say the word in both Spanish and English. If you like, you can also watch a video of the word being spoken in context. Any word that is spoken is also written on-screen. To keep yourself honest, you can digitally record your voice with a microphone and hear how it sounds compared with the same word spoken by the CD. (The Rosetta Stone series provides a similar function.)

After the vocabulary lesson, you can visit ten additional screens that test your knowledge and help you apply it. For example, in The Action screen shown in Figure 22-10, you learn about Spanish culture and how, unlike your typical American, a Latin fellow might not hanker to your walking up to him and saying, "Yo, Fathead, where the heck is closest place to buy some of that Monopoly money youse guys pass off as cash?" Instead, you're supposed to say the equivalent of "Pardon me, Bub" and maintain a more or less courteous composure. If you can't remember a word in this Spanish-only section, just click on it. Every Spanish word is linked to its English equivalent for handy reminders. As you can see in the figure, *¿Dígame?* means *What in the world do you want?*

Figure 22-10: To figure out what these crazy folks are saying, you can click your way through the Spanish sentences and see English translations above.

For me, The Rosetta Stone approach seems a better way to learn. But if you've had success with traditional techniques in the past or you're trying to build on a language you learned in school, there is absolutely nothing wrong with Learn to Speak Spanish 5.0. It offers step-by-step chapters, lots of real-world examples, and some very good-looking speakers who might use a little too much gel in their hair. If they had this kind of stuff when I was in school, I might have actually learned something. Then again, I was a pretty lazy student, so you never know.

Learn to Speak Spanish 5.0, HyperGlot Software, 800-726-5087, 615-558-8270. Estimated street price: $135.

The Next-Best Ten

If I were to say I *loved* the previous ten CDs, I guess I'd describe my feelings for these next ten as *very pronounced affection,* or *strong approval,* or perhaps *right ho, what?* Well, whatever my exact feelings might be, I want to strongly urge you not to dismiss these titles just because they get small write-ups. One of them, Microsoft's Encarta, is one of the best-selling CDs ever, and the rest deserve to do equally well.

- **ITN World News,** Media Design Interactive, UK: 44-1252-737630. Estimated street price: $50. ITN is a news service featured on independent television stations. Its stories also occasionally manage to find their way onto ABC and CNN. This two-CD set documents more than 3,500 ITN news stories through a combination of text, photographs, and video. It's easily the best news CD I have seen. The only problem: It covers the years 1992 and 1993. Those were eventful years, but I'd love to see the series updated.

- **How Computers Work,** Time Warner Interactive Group, 800-482-3766, 818-955-9999. List price: $80. Time-Life produces a series of books called *Understanding Computers* that follows the evolution of thinking machines throughout this century. It's a fine series, and I confess that I refer to it often. Unfortunately, Time has been haranguing me for about 18 months now to pay $35 for some books in the series that I never received. So imagine my relief when the How Computers Work CD, which is based on *Understanding Computers,* arrived on my doorstep. Though it lacks any QuickTime movies, the CD is significantly more reasonably priced than the book series and just as jam-packed with information. My days of waiting for those missing volumes are over.

- **Bookshelf '94,** Microsoft, 800-228-6270, 206-882-8080. List price: $70. If you've ever dreamed of having Roget's Thesaurus, the Columbia Book of Quotations, the American Heritage Dictionary, and the World Almanac Book of Facts assembled together on your desktop for immediate reference, then you have some pretty piddly little dreams. Just the same, this particular dream is answered by Bookshelf '94, which provides all these resources and more. There isn't much here in the way of multimedia, and the dates in the People's Chronology aren't quite in order, but for sheer convenience, it can't be beat.

- **Leonardo the Inventor,** Future Vision Multimedia, 800-472-8777, 914-426-0400. List price: $50. In addition to painting the *Mona Lisa* and the *Last Supper,* Leonardo da Vinci seems to have invented just about everything we use today short of the garbage disposal and Pogs. In page after page, he sketched plans for the tank, the parachute, the suspension bridge, the snorkel, and heaps more. He didn't actually make any of this stuff, mind you, but he had some very big ideas. This CD looks at his life, examines his art, and shows three-dimensional, working versions of his inventions. It even comes with a pair of 3-D glasses. Now that's multimedia.

- **Who Built America?,** Voyager, 800-446-2001, 914-591-5500. List price: $50. This CD is a lesson in turn-of-the-century American history, from the centennial celebration of 1876 to the beginning of World War I in 1914. The grayscale interface has a very academic feel and is at times a little unfriendly, but it houses a wealth of textual information that rivals an encyclopedia. And unlike the encyclopedias, which sometimes have a thrown-together feel, the historical images and archival sound and video on this CD are thoughtfully integrated, and the search and index features are top-notch. If you value quality over glitz, and you don't mind a challenge, this CD is well worth looking into.

- **Weekend Home Projects,** IVI Publishing, 800-432-1332, 612-996-6000. Estimated street price: $40. Modeled after the PBS fix-it-yourself television series "Hometime," Weekend Home Projects shows you how to make your home a little safer and more desirable place to live. It contains 60 high-quality videos that show you how to reseat your toilet, install a garage door opener, or build a deck. The CD also offers advice about tools and materials as well as general tips in written form. The links to related topics are a little iffy, and many options don't become highlighted when you click on them, but the videos are friendly and well presented. I actually feel like I might be able to pull off one of these projects after watching one.

- **Prehistoria,** Grolier Electronic Publishing, 800-285-4534, 203-797-3530. List price: $70. Earlier in this chapter, I mentioned that the Microsoft Dinosaurs CD features animated sequences from the PBS "Dinosaurs" series. Prehistoria, on the other hand, contains much of the live-action stuff from the series. In addition to these videos, the CD contains information on hundreds of dinosaurs, early primates and mammals, and lots of other ancient creatures. The CD pronounces the name of each critter and shows how big it was compared to a stylized human symbol or a silhouette of a guy with his hands in his pockets. Getting around can be a little painful — you can't always go back to the last slide, for example — but if the dinosaur fancier in your family isn't satisfied by the Microsoft CD, Prehistoria is a good follow-up.

- **Exotic Japan,** Voyager, 800-446-2001, 914-591-5500. List price: $50. Exotic Japan is a comprehensive visitor's guide to the Land of the Rising Sun, examining the language, explaining the customs, and throwing in a few traveling tips for good measure. The CD is filled with the typical pronunciation sounds and tips on how to behave yourself abroad. What really distinguishes it are the animated Kanji characters. An everyday object transforms itself into a written word to help you remember these complex and plentiful characters.

- **Encarta 1994 Edition,** Microsoft, 800-228-6270, 206-882-8080. List price: $100. I have to admit that I'm disappointed by the CD encyclopedias I've seen so far. It's certainly remarkable that 20 or 30 volumes of encyclopedia text takes up less than 5 percent of the space on a CD-ROM, leaving lots of room for still images, sound, and video. My frustration is that, for the present, this extra space is generally wasted on some pretty questionable material. Encarta is the most successful CD-ROM encyclopedia, offering good text links, a fast search command, and lots of audio clips. But the occasional videos are little more than slide shows, the animation is crude, and the content needs work. Microsoft tells me that an updated Encarta for 1995 will be out by time you read this and that it will be much better. I look forward to it.

- **The 1995 Grolier Multimedia Encyclopedia,** Grolier Electronic Publishing, 800-285-4534, 203-797-3530. List price: $150. Frankly, this encyclopedia is a below-average work of multimedia, not nearly so well presented or so easy to navigate as Encarta. But it also contains more information than Encarta, and the coverage is more balanced. In fact, it is one of the few CDs and the only encyclopedia that lives with me here at my office. (Most hang out at my home, where I'm not tempted to play with them when I should be working.) If all you care about is the facts, Jack, then this is the encyclopedia to buy.

Chapter 23
Top Ten CDs — Games and Entertainment

In This Chapter
▶ The Lost Mind of Dr. Brain
▶ Star Trek: The Next Generation Interactive Technical Manual
▶ The Daedalus Encounter
▶ Myst
▶ Gadget
▶ The Residents Freak Show
▶ SimCity Enhanced
▶ Lode Runner: The Legend Returns
▶ This Is Spinal Tap
▶ Rebel Assault
▶ The Next-Best Ten

Every once in a while, I'll be hanging out in a computer store and overhear a salesman conning some poor soul into buying a PC instead of a Mac because there's less software for the Mac. "All the software developers are developing stuff for the PC," goes the Grinchy lie, "because that's where all the users are." As a user of both kinds of machines (with prejudices in the Mac's favor, I admit), I can attest that this line is a big ball of hooey — with a candy coating of truth around the edges. Nearly all major business, graphics, and multimedia programs exist on both platforms. Where the PC has the edge is in the fringe categories, and one of these categories is CD-ROM games.

The bad news is that PC users can choose from two to three times as many game titles as their spunkier, savvier, Macintosh-using counterparts. The good news is, Mac users have access to nearly all the games that are worth playing. And lots of games are developed on the Mac and ported over to the PC. Furthermore, every game vendor I talked to assured me that the Mac is top priority from now on. There's simply no sense in ignoring the 15 percent of the market that buys 25 percent of the software.

Feeling smug? Well, rightly so. You're an important, vocal minority, and you deserve the best.

In addition to games, I also cover general entertainment CDs in this chapter. From my perspective, one way of wasting time is just as valuable as the next. Just because you aren't blasting every alien within a ten-mile radius doesn't mean that you aren't having a blast. I cover CD-ROMs that contain movies, music videos, and virtual tours through 3-D environments — they're not quite games, but they clearly amount to a good time. Game or no game, if it's designed to entertain, it's in this chapter.

The Lost Mind of Dr. Brain

Brain teasers are amazing things. In addition to wasting all kinds of valuable time, they actually enhance your thinking power. While synapses that go unused grow cold, firing synapses keep old trails open and forge new ones. Problem solving, in other words, not only keeps you on your toes, but can actually alter the physical composition of your brain and build new connections. Puzzles make you smarter.

At least, that's the idea behind The Lost Mind of Dr. Brain, a delightful series of puzzles that encourage you to test your seven different kinds of intelligence — verbal, logical, spatial, kinetic, musical, interpersonal, and intrapersonal. The game starts out with the puzzle-obsessed but lovable Dr. Brain trying to figure out the ultimate puzzle: how to transfer intelligence from one critter to another. When the experiment goes haywire, as experiments always do, his mind ends up inside the body of his rat Rathbone, and Dr. Brain is left witless. Your job is to solve the puzzles, with the help of the doctor's niece (a renowned scientist in her own right), and restore the good doctor's brain.

So much for the silly plot. The real fun is in solving the puzzles. You get ten kinds of puzzles that test different types of intelligence (with some overlap, obviously). You can control the level of difficulty, and if you solve the harder puzzles, you fix Dr. Brain's brain that much faster. The harder puzzles also provide better challenges. In Figure 23-1, I'm playing the toughest level of the Train of Thought game, where you have to manage little balls rolling along a track. You flip switches to guide the balls toward a destination as Rathbone (shown hanging out in a barrel) calls for the balls. It's very hectic, and it requires you to keep an eye out on as many as seven balls at a time.

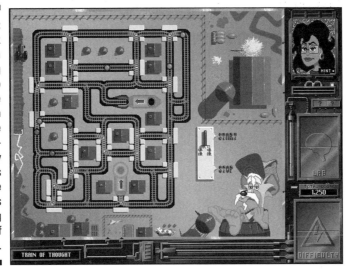

Figure 23-1: As you work like a whirling dervish to keep the balls in order, the rat occasionally harasses you, and the niece offers motivating quips of wisdom.

What I absolutely love about The Lost Mind of Dr. Brain is that not a single one of these puzzles could be written down on a sheet of paper, recorded on videotape, or explained on an audio CD. Every one takes full advantage of the give and take of human and machine, making for a thoroughly satisfying and challenging experience. The game is funny; Rathbone adds hilarious commentary, and when he and the brainless Dr. talk at once — their brains are linked, you see — each voice comes out of a different speaker. And though the games are thoroughly addictive, you emerge feeling sharp as a tack instead of drained and dulled. Oh, sure, it's still a waste of time, but I think that your mom would approve of the fact that you're finally exercising your mind.

The Lost Mind of Dr. Brain, Sierra On-Line, 800-757-7707, 206-649-9800. List price: $45.

Star Trek: The Next Generation Interactive Technical Manual

When you ask folks whether they like the TV show "Star Trek: The Next Generation," you usually get one of two answers:

1. An unabashed, "What are you, nuts? I love it!"

2. Or a hesitating, "Yeah, I like it. I mean, I'm not *obsessed* with it like some people, but I like it," which translates to, "What, are you nuts? I love it! I just don't want to be associated with those wackos who dress up like the characters and go to science-fiction conventions."

Now, now, I'm just presenting points of view, here. If you *like* to dress up like the characters and go to conventions, more power to you. My only point is, most everyone seems to like the show. Oh sure, there are a couple of naysayers, folks who haven't quite caught on, but most of us have all but forgotten the original "Star Trek" — once so clearly emblazoned in our collective psyche — and taken the new one to heart.

As a result, STNG Technical Manual is bound to have fairly universal appeal. If you're a Trekker, you've probably already purchased six or seven copies. But if not, this CD, which offers an exhaustive examination of the U.S.S. Enterprise, is decidedly worth a look. You can visit just about all points of interest inside and outside the ship — including several private cabins — and find out all kinds of information about the different areas. You can enjoy semi-believable discussions about how the transporter and holodeck work, learn why Ten Forward is called Ten Forward, and even see how the bridge and other areas appear from outside the ship. You can spin the ship in 3-D space and — as I mentioned in the "QuickTime's Virtual World" section of Chapter 16 — meander through the rooms, which are depicted with astounding accuracy. It's all just a Hollywood set and a bunch of models, but I, for one, find it absolutely enthralling.

Actor Jonathan Frakes (Number One) narrates guided tours through the ship, while the widow of series creator Gene Roddenberry, Majel Barrett Roddenberry (who appeared as different characters on both *Star Trek* series) explains parts of the ship as you explore at your own pace. But the real pleasure in STNG: Interactive Technical Manual is in the details. As you can see in Figure 23-2, the interface looks just like the monitors for the on-board computer. The sound effects — from the blippity blip of the computer to the swish of the cabin doors — are right on. The interface is constantly adjusting itself and offering new information. Barely moving your mouse can send messages scurrying around on-screen. And some of the interface elements, including the scroll bar, offer some attractive advantages over their standard Macintosh counterparts. If you find the show convincing, the CD-ROM is bound to feel like the real thing.

Star Trek: The Next Generation Interactive Technical Manual, Simon and Schuster, 800-983-5333, 212-698-7000. List price: $70.

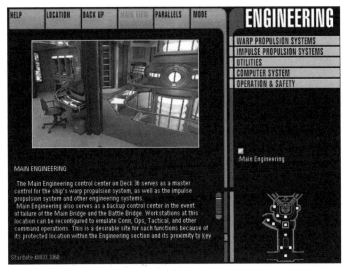

Figure 23-2: My peaceful stroll through engineering is punctuated by the melodious rumblings of the ship and the chirps of the computer.

The Daedalus Encounter

There's been a lot of speculation that virtual reality might have the same effect on folks in the future that forces such as drugs and gambling have now. VR junkies will plug into imaginary scenarios and lose themselves for days, while their families, jobs, and lives go to pot. I submit The Daedalus Encounter as early confirmation that these fears are 100 percent justified. I don't mean to say that this particular game is addictive — at least I haven't had any compulsions to play it for days on end — but it gives you a good idea of what virtual games may hold in store for the future.

In this game, you are a character in a state-of-the-art, interactive science-fiction movie that takes up three — count 'em three — CDs. The movie stars the lovely Tia Carrere (*Wayne's World*, *True Lies*) and the not-so-lovely though entirely acceptable-looking Christian Bocher (a regular on the Comedy Central cable network). You play Casey O'Bannon, a gunner aboard a patrol ship. Unfortunately, before you're even given a chance to start playing the game, you go and get yourself killed. Bummer. Thank golly you get a second lease on life when your buddies Ariel and Zack (Carrere and Bocher) are able to rescue your brain and plop it into an obliging robot. Wouldn't be much of a game if you just laid there dead.

The robot thing is really just an excuse to display a quarter-screen movie inside an interface filled with navigational and action options, as shown in Figure 23-3. Computer games aren't yet set up for you to start carrying on real conversations with your virtual buddies, so you're permitted to click on "Yes" and "No" buttons, analyze items, pick up stuff with your grappling arm, and fly around inside your remote-controlled probe.

Your time in Daedalus Encounter is about equally split between sitting back and watching five- to ten-minute increments of the movie and actively solving puzzles and saving your cohorts from certain death. In Figure 23-3, for example, Ariel is being attacked by piranha-like krin, who fly through the air and chomp through everything they come in contact with. If you allow Ariel or Zack to die, the game's over, and you have to take up from the last significant point in the game (wherever that may be). I should point out that there is one maze in which you fly through narrow passages and get lost unless you carefully map out your route. I hate mazes and think that they should be banned from games as a matter of course. But if you're a maze fan (you sicko), you may like it.

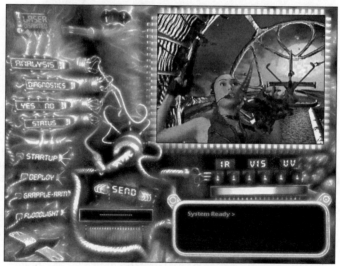

Figure 23-3: Thanks to the fact that I was irresponsibly trying to take a screen shot instead of fighting our current enemy, I allowed a savage krin to toast Tia.

As an interactive movie, The Daedalus Encounter is about the best I've seen, offering excellent 16-bit graphics, alluring 3-D animation, and a seamless blend of live-action camera work and computer-generate fakery. The sound is also exceptional. The game is pretty linear — you have to do your bits in the order dictated by the movie — so there isn't a lot of room for personal interpretation, as there is in a game such as Myst (up next). But I can honestly say that no other CD so thoroughly engulfs you in a big-production cinematic experience as The Daedalus Encounter.

The Daedalus Encounter, Virgin Interactive Entertainment, 800-874-4607, 714-833-1999. List price: $60.

Chapter 23: Top Ten CDs — Games and Entertainment   325

Myst

Myst is the Pastoral Symphony of CD-ROM games. At its heart, it's a series of a few thousand three-dimensional graphics with some isolated QuickTime movies to provide movement; a continuous, slender musical sound track; and understated sound effects. The result of this seemingly simple structure is one of the most captivating games on record. As illustrated in Figure 23-4, the tableaus are lush and enchanting, thanks as much to the talents of artist Chuck Carter as to brothers Rand and Robyn Miller, who dreamed up the game. And the thin veil of music never seems to get old, possibly because you never quite consciously pay attention to it in the first place.

Figure 23-4: Myst rewards your every move with full-screen picture postcards that soon have you believing you really are stranded on a cloudy island.

Now that I'm through waxing hyperbolic, let me explain how the game works. Everything in Myst is related to a book. In the game's introduction, you find a book that actually weaves the island world of Myst around you. (It's an offbeat pretext, and it never makes all that much sense, but it's as good a plot as any game offers.) Later, you discover within this book more books that take you to other islands. All the books were written by this fellow named Atrus, who has a couple of sons, Sirrus and Achenar, both of whom are out of their respective skulls. Each son is trapped in a book and encourages you to free him while suggesting that you needn't bother with the other one. Your mission is . . . well, that's for you to figure out.

Myst contains plenty of puzzles, but you'll likely be able to solve all of them without help. And you can never die or make an entirely irrevocable error, as you can in many other adventure games. Like The Daedalus Encounter, Myst includes a maze, which is potentially the hardest and easily the most boring part of the game to get through. (Pay attention to the sounds; they tell you where to go.) And the ending is something of a dud. If you were to remove the maze and modify the ending, you'd have yourself a perfect game, but even with those elements, it's not too shabby.

Myst, Broderbund Software, 800-521-6263, 415-382-4400. Estimated street price: $60.

Gadget

Gadget is the third Macintosh CD-ROM game from Japanese artist Haruhiko Shono. Following Alice and the beautifully rendered L-Zone, this game is his first that has a plot, which makes a world of difference. Although his other games are fascinating to look at, your interest is liable to falter once you discover that nothing you do makes a lick of difference. In Gadget, the story, the graphics, and the bold music of Koji Ueno merge to create a feast for the eyes, ears, and (finally) the imagination.

Gadget is a dark and rather sinister game that looks like it's set in an Eastern Block country during a particularly nasty nuclear winter. From word one, events seem to conspire against you. An ashen little kid switches briefcases with you in the elevator. When you try to pursue him, the elevator doors close, and you are sent down to ground level. A sinister fellow who waits for you in the lobby insists that you and he have spoken before and that you have a mission — to find a man named Horselover and his team of mad scientists (all of whom, if the picture you receive is any indication, can be identified by their prominent ears). Is Horselover an evil fiend intent upon corrupting the world or a man trying to save those around him from a forthcoming catastrophe? This is one of the many gloomy riddles you have to unravel in this thick and riveting game.

What amazes me most about Gadget is the handling of the characters, two of which found their way in Figure 23-5. Though they aren't the handsomest bunch, they sport realistic faces with roughly carved features — quite a departure from the geometric humanoids you normally encounter in computer graphics. The still images in the game appear in color, but the transitional animations of belching trains and other fast-moving machinery fly by in black-and-white, heightening the element of dread and suspense. You could cut the mood of this game with a knife, which is precisely what I like about it. Dark and gruesome underworld, here I come.

Gadget, Synergy Interactive, 213-687-2905. List price: $80.

Figure 23-5: A couple of holly-jolly customers who populate the outrageously cheerful world of Gadget.

The Residents Freak Show

On the off that chance you haven't been boning up on your avant-garde pop bands, The Residents are a San Francisco-based performance-art group that have been milling about since the mid '70s. The members of the band are probably best known for appearing in some of the earliest music videos wearing large eyeballs over their heads, garnished with top hats. Two of these videos are part of the permanent collection in the Museum of Modern Art in New York, which recognizes The Residents as among the originators of "the music video form." And if you ever watched "Pee Wee's Playhouse," you heard the band playing its twittering, sometimes repetitive music in the background.

Though prominent and highly respected in certain circles, The Residents are clearly not everyone's cup of tea, and neither is the Freak Show CD. It permits you to visit "the down-and-out inhabitants of a fantasy freak show." Sound depressing, even exploitive? I guess that it could be construed that way, but I found it to be both fascinating and occasionally sympathetic. Artist Jim Ludtke's 3-D graphics are on par with the work in Myst and Gadget, though they do have something of a demented quality about them. And the artwork from the comic book descriptions of the characters — which you have to hunt for inside each entertainer's trailer — is equally imaginative and well executed. Figure 23-6 supplies examples of both the comic book and 3-D versions of one of the entertainers, Harry the Head. Though once a charismatic member of sideshow society, he now resides in a jar of formaldehyde. (Chock up the fact that the two Harrys don't look the least bit alike — and that the Ludtke Harry has misplaced his ears — to artistic license.)

In addition to the folks in the show, you can research the lives of nearly 100 real-life sideshow entertainers from this country's past. One of my favorite stories involves one Dolly Dimples, who joined sideshow life when her weight tipped 500 pounds. After a successful career making as much as $300 a day in the early portion of this century, she was warned that if she didn't lose weight, her days were numbered. Lose weight she did, returning to the 100-pound range in just over a year. She then switched careers inside the circus and became Madame Celeste, Teller of Fortunes. Not all the stories are this optimistic, of course. Though many entertainers raked in the cash and lived normal lives, others were exploited or treated as something less than human, their deaths never recorded.

If you're a Residents fan — and who isn't? — the CD displays all the band's albums, shows many of its videos, and offers the occasional concert footage, some of which is narrated by the gravel-voiced Penn Jillette of the magic duo Penn and Teller.

Granted, the CD is a little unusual, even peculiar, and it may not be the kind of entertainment you'll want to share with the whole family (unless your family's name happens to be Addams). But I must say, between the idiosyncratic music and the extraordinary graphics, Freak Show never fails to hold my rapt attention. And just think of the investment possibilities. You know this unusual fragment of entertainment history is going to be worth a fortune one day. (Madame Celeste told me so.)

The Residents Freak Show, Voyager, 800-446-2001, 914-591-5500. List price: $50.

Chapter 23: Top Ten CDs — Games and Entertainment

Figure 23-6: Harry the Head of yesterday (top) and today (bottom), as rendered by artists Brian Bolland and Jim Ludtke, respectively.

SimCity Enhanced

There's a lot of confusion about this game. About whether or not the game exists, that is. I know that it does, because I'm holding it in my hot little hands. But I was assured by a PR person at Maxis — which handles SimCity, SimEarth, SimAnt, and all those other simulation titles — that SimCity did not and never would exist on CD-ROM. Later, we tracked down the CD at a game company called MacPlay. But when I called those folks to confirm the price — because the CD isn't in the catalog — I learned that they don't have it listed under SimCity Enhanced in their computers, just SimCity on CD-ROM.

Well, this kind of stuff happens with new titles sometimes. So if you run into problems, I just want you to know the following:

- SimCity Enhanced definitely does exist.
- It's lots and lots of fun.

If you've never played SimCity, it goes like this: You are the mayor of a city, and it's your job to keep everything running smoothly. You bulldoze the land, establish residential and commercial sites, hook up electricity, construct roads, create airports and train stations, build parks and schools, and tax your constituents at a sufficient rate to keep everything funded but not so high that everyone moves out of town. You're looking for a happy, well-oiled machine.

As an added bit of fun, you can introduce random acts of disaster. Perhaps you'd like to test you wits against a flood. Or maybe a tornado sounds fun. How about a monster trashing your city and toppling over buildings? In Figure 23-7, I'm trying out one of the predefined scenarios, the San Francisco earthquake of 1906. Half the city is on fire, and just for fun, I've completely cut off funding to the fire and police departments for four consecutive years. I'm interested in seeing what happens when folks live in an inferno and everyone riots without an honest cop in sight. In addition to listening to a series of thundering explosions as one natural gas silo after another bursts into flames, I am hounded by videos of the fire and police chiefs recounting their petty concerns. And as if that's not enough, my approval rating is in the toilet (as the City Evaluation window in the figure shows). Maybe if I let the fires consume the whole city, they'll all realize how lucky they used to be when only half the place was ablaze. Ah ha-ha-ha, I'm *maaaad* with power!

Figure 23-7: Man, my fire chief will not get off my back, and the voters hate me. What a bunch of ingrates.

SimCity has long been one of the most fun games on the Mac, and the Enhanced version makes it more fun than ever, adding sound effects and videos of the complaining or congratulatory civil servants. (In my tight-fisted games, some city employee or other is forever nagging me to better fund a pet department. Hey, you think money grows on trees around here? I'm trying to balance my budget.) And you can look in on the little people in your town by clicking on an eyeball icon. So before you write that outraged letter to your real-life mayor, give SimCity a try and see whether you can do any better.

SimCity Enhanced CD-ROM, MacPlay, 800-462-2752, 714-553-3530. List price: $50.

Lode Runner: The Legend Returns

One of the most diverting arcade games ever designed, Lode Runner has enjoyed popularity on the Mac ever since the black-and-white days. You're a little guy called the Lode Runner, and your objective is to grab all the treasure on each level without being gobbled up by the menacing mad monks. As shown in Figure 23-8, you navigate from one clump of grass (or ice or what have you) to the next via ladders and ropes. You can also jump off the edge of a clump without damaging yourself.

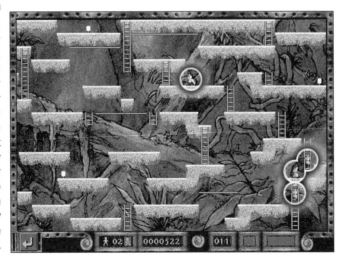

Figure 23-8: I circled my character, the lode runner (upper middle), and the three monks that are on my tail (lower right) to make them slightly more recognizable.

All in all, the CD-ROM version of Lode Runner provides a total of 10 so-called underworlds that offer 15 levels apiece. Figure 23-8 shows level 11 of underworld 1. (Confusing as this scene may appear, rest assured that things get much more challenging.) Each underworld provides you with a new tool. In underworld 1, for example, you have a laser gun that you can use to blast holes in the clumps. This is a great way to access lower clumps or trap monks who are in hot pursuit. Later underworlds offer bombs, jackhammers, pick axes, and, my favorite, slime buckets.

After you finish each level, you're treated to a little bit of animation. The game is also well equipped with sound effects. And if you get sick of the 150 levels of play that the CD provides — which means that you're probably playing the game a little too much — you can design you own levels using the Game Generator feature. You select the background, you position the clumps, you make the ladders, and on and on. Okay, so you probably won't ever take advantage of that feature, but it's there if you need it. You never know when you might become completely obsessed by Lode Runner.

Lode Runner: The Legend Returns, Sierra On-Line, 800-757-7707, 206-649-9800. List price: $45.

This Is Spinal Tap

The first CD in this two-CD set contains the complete movie *This Is Spinal Tap*, which chronicles the failing careers of the aging members of a heavy metal rock band comprising comic actors Michael McKean, Harry Shearer, and (the vastly underrated) Christopher Guest. After achieving the pinnacle of popularity with a sappy '60s ballad called "Listen to the Flower People" — which vaguely approximates the Lemon Pipers singing "To Sir with Love" — the band has been experiencing something of a prolonged decline. By the time rockumentary filmmaker Marty Di Bergi (Rob Reiner) arrives on the scene, the decline has turned into a roller coaster of tears, though our heroes possess too insufficient a grasp on reality to cry. By the movie's close, they're resorting to playing an amusement park as second billing to a puppet show.

A second CD contains about 90 minutes' worth of footage that was deleted from the movie, during which you learn more about Guest's unhealthy affections for Gumby and see Bruno Kirby — who plays a limo driver — sing Frank Sinatra tunes in his underwear (truly one of the funniest sequences ever recorded). You'll also find still pictures, a 20-minute demo film used to sell the movie to Embassy Pictures, and a couple of the most off-the-wall trailers ever proffered to entice the movie-going public. (To give you an idea, Ed Begley, Jr., plays a champion cheese roller.)

Throughout the first CD, you can listen to commentary from the writers, director Rob Reiner, and others who were involved in making the film. But this element and everything else I've mentioned so far is also included on the Criterion laserdisc version of the movie (also available from Voyager), with much better video resolution. As demonstrated in Figure 23-9, the main advantage of the CD-ROM is that you can do word searches to skip to different spots within the movie. You can search for spoken lines of dialog ("bizarre gardening accident," "keep the dwarves clear"); bits of written text ("Smell the Glove," "Spinal Pap"); actors (Anjelica Houston, Paul Shaffer); or even props (Stonehenge, cricket bat). I wasn't able to find a couple of crucial bits, such as "Gumby" and "cold sore," but I was surprised by how much worked. You can also skip from one search point to the next by pressing the arrow keys.

Figure 23-9: The result of searching for a particular lyric in a particular song.

Another point in the CD's favor is that it's considerably cheaper than the laserdisc — about a third of the price, in fact. Given the current state of technology, I'd say that the coarse quality of the movie is bearable when weighed against the considerable cash savings. In any case, the CD is a laugh riot, and it provides a glimpse of how we'll be watching movies a few years from now. And just think how hip you'll seem to your friends (or not).

This Is Spinal Tap, Voyager, 800-446-2001, 914-591-5500. List price: $35.

Rebel Assault

Created in 1993, Rebel Assault is starting to show its age, but it's still a great arcade game. Based on the *Star Wars* movies, this CD finds you flying through canyons on the dusty planet of Tatooine, taking pot shots at an Imperial Cruiser, flying through asteroid fields, and blasting TIE fighters. It's one of those keep-your-finger-plastered-against-the-fire-button-and-hope-for-the-best games. You may feel too superior for that kind of thing anymore, but anything in the name of mindless computer fun is A-OK with me.

In Rebel Assault, you play Rookie One, a Luke Skywalker-like character who knows how to fly but has never been in combat. Your first few missions are pure training exercises in which you maneuver inside canyons and shoot target droids as they scurry about the rocks and crags below. Your first real assignment is to go on a shooting spree around a Star Destroyer. The route is predetermined, so all you have to do is aim and fire. Later, you revisit the familiar Tatooine canyon, but you're in a larger X-Wing fighter and firing like a madman in pursuit of the enemy. In order to maintain a semblance of plot, Rebel Assault has you talk to a few characters, as shown in Figure 23-10. But the fun of the game is the vintage arcade stuff, with each new scenario getting tougher than the one before it.

Figure 23-10: When I wasn't busy firing my brains out and dodging asteroids, I took a few moments out to snap these screen shots.

Rebel Assault provides computer-generated sound throughout, and the action is 320 × 240 pixels in 256 colors. Those aren't exactly state-of-the-art specifications, but it's a safe bet that the game will run well on old and new machines alike. I had some consistent problems with the sound not matching up with the lip movements of the speaker, but as I said, the plot is entirely superfluous, so you're better off skipping that junk anyway. No doubt, some would argue that there are more deserving games out there that provide better graphics, stereo sound, tighter programming, and yada yada ya. But Rebel Assault has something that the games I don't recommend in this chapter lack — great action. The second I started playing, I was hooked. If that's not the ultimate determination of a terrific game, I don't know what is.

By the way, if you're a *Star Wars* fan, keep an eye out for Dark Forces, the next game in the series. When I finished this book, the game was still about two weeks away from being released, so it should definitely be out and about by the time you read this.

Rebel Assault, LucasArts, 800-782-7927, 415-721-3300. List price: $70.

The Next-Best Ten

We all have fun in different ways. My wife, for example, would have ranked this chapter completely differently. She doesn't have enough patience for Myst and Gadget, and she thinks that arcade games are a total waste of time, so there go Lode Runner and Rebel Assault. We also have different preferences based on who we're with. If I were selecting one of these CDs to play with my wife, I would definitely go with The Lost Mind of Doctor Brain or the Star Trek title; if I were alone, I'd probably grab Gadget because I haven't finished playing it yet. If I were tired, I might play a few rounds of Lode Runner and call it a day.

The point is, you may be interested in only a couple of the CDs I've mentioned so far. I just hate the idea of leaving you with so few alternatives, so here are some more to consider:

- **Marathon,** Bungie Software, 312-563-6200. List price: $70. This game *just* arrived on my doorstep, yet I was so immediately impressed by it that I bumped another title off the list to squeeze this one in. If I had had more time, I might have substituted Marathon in place of Rebel Assault as one of my top ten titles. Marathon is a dense shoot-em-up game with splendid 16-bit graphics and 22 kHz stereo sound. The game has the feel of the movie *Aliens,* with praying mantis-like bad guys coming at you from all directions, even dropping down on you from the ceiling. You die a lot, but you can immediately rejoin the game, or you can just lie there and watch the aliens shift around above you. Marathon is the only CD I recommend that accommodates network play so that you and the other folks at the office can blast each other to smithereens during lunch.

- **Iron Helix,** Spectrum Holobyte, 510-522-1164. Estimated street price: $70. During a war game simulation, the computer on-board one of the ships goes nuts and targets — wouldn't you know it — a peaceful, nonagressive planet that is entirely without defenses. (Will these peaceful, nonagressive planets never learn?) Rather conveniently, all the crew members of the renegade ship contract a horrible virus and die. But before they do, they plant secret codes that will trigger the ship's self-destruction in places where the computer cannot find them. Enter you, a probe whose mission it is to hunt down the DNA from the dead crew. You use this DNA to enter secure areas and locate the trigger codes. But watch out for the security robots, because they'll nail you if they find you. Great graphics, good music, a bit weak on the plot, but still very good fun.

- **Xplora 1: Peter Gabriel's Secret World,** MacPlay, 800-462-2752, 714-553-3530. List price: $50. Xplora has a tendency to be a little too arty for its own good. The navigation buttons in this CD, for example, are a bunch of unlabeled colored squares. What kind of operation does green suggest versus, say, light blue? But once you get beyond the initial disorientation, this CD really takes off. It's well supplied with the marvelous videos that transformed Gabriel's career. You can also see how a few of the videos were made, remix the music, and crash in on Peter and friends in their virtual studio. To its credit, the CD rarely slips into the hero-worship that seems to be the primary distinguishing characteristic of other pop-star CDs. In the world-beat area, you're even permitted to sample music from *other* artists, independent of any participation from Gabriel. Frankly, this one section of the CD is enough to justify the purchase.

- **Who Killed Brett Penance?** and **Who Killed Taylor French?,** Creative Multimedia, 503-241-4351. Estimated street price: $30 apiece. The Who Killed CDs are a series of whodunit games in which you are chief detective. You question witnesses, dig up clues, and check up on the suspects' alibis with the help of your assistant, Sheryl Lee (who played the dead Laura Palmer on "Twin Peaks"). Before you can get a warrant or charge the suspect, you have to face a press conference. Answer seven out of ten questions correctly, or it's back to the interview rooms. Oh, and one other thing — you have just six hours to solve the mystery. These are some of the most thoughtfully organized, logically presented games for the Mac. The videos are a little rough, but the acting is first-rate (quite the departure from what passes for acting in most games). And when it's all over, the solution makes sense. Needs some tweaking, but bravo.

- **Return to Zork,** Activision, 800-477-3650, 310-473-9200. List price: $80. If you've owned a computer for more than five years, you may remember an adventure game called Zork. It was the best-selling adventure game ever, and yet it was made up entirely of text. If the game were to tell you, "You see a box," for example, you'd respond by typing, "Pick up box," and so on. It required lots of imagination, but it was great fun. Return to Zork is sequel number six and the first Zork to break with text and go the full multimedia route. Happily, it retains the same humor and weird logic that marked the earlier Zorks. I played the original Zork about ten years ago, so this was a real walk down memory lane. But I have the same complaint now that I did then — you need a hint book (which you can purchase separately) to get through it.

✔ **Wrath of the Gods,** Luminaria, 415-284-6464. List price: $50. Wrath of the Gods reminds me a lot of Return to Zork, except that you never die, and the hints are built into the game. In fact, if it weren't for the fact that Zork hearkens me back to younger days, I might like Wrath of the Gods better. Ah, but it's pointless to speculate. In this game, you wander through Greek landscapes, fight hydras, steal from dragons, hang out with fetching nymphs, consult an oracle, and engage in many more mythological activities. The action can drag a little at times, but at its best, the CD offers light-hearted, sometimes comical entertainment. If you like old Ray Harryhausen films (*Jason and the Argonauts*, *Clash of the Titans*), it's a cinch you'll like Wrath of the Gods. It's good, wholesome gaming for the whole family.

✔ **Maniac Sports,** The Software Toolworks, 800-234-3088, 415-883-3000. List price: $50. If you're like most people, you haven't experienced sky diving, windsurfing, whitewater kayaking, or bungee jumping. Nor have you biked, skied, climbed, skateboarded, or surfed like the lunatics featured on this CD. Experience vicarious thrills as people with tremendous athletic capabilities and nothing upstairs attempt some of the most daring stunts on record. It's a lot of fun to watch, and there are even some useful tips in case you decide to (stupidly) pursue one of these avenues on your own. The games are hilarious, the videos are top-notch. The surfer-dude host, however, can't even do a decent surfer dude. For shame, for sure, man.

✔ **Club Dead,** Viacom New Media, 800-469-2539, 212-258-6000. List price: $60. It's fitting that the box for this game is inscribed with the MTV logo, because the game itself has the look and feel of one of those 30-second station ID spots the channel is so (in)famous for. In other words, it gets right in your face. You are Sam Frost, ex-con and virtual reality addict (see, told you it was real). The sinister conglomerate Metacorp has hauled your sorry carcass out of the joint because they need a cyberplumber, and you just happen to be the best there is. Translation? You're trying to solve a mystery by hunting around for clues. It's weird, it's dark, it's full of irritating music. But turn off the music, give the game a chance, and it kind of grows on you.

✔ **The 7th Guest,** Virgin Interactive Entertainment, 800-874-4607, 714-833-1999. List price: $60. In this two-CD set, you visit a haunted castle and attempt to solve the puzzles therein. The house belongs to a master toymaker who has somehow managed to kill a bunch of children with his toys. (Why do they even bother with these plots?) The toymaker is dead now, but his caustic spirit continues to permeate the castle. He tests you, offering you one puzzle after another until . . . you're quite thoroughly amused. The scenarios are goofy, but the graphics are excellent, and the puzzles are challenging. There's even a hint book on a table in the library to help you if you get stuck. (Every game should have one of these!) Unfortunately, you can't cancel the movies. In fact, if you click on a movie in an attempt to stop it, it just plays over again after it finishes. Still, this CD is a high-quality piece of entertainment.

✔ **Jewels of the Oracle,** Discus, 800-567-4321, 416-250-6537. List price: $60. The pretext of this game is so vague that I didn't even know there was one until I read the back of the CD case. It has something to do with some ancient, really smart Sumerians in the Fertile Crescent. What really counts, though, are — you guessed it — the puzzles, puzzles, puzzles, and more puzzles. These babies are hard, too. You get number puzzles that have multiple solutions, for example, and spatial puzzles that require you to map movement patterns. It took me an hour to figure out the first puzzle alone, and that was at the Easy setting. For each correctly solved puzzle, you are awarded with a jewel. The graphics, which include depictions of actual historical artifacts, are well rendered, and the play is rigorous, to say the least. If you're looking for a challenge, this CD will not disappoint.

Chapter 24
Top Ten CDs — Great Stuff for Kids

In This Chapter
- Gahan Wilson's The Ultimate Haunted House
- The Trail Series
- Mario is Missing! Deluxe
- Welcome to Bodyland
- Putt-Putt Joins the Parade
- Bailey's Book House (and Friends)
- Math Workshop
- SimTown
- 3-D Dinosaur Adventure
- The Living Books Series

This chapter requires a bit of explanation. You see, I know that I'm not a kid, and I'm guessing that you're not a kid, either. So it didn't seem to make sense to try to judge kids' CDs totally from an adult perspective — after all, it's the little citizens of your house who are going to be using these things.

If I had any kids of my own, I could sit down with them and balance what they liked with what I thought was good for them. But my wife and I have been going the peaceful, childless route and loving every second of it.

So I did what any rational reviewer would do in my place. I rounded up a kid — one nine-year-old Jessica Deiter. Jessica is very bright and struck me as being fully able to judge kids' CDs from a kid's perspective without any interference from me. So I threw a bunch of CDs at her and left her alone. With able assistance and occasional supervision from her mom, Mrs. Deiter (all right, I guess you're old enough to call her Tonya), Jessica graded the CDs based on four criteria:

- How fun is the CD?
- How educational is it?
- How easy is it to use?
- Is it sufficiently captivating to retain my interest over the long haul?

After awarding each CD up to 25 points in each of these areas, she added the points and came up with the winners. *Very* scientific, and she did it all without any meaningful direction from yours truly. But even so, keep in mind that the results are just one kid's choices. And the choices aren't necessarily what an adult might think is good for kids, but what a kid thinks is good for kids.

All I did was come in and tighten things up a bit. I combined different titles in the same CD series — like the well received Oregon Trail, Yukon Trail, and Amazon Trail from MECC — into one entry. And I discussed with Jessica whether or not we might have a few too many Mario CDs on our list. (I'm sure that Nintendo wouldn't approve, but we ultimately narrowed down our recommendations to just one CD, Software Toolwork's Mario is Missing.) Oh, yeah, and *I* went ahead and wrote the chapter. Much as I tried, I wasn't able to pawn that part off on Jessica.

Because I combined CD series titles into one listing, and because kids are ruthless judges, I have only ten recommendations in this category. This chapter has no "The Next-Best Ten" section, as do the other CD review chapters. That's not going to please the vendors, either. I told Jessica that when they start calling in to complain, I'd pass them along to her. She figures she's up to it.

Gahan Wilson's The Ultimate Haunted House

I couldn't agree more with Jessica's choice for favorite CD: The Ultimate Haunted House. Created by cartoonist Gahan Wilson, this game takes place — where else? — inside a spooky mansion. The trick is to acquire 13 keys before the witching hour of 13 o'clock (way past the kids' bedtimes). If you make it, you win a cartoon, a sound, or an animation file (your choice), which is copied to your hard drive. You can open the cartoon in SimpleText, and you can play the sound by double-clicking on it. To look at an animation file, you have to have a special program, such as the screen saver After Dark from Berkeley Systems.

To play, you roam around the house with your trusty carpetbag in tow. Each of the 13 rooms in the mansion contains lots of objects and monsters, as shown in the particularly crowded Figure 24-1. You collect all the objects you can and put them in your bag. Examples include a dead rat, a brain, and a plateful of worms. Mmm, just thinking about all that yummy stuff makes me hungry. When you come across a ghost or a monster, you click on it to get hints. Or you might offer it one of those scrumptious treats from your bag. Every so often, something somewhere gives you a key for your troubles.

Figure 24-1: A monster in a cage, a piranha in a tank, and a hanging guy with a pumpkin head. What more could you want?

Jessica assured me that the CD is fun, not scary. She also admired what she called "the authentic music," which features "Monster Mash" and other ghoulish tunes. In one of my favorite rooms, you can play your own tunes on an organ. You click on the stops to get different organ sounds such as howls, screams, and burps. The game changes from one play to the next, and you can save your spot whenever it's quitting time.

I'm not quite sure how The Ultimate Haunted House managed to rack up any points in the education area, but Jessica awarded this CD a whopping 97 out of 100 total points. Perhaps the monsters teach you things if you're young enough to listen. But, as far as I'm concerned, this wonderful little game is the next best thing to having Halloween all year 'round.

Gahan Wilson's The Ultimate Haunted House, Microsoft, 800-228-6270, 206-882-8080. List price: $50. Designed for ages 8 and up.

The Trail Series

The Trail series CDs from MECC (pronounced *meck*) are the kind of kids' CDs that moms and dads are sure to approve. The CDs are highly educational, possibly more so than any of the other titles in this chapter, as well as interesting to explore. In a matter of days, your kids will know more about going West in the 19th century, panning for gold in the Yukon, or paddling down the Amazon on the way to the river's source in the Andes than you ever learned. And if you take the time to sit down with them, you'll be pleasantly surprised by how much you enjoy yourself.

Take Oregon Trail II, for example, the best Trail CD of the bunch. A follow-up to the original Oregon Trail — a game that was written for big mainframe computers more than 20 years ago — Oregon Trail II offers realistic graphics, lots of people to meet, and three hours of speech and music. The result is a thorough and exciting account of traveling from the Midwestern states of Illinois or Missouri across the Overland Trail in the mid-1800s.

You start your journey in town, searching for supplies. You can click on passers-by to seek out advice or trade with them. You can also visit the local merchants to purchase wagons, weapons, draft animals, and all the other rustic stuff you need to stay alive on the trail. After you're satisfied that you're ready for the journey, you head out with a wagon train for the lone prairie.

The trail itself is slow going, and you run into many hardships. In Figure 24-2, for example, little Peggy has died of a snake bite. I told her to stay away from anything that rattled. Maybe that'll learn her. Anyway, it can't help but make you feel sad when one of your virtual pals kicks the bucket, but if you take a close look at the Health Status window, you'll find some good news. Deke is listed as "Feeling good." Looks like everything's okay after all.

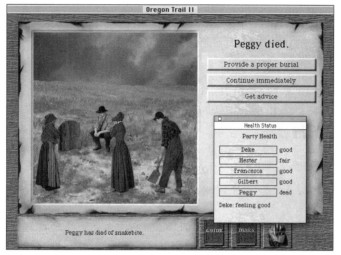

Figure 24-2: Out of the deepest respect for dear Peggy, I clicked on the Continue Immediately button.

All the Trail CDs are challenging. You're constantly breaking down, getting sick, running out of money, and having things stolen. Sometimes, you even have to turn back. And, as Jessica thoughtfully warned me, sights like the Dead Horse Trail from The Yukon Trail CD "can be very graphic for little children." But as far as I'm concerned, any CD that teaches kids the value of planning while bringing history to such vivid life is an absolute winner. These are truly remarkable CDs.

The Oregon Trail, The Yukon Trail, The Amazon Trail, Oregon Trail II, MECC, 800-685-6322, 612-569-1500. List price: $70 per title, except Oregon Trail II, $90. Designed for ages 10 and up.

Mario is Missing! Deluxe

So far, I agree 100 percent with Jessica's choices. But Mario is Missing is a different story. I can honestly say that I wouldn't have recommended it in a million years. Ripe with completely random dialog, video arcade music, and smallish graphics, it holds about as much interest for adults as a typical episode of "Mighty Morphin Power Rangers." But at least one nine-year-old loved it.

The scene begins with plumber Mario and brother Luigi paying a visit to the castle of the fiendish Bowser, who is trying to melt all the snow in Antarctica. I was unable to discover anything of Bowser's motives. From what I gathered from Jessica's somewhat impatient analysis, Bowser has displayed a penchant for doing bad things without provocation in the past, so his newest scheme is accepted without question. Mario rather naively enters the castle alone — again, the reasons for his actions are a bit unclear — and is immediately kidnapped and shuttled off to whereabouts unknown. When Luigi follows roughly 20 seconds later, he is informed by Bowser that his only hope is to scour the world for Mario and perhaps learn a bit about geography while he's at it. (This terrific scene is captured in Figure 24-3.) Why Bowser shows no interest in kidnapping Luigi and why Luigi doesn't simply wring Bowser's neck are riddles that will forever escape us.

Figure 24-3: The spine-chilling initial encounter between Bowser and Luigi (top) and a communiqué received from Mario minutes later (bottom).

As Luigi, you select a door in Bowser's castle and are whisked randomly to one of 25 cities in the world. There, you do your best to intercept Bowser's henchmen, the turtlelike Koopas, as they attempt to make off with historic artifacts. You then return these artifacts to their rightful owners and collect rewards. As you make your way, you may acquire newsletters covering the day's events as well as educational pamphlets about regional landmarks, and you converse with people on the street. All newspapers, pamphlets, and conversations are duly noted on the PowerBook that you carry along with you. You also receive calls from city officials on your videophone. You may even get a call from Mario offering advice. (Nothing like hearing a tip or two from the guy you're looking for.)

Frankly, try as I might, I never grasped the big picture behind Mario is Missing. Oh, sure, I snared my share of Koopas, returned a couple of artifacts, and learned a thing or two about the cities I happened to land in, Nairobi and

Bombay. But I never exactly caught the Mario bug, if you know what I mean. Jessica, quite by contrast, was completely captivated, awarding it an enthusiastic 92 points. I guess this is one of those areas where I just have to accept the fact that although I may sometimes act like a nine-year-old, I don't quite think like one.

Mario is Missing! Deluxe, The Software Toolworks, 800-234-3088, 415-883-3000. List price: $50. Designed for ages 7 and up.

Welcome to Bodyland

In this charming CD, you visit an amusement park dedicated to the inner workings of the human body. Your tour guides are Ricki, a girl who seems to be the same age as a typical baby sitter, and her parrot Hiccups, who, frankly, gets a little tiresome but is tolerable. They escort you around 12 rides, including such sure-fire hits as Bony Boulevard, Mouthopolis, and Nose Run. To enter one of the rides, you simply click on its icon on the main screen, shown in Figure 24-4. (The Nose Run plane and Land A'Head submarine are constantly moving around, making them hard to click on. Fortunately, you can alternatively click on the boy's nose or head to access the rides.)

Figure 24-4: This aerial view of Bodyland provides access to all 12 rides plus the Discovery Tower, where you can test your knowledge.

Inside each ride, you are treated to an original song, and the songs are both amusing and educational for the younger set. In Nose Run, for example, a country singer drawls, "My mucus membranes are drippin', so my nose I'm a grippin'." He later explains that he always uses a handkerchief and never picks anything but his guitar. Words to live by. You can then explore how the body functions by clicking on the different items you see.

When you think you've learned everything there is to learn, you can visit the Discovery Tower, which contains three levels of questions, each getting progressively harder. If you answer all 90 multiple-choice questions correctly — for a total of 9,999 points! — Bodyland treats you to a special animated fireworks show.

Bodyland is great fun, and I learned a thing or two myself. The animation is a bit rudimentary — especially when compared with the highly polished songs — and Ricki and Hiccups are a tad slow with their cues, but I doubt that your youngster will much notice these problems. Though the vendor, IVI Publishing, recommends the CD to children ages 5 through 11, Jessica made a special point of telling me that she thinks it's for kids 7 or younger, and I tend to agree.

Welcome to Bodyland, IVI Publishing, 800-432-1332, 612-996-6000. Estimated street price: $30. Designed for ages 5 through 11.

Putt-Putt Joins the Parade

This CD is part of Humongous Entertainment's Junior Adventures series. Sadly, Putt-Putt Joins the Parade was the only title Humongous sent us for review, but the series also includes CDs about Fatty Bear and Freddi Fish. If they're anywhere as good as Putt-Putt Joins the Parade, and if you have a 3- to 8-year-old in the family, I would buy up every single title. I have to confess, I am totally in love with Putt-Putt.

This CD has everything going for it. Putt-Putt is a vibrant and sympathetic character, reminiscent of *Bambi's* Thumper and other memorable animated characters from the big screen. And everything around him is ready to jump about at your child's command. Click on the frog, and he slurps down a fly that's been bothering you. Click on Putt-Putt's horn, and he scrunches up his face and honks. Click on two flowers by the side of the road, and they turn and kiss each other. You can even click on multiple items at a time and have them all hopping around at once. In the top scene in Figure 24-5, for example, I clicked on every one of the five apples on the apple tree, and sure enough, every one of them did its own special action without slowing down one bit. This may be the only CD I've seen that can handle every click your rambunctious kid throws at it without complaining.

Figure 24-5: Two early scenes from Putt-Putt Joins the Parade, showing five simultaneously animated apples (top) and Putt-Putt's garage-sweet-garage (bottom).

If Putt-Putt has a problem — and I'm really picking nits here — it's that the screen holds only 320 × 240 pixels, doubled in size to fill a 14-inch screen. You can make things appear a little less blocky by choosing a Smooth Graphics command, but still, more real pixels would be nice. Even without those pixels, though, your kids are going to go nuts for this little car.

Most every kids' CD supplies children with encouragement — "You're so smart," "Way to go," and so on — but this CD is forever cheerful and obliging. If you're at the gas station and you click on the pump, Putt-Putt thinks about it and reckons, "I think I need some gas." Click on the pump five seconds later, and he says, "I think I'll have some more." The speedometer only goes up to 35, the car wash costs 2¢, and the gas seems to be totally free (not to mention nonpolluting). What a groovy, feel-good world! Putt-Putt and his friends are generous, agreeable, enthusiastic, and never for a second saccharine. I wish my car were half as fun.

Putt-Putt Joins the Parade, Humongous Entertainment, 206-485-1212. Estimated street price: $40. Designed for ages 3 through 8.

Bailey's Book House (and Friends)

Bailey's Book House is part of a series from Edmark that includes Millie's Math House and Sammy's Science House. All are exemplary educational CDs designed for home schooling of very young children. And like Putt-Putt, they are extremely obliging programs, instructive without being judgmental.

In Bailey's Book House (Jessica's personal favorite of the three), little minds learn the fundamentals of literacy by selecting words and assembling phrases that talk out loud. You visit Bailey, a young cat, and click on items inside his house to visit one of five learning areas. Three areas — Read-A-Rhyme, Letter Machine, and Edmo & Houdini — provide both divergent (many possible answers) and convergent (one correct answer) modes.

For example, Edmo the clown and Houdini the dog allow you to experiment with prepositions. In the divergent mode, Edmo can instruct Houdini to act out the prepositions you click on (*over*, *behind*, *in*, and so on) with respect to his dog house. Or, if you prefer, Houdini can tell Edmo what to do. In the convergent mode, a bug asks you, "Can you put Houdini in the dog house?" You have to click on the word *In*. If you click on a different word, the bug informs you what this different word is and once again poses the question regarding *In*.

The two other areas are altogether exploratory. In one, you build a story by selecting from different options. If you decided to create a story about Harley the Horse, for example, you would then select what kind of vehicle Harley likes to ride in, as in the top of Figure 24-6. After informing the software that Harley's preferred mode of transportation is the bathtub, you would be asked to select a destination for horse and bathtub, and so on. In the last area, you can build greeting cards by selecting from various text and related graphic options.

Figure 24-6: Harley flies his bathtub into outer space in this exciting little tale that I've devised for my own amusement.

Bailey's voice is a child's voice, just as his Book House is a child's world. Left to their own devices and without the performance expectations that Mom or Dad might be tempted to bear, children can explore at their own speeds and in their preferred directions. And what a wonderful time they'll have. If these CDs continue to be this good, I'm going to have to call 1-800-555-KIDS and see if I can get a little duffer delivered.

Bailey's Book House, Millie's Math House, and *Sammy's Science House,* Edmark, 800-320-8379, 206-556-8484. List price: $50 per title. Designed for ages 2 through 6.

Math Workshop

Though it covers math rather than word associations (as you may have surmised from the title), this CD takes up where the Edmark series leaves off. It covers arithmetic, fractions, spatial reasoning, and other fine points of basic math. The CD also includes a Parent's Video Guide that explains how Mom and Dad can help their kids develop math skills in everyday life. The guide specifically covers indoor and outdoor noncomputer activities, as the Math Workshop generally speaks for itself.

The host of Math Workshop is a baby-sitter-aged girl named Polygonzales. (Love that name.) She makes you sign in at the door and explains puzzles to you when and if you need help. There are six puzzle areas in all, including three sections of geometric and spatial pattern puzzles, a fractions area, an arithmetic game in which contestants are awarded bowling pins, and a planning game in which you and an opponent take turns launching rockets. The pattern puzzles and the bowling game are the most successful. In addition to answering arithmetic questions in the bowling section, for example, you can click on an equal button to test equivalencies or an approximately-equal button to test estimates. In Figure 24-7, I am asked to estimate how many pencils an orange weighs. Though the question may seem frivolous, it forces kids to establish relationships between the real-world objects they've encountered. Math is, after all, about quantitative relationships, and these estimates demonstrate in a fun and off-beat way how math fits into everyday life. For each correct answer, a frightened-looking bowling pin plops down at the end of the lane. When you collect ten pins, the gorilla flings his ball and knocks them all down.

Figure 24-7: The answer to this puzzling question, incidentally, is 20.

Though Math Workshop is a very strong CD, I'm not sure that it always hits the mark. The music, for example, is a little grating after a while, compared with the highly listenable tunes included with the Edmark CDs. I found the fractions section a real challenge to learn, and if you get stuck in a patterns puzzle, the CD doesn't suggest exactly where you've gone wrong. Also, the CD has a little fun-facts section, but some of the topics — such as the Pythagorean theorem, which explains that the hypotenuse of a right triangle is equal in length to the square root of the sum of each side squared — are so casually and quickly discussed that I doubt that any but the brightest of kids is going to pick up on it. (Most adults might even feel their jaws dropping a bit.)

None of these concerns had any impact on Jessica's enthusiasm for Math Workshop, and, as a nine-year-old, she falls smack dab in the middle of the age group the CD is aimed at. (For the record, Jessica gave this title 84 points.) As a big-time math enthusiast myself, I am very much in favor of any program that makes learning math fun, and — my complaints notwithstanding — I have not seen any program that does a better job of covering all the basics. To its credit, the CD offers three or more levels of difficulty inside each section, and you can switch back and forth on the fly, without having to return to the main area. So, although Math Workshop may not be perfect, it is undoubtedly a powerful learning tool that inspires, educates, and encourages repeat visits.

Math Workshop, Broderbund Software, 800-521-6263, 415-382-4400. Estimated street price: $40. Designed for ages 6 through 12.

SimTown

SimTown is a SimCity game for kids, and we had an absolute blast playing it. Starting with one of three kinds of towns — Road Town, Park Town, or Bike Town — or a mix of the three, you add houses, entertainment attractions, eateries, and even (gulp) schools. The idea is to keep your budding population as happy as possible by balancing homes and businesses and avoiding the dreaded Eco-Villains, who hog too many resources for themselves.

As you build homes — which include such enviable abodes as haunted houses, futuristic houses, and castles — your population immediately begins to move in. You can spy them walking, skateboarding, or riding their bikes up and down the streets. You can also zoom in on the individual houses and double-click on a house to open it up for inspection. In Figure 24-8, I've opened up a tribal-style grass shack to see what the little family inside is up to. Many folks are home, which is a bad sign. (It generally means that they're unemployed and need you to build places for them to work.) Click on a family member to find out the person's name and hobbies. You can even click on pets, such as Napoleon the pig in Figure 24-8.

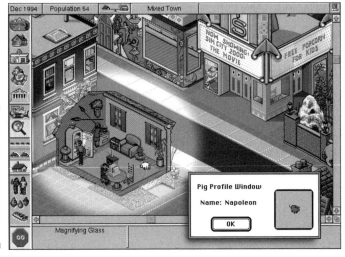

Figure 24-8: You can pop the top of any house in your town and take a peek at the inhabitants.

SimTown is one of those rare children's games that you will enjoy every bit as much as the kids. Very little bad ever happens, but it's a challenge to keep the townsfolk employed, the kids in school, and the houses and businesses in balance. And SimTown conveys that same magical quality that we got from Legos and Matchbox cities when we were kids. You are in control of a little town; you can examine that town from any angle and add to it or demolish it in any way you choose. All you and your children have to supply is the imagination.

SimTown, Maxis, 800-336-2947, 510-254-9700. List price: $40. Designed for ages 8 through 12.

3-D Dinosaur Adventure

Imagine having a little 3-D *Jurassic Park* on your computer, and you have an approximate idea of what this entertaining CD is all about. After a short movie — that you watch with your 3-D glasses — you enter the park by clicking on the gates. The software permits you to move around inside a magical 3-D environment in the direction you move your mouse. Or, if you find the mouse technique a little cumbersome — as I did — you can press the arrow keys on the keyboard. After a few minutes of experimentation, you'll be moving around with the best of them.

As you travel through the three major areas of the park — Triassic Tour, Jurassic Jungle, or Cretaceous Corner — you come across various exhibits that you can explore by clicking on them. For example, you can watch a series of dinosaur movies, look at a narrated storybook, or visit a 3-D museum. In Figure 24-9, I'm painting a 3-D dinosaur in the Create-A-Saurus exhibit. After selecting a dinosaur and applying one of the ten skin patterns available at the top of the screen, I can spin the creature around to get a good view of my creation.

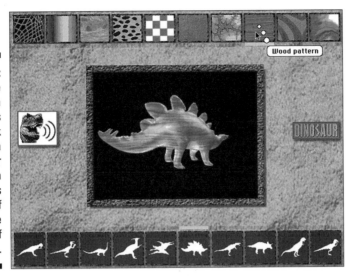

Figure 24-9: You can see how a triceratops might look with zebra stripes or how a stegosaurus would look if it were made out of wood.

As an adult, you may be a little perturbed that the software dumps you back at the beginning of the tour each time you exit an exhibit. And you can't help but notice that the same ten dinosaurs keep showing up in different places. But the movies are fun, and the 3-D images are likely to keep the kids mesmerized throughout several visits.

I should mention that Knowledge Adventure also makes an Undersea Adventure CD for the Mac. It offers many similar games and learning activities, but it doesn't allow you to navigate through a 3-D environment, which seems to be the major point in favor of 3-D Dinosaur Adventure.

3-D Dinosaur Adventure, Knowledge Adventure, 800-542-4240, 818- 542-4200. List price: $80. Designed for ages 3 through 10.

The Living Books Series

Okay, that's it. This is the last straw. We were totally ripped off as kids, and that's all there is to it. Broderbund's Living Book series proves that our formative years were altogether wasted. Remember when the teacher would read to the entire class? Great stuff, huh? Well, now imagine that the entire scene magically materialized in front of you and that you could examine each character and every prop in detail, as well as replay every word in the story. Needless to say, today's children have exactly these kinds of advantages in the form of Living Books. And our parents thought *we* were spoiled.

Take but one of the many Living Books titles, Marc Brown's Arthur's Teacher Troubles. Arthur is a little kid who has been cursed with the strictest teacher in school, Mr. Ratburn. He has homework, an irritating little sister, and a spelling bee to worry about. Ah, but you can read the story for yourself some time. What counts is not so much the wonderful story itself, but how the story comes to life on-screen.

You can either have the story read to you (if you're feeling in a particularly passive mood), or you can play inside the story. Either way, the entire text of the story is read out loud in many different voices, and the words appear highlighted on-screen as they are pronounced. If you have selected to play inside the story, you can hang around each page after the reading is complete. You can then click on items and people on the page to make them wiggle about or share their innermost thoughts. If you click on the swordfish on the bulletin board in Figure 24-10, it pops the tire of the motorcycle in front of it. Click on the children to hear what they're thinking.

Figure 24-10: These two pages from Arthur's Teacher Troubles contain hundreds of voices and animations that you can discover by clicking around on-screen.

Unlike the Putt-Putt CD, these CDs let only one event occur at a time. If you click on Arthur (the kid with the glasses), for example, you have to wait for him to finish talking before you click on anything else. Even so, these are very special CDs that go well beyond simple storytelling. The sheer depth of information encourages your children to both scrutinize the pages and invest themselves in the action. Each title is designed for a slightly different age group, but young and old are sure to be delighted.

Just Grandma and Me, The Tortoise and the Hare, Arthur's Teacher Trouble, Arthur's Birthday, The New Kid on the Block, Little Monster at School, Harry and the Haunted House, Ruff's Bone, Broderbund Software, 800-521-6263, 415-382-4400. Estimated street price: $40 per title. Designed for ages 3 through 12, depending on specific title.

Index

• Symbols •

3-D Dinosaur Adventure, 354–355
7th Guest, The, 337–338
8-bit sound, 175–176
8-bit, 22 kHz sound, 177
  junior AV Macintosh, 241
8-bit, 44 kHz sound, 178
16-bit color, 55
16-bit sound, 175–176
16-bit, 22 kHz sound, 178
16-bit, 44 kHz sound, 177–178
  AV Macintosh, 241
25-pin connector, 33
50-pin connector, 34
1995 Grolier Multimedia Encyclopedia, The, 317

• A •

About This Macintosh command, 244
access time, 28
active matrix, 21
A.D.A.M.: The Inside Story, 303–304
Adobe Fetch. *See* Fetch
Adobe Photoshop *See* Photoshop
Adobe Premiere, 111, 235–265
  ⌘-1 (Construction Window Options) keyboard shortcut, 254
  ⌘-6 (Transitions) keyboard shortcut, 259
  ⌘-F (Filters) keyboard shortcut, 258
  ⌘-I (Import File) keyboard shortcut, 252
  ⌘-K (Make Movie) keyboard shortcut, 263
  ⌘-M (Print to Video) keyboard shortcut, 273
  ⌘-N (New Project) keyboard shortcut, 251
  ⌘-S (Save) keyboard shortcut, 254
  ⌘-W (Clip Window) keyboard shortcut, 256–257
  assigning memory to, 244
  Cinepak option, 264–265
  clean cut, 259
  Clip⇨Filters command, 258
  clips, 254
  Component Video option, 238–239, 265
  Compression Settings dialog box, 265
  cutting movies, 254–257
  deleting clips, 257–
  editing movie, 252–253
  F10 (Movie Capture) function, 236
  fading clips into each other, 259–261
  fading sound in and out, 258
  File⇨Capture⇨Movie Capture command, 236
  File⇨Export⇨Frame as PICT command, 243
  File⇨Export⇨Print to Video command, 273
  File⇨Import⇨File command, 252
  File⇨Import⇨Multiple command, 252
  File⇨New⇨New Project command, 251
  File⇨Save command, 242, 254
  grabbing frames from movie, 243
  independent scenes, 254
  Make⇨Movie command, 263
  making recordings, 236–242
  Movie Analysis function, 251
  Movie Capture⇨Recording Settings command, 242, 244
  Movie Capture⇨Sound Input command, 240
  Movie Capture⇨Video Input command, 237
  movie size, 242
  movie window, 242
  moving clips, 257
  New Projects Presets dialog box, 236
  previewing transition effects, 261–262
  Project⇨Preview command, 262
  projects, 250–251
  QuickTime Composite option, 264
  QuickTime movie from project, 263–265
  realigning sound and clips, 258
  recording sound, 169
  recording sound with movie, 240–241
  returning edited movies to videotape, 273–274
  saving movie, 254
  selecting Presentation, 251
  special effects, 258
  starting, 251
  thumbnails, 254–255
  transition effects, 259–262
  Video option, 265
  Windows⇨Construction Window Options command, 254
  Windows⇨Transitions command, 259
  work area bar, 261–262
alert boxes, speaking contents of, 201

Mac Multimedia & CD-ROMs For Dummies

alert sounds
  naming, 165
  recording, 163–167
  scale, 167–169
  tips, 165–167
Altair computer, 51
American Visions: 20th Century Art from the Roy R. Neuberger Collection, 285–286
amplitude, 175
answering machine on AV Macintosh, 67
Apple CD–ROM extension, 38
Apple menu, 56, 140, 244
Apple Menu Options control panel, 57
Apple Microphone, 159–160
Apple Multimedia Tuner, 225
Apple Photo Access extension, 39, 97
Apple Presentation System, 68, 268
Apple TV/Video System, 68, 208
Apple Video Player, 210–219
  ⌘-4 (Show Controls Window) keyboard shortcut, 216
  ⌘-C (Copy Video Display) keyboard shortcut, 218
  ⌘-M (Mute) keyboard shortcut, 211
  ⌘-Q (Quit) keyboard shortcut, 217
  adding channels, 213
  Channel buttons, 210–211
  Channel pop–up menu, 211
  closed captioning, 217
  determining signal kind, 216–217
  Edit⇨Copy Video Display command, 218
  File⇨Quit command, 217
  fine–tuning channel list, 212–213
  grabbing single frame, 218–219
  locking out channels, 213–215
  Mute icon, 211
  named channels, 213
  quitting, 217
  removing channels, 213
  SAP (Second Audio Program) button, 217
  scanning for active channels, 211–212
  Setup⇨Channel Setup command, 211–213
  Setup⇨Set Channel Password command, 214
  Setup⇨TV Reminders command, 216
  switching between window sizes, 216
  taping TV, 218
  volume slider, 211
  Windows⇨Other Size command, 215
  Windows⇨Show Controls Window command, 216
Apple⇨Control Panels command, 64
Apple⇨Control Panels⇨Monitors command, 57, 269
Apple⇨Control Panels⇨Sound command, 161
AppleCD 300i CD–ROM drive, 12
AppleCD Audio Player, 143–144, 166
  ⌘-E (Eject) keyboard shortcut, 148
  customizing tracks, 149–150
  Eject button, 148
  Indicator Color command, 151
  naming tracks, 149
  Normal, Shuffle, and Prog buttons, 149
  options, 148–152
  Play/Pause button, 148
  Repeat button, 149
  Scan button, 148
  Sound command, 152
  Startup CD Drive command, 152
  Stop button, 148
  Time menu, 149
  Track button, 148
  Track menu, 149
  Volume button, 148–149
  Window Color command, 151
AppleTalk, turning off, 244, 278
Arthur, Ken, 174
Audio CD Access extension, 39
audio CDs, 24, 33, 39
  CD-quality sound, 177
  checked tracks only, 146
  customizing tracks, 149–150
  ejecting, 146, 148
  external speakers, 41
  fast-forward or -reverse, 145
  forward or backward inside track, 148
  how much it holds, 26
  list of song titles, 146–147
  listening to, 139–152
  listing track names, 149
  naming tracks, 149
  only one channel, 145
  order of tracks, 149
  pausing, 145, 148
  playing, 10, 148
  random order tracks, 146
  recording first track of, 145
  recording from, 152
  repeating, 149
  repeating one song or entire CD, 145
  repeating segment of track, 146
  software to play them, 143
  song length, 152–153

Index 361

sound cutting out, 153
stopping, 148
switching tracks, 148
time display, 149
time track changes, 146
track being played, 145
volume, 146, 148–149
AudioVision monitor
 microphone, 157–158
 volume for audio CDs, 142
AV Macintoshes, 65
 16-bit, 44 kHz sound, 241
 answering machine from, 67
 AV Power Macintoshes, 69–71
 AV Quadras, 69–71
 bad sound, 220
 Built-In Video dialog box, 269
 capabilities, 67
 capturing frames from movies, 67
 changing number of colors displayed, 235–236
 computer signals to VCR, 75–76
 DAV (digital audio/video) connector, 77–79
 displaying live video, 235–236
 FusionRecorder program, 235–236
 hardware for video out, 268
 hearing what VCR is recording, 76
 hooking up camcorder, 72–73
 hooking up VCR, 71–75
 internal CD-ROM drive, 67
 junior models, 68–69. *See also* junior AV Macintoshes
 laserdisc player, 75
 models, 66–67
 MoviePlay, 272–273
 picture discolored and jiggly, 220
 playing video in, 73–74
 RCA jacks, 72–73
 recording CD-quality sound, 177
 recording QuickTime movies, 67, 233
 recording sound, 67
 resizing video window, 221
 SCSI Manager 4.3 extension, 88
 seeing what VCR sees, 76
 speech recognition, 67
 splitting VRAM in half, 235
 trading in Macintosh for, 79–80
 unable to see video on display, 219
 videotaping edited movies, 67
 watching TV on, 219–221
AV Power Macintoshes, 69–71

RCA jacks, 74
SpigotPower AV (SPAV) board, 78
AV Quadras, 69–71
 RCA jacks, 73
 SpigotPower AV (SPAV) board, 78
 S-video jacks, 73
AV Technologies card, 12, 70–71

• B •

Bailey's Book House (and Friends), 349–351
bass response, 48
Big Green Disc, The, 297
binary digit, 84
bits, 55, 84
 sound, 175–176
boards, 60
 bus slot, 63
 PCI, 63
 PDS (Processor Direct Slot), 63–64
 video, 60–64
Bookshelf '94, 315
bus, 63
bus slot, 63
bytes, 84

• C •

cable–ready TV tuner and junior AV Macintosh, 68
cables
 external CD-ROM drives, 31
 minijack-to-RCA conversion cable, 45–46
 minijacks, 43
 miniplugs, 43–45
 RCA plugs, 45
 RCA plugs at both ends, 46–47
 Y, 45–46
CalcTalk, 201
camcorder
 as digital camera, 110–111
 hooking up to AV Macintosh, 72–73
Canvas, 100
cards, 60
Cartoon History of the Universe, The, 304–306
cassettes, recording sound on, 155–156
CD Remote, 143–147, 166
 AB button, 146
 Audio Channels button, 145
 Eject button, 146
 list of song titles, 146–147
 options, 145–147
 Program button, 146

(continued)

Mac Multimedia & CD-ROMs For Dummies

CD Remote *(continued)*
  Repeat button, 145
  Scan button, 145
  Shuffle button, 146
  Stop, Play, and Pause buttons, 145
  Time button, 146
  Track button, 145
  Volume button, 146
CD Remote INIT extension, 147
CD-quality sound, 177
  stereo sound, 13
CD-ROM drives, 23–28
  access time, 28
  AppleCD 300i, 12
  CDs, 23–26
  cost, 27
  drivers, 38
  extensions, 38–39
  external, 29–33
  inserting Photo CD, 97
  internal, 12, 17, 27, 29, 37
  purchasing, 27
  removing CDs, 39–40
  SCSI connections, 33–35
  SCSI-ID conflicts, 29
  single-speed drive, 28
  speed, 27–28
  spin rate, 28
  used, 27
CD-ROMs (Compact Disc, Read Only Memory).
    See CDs
CDs, 23–24
  buying vs. pirating, 25
  care of, 25–26
  clicking on buttons, 280–281
  color and, 54, 56
  copying files from, 27
  copying main program file to hard drive, 279
  durability, 25
  editing photographs stored on, 10
  educational resource, 299–317
  games and entertainment, 319–338
  giving HyperCard Player more
    memory, 278–279
  great for children, 341–357
  how much it holds, 26
  installing QuickTime, Multimedia Tuner, and
    Sound Manager, 278
  interactive, 10
  interactive coffee-table books, 283–298
  manufacturing costs, 25
  Monitors control panel and colors set to
    thousands, 279
  mounting, 38
  movies on, 229
  moving cursor away from QuickTime movie, 281
  playing, 10
  properties of, 24–25
  putting photo album on, 93–102
  removing from drive, 39–40
  skipping closing credits, 281
  skipping introductory movie, 280
  storage capacity, 25
  tips for better performance, 277–282
  tracking problems, 282
  translators, 39
  turning off AppleTalk, file sharing, extensions,
    and control panels, 278
  unable to mount, 282
  unmounting, 40
  will not play if color is set too high, 64
CDs (titles)
  1995 Grolier Multimedia Encyclopedia, The, 317
  3-D Dinosaur Adventure, 354–355
  7th Guest, The, 337–338
  A.D.A.M.: The Inside Story, 303–304
  American Visions: 20th Century Art from the
    Roy R. Neuberger Collection, 285–286
  Bailey's Book House (and Friends), 349–351
  Big Green Disc, The, 297
  Bookshelf '94, 315
  Cartoon History of the Universe, The, 304–306
  Cinemania '95, 298
  Clinton: A Portrait of Victory, 298
  Club Dead, 337
  Comic Book Confidential, 295–296
  Complete Maus, The: A Survivor's Tale, 291
  Crucible, The, 301–303
  Daedalus Encounter, The, 323–324
  Encarta 1994 Edition, 316
  Exotic Japan, 316
  Exploring Ancient Cities, 310–311
  First Emperor of China, The, 300–301
  For All Mankind, 288–289
  Four Paws of Crab, 292–293
  Gadget, 326–327
  Gahan Wilson's The Ultimate Adventure, 342–344
  How Animals Move, 306–307
  How Computers Work, 315
  Iron Helix, 336

Index

ITN World News, 315
Jewels of the Oracle, 338
Learn to Speak Spanish, 313–314
Leonardo the Inventor, 315
Lively Books Series, The, 355–357
Lode Runner: The Legend Returns, 331–332
Lost Mind of Dr. Brain, The, 320–321
Macbeth, 312–313
Maniac Sports, 337
Marathon, 335
Mario is Missing! Deluxe, 345–347
Martial Arts Explorer, The, 298
Material World: A Global Family Portrait, 284–285
Math Workshop, 351–352
Microsoft Exploration Series, 307–309
MPC (Multimedia PC), 282
Myst, 325–326
Nine Month Miracle, 303–304
OceanLife: Volumes 2 through 4, 287–288
Oceans Below, 296–297
Passage to Vietnam, 289–291
Prehistoria, 316
Putt-Putt Joins the Parade, 348–349
QuickTime: The CD, 226
Rebel Assault, 334–335
Residents Freak Show, The, 327–328
Return to Zork, 336–337
Rosetta Stone Language Library, The, 309–310
Seven Days in August: Unfold the Drama of the Cold War, 293–295
SimCity Enhanced, 329–331
SimTown, 353–354
Small Blue Planet: The Cities Below, 297
Small Blue Planet: The Real Picture Atlas, 297
Space: A Visual History of Manned Spaceflight, 298
Sports Illustrated Multimedia Almanac, 298
Star Trek: The Next Generation Interactive Technical Manual, 230–322
Street Atlas USA, 297
This Is Spinal Tap, 332–333
Trail Series, The, 344–345
Warplanes, 297
Weekend Home Projects, 316
Welcome to Bodyland, 347–348
Who Built America?, 315
Who Killed Brett Penance?, 336
Woodstock: 25th Anniversary CD-ROM, 298
Wrath of the Gods, 337
Xplora 1: Peter Gabriel's Secret World, 336

Centris 660AV, 12, 66
  recording movies, 239
channel-splitting, 45–46
channels, 43
children's CDs, 341–357
  3-D Dinosaur Adventure, 354–355
  Bailey's Book House (and Friends), 349–351
  Gahan Wilson's The Ultimate Adventure, 342–344
  Lively Books Series, The, 355–357
  Mario is Missing! Deluxe, 345–347
  Math Workshop, 351–352
  Putt-Putt Joins the Parade, 348–349
  SimTown, 353–354
  Trail Series, The, 344–345
  Welcome to Bodyland, 347–348
Chooser desk accessory and turning off AppleTalk, 244
chrominance, 73
Cinemania '95, 298
ClarisWorks, 100
clasps on external CD-ROM drives, 31
clicking, 2
Clinton: A Portrait of Victory, 298
clips, 254
ClockTalk, 201
Club Dead, 337
codecs (compression/depression), 238
color
  16-bit, 55
  CDs and, 54, 56
  changing number displayed, 235–236
  dithering, 53
  finding out how many can be displayed, 56–58
  getting more, 59–64
  laptops, 12, 20–21
  maximum that can be displayed, 18
  number displayed on-screen, 52–56
  options, 58
  thousands of, 13
Color It!, 123
Comic Book Confidential, 295–296
commands
  About This Macintosh, 244
  Apple⇨Control Panels, 64
  Apple⇨Control Panels⇨Monitors, 57, 269
  Apple⇨Control Panels⇨Sound, 161
  choosing, 3
  Control Panels, 56–57, 140
  File⇨Find, 194, 196
  File⇨Get Info, 102, 152–153, 244

(continued)

commands *(continued)*
    File➪Put Away, 40
    Special➪Restart, 196
    View➪By Icon, 234
Complete Maus, The: A Survivor's Tale, 291
composite video, 73
computer video vs. TV, 72
computerized Polaroids, 104–107
computerized stereo, 41–50
    channel-splitting, 45–46
    minijack-to-RCA conversion cable, 45–46
    powered speakers, 47–50
    RCA plugs, 45–47
    sound-out port, 42–47
computers
    Altair, 51
    conversing with, 193–203
    speaking date and time while booting up, 201
control panels
    Monitors, 269
    Sound, 140–143
    turning off, 278
Control Panels command, 56–57, 140
Crucible, The, 301–303

• D •

Daedalus Encounter, The, 323–324
daisy chaining, 35
DAV (digital audio/video) connector, 77–79
desk accessories (DAs), CD Remote, 145–147
desktop, 2
    CD icon, 152
digital audio tape (DAT), 89
Digital Camera 40 vs. QuickTake 150, 107–108
digital cameras, 103–110
    batteries, 110
    camcorder as, 110–111
    Digital Camera 40, 107–108
    full-screen, 105
    quarter-screen, 105
    QuickCam, 233
    QuickTake 150, 104–108
    taking photos, 108–109
    where they are useful, 106–107
digital images, organizing, 113–120
disks, recording sound to, 156
dithering, 53
double-clicking, 2
dragging, 2
drivers and CD-ROM drives, 38

Duos and docking stations, 21

• E •

EasyPlay, 226
editing photos, 123–136
    color balance, 133–136
    cropping images, 129–130
    rotating images, 127–129
    sharpening focus, 131–133
    straightening images, 126–129
editing sound, 173–192
    from other programs, 191–192
    refining sounds, 188–191
    sound quality, 175–176
educational resource CDs, 299–317
    1995 Grolier Multimedia Encyclopedia, The, 317
    A.D.A.M.: The Inside Story, 303–304
    Bookshelf '94, 315
    Cartoon History of the Universe, The, 304–306
    Crucible, The, 301–303
    Encarta 1994 Edition, 316
    Exotic Japan, 316
    Exploring Ancient Cities, 310–311
    First Emperor of China, The, 300–301
    How Animals Move, 306–307
    How Computers Work, 315
    ITN World News, 315
    Learn to Speak Spanish, 313–314
    Leonardo the Inventor, 315
    Macbeth, 312–313
    Microsoft Exploration Series, 307–309
    Nine Month Miracle, 303–304
    Prehistoria, 316
    Rosetta Stone Language Library, The, 309–310
    Weekend Home Projects, 316
    Who Built America?, 315
eject button on external CD–ROM drives, 31
Eliza, 202
Encarta 1994 Edition, 316
EPS file format, 120
ExcuseMe system extension, 201
Exotic Japan, 316
Exploring Ancient Cities, 310–311
extensions
    Apple CD-ROM, 38
    Apple Multimedia Tuner, 225
    Apple Photo Access, 39, 97
    Audio CD Access, 39
    CD Remote INIT, 147
    ExcuseMe, 201

Foreign File Access, 39, 97
High Sierra File Access, 39
ISO 9660 File Access, 39
MacinTalk Pro, 196
QuickTime, 98, 225
QuickTime Musical Instruments, 226
QuickTime PowerPlug, 225
SCSI Manager 4.3, 87–88
System Manager, 196
turning off, 278
external CD-ROM drives, 29
  cables, 31
  clasps, 31
  eject button, 31
  force eject hole, 31
  front of, 30–31
  headphone jack, 30
  hooking to stereo, 46–47
  jumpers, 32
  listening to audio CDs, 139
  minijack, 30
  miniplugs, 30
  power cord socket, 32
  power light, 31
  power switch, 32–33
  RCA jacks, 32
  rear of, 31–33
  recording sound, 160–161
  SCSI connectors, 31
  SCSI-ID switch, 32
  speakers, 49
  testing used, 33
  tray/caddy door, 30
  volume control, 31
  what to look for in, 29–33
external hard drives, 87–88
external microphones, 159–160

• F •

Fetch, 113–114, 117
  ⌘-E (Add/Update Items) keyboard shortcut, 116–117
  ⌘-F (Find) keyboard shortcut, 119
  ⌘-G (Edit Original) keyboard shortcut, 119
  ⌘-N (New) keyboard shortcut, 116
  ⌘-period (Cancel) keyboard shortcut, 117
  ⌘-quote (Display All) keyboard shortcut, 119
  ⌘-U (Description) keyboard shortcut, 119
  ⌘-Y (Keywords) keyboard shortcut, 119
  adding captions, 119

  Admin⇨Add/Update Items command, 116, 119
  displaying all images in catalog, 119
  Edit⇨Description command, 119
  Edit⇨Keywords command, 119
  editing images and, 119
  File⇨New command, 116
  Item⇨Edit Original command, 119
  keywords for searching, 119
  naming catalog file, 116
  on-screen image album, 116–117
  printing thumbnails, 120
  removing/restoring image from catalog, 119
  saving catalog to disk, 117
  Search⇨All command, 119
  Search⇨Find command, 119
  searching for images, 119
  usable file formats, 120–121
file formats
  EPS, 120
  GIF, 121
  JPEG, 120
  Photo CD, 121
  Photoshop, 120–121
  PICT, 120
  RIFF, 121
  TIFF, 120
file sharing, turning off, 278
File⇨Find command, 194, 196
File⇨Get Info command, 102, 152–153, 244
File⇨Put Away command, 40
files, copying from CDs, 27
Find (⌘-F) keyboard shortcut, 194, 196
Finder desktop, 2
  CD icon, 152
First Emperor of China, The, 300–301
FlexCam, 246–247
For All Mankind, 288–289
force eject hole on external CD-ROM drives, 31
Foreign File Access extension, 39, 97
Four Paws of Crab, 292–293
Fractal Design Painter, 121, 123
freeware
  Sound Editor, 174
  SoundBuilder, 174
  SoundHandle, 174
FusionRecorder, 235–242
  ⌘-C (Copy) keyboard shortcut, 243
  assigning memory to, 244
  Edit⇨Copy command, 243
  File⇨Save command, 242

(continued)

FusionRecorder *(continued)*
  grabbing frames from movie, 243
  making recordings, 236–242
  movie size, 242
  movie window, 242
  record window, 236
  Record⇨Record Preferences command, 244
  Record⇨Record Window Size command, 242
  Record⇨Sound Settings command, 240
  Record⇨Video Settings command, 237
  recording movies, 238–242
  recording sound with movie, 240–241

• G •

Gadget, 326–327
games and entertainment CDs, 319–338
  7th Guest, The, 337–338
  Club Dead, 337
  Daedalus Encounter, The, 323–324
  Gadget, 326–327
  Iron Helix, 336
  Jewels of the Oracle, 338
  Lode Runner: The Legend Returns, 331–332
  Lost Mind of Dr. Brain, The, 320–321
  Maniac Sports, 337
  Marathon, 335
  Myst, 325–326
  Rebel Assault, 334–335
  Residents Freak Show, The, 327–328
  Return to Zork, 336–337
  SimCity Enhanced, 329–331
  Star Trek: The Next Generation Interactive Technical Manual, 321–322
  This Is Spinal Tap, 332–333
  Who Killed Brett Penance?, 336
  Wrath of the Gods, 337
  Xplora 1: Peter Gabriel's Secret World, 336
GeoPort Telecom Adapter, 67
Get Info (⌘-I) keyboard shortcut, 102, 152–153, 244
GIF file format, 121
gigabyte (GB), 84
Gahan Wilson's The Ultimate Adventure, 342–344
Greetings, 201

• H •

hard drives
  checking size of internal, 86
  copying CD main program file to, 279
  external, 87–88
  milliseconds (ms), 87
  purchasing tips, 87–88
  seek time, 87
  speed, 87
  sustainable read and write rate, 87
hardware
  Apple Presentation System, 268
  SCSI-ID number, 32
  Spigot II Tape, 268
headphone jacks
  external CD-ROM drive, 30
  junior AV Macintosh, 68
  volume controls, 12
headphones and powered speakers, 50
hertz (Hz), 72
High Sierra File Access extension, 39
histogram, 134–135
How Animals Move, 306–307
How Computers Work, 315
HyperCard Player and more memory, 278–279

• I •

icons used in this book, 4–6
images, organizing, 113–120
Input Source dialog box, 141, 162–163
interactive CD coffee-table books, 283–298
  American Visions: 20th Century Art from the Roy R. Neuberger Collection, 285–286
  Big Green Disc, The, 297
  Cinemania '95, 298
  Clinton: A Portrait of Victory, 298
  Comic Book Confidential, 295–296
  Complete Maus, The: A Survivor's Tale, 291
  For All Mankind, 288–289
  Four Paws of Crab, 292–293
  Martial Arts Explorer, The, 298
  Material World: A Global Family Portrait, 284–285
  OceanLife: Volumes 2 through 4, 287–288
  Oceans Below, 296–297
  Passage to Vietnam, 289–291
  Seven Days in August: Unfold the Drama of the Cold War, 293–295
  Small Blue Planet: The Cities Below, 297
  Small Blue Planet: The Real Picture Atlas, 297
  Space: A Visual History of Manned Spaceflight, 298
  Sports Illustrated Multimedia Almanac, 298
  Street Atlas USA, 297
  Warplanes, 297
  Woodstock: 25th Anniversary CD-ROM, 298

Index *367*

interactive CD-ROMs, 10
internal CD-ROM drives, 17, 27, 29
  AV Macintosh, 67
  internal speaker, 37
  junior AV Macintosh, 69
  listening to audio CDs, 139–152
  monophonic Macintoshes, 43
  recording CD-quality sound, 177
  SCSI-ID number, 37
  self installation, 37
  what to expect from, 37
internal microphones, 157–158
internal speakers, 11
  internal CD-ROM drives, 37
interneg, 95
Iron Helix, 336
ISO 9660 File Access extension, 39
ITN World News, 315

• J •

Jewels of the Oracle, 338
JPEG file format, 120
jumpers, 32
junior AV Macintoshes, 68
  8-bit, 22 kHz sound, 241
  Apple Presentation System, 268
  cable-ready TV tuner, 68
  headphone jack, 68
  internal CD-ROM drives, 69
  recording movies, 239
  recording QuickTime movies, 233
  recording sound, 177
  recording videos, 68
  reminders for shows, 216
  remote controls, 69
  resizing window, 215
  stereo speakers, 68
  TV remote control, 208–210
  TV tips, 215
  watching TV on, 208–219

• K •

keyboard shortcuts
  ⌘-F (Find), 194, 196
  ⌘-I (Get Info), 102, 152–153, 244
  ⌘-Option-P-R (Zapping PRAM), 271
  ⌘-Y (Put Away), 40
kilobytes (K), 84
kilohertz (kHz), 177
Kodak Photo CD. *See* Photo CD

• L •

laptops
  maximum number of colors, 20–21
  microphones, 20
  multimedia and, 18–21
  screen matrix, 21
  sound-output jacks, 20
laserdisc player and AV Macintosh, 75
laying down black, 273
Learn to Speak Spanish, 313–314
Leonardo the Inventor, 315
line-level signal, 160
live video cameras, 244–247
Lively Books Series, The, 355–357
Lode Runner: The Legend Returns, 331–332
logic board, 70
Lost Mind of Dr. Brain, The, 320–321
luminance, 73

• M •

Macbeth, 312–313
MacinTalk Pro
  ⌘-H (Speak) keyboard shortcut,
    197–198, 200
  ⌘-period (Cancel), 200
  hardware requirements, 196
  intonation and pronunciation, 198
  Sound⇨Speak All command, 197
  Sound⇨Speak Selection command, 200
  Sound⇨Stop Speaking, 200
  Sound⇨Voice submenu, 197
  speaking tips, 200
  voice differences, 198–200
MacinTalk Pro system extension, 196
Macintosh
  AV models. *See* AV Macintoshes, junior AV
    Macintoshes and AV
   Quadra
  black-and-white only, 52
  headphone jack with volume controls, 12
  hooking up speakers, 41–42
  internal CD-ROM drive, 12, 17
  internal speaker, 11
  laptop multimedia, 18–21
  laptops with color and video-out ports, 12
  LCD screen, 13
  left and right RCA jacks, 12
  maximum number of colors, 18
  microphones, 12

(continued)

Macintosh *(continued)*
  milestones in multimedia, 11–13
  model multimedia capability, 14–18
  models that don't rate very high, 21–22
  multimedia and, 10–22
  SCSI port, 11
  sound-input jack, 12, 17
  sound-output jack, 18
  stereo microphone minijack, 12
  stereo sound, 11
  stereo speakers, 12
  television in and out, 18
  thousands of colors, 13
  trading in for AV Macintosh, 79–80
  TV tuner, 13
  upgrade boards, 11
  video capture card, 13
  video boards and odd-ball models, 63–64
  video ports, 12, 18
  watching TV on, 207–221
Macintosh II, 11
Macintosh IIci, 12
Macintosh IIsi, 12
Macintosh LC, 12
Macintosh LC630, 13, 68
Macintosh LC520, 12
Macintosh Plus, 11
Macintosh TV, 13
MacRecorder, 79
magnetically shielded speakers, 49
magneto-optical drives, 88–89
Maniac Sports, 337
Marathon, 335
Mario is Missing! Deluxe, 345–347
Martial Arts Explorer, The, 298
Material World: A Global Family Portrait, 284–285
Math Workshop, 351–352
megabytes (MB), 84
memory, 82–83. *See also* RAM (random access memory)
  assigning to programs, 244
  bits, 84
  bytes, 84
  gigabyte (GB), 84
  HyperCard Player and, 278–279
  kilobytes (K), 84
  megabytes (MB), 84
  removable media, 88–89
  storage, 85–88
  terabyte, 84

microphones, 12
  Apple Microphone, 159–160
  AudioVision monitor, 157–158
  desktop models, 157
  external, 159–160
  internal, 157–158
  laptops, 20
  line-level signal, 160
  mike-level signal, 160
  PlainTalk Microphone, 159–160
  PowerBooks, 157
Microsoft Exploration Series, 307–309
Microsoft Word, 100
  Insert⇨Annotation command, 170
  recording sound, 169–171
  voice annotation, 169–171
mike-level signal, 160
milliseconds (ms), 87
minijack, 30, 43
minijack-to-RCA conversion cable, 45–46
miniplugs, 30, 43–45
  mono, 44–45
  stereo, 44–45
monaural sound, 43
monitors, 51–64
  finding out how many colors can be displayed, 56–57
  redraw rate, 72
  sizes, 58
  vs. TVs and viewing movies, 271–272
Monitors control panel, 56–58, 64, 269
  colors set to thousands, 279
  number of colors displayed, 235–236
mono miniplug, 44–45
monophonic sound, 43
  recording, 178–182
motherboard, 70
mouse
  clicking, 2
  double-clicking, 2
  dragging, 2
MoviePlay, 272–273
  ⌘-4 (Screen Size) keyboard shortcut, 272
  ⌘-O (Open) keyboard shortcut, 272
  File⇨Open command, 272
  Movie⇨Screen Size command, 272
  playing movies, 272–273
MoviePlayer, 226
movies, 223–226
  AV Macintosh, 67

Index

back a frame, 228
compression, 244
editing from videotape, 249–265
file sizes, 233
grabbing frames, 242–243
interlacing, 243
laying down black, 273
moving from one point to another, 228
on CD-ROM, 229
on-line services, 226
overscanning, 272
player program options, 227–228
playing/pausing, 10, 227
programs to play them, 226–228
recording QuickTime, 11, 233–247
resizing, 228
returning edited to videotape, 267–274
saving to disk tips, 243–244
sending to VCR, 268–271
TVs vs. monitors, 271–272
underscanning, 272
volume, 227
where to find them, 226
multimedia, 9–10
  Macintosh and, 10–22
  uses of, 10–11
Multimedia Tuner installation tips, 278
music CDs. *See* audio CDs, 42
music. *See* audio CDs
Myst, 325–326

 N

networks and turning off file sharing, 244
Nine Month Miracle, 303–304
NTSC standard, 72
NuBus, 63
NuBus connector to video boards, 61
NuBus slots and Power Macintosh, 71

 O

O'Connor, Michael, 226
OceanLife: Volumes 2 through 4, 287–288
Oceans below, 296–297
on-line services and movies, 226
on-screen image album, 114–117
  what you can do with it, 118–120

 P

PAL standard, 72
Passage to Vietnam, 289–291

passive matrix, 21
PCI bus, 63
PDS (Processor Direct Slot) board, 63–64
  AV Technologies card, 70–71
Performa 600, 12
Performa 630, 68
Performa 630 through 636, 13
Performa 635, 68
Performa 636, 69
Performa 636D, 69
Performa 6100
  QuickTime PowerPlug system extension, 225
  recording CD-quality sound, 177
  Sound control panel, 143
phono jacks. *See* RCA jacks
photo album on CD, 93–102
Photo CD, 94
  advantages, 94
  costs, 95
  disadvantages, 94
  enlarged picture quality, 106
  enlarging photos, 100–101
  file format, 121
  getting pictures onto, 95–96
  interneg, 95
  PICT format, 100
  printing photos, 102
  proof sheets, 96
  putting in CD-ROM drive, 97
  resolution, 101
  reusage, 96
  rotating images, 127
  saving photo editing to, 102
  thumbnails, 96
  viewing photos, 33, 39, 98–99
  when photos were scanned, 102
PhotoFlash, 113–116, 124
  ⌘-I (Get Info) keyboard shortcut, 119
  ⌘-N (New) keyboard shortcut, 114
  ⌘-S (Save) keyboard shortcut, 116
  adding captions, 119
  adding photos to catalog, 115
  catalog, 114–116
  File⇨Add to Catalog command, 115, 119
  File⇨Get Info command, 119
  File⇨New command, 114
  File⇨Save command, 116
  modifying images, 119
  on-screen image album, 114–116
  printing thumbnails, 120
  removing/restoring image from catalog, 119

(continued)

PhotoFlash *(continued)*
  saving edited image, 119
  searching for images, 119
  thumbnails, 115
  usable file formats, 120–121
photographs
  direct to disk, 103–110
  editing, 10, 123–136
  organizing, 113–120
Photoshop, 100, 111, 123
  ⌘-J (Float) keyboard shortcut, 128
  ⌘-L (Levels) keyboard shortcut, 134, 136
  ⌘-V (Paste) keyboard shortcut, 243
  ⌘-Z (Undo) keyboard shortcut, 128
  color balance, 133–136
  cropping images, 129–130
  Edit⇨Paste command, 243
  Edit⇨Undo command, 128
  editing Fetch images, 119
  file format, 120–121
  Filter⇨Sharpen submenu, 131
  Filter⇨Sharpen⇨Unsharp Mask command, 132
  floating selections, 128
  grabbing frames from movie, 242–243
  histogram, 135
  Image⇨Adjust⇨Brightness/Contrast command, 134
  Image⇨Adjust⇨Levels command, 134, 136
  Image⇨Rotate submenu, 127
  Image⇨Rotate⇨Arbitrary command, 127–129
  Levels dialog box, 134–136
  rotating images, 127–129
  Select⇨Float command, 128
  sharpening focus, 131–133
  straightening images, 126–129
  what it can do, 124–126
PICT file format, 100, 120
pitch, 175, 182
PixelPaint Pro, 124
pixels, 55
PlainTalk, 193
  Install Speech dialog box, 195
  installing, 194–196
PlainTalk Microphone, 159–160
player programs, 226
  options, 227–228
Popcorn, 226
ports, 42
power cord socket and external CD-ROM drives, 32
power light and external CD-ROM drives, 31
Power Macintosh, 13

6100AV, 67
7100AV, 67
8100AV, 67
AV hardware, 13
CD-quality sound, 70
NuBus slots, 71
QuickTime PowerPlug system extension, 225
recording CD-quality sound, 177
recording movies, 239–242
Sound control panel, 143
Power Macintosh 5200 LC, 13, 68
  RCA jacks, 73
  S-video jacks, 73
power switch and external CD-ROM drives, 32–33
PowerBook 140, 12
PowerBook 160, 12
PowerBook 170, 12
PowerBook 180, 12
PowerBook 500 series, 13
PowerBook Duo 270C, 13
PowerBooks
  microphones, 157
  multimedia and, 18–21
  sound-input jacks, 20
powered speakers, 47–50
  automatically shutting off, 49–50
  bass response, 48
  controls, 49
  headphones, 50
  magnetically shielded, 49
  subwoofer, 48–49
  watts per channel, 49
Prehistoria, 316
Presentation System, 80
printing photos, 102
programs
  Adobe Premiere, 111, 235–265
  Apple Video Player, 210–219
  AppleCD Audio Player, 143–152
  CalcTalk, 201
  Canvas, 100
  CD Remote, 143–147
  ClarisWorks, 100
  ClockTalk, 201
  Color It!, 123
  EasyPlay, 226
  Eliza, 202
  Fetch, 113–114, 116–117
  Fractal Design Painter, 121, 123
  freeware, 174
  FusionRecorder, 235–242

Greetings, 201
Microsoft Word, 100
MoviePlay, 272–273
MoviePlayer, 226
opening Photo CD photos, 100
PhotoFlash, 113–124
Photoshop, 100, 111, 119, 123–136
PixelPaint Pro, 124
PlainTalk, 193–196
Popcorn, 226
QuicKeys, 202–203
SayIt, 201
shareware, 174
SimpleText, 196–197, 226
Slide Show, 97
Slide Show Viewer, 97–102, 229
SmartVoice, 194–195
sound resources from, 191–192
SpeechLab, 202
starting up, 2
TeachText, 196
to play movies, 226–228
Video Monitor, 219–221
VideoFusion, 250
VideoShop, 250
proof sheets, 96
Put Away (⌘-Y) keyboard shortcut, 40
Putt-Putt Joins the Parade, 348–349

Quadras
  recording movies, 239
Quadra 630, 13, 68
  microphone, 158
  recording sound, 177
Quadra 660AV, 12, 67
  DAV (digital audio/video) connector, 77
Quadra 840AV, 12, 66
  DAV (digital audio/video) connector, 77
Quadra 900, 12
QuickCam, 233, 245–247
QuickKeys
  Define⇨Extensions⇨System Tools⇨Speak Ease command, 202
  voice recognition, 202–203
QuickMail, recording sound, 169
QuickTake 150, 104–105
  enlarged picture quality, 106
  full-screen, 105
  quarter-screen, 105
  speed, 105
  vs. Digital Camera 40, 107–108
QuickTime, 10, 98, 223–226
  installation tips, 278
  movies on CDs, 229
  playing movies, 226
QuickTime movies
  compression, 244
  file sizes, 233
  from Adobe Premiere project, 263–265
  grabbing frames, 242–243
  hardware checks for, 234
  interlacing, 243
  movie editors, 249–250
  moving cursor away from, 281
  recording to disk, 233–247
  saving to disk tips, 243–244
QuickTime Musical Instruments system extension, 226
QuickTime PowerPlug, 225
QuickTime system extension, 225
QuickTime VR (virtual reality), 230–231
QuickTime: The CD, 226

• R •

RAM (random access memory), 59, 82–85
  how much is enough, 83
  SIMMs, 84
RCA jacks
  AV Macintosh, 72–73
  AV Power Macintosh, 74
  AV Quadras, 73
  composite video, 73
  external CD-ROM drives, 32
  left and right, 12
  Power Macintosh 5200 LC, 73
  VCR, 71
RCA plugs, 46–47
  color coding, 45–46
Rebel Assault, 334–335
recording sound, 155–156
  Adobe Premiere, 169
  alert sounds, 163–167
  external CD-ROM drive, 160–161
  levels, 164
  microphones, 157–160
  Microsoft Word, 169
  naming alert sounds, 165
  QuickMail, 169
  recording session setup, 161–163

(continued)

recording sound *(continued)*
  ResEdit, 167–169
  SoundEdit 16, 169
  WordPerfect, 169
redraw rate, 72
remote controls and junior AV Macintosh, 69
removable media, 88
  digital audio tape (DAT), 89
  magneto-optical drives, 88–89
  SyQuest drives, 88–89
  Zip drive, 89
ResEdit
  alert scales, 167–169
  Snd icon, 168
  Snd⇨Try Scale with Sound command, 168
Residents Freak Show, The, 327–328
resolution and sound, 175
Return to Zork, 336–337
RGB (red, green, blue), 55
RGB composite video, 72
Ricci, Alberto, 174
RIFF file format, 121
Rosetta Stone Language Library, The, 309–310

• S •

S-video jacks
  AV Quadras, 73
  Power Macintosh 5200 LC, 73
samples, 175
sampling, 175
SayIt, 201
screen, 51–58
  black-and-white only, 52
  dithering, 53
  finding out how many colors can be displayed, 56–58
  laptop matrix, 21
  more colors, 59–64
  number of colors displayed on, 52–56
  pixels, 55
  sizes, 58
SCSI (Small Computer System Interface), 31
  connections and CD-ROM drives, 33, 34, 35
  daisy chaining devices, 35
  port, 11
  termination, 36
  terminator, 36
SCSI connectors and external CD-ROM drives, 31
SCSI Manager 4.3 extension, 87–88

SCSI-ID
  conflicts, 29
  number, 32
  internal CD-ROM drives, 37
  external CD-ROM drives and switch, 32
SECAM standard, 72
seek time, 87
Seven Days in August: Unfold the Drama of the Cold War, 293–295
shareware, 174
  EasyPlay, 226
  Popcorn, 226
  Sound Sculptor, 174
  SoundEffects, 174
Sharing Setup control panel, turning off sharing, 244
SimCity Enhanced, 329–331
SIMMs
  how many have to be added at once, 85
  pins, 85
  sizes, 84
  speed, 85
SimpleText, 101, 196–197
  playing movies, 226
  speaking text from, 196–197
SimTown, 353–354
single-speed drive, 28
Slide Show, 97
Slide Show Viewer, 97–99, 229
  ⌘-E (View Photo) keyboard shortcut, 101
  ⌘-P (Print) keyboard shortcut, 102
  enlarging photos, 100–101
  File⇨Preferences command, 100
  File⇨Print command, 102
  Photo⇨View command, 101
  Preferences dialog box, 100
  printing photos, 102
  will not run, 98
Small Blue Planet: The Cities Below, 297
Small Blue Planet: The Real Picture Atlas, 297
SmartVoice, 194–195
  CalcTalk program, 201
  ClockTalk program, 201
  Eliza program, 202
  ExcuseMe system extension, 201
  Greetings program, 201
  MacinTalk 2, 196
  SayIt program, 201
  SpeechLab program, 202
Smith, Jeff, 174

sound
  8-bit, 175–176
  8-bit, 22 kHz, 177
  8-bit, 44 kHz, 178
  16-bit, 175–176
  16-bit, 22 kHz, 178
  16-bit, 44 kHz, 177–178
  amplitude, 175
  AV Macintosh, 67
  bits, 175–176
  channels, 43
  copying from programs, 191–192
  editing, 173–192
  kilohertz (kHz), 177
  loudness, 182
  monaural, 43
  monophonic, 43
  monophonic recording, 178–182
  pitch, 175, 182
  Power Macintosh and CD–quality, 70
  quality, 175–176
  reading sound wave, 181–182
  recording, 155–171
  recording CD-quality stereo, 13
  resolution, 175–176
  samples, 175
  sampling, 175
  sampling rate, 177
  speed of, 177
  stereo, 11, 42–43
  stereo recording, 183–186
  vibration, 182
Sound control panel, 140–143
  Add button, 164
  Alert Sounds option, 143, 153
  older versions, 140
  Options button, 162
  Play button, 165
  Record button, 165
  setup for recording session, 161–163
  Sound In option, 140, 161
  Sound Out options, 143
  Sound Resources window, 191
  Stop button, 165
  Volumes option, 142
Sound Editor, 174
Sound Manager, 142
  installation tips, 278
sound resources, 188
Sound Sculptor, 174

sound-in port and recording session setup, 161
sound-input jacks, 12, 17
  PowerBooks, 20
sound-out port (jack), 18, 42–47
  laptops, 20
  miniplugs, 43–45
  plugging into, 43–45
  stereo sound, 42–43
SoundBuilder, 174
SoundEdit 16, 173
  ⌘-A (Select All) keyboard shortcut, 183
  ⌘-C (Copy) keyboard shortcut, 192
  ⌘-D (Delete Track) keyboard shortcut, 185
  ⌘-I (Sound Format) keyboard shortcut, 179
  ⌘-L (Make Label) keyboard shortcut, 186
  ⌘-N (New) keyboard shortcut, 179
  ⌘-O (Open) keyboard shortcut, 188, 191
  ⌘-R (Record) keyboard shortcut, 180
  ⌘-S (Save) keyboard shortcut, 181, 185, 190
  ⌘-T (Add Track) keyboard shortcut, 183
  ⌘-V (Paste) keyboard shortcut, 187, 192
  ⌘-X (Cut) keyboard shortcut, 187
  ⌘-Z (Undo) keyboard shortcut, 187
  deleting selections, 187
  Edit➪Copy command, 192
  Edit➪Cut command, 187
  Edit➪Make Label command, 186
  Edit➪Paste command, 187, 192
  Edit➪Select All command, 183
  Edit➪Undo command, 187
  editing sound, 10, 186–188
  File➪New command, 179
  File➪Open command, 188, 191
  File➪Save As command, 190
  File➪Save command, 181, 185, 190
  independently editing tracks, 188
  Input Source dialog box, 179
  labeling selections, 186–187
  level controls, 180
  magnifying sound wave, 187
  mixing sounds, 187–188
  monophonic sound recording, 178–182
  naming tracks, 184
  no active track, 185
  playing selections, 186
  reading sound wave, 181–182
  recording sound, 10, 169
  refining sounds, 188–191
  reinstating deleted selections, 187
  renaming sounds, 190–191

(continued)

SoundEdit *(continued)*
  reordering dialog, 187
  selecting selections, 186
  Shift-spacebar (Play) keyboard shortcut, 185
  sound resources, 188
  Sound⇨Add Track command, 183
  Sound⇨Delete Track command, 185
  Sound⇨Recording Options command, 179
  Sound⇨Sound Format command, 179
  sounds from other programs, 191–192
  special effects, 187
  stereo sound recording, 183–186
  switching channels, 186
  taking sound out of System file, 188–191
  tracks, 183
  View⇨Display Options command, 183
SoundEffects, 174
SoundHandle, 174
Space: A Visual History of Manned Spaceflight, 298
SPAV board, 239
speakers
  hooking up to Macintosh, 41–42
  powered, 47–50
  sound cutting out, 153
special effects and movies, 249–265
  Adobe Premiere, 258
  transition effects, 259–262
Special⇨Restart command, 196
Speech Manager system extension, 196
SpeechLab, 202
Spigot II Tape, 268
Spigot II Tape board, 80
SpigotPower AV (SPAV) board, 77–79
SpigotPro AV board, 79
spin rate, 28
Sports Illustrated Multimedia Almanac, 298
Star Trek: The Next Generation Interactive Technical Manual, 230–231, 321–322
stereo
  computerized, 41–50
  hooking external CD-ROM drive, 46–47
  microphone minijack, 12
  miniplug, 44–45
  sound, 11, 42–43, 183–186
  stereo speakers, 12–13
  junior AV Macintosh, 68
storage, 85
  hard drives, 86–88
  removable media, 88–89
Street Atlas USA, 297

subwoofer, 48–49
SyQuest drives, 89
  cartridges, 88
System 7.1
  PlainTalk Installer program, 195
  QuickTime, 98
  TeachText, 101
System 7.5
  Apple⇨Control Panel⇨Sound command, 140
  AppleCD Audio Player, 143–144
  CD-ROM extensions, 38
  Control Panels command, 57
  MoviePlayer, 226
  PlainTalk Installer program, 195
  Power Macintosh and Performa 6100, 143
  QuickTime, 98
  SCSI Manager 4.3 extension, 87–88
  SimpleText, 101
  Sound Manager, 142
  voice recognition, 194
system extensions
  Apple Multimedia Tuner, 225
  ExcuseMe, 201
  MacinTalk Pro, 196
  QuickTime, 98, 225
  QuickTime Musical Instruments, 226
  QuickTime PowerPlug, 225
  SCSI Manager 4.3, 87–88
  Speech Manager, 196
  turning off, 278
System file, taking sound out of, 188–191

• T •

talking calculator, 201
TeachText, 101, 196
ten educational resource CDs, 299–317
ten games and entertainment CDs, 319–338
ten great CDs for children, 341–357
ten interactive CD coffee-table books, 283–298
ten tips for better CD-ROM performance, 277–282
terabyte, 84
termination, 36
terminator, 36
This Is Spinal Tap, 332–333
thumbnails, 96
  Adobe Premiere, 254–255
  PhotoFlash, 115
TIFF file format, 120
Trail Series, The, 344–345
tray/caddy door, 30

Index 375

TV, 207–221
  adjusting volume, 211
  changing channels, 210–211
  closed captioning, 217
  displaying broadcast schedules, 217
  favorite channels, 211
  fields, 243
  fine-tuning channel list, 212–213
  locking out channels, 213
  Macintosh and, 10
  muting, 211
  NTSC standard, 72
  PAL standard, 72
  reminders for shows, 216
  resizing window, 215
  scanning for active channels, 211–212
  SECAM standard, 72
  second program soundtrack, 217
  startup, 210
  switching between channels, 215
  switching between window sizes, 216
  taping through Apple Video Player, 218
  vs. computer video, 72
  vs. monitors and viewing movies, 271–272
TV tuner, 13

• U •

underscanning, 272

• V •

VCR
  computer signals to, 75–76
  hooking to AV Macintosh, 71–75
  RCA jacks, 71
  S-video jacks, 73
  sending video to, 268–271
Veeneman, Dale, 174
Veldhuizen, David, 174
video
  chrominance, 73
  composite, 73
  computer, 72
  junior AV Macintosh, 68
  luminance, 73
  playing into AV Macintosh, 73–74
  RGB composite, 72
video boards, 60–64
  installing, 62–63
  NuBus connector, 61
  odd-ball Macintoshes and, 63–64
  video-out port, 61
video cameras, 244
  FlexCam, 246–247
  QuickCam, 245–247
Video Monitor, 219–221
  ⌘-C (Copy) keyboard shortcut, 221
  ⌘-O (Open) keyboard shortcut, 221
  ⌘-Q (Quit) keyboard shortcut, 221
  Edit⇨Copy command, 221
  File⇨Open command, 221
  File⇨Preferences command, 221
  File⇨Quit command, 221
  grabbing frames, 221
  Monitor⇨Sound Settings command, 220
  Monitor⇨Video Settings command, 219–220
  picture discolored and jiggly, 220
  quitting, 221
  redisplaying window, 221
  resizing video window, 221
  unable to see video on display, 219
video ports, 12, 18
video-capture card, 13
video–input board and recording QuickTime movies, 233
video-out ports
  laptops, 12
  video boards, 61
VideoFusion, 250
VideoShop, 250
VideoSpigot boards, 80
videotapes
  editing movies from, 249–265
  returning edited movies to, 267–274
  special effects, 249–265
View⇨By Icon command, 234
virtual reality (VR) and QuickTime, 230–231
voice recognition, 193–202
  altering voices, 202
  AV Macintosh, 67
  differences in voices, 198–200
  making computer talk, 196–197
  practical usage, 201–202
  QuicKeys, 202–203
  speaking date and time during bootup, 201
  speaking text, 201
  talking calculator, 201
  telling time, 201

volume control and external CD-ROM drives, 31
VRAM (video RAM), 59–60
   limits, 59–60
   splitting in half, 235

• W •

Warplanes, 297
watts per channel, 49
Weekend Home Projects, 316
Welcome to Bodyland, 347–348
Who Built America?, 315
Who Killed Brett Penance?, 336
Woodstock: 25th Anniversary CD-ROM, 298
WordPerfect and recording sound, 169
Wrath of the Gods, 337

• X •

Xplora 1: Peter Gabriel's Secret World, 336

• Y •

Y cable, 45–46

• Z •

zapping PRAM (⌘-Option-P-R) keyboard
       shortcut, 271
Zip drive, 89

Notes

ORDER FORM

Order Center: **(800) 762-2974** *(8 a.m.–6 p.m., EST, weekdays)*

Quantity	ISBN	Title	Price	Total

Shipping & Handling Charges				
	Description	First book	Each additional book	Total
Domestic	Normal	$4.50	$1.50	$
	Two Day Air	$8.50	$2.50	$
	Overnight	$18.00	$3.00	$
International	Surface	$8.00	$8.00	$
	Airmail	$16.00	$16.00	$
	DHL Air	$17.00	$17.00	$

*For large quantities call for shipping & handling charges.
**Prices are subject to change without notice.

Ship to:

Name _____

Company _____

Address _____

City/State/Zip _____

Daytime Phone _____

Payment: ☐ Check to IDG Books (US Funds Only)
☐ VISA   ☐ MasterCard   ☐ American Express

Card # _____ Expires _____

Signature _____

Subtotal _____

CA residents add
applicable sales tax _____

IN, MA, and MD
residents add
5% sales tax _____

IL residents add
6.25% sales tax _____

RI residents add
7% sales tax _____

TX residents add
8.25% sales tax _____

Shipping _____

Total _____

Please send this order form to:

IDG Books Worldwide
7260 Shadeland Station, Suite 100
Indianapolis, IN 46256

*Allow up to 3 weeks for delivery.
Thank you!*